Global Food Trade and Consumer Demand for Quality

Global Food Trade and Consumer Demand for Quality

Edited by

Barry Krissoff
Mary Bohman

Economic Research Service/USDA
Washington, D.C.

and

Julie A. Caswell

University of Massachusetts
Amherst, Massachusetts

Kluwer Academic / Plenum Publishers
New York, Boston, Dordrecht, London, Moscow

Library of Congress Cataloging-in-Publication Data

Global food trade and consumer demand for quality/edited by Barry Krissoff, Mary Bohman, and Julie Caswell.

p. cm.

Based on the proceedings of a conference held in June 2000 under the cosponsorship of the International Agricultural Trade Research Consortium and Regional Research Project NE-165: Private strategies, public policies, and food system performance.

Includes bibliographical references and index.

ISBN 0-306-46754-2

1. Produce trade—Government policy. 2. Agriculture—Economic aspects. 3. Consumption (Economics) 4. Consumer protection. 5. Globalization. I. Krissoff, Barry. II. Bohman, Mary. III. Caswell, Julie A. IV. International Agricultural Trade Research Consortium. V. Regional Research Project NE-165

HD9000.5 .G583 2002
382′.456413—dc21

2001057977

Proceedings of the conference Global Food Trade and Consumer Demand for Quality, held June 26–27, 2000, in Montreal, Canada

ISBN 0-306-46754-2

233 Spring Street, New York, NY 10013

http://www.wkap.nl

10 9 8 7 6 5 4 3 2 1

A C.I.P. record for this book is available from the Library of Congress

Printed in the United States of America

PREFACE

Consumers have always been concerned about the quality, and particularly the safety, of the foods they eat. In recent years this concern has taken on additional prominence. Consumer focus on food safety has been sharpened by reports about new risks, such as that posed by "mad cow" disease, and about more familiar sources of risk, such as food-borne pathogens, pesticides, and hormones. At the same time, some consumers are increasingly interested in knowing more about how their food is produced and in selecting products based on production practices. Some of the questions consumers are asking include whether food is produced with the use of modern biotechnology, whether it is organically produced, how animals are treated in meat and egg production systems, and whether food is produced using traditional methods.

Recent trends also show increased consumer demand for a variety of food products that are fresh, tasty, and available on a year-round basis. This has fostered increased global trade in food. For example, consumers in temperate climates such as North America are able to buy raspberries throughout the year, and Europeans can enjoy South American coffee. Trade in processed food products is actually increasing more rapidly than trade in agricultural commodities, further addressing the demand for variety among consumers. Trade may also make food more affordable. However, trade may also threaten the ability of consumers to purchase the products they want because imported products are less safe, are produced in undesired ways (e.g., with the use of hormones), or do not meet other quality standards. Thus the question arises of how well the global food trade serves consumer demand for quality.

Trade presents both an opportunity and a challenge in meeting consumer demand for products increasingly differentiated by a wide range of quality attributes. Companies profit from selling new products or supplying quality characteristics that consumers want and for which they will pay a premium. For example, supermarket chains in Britain responded to concerns about biotechnology by pledging to remove products made with the use of biotechnology from their shelves. Many quality characteristics pose a challenge in marketing because they are difficult or impossible for consumers to verify even after consumption (in economics, these are known as credence goods). Here companies must rely on information such as certification, labeling, and brand names to reassure consumers. In some cases, trade can increase problems in conveying information about quality to consumers as products travel over longer distances and, frequently, through more hands.

Both consumers and businesses have turned to government for policies to meet demands for quality, to provide information about quality, and to facilitate trade where quality standards differ among countries. For example, some consumer organizations have called for government action ranging from bans on certain types or qualities of products to mandatory labeling. Business has asked the government to define, establish, and provide quality standards or third-party certification because of the government's credibility with consumers. Both expect government to play a prominent role in reconciling different standards for quality across countries, although their expectations for this role differ. Consumers want to be assured that trade in food products will not threaten quality standards or pose new risks. Industry wants to know that imported products will not unfairly compete against domestic products and that its own exports will enjoy ready access to markets in other countries. Governments' choices of policy options have implications for consumer and producer welfare, the structure of the food industry, and the flow of foods across international borders. The possibility exists too that consumer concerns about quality will be exploited by business to promote policies regarding imports that are protectionist and pose barriers to trade rather than provide legitimate consumer protection.

Another important issue in the global food trade is the trade relationship between industrialized and developing countries. The regulations of industrialized countries are becoming stricter and are expanding into new areas such as biotechnology and organic foods. Standards and regulations diverge across industrialized countries because of differences in income, tastes, risk preferences, geography, culture, and religion. The divergence between industrialized and developing country standards is even greater. In this environment, are developing countries disadvantaged in meeting the quality criteria to be able to import into industrialized countries? How developing countries respond to export challenges and opportunities is an important aspect of the interaction between consumer demand and the global food trade.

While economists have begun to analyze the relationship between consumer demand for quality and international trade, there has not been a systematic treatment of the various components of the issue. This volume helps fill that gap. In 2000, the International Agricultural Trade Research Consortium (a group of agricultural trade economists) and Regional Research Project NE-165: *Private Strategies, Public Policies, and Food System Performance* (a group of agricultural consumer and industrial organization economists) jointly organized a conference on the economics of trade and consumer demand for quality. The conference was cosponsored by the Economic Research Service of the U.S. Department of Agriculture and the Farm Foundation. Participants included leading researchers and practitioners from North America, Europe, Latin America, and Asia.

Leading experts in international trade, political science, and consumer demand were commissioned to contribute overview papers to frame the issues. Three case studies were also commissioned based on a review of proposals submitted to the organizing committee. These case studies focus on European Union (EU) animal welfare policies, food safety problems in the trade of Guatemalan raspberries to the United States and Canada, and the development of the beef export sector in Uruguay. Each applies economic theory to explain private and public responses to issues associated with global trade in food products. In addition, papers were selected for presentation at the conference from the many that were submitted. Several of the selected papers are included in this volume. All the commissioned papers, case studies, and selected papers were peer-reviewed and edited for inclusion in this book. While discussants' comments are not published, the authors have incorporated these comments into the revised versions of their papers.

The book begins with the overview papers designed to define the issues and lay out alternative conceptual models. The case studies follow, showing how some of these concepts can be applied to real-world problems and also raise challenges for future theoretical analysis. For example, the animal welfare case points to the need for additional research to incorporate ethical issues into trade models, while the Guatemalan raspberry case highlights the need to pay more attention to the public good aspects of food safety reputations. The papers in the final section of the book tackle specific issues and develop new conceptual and empirical approaches. Topics include development of models of the impacts of divergent food safety regulations on trade and of agricultural price support policies on the quality of products produced and consumed. These papers place a strong emphasis on the role of standards, certification, and labeling in trade in differentiated food products, including those differentiated on the basis of the use or nonuse of biotechnology, organic production methods, and geographically distinct production practices.

An important objective of this book is to survey and extend the available economic tools to analyze the interface between trade and consumer issues. For example, Bureau, Jones, Gozlan, and Marette survey the economic literature that has been applied to trade and quality issues, while Caswell, Noelke, and Mojduszka unify the economic and marketing literature approaches to analyzing quality and quality assurance. Orden, Josling, and Roberts and Lohr and Krissoff develop empirical trade models to analyze differences in the effects of domestic regulation of the poultry and organic markets, respectively. Alston and James show how quality can be incorporated into models of agricultural policies, while Roe and Sheldon develop a model of vertical differentiation in markets with trade and imperfect competition or information.

The first section of the book presents four chapters that provide overviews of the international trade, political science, and consumer demand dimensions of the nexus between trade and consumer demand for quality. Bureau and his colleagues (Chapter 1) start by presenting a discussion of the most controversial issues involving trade, regulation, and quality: the role of risk and the use of the precautionary principle, the approach to the introduction of biotechnology, animal welfare policies, and the use of geographical indications on labels for food products. Their analysis of the economic literature finds that, in general, the different demands for quality across countries do not undermine the potential benefits from free trade. However, three sources of market failure—imperfect competition, imperfect information, and risk—can create specific cases where trade reduces welfare. In order to maintain public support for trade liberalization, Bureau and colleagues conclude that rules governing international trade need to be consistent with consumer demand for quality. While not without its pitfalls, cost-benefit analysis is proposed as an economic framework that could be used to evaluate cases in which differences in demand for quality potentially conflict with trade liberalization. The authors argue that application of cost-benefit analysis to trade and quality conflicts is lagging 20 years behind its application to environmental disputes.

Victor and Weiner (Chapter 2) place trade and consumer issues in the context of the politics underlying the transformation of world trade rules in the Uruguay Round that led to the formation of the World Trade Organization (WTO). They characterize the process as a "sea-change in international law" from an exclusive focus on controlling producer distortions of trade (e.g., tariffs and quotas) to asserting some international jurisdiction over domestic regulations, such as on food safety, that may constitute protectionism rather than legitimate consumer protection. The new areas of oversight are no longer simple border measures such as tariffs but include domestic regulations covering core functions of governments. A dispute settlement process that follows a strict timetable and produces definitive judgments now enforces WTO rules. This process does not permit governments to ignore decisions against their regulations, which may require unpopular changes in domestic policies, although countries have the option of maintaining their policy and paying compensation to affected trading partners. The broader scope of the WTO juxtaposes the opportunity to reduce trade barriers with the potential for strong domestic opposition to the prescribed resolutions of trade disputes. The beef hormone case is cited as an example where dispute decisions by the WTO and implementation of trade sanctions only serve to strengthen EU resolve to maintain current regulations. Victor and Weiner argue that too many intractable cases like the beef hormone case could undermine the WTO itself. They offer several solutions that involve trade-offs between using objective criteria to establish credible international legal precedent and not forcing governments to choose between domestic political opinion and international trade rules.

Caswell, Noelke, and Mojduszka (Chapter 3) unify the economic and marketing literature approaches to analyzing quality perception and quality assurance. They begin by contrasting the strengths and weaknesses of each approach. Economic models frequently assume a one-dimensional view of product quality based on whether buyer information about quality is of a search, experience, or credence nature. Search goods are products for which consumers can obtain information to judge quality prior to purchase, experience goods are those for which quality can be judged after purchase and use, and credence goods are those for which quality cannot be accurately judged even after purchase and use. They argue that this breakdown is a powerful tool for analyzing the role of quality and quality signaling in markets but is too narrow for understanding the full scope of quality and quality assurance activities in markets. Marketing models allow for a richer definition of quality and provide valuable insights into the purchase decisions of consumers. Goods can have multiple attributes with different quality levels and information environments. For example, the tenderness of beef is an experience attribute, but the conditions under which the animal was raised is a credence attribute. Empirical applications of marketing models find that consumers base decisions on both the appearance of a product (called intrinsic cues) and information provided about the product such as labels (extrinsic cues). Caswell, Noelke, and Mojduszka argue that a unified quality framework that systematically analyzes several dimensions of quality and quality assurance is particularly important in a trade environment where the dimensionality of the issues grows rapidly as buyers in different countries place different values on individual attributes of food products.

Unnevehr (Chapter 4) focuses on the challenges facing developing countries in exporting food products, particularly to industrialized countries. This ability is a key dimension of the impact of demands for quality on international trade and on the prospects for individual countries to participate in this trade. She examines how developing countries can meet the food safety, sanitation, and good agricultural and manufacturing practice standards of the higher income countries and the possible roles of the private and public sectors in achieving these standards. For the private sector, the key is managing food safety hazards through vertical coordination from the farm to the export market. For the public sector, the roles may include policymaking, provision of information, prevention and control of hazards, and investment in infrastructure and research. Decisions about intervention need to take into account private actions because public actions are unnecessary if they simply displace private activities. Unnevehr finds factors supporting public intervention to facilitate developing country exports include the lack of information about private actions, the fact that hazard control provides a public good, and potentially large spillover benefits for domestic consumers. Unnevehr's approach to assessing the roles of the public sector in quality assurance is very relevant to the two case studies on trade in raspberries from Guatemala and beef from Uruguay.

The second section presents three in-depth case studies that assess specific food quality issues. Each case study has some common elements. They all examine demands for quality attributes and private industry and public response to those demands. They analyze the implications of changes in production and distribution processes that were established based on quality concerns. They also address the effects on competition and global trade, not just for the countries that are directly involved in buying and selling but for third-country competitors as well.

In the first case study, Blandford and his colleagues (Chapter 5) focus on the interest of European consumers in protecting animal welfare. Although in surveys consumers do not mention animal welfare as frequently as other concerns about hormones or genetically engineered food, both government legislation and private initiatives have emerged regarding the treatment of farm animals. In the European Union, minimum animal welfare standards are determined by legislation, and the scope and level of these standards have been increasing. Standards have been established for chickens, pigs, and veal calves. Some in the private sector have chosen to go beyond the minimum standards in response to consumer demand and are backed by government labeling standards. For example, there has been an increase in the demand for and sale of free-range eggs in response to concern about confining chickens in specialized housing with limited space, a production method common in modern intensive agriculture. Stricter animal husbandry standards are likely to increase costs for EU producers and may pose trade difficulties such as a reduction in the ability of EU producers to compete in international markets. EU industry and government may have an interest in restricting imports into the EU to only those foreign producers that follow the stricter standards or in requiring labeling of production practices, which may be difficult to verify and enforce. Ultimately, consumer willingness to purchase and pay a premium for animal-friendly production practices will determine the extent to which consideration of animal welfare attributes will be incorporated into production practices.

The second and third case studies, by Calvin and colleagues (Chapter 6) and Marshall and colleagues (Chapter 7), address food safety and quality issues related to the ability of developing countries to export to industrialized countries. In each case, the public and private sectors worked together to meet the quality demands of the industrialized countries. Calvin and colleagues examine the reaction of Guatemalan growers, public officials, and the international community to U.S. and Canadian outbreaks of cyclosporiasis, an illness caused by the foodborne pathogen *Cyclospora*. Outbreaks of cyclosporiasis traced to Guatemalan raspberries were reported in the United States and Canada in the spring and early summer of 1996 and again in 1997. Calvin and colleagues explain how the Guatemalan Berry Commission and the Guatemalan government, in conjunction with U.S. and Canadian health and food safety agencies and the Food Marketing Institute (an association that represents retail buyers), developed a specific plan of excellence for agricultural practices to address the problem. The United States allowed entry of raspberries produced under the Model Plan of Excellence beginning in the spring of 1999. The plan also establishes a process for traceback to individual growers, a critical element in a foodborne illness outbreak. Other exporters of raspberries to the United States, such as Chile and Mexico, as well as U.S. producers have also adopted higher standards of food safety readiness, although the disease has only definitely been traced to Guatemalan raspberries. Guatemala lost U.S. raspberry market share to Mexico, although it is not clear whether the change is related exclusively to food safety problems or to a combination of food safety and other profit-related considerations.

Marshall and colleagues examine the development of Uruguayan beef exports to the European Union. Uruguayan public and private sector interests have worked to position the beef industry favorably in order to expand exports to the European Union. The opportunity occurred because of the EU ban on imports of beef produced with hormones and requirements for the traceability of products. The reliance of the Uruguayan industry on pasture grazing systems rather than feedlot operations and the establishment of the Dicose system for traceability produced beef consistent with European demands. In addition, the pronouncement of Uruguay as free of foot-and-mouth disease in 1995, based on sanitary improvements, also promoted the export potential of the industry. Marshall and colleagues also describe the efforts of a cooperative to offer incentives to producers to go beyond the base quality requirements. In contrast to the study of Guatemalan raspberries, which focused on public and private sector reaction to a foodborne illness outbreak, Chapter 7 shows how the public and private sectors in a developing country can work proactively to augment exports.

The third section of the book presents six papers covering specific issues and methodological challenges in modeling the interface between trade and quality. The section begins with two papers by Orden, Josling, and Roberts (Chapter 8) and Alston and James (Chapter 9). Orden, Josling, and Roberts develop a model of world poultry markets that takes into account traditional barriers to trade such as tariffs as well as potential barriers arising as a result of regulations intended to protect human and avian health. They explicitly recognize that the world market is differentiated into low- and high-value products, and that a small number of countries are the major players in the trade. This approach allows the authors to evaluate the effects of sanitary barriers related to avian and human health in the context of the broader set of economic factors and policy decisions that affect trade flows. Based on an analysis of different scenarios of policy change, the authors conclude that there may be sufficient opportunities for arbitrage (i.e., opportunities to divert sales to other markets) so that imposition of stricter sanitary standards in one market may not have a significant impact on exports. However, the size of the impact and its distribution among countries depend on how widespread such restrictions become in the market. Thus Orden, Josling, and Roberts argue that multicountry trade arbitrage should be considered in assessing the impact of safety-related standards.

Alston and James point out that the assumption that agricultural commodities are homogeneous, an assumption almost universally made in trade modeling, may no longer hold in our global food economy. Commodities are in fact becoming more differentiated. When this differentiation is taken into account, analysis of alternative trade regimes may provide substantially different results than under the assumption of homogeneity. Alston and James develop a theoretical multimarket model that allows for quality differences. They then undertake numerical simulations to demonstrate how alternative policy scenarios could influence the wheat market in the European Union when it is differentiated based on quality. For example, they demonstrate that with a per unit import tariff reduction, consumption of the low-quality product is greater and the reduction in consumption of the high-quality product is smaller than would be predicted without taking quality differentiation into account. Furthermore, total consumption and the average quality of products consumed may change in different ways than as predicted in the no-quality differentiation case.

The last four chapters focus on the role of differentiation via standards, certification, and labeling on quality and quality assurance in international markets. Roe and Sheldon (Chapter 10) present a generalized model of vertical quality differentiation in a trade environment. The following three chapters deal with specific examples of the use of certification and labeling in markets with international trade: Golan and Kuchler (Chapter 11) discuss labeling of foods produced with the use of biotechnology, Lohr and Krissoff (Chapter 12) analyze the operation of organic standards that differ across countries, and Zago and Pick (Chapter 13) examine the welfare impacts of differentiation of food products based on geographical origin.

Roe and Sheldon focus on the role of labeling programs in markets for products with credence attributes that are vertically differentiated. In such markets, consumers agree on what constitutes high and low quality and will purchase products of different quality, when they can identify that quality, based on their income levels. In the absence of trade, Roe and Sheldon's model shows that credible private or public certification and labeling programs can increase welfare by allowing consumers to evaluate quality and facilitating the existence of a market for high-quality products. In addition, they explore whether and how this effect is altered based on whether the labeling program is binary (if the product meets a threshold level of quality it can be labeled) or continuous (products are rated and labeled on a continuous scale). They then address the effect of trade among countries with the same income levels (e.g., north-north trade) on industry structure, trade levels, and consumer welfare with both types of labeling programs and harmonization versus mutual recognition of labeling programs among countries. Roe and Sheldon conclude, based on their modeling efforts, that the consumer welfare effects of trade depend on the circumstances in individual cases.

Golan and Kuchler address the contentious issue both within the United States and between the United States and its trading partners of whether or not biotech agricultural products should be labeled. Economists tend to argue that labeling and market differentiation of biotech and nonbiotech commodities and food product would expand consumer welfare. Golan and Kuchler argue that, although labeling may redress problems of asymmetric or missing information, thereby increasing consumer welfare and market efficiency, labeling will rarely be sufficient to correct problems of production externalities. They demonstrate that production externalities associated with biotech cultivation and production reduce the value of labeling as a tool to increase market efficiency. The observation that labeling is not a "cure-all" solution helps shed light on a basic confusion underlying the biotech labeling debate.

Lohr and Krissoff consider the trade and welfare implications of multiple regional and national organic standards that have been enacted worldwide. The authors suggest that establishing credibility of a single minimum standard can reduce consumers' costs of obtaining information about the production process—an otherwise unobservable characteristic—and improve consumer welfare. To illustrate, Lohr and Krissoff simulate a partial equilibrium model of trade in organic wheat between the United States and Germany. The authors examine six cases—no equivalency in standards (the status quo), equivalency of standards with complete or incomplete import acceptance, exporters certifying in the importing country with complete or incomplete import acceptance, and exporters paying educational costs with incomplete import acceptance. When there is less uncertainty about standards, importing country consumers are better off accepting imports as equivalent to domestically produced organic foods. Moreover, the authors show that strategies to reduce resistance such as educational programs or foreign certification add costs to production that reduce quantity traded and impose welfare losses on exporting country producers and importing country consumers.

Zago and Pick (Chapter 13) examine the issue of quality differentiation based on linking a food product or its attributes to specific geographic origins. In the European Union, the goal of this linkage is to provide higher incomes to farmers and improve the quality of food items enjoyed by consumers. Zago and Pick develop a model to analyze the actual effect of EU regulations establishing and protecting products with geographical indications and products with designations of origin on producer and consumer welfare when the attributes being certified are credence in nature. They consider the case before and after regulation (including *ex post* labeling) that distinguishes the variety of the product offered. An interesting aspect of Zago and Pick's specification is that they allow high-quality producers (those with the designation) to exercise a degree of market power. They then compare the producer and consumer welfare effects given a competitive market for low-quality producers and a monopolistic market for high-quality producers. Moreover, with a goal of the EU regulations being to improve welfare in rural communities, Zago and Pick discuss the implications of these policies for producers in different geographic regions.

Overall, the chapters of this book underline the complex relationship between global food trade and consumer demand for quality. Trade can offer benefits to consumers in the form of access to products at lower prices, in greater variety, throughout more of the year, at higher quality. At the same time, trade can pose risks—for example, from products that are less safe or that undermine the quality of foods offered in the domestic market. Governments enact policies to manage these positive and negative effects, and may also be pressured to use quality, particularly safety, regulation to protect domestic industries. The WTO trade disciplines attempt to oversee this decisionmaking process at the national level to ensure that regulations serve legitimate ends. However, the WTO must tread lightly or risk losing support in countries that wish to enact stricter regulations on an increasingly broad array of food product attributes. The weight of the analysis presented here clearly shows that the welfare impacts of global food trade, in markets where consumer demand for quality is increasingly differentiated, deserves detailed and nuanced consideration.

Mary Bohman
Julie A. Caswell
Barry Krissoff

ACKNOWLEDGMENTS

This book is based on the proceedings of a conference held in June 2000 under the cosponsorship of the International Agricultural Trade Research Consortium and Regional Research Project NE-165: *Private Strategies, Public Policies, and Food System Performance*. The Department of Applied Economics at the University of Minnesota provided administrative support for the conference. Financial support was provided by the Economic Research Service and the Foreign Agricultural Service of the U.S. Department of Agriculture, Agriculture and Agri-Food Canada, and the Farm Foundation.

The International Agricultural Trade Research Consortium (IATRC) is an organization of more than 180 economists from 25 different countries, interested in research, policy analysis, and current developments in international agricultural trade. The objectives of the IATRC are to enhance the quality and relevance of international agricultural trade research and policy analysis; encourage collaborative research; facilitate communication among trade researchers and analysts drawn from universities, government agencies, and the private sector; and improve public understanding of international trade and trade policy issues. Each summer, the IATRC sponsors a symposium on a topic related to trade and trade policy from which proceedings are published. Additional information about the IATRC is available at http://iatrcweb.org.

NE-165 does research on the impacts of changes in strategies, technologies, consumer behavior, and policies on the economic performance of the food system, and on how private and public strategies influence improvement in food safety and other quality attributes. It has over 100 members around the world, primarily from universities and government agencies, and a core research group at the Food Marketing Policy Center located at the University of Connecticut and by subcontract at the University of Massachusetts. NE-165's specific research areas in the food system are industrial organization, competition policies, strategic decisionmaking and marketing, cooperative strategy, consumer risk perception and demand, risk assessment and benefit–cost analysis, and food quality and safety. Additional information about NE-165 is available at http://www.umass.edu/ne165.

The editors wish to thank Laura Bipes of the University of Minnesota for her pure competence in arranging the Montreal symposium. Nita Congress was our production editor and Bernice Eisen our indexer. We appreciate their professionalism in preparing this book in a timely and precise manner.

CONTENTS

SECTION I.
OVERVIEW AND CONCEPTUAL FOUNDATION

1. ISSUES IN DEMAND FOR QUALITY AND TRADE 3
Jean-Christophe Bureau, Wayne Jones, Estelle Gozlan, and Stephan Marette

2. A GREAT TRANSFORMATION IN WORLD TRADE LAW: CAN THE WTO STAY AFLOAT? 33
David G. Victor and Rebecca U. Weiner

3. UNIFYING TWO FRAMEWORKS FOR ANALYZING QUALITY AND QUALITY ASSURANCE FOR FOOD PRODUCTS 43
Julie A. Caswell, Corinna M. Noelke, and Eliza M. Mojduszka

4. LDC FOOD EXPORTS AND FOOD SAFETY STANDARDS IN HIGH-INCOME COUNTRIES: WHAT ROLE FOR THE PUBLIC SECTOR IN OVERCOMING BARRIERS TO TRADE? 63
Laurian J. Unnevehr

SECTION II.
CASE STUDIES

5. POTENTIAL IMPLICATIONS OF ANIMAL WELFARE CONCERNS AND PUBLIC POLICIES IN INDUSTRIALIZED COUNTRIES FOR INTERNATIONAL TRADE 77
David Blandford, Jean-Christophe Bureau, Linda Fulponi, and Spencer Henson

6. RESPONSE TO A FOOD SAFETY PROBLEM IN PRODUCE: A CASE STUDY OF A CYCLOSPORIASIS OUTBREAK 101
Linda Calvin, William Foster, Luis Solorzano, J. Daniel Mooney, Luis Flores, and Veronica Barrios

7. A CASE STUDY OF BEEF PRODUCTION AND EXPORT IN URUGUAY 129
María I. Marshall, Michael Boland, Daniel Conforte, and Deborah Cesar

SECTION III.
SPECIFIC ISSUES AND METHODOLOGICAL CHALLENGES

8. PRODUCT DIFFERENTIATION, SANITARY BARRIERS, AND ARBITRAGE IN WORLD POULTRY MARKETS 147
David Orden, Timothy Josling, and Donna Roberts

9. PRICE POLICIES AND THE DOMESTIC AND INTERNATIONAL DISTRIBUTION OF COMMODITY QUALITY: THEORY AND APPLICATION TO EU WHEAT 165
Julian M. Alston and Jennifer S. James

10. THE IMPACTS OF LABELING ON TRADE IN GOODS THAT MAY BE VERTICALLY DIFFERENTIATED ACCORDING TO QUALITY 181
Brian Roe and Ian Sheldon

11. LABELING BIOTECH FOODS: IMPLICATIONS FOR CONSUMER WELFARE AND TRADE 197
Elise Golan and Fred Kuchler

12. CONSUMER EFFECTS OF HARMONIZING INTERNATIONAL STANDARDS FOR TRADE IN ORGANIC FOODS 209
Luanne Lohr and Barry Krissoff

13. THE PUBLIC PROVISION OF INFORMATION: A WELFARE ANALYSIS OF EUROPEAN PRODUCTS WITH GEOGRAPHICAL INDICATIONS AND PRODUCTS WITH DESIGNATIONS OF ORIGIN 229
Angelo Maria Zago and Daniel Pick

INDEX 245

Global Food Trade and Consumer Demand for Quality

SECTION I

OVERVIEW AND CONCEPTUAL FOUNDATION

ISSUES IN DEMAND FOR QUALITY AND TRADE

Jean-Christophe Bureau, Wayne Jones, Estelle Gozlan, and Stephan Marette*

International trade flows in agro-food products have increased dramatically over the last three decades. Trade is likely to continue expanding now that agriculture is integrated into the overall framework of the General Agreement on Tariffs and Trade (GATT). In addition to the increase in the volume of trade, there has been a considerable increase in the diversity of products traded. Food products now come from more distant and more various origins. They are imported from countries that differ in institutional structure and regulatory framework and, therefore, in their perceived ability to protect consumers from unsafe products and deceptive practices. As a result, the ongoing process of trade liberalization raises consumer concerns about the safety of food products.

The issue of food safety has been particularly sensitive in recent years because of a number of outbreaks of foodborne diseases, e.g., bovine spongiform encephalopathy (BSE), *Escherichia coli*, *Salmonella*, *Campylobacteria*, and *Listeria* (OECD 1999). In a limited number of cases, these outbreaks were traced to imports, although statistics suggest that the safety of imported products is on average similar to that of domestic products. However, highly publicized cases linked to imports have spread the idea that globalization magnifies risks linked to food safety. Some consumer organizations have suggested that international standards are less protective of consumers than domestic and have expressed displeasure with international trade rules on food safety and quality (Silverglade 1998; see also the web pages of organizations such as the Center for Science in the Public Interest, Safe Tables Our Priority, or Public Citizen Inc.).

The development of trade also raises concerns that go beyond basic food safety. Broader aspects of the quality of food (taste, integrity) and the way it has been produced (the use of

* Jean-Christophe Bureau is with the Institut National Agronomique Paris-Grignon, Unité Mixte de Recherches en Economie Publique, Paris, and was with the Department of Economics of Iowa State University when this work was finalized. Wayne Jones is with the Food, Agriculture and Fisheries Directorate of the Organisation for Economic Co-operation and Development and secretary to that organization's Ad Hoc Group on Food Safety. Estelle Gozlan and Stephan Marette are with the Institut National de la Recherche Agronomique, UMR Economie Publique, Grignon, France. The views expressed in this chapter are those of the authors and do not necessarily represent the views of their respective institutions.

Global Food Trade and Consumer Demand for Quality, edited by Krissoff *et al.*
Kluwer Academic/Plenum Publishers, New York, 2002.

genetically engineered material, the impact on the environment, the impact on values such as animal welfare) have become issues in the public debate over regulation of the food industry.[1] New production methods driven by technology have added to consumer unease, fuelled by a growing mistrust of science and its interpretation in terms of food regulation (OECD 1999). This is particularly true in countries where food is closely associated with cultural values.

Consumer pressures to ensure food quality could give rise to new trade barriers, although the 1994 Uruguay Round introduced constraining disciplines. The World Trade Organization (WTO) addresses potential nontariff trade barriers associated with food quality primarily through the Sanitary and Phytosanitary (SPS) Agreement and a strengthened Technical Barriers to Trade (TBT) Agreement. Barriers to imports must now be based on scientific grounds. (See Annex I of OECD 1999 for a description of the SPS and TBT Agreements and the WTO Dispute Settlement Body.) However, enforcement of international rules based purely on science has resulted in some controversies. Countries differ in their culture as well in their technical skills and ability to enforce regulations. Domestic regulations often result from history, correspond to specific demands from consumers, or are designed to cope with a specific legal system which provides particular incentives for firms as far as product quality is concerned. This raises the question of the setting of international rules that enhance the process of trade liberalization while ensuring an adequate level of protection for consumers. (For a review of what is being done at the national and international levels to address food safety issues, see OECD 2000a.)

Several authors have emphasized the possible contribution of economists in addressing these concerns. They have argued that economics could be part of the science-based, rules-based approach that could be used for assessing the legitimacy of trade restrictions. Economics could contribute to clarifying international rules if disputes were resolved using economically based definitions of a nontariff barrier and of a genuine correction of market failure (Mahé 1997). The need for an increased role of cost-benefit analysis in designing sanitary and phytosanitary legislation has also been emphasized (Arrow et al. 1996, James and Anderson 1998). Others have suggested that economics could help quantify consumer concerns (through the use of economic valuation of their preferences) and that the whole process of economic assessment could be a useful negotiation tool (Bureau and Marette 2000). These authors have also raised the question of explicitly incorporating the economic analyses of the gains and losses caused by trade (and of the distribution of these gains) into international rules such as the WTO's procedure for settling disputes.

The following section presents a number of current issues related to consumer demand for quality in which the various policy responses have, or may, become trade issues. The chapter next illustrates some possible market inefficiencies linked to consumer's demand for quality that could arise with trade liberalization. The subsequent section examines more closely the use of economic criteria in setting international trade rules. The final section provides a summary and conclusions.

POLICY ISSUES IN FOOD QUALITY AND TRADE[2]

Establishing the Appropriate Level of Risk

With respect to food safety and human health, there are differences across countries as to the appropriate level of protection (acceptable level of risk). Establishment of this level in national law is inherently a political choice. WTO members may adopt sanitary and phytosanitary measures to achieve higher levels of protection than that provided by the international standards if they have a scientific justification based on risk assessment. The SPS Agreement identifies some of the factors that should be considered in the assessment of risk; there is no agreement, however, on what constitutes justifiable or acceptable risk.

To date, five SPS disputes have been examined by the WTO dispute settlement panels and the Appellate Body. Separate U.S. and Canadian complaints against the European Union's (EU's) ban on imports of meat treated with growth-promoting hormones are the only cases involving food safety concerns. Separate Canadian and U.S. complaints against Australian restrictions on imports of salmon addressed animal health protection, whereas a U.S. complaint against Japan involved protection of plants from insect damage. The WTO dispute settlement panels have examined and judged both the risk assessments undertaken by governments and their risk management decisions, in light of the obligations of the SPS Agreement.

The 1997 WTO panel that found against the EU hormone ban based its decision on science. However, some EU consumers saw the decision as a violation of national sovereignty and associated trade liberalization in the beef sector with the forced acceptance of unwanted foods. In some European countries, the panel's finding played a significant role in the rejection of globalization by a share of the population, who became opponents to the opening of a new round of multilateral trade negotiations in Seattle in December 1999.

In effect, the SPS Agreement references the standards, guidelines, and recommendations established by the Codex Alimentarius Commission relating to food additives, veterinary drug and pesticide residues, contaminants, methods of analysis and sampling, and codes and guidelines of hygienic practice. For animal health and epizootics, the SPS Agreement references the guidelines developed by the International Office of Epizootics. For plant health, the international standards developed under the auspices of the International Plant Protection Convention are referenced. For matters not covered by the above organizations, the SPS Committee may identify appropriate standards promulgated by other relevant international organizations open for membership to all members.

Although the term "risk management" does not appear in the SPS Agreement, the focus of the agreement is on the measures taken by WTO member governments to address sanitary and phytosanitary risks that may have an effect on international trade, rather than on the risks per se. A WTO member has the right to determine what level of sanitary protection it considers appropriate within its territory, but the objective of minimizing negative trade effects should be taken into consideration. Governments must avoid arbitrary or unjustifiable distinctions in the levels of risk they consider acceptable in different situations if these differences result in discrimination or are a disguised restriction of trade. In addition to the requirements that measures be based on scientific principles and not maintained against available scientific evidence, the measures cannot be more trade restrictive than necessary to achieve the desired level of health protection, taking into account technical and economic feasibility.

Applying the Precautionary Principle

Many consumer and environmental interest groups, promoting a "better safe than sorry" approach, argue that a more stringent precautionary approach should be applied to food safety; that is, measures should be taken to avoid potential injury to human health where scientific information is inconclusive. The role of precaution is currently being debated at the national and international levels, but there is little agreement on the definition of precaution or how it should be applied. Initiatives are under way within the Codex Alimentarius Commission to develop international guidelines on appropriate use of precaution in dealing with scientific uncertainty.

A precautionary approach is applied to the regulation of food safety in virtually all countries, but there are significant differences in how and where it is incorporated into food safety decisions. Precaution is generally regarded as an integral part of risk analysis. For example, maximum residue levels for pesticides typically include a wide safety margin such that legal limits are lower than those considered acceptable from a purely toxicological perspective. In some countries, however, explicit reference is made to an additional facet of precaution, referred to as the "precautionary principle," which is seen as an element of risk management and is applied when scientific information on risk is incomplete and there is sufficient evidence of potential unacceptable health effects.

The relevance of the precautionary principle in the interpretation of the SPS Agreement was raised by the parties to the dispute over the European Community ban on imports of meat treated with growth-promoting hormones. The European Community asserted that the precautionary principle was already a general customary rule of international law and, as such, would override obligations by virtue of SPS Articles 5.1 and 5.2 to base SPS measures on risk assessment based on available scientific evidence. The United States considered that there was not a precautionary principle in customary international law but simply a precautionary approach already incorporated in the SPS Agreement, while Canada viewed the concept as an emerging principle that might in the future crystallize into one of the "general principles of law recognised by civilised nations," within the meaning of Article 38(1)(c) of the Statute of the International Court of Justice.

In the EU hormone case, neither the dispute panel nor the Appellate Body made a definitive finding with regard to the status of the precautionary principle in international law. However, the Appellate Body made some observations on the relationship of the precautionary principle to the SPS Agreement, while noting that "the 'precautionary principle,' at least outside the field of international environmental law, still awaits authoritative formulation."[3]

Although no explicit reference is made to a precautionary principle or approach in the SPS Agreement, it has been recognized that it is given expression in the provision of Article 5.7.[4] This provision is thus among the first in international law to introduce the concept of precaution in an area other than the protection of the environment. At the same time, it further specifies the concept by elucidating its scope and conditions of implementation. In the context of the multilateral trading system, precaution in the adoption and enforcement of sanitary and phytosanitary measures takes on a provisional character and implies an active research for scientific evidence that could back up the provisionally adopted measures. Furthermore, unlike provisions in international environmental agreements, SPS Article 5.7 does not institute an obligation to act in the absence of scientific certainty, but rather the possibility not to refrain from acting as long as the scientific evidence requested by the agreement (Article 2.2) is not yet available.

The adoption of provisional measures on the basis of Article 5.7 is not limited to the cases where scientific evidence does not sufficiently support the existence of risk but can also take place where a member decides, in accordance with SPS Article 3.3 "to introduce or maintain sanitary or phytosanitary measures which result in a higher level of sanitary or phytosanitary protection than would be achieved by measures based on the relevant international standards, guidelines or recommendations..." In this case, the member can adopt stricter provisional measures, even if there is not enough scientific information to suggest that relevant international standards, guidelines, or recommendations would not be sufficient to achieve the level of sanitary or phytosanitary protection the member determined as appropriate.

Regulating Modern Biotechnology

Consumer response to genetically modified (GM) foods depends on perceived product benefits versus costs, confidence in government regulations, evaluations of possible health and environmental risks, and an individual's own ethical stance toward genetic engineering in general (OECD 2000b). Differences are particularly marked between North America and Europe. North Americans are overall quite favorable to the use of agricultural biotechnology for food production: two-thirds to three-quarters of them believe the technology can bring benefits to the environment as well as to nutrition (Hoban 1998). In contrast, Europeans are quite skeptical about the net benefits to be had from the technology in agriculture in its present state (Joly and Lemarié 1998). Governments take into account certain of these public concerns along with other important information in deciding if there is a need for specific policies about biotechnology.

In early 2000, the Organisation for Economic Co-operation and Development (OECD) held a conference on the scientific and health aspects of GM foods attended by some 400 scientists, regulators, nongovernmental organizations, and industry representatives from more than 25 developed and developing countries.[5] Although it was agreed that no adverse effects on human health have been reported in peer-reviewed scientific literature, there remains uncertainty about the potential long-term effects of GM food. These concerns fall under three general headings:

- *Human health.* There are concerns about the possible adverse effects on human health (e.g., allergic reactions, resistance to antibiotics) of introducing genetic material from a wide variety of sources into foodstuffs. Current methods for testing toxicity and allergenicity leave some uncertainties and need to be improved. Though feeding trials in animals may in some cases offer supplementary safety guarantees, it is unclear whether they will be applicable or useful for GM foods.
- *Environmental risks.* There are concerns that transgenic plants could generate negative effects on the environment either directly or through interaction between existing and new genes (e.g., introduction of new plants, creation of "super weeds" through "outcrossing," loss of biodiversity). The impact in tropical zones is particularly uncertain, as most field trials have been carried out in temperate zones.

- *Ethical considerations.* There are concerns about the use and patenting of genetic materials linked to issues of intellectual property rights, implications for developing countries, dietary intake, and religious convictions (e.g., crossing species boundaries, "terminator" seeds that are genetically made sterile, excessive industrial concentration due to genes patenting). The valuation of acceptable levels of different types of risks is also part of the ethical considerations involved in the determination of the acceptability of GM foods.

These concerns or uncertainties have generated a demand in many countries for labeling products containing or made through genetic modification. Most countries have food labeling requirements with respect to food content, but, with the advent of GM foods, the issue of labeling according to process or production methods has arisen in a number of countries. In 1999, Japan, South Korea, Australia, and New Zealand joined the EU and Switzerland in requiring GM food labeling to be applied in the near future. These regulations contrast with those in the United States and Canada, which do not require GM labeling unless the food or food ingredient is no longer substantially equivalent to the corresponding existing food or food ingredient with regard to composition, nutritional value, or intended use, or if potential allergens are identified.[6]

Modern biotechnology has not been a major issue of discussion in the WTO to date, although countries have been notifying biotechnology-related measures under both the SPS and TBT Agreements. With respect to labeling requirements on GM foods introduced by several WTO members, discussions have occurred primarily in the TBT Committee. The TBT Agreement permits governments to impose labeling requirements necessary to fulfill legitimate objectives, although members disagree as to whether providing information on the method of production to consumers is a legitimate objective.

Addressing Socioeconomic Concerns

The extent to which socioeconomic concerns influence risk decisions varies across countries. In some countries, there is a recognition that consideration should be given to the economic costs that food safety regulation imposes on consumers and food businesses (and the consequent impact on international competitiveness) as well as on society as a whole. These costs are frequently assessed as part of the risk analysis process. For example, regulatory impact analysis may be applied to new regulatory or legislative proposals in order to assess the associated costs and benefits. Concerns about the costs of not regulating are also considered, including the societal costs of medical care, lost productivity, and premature mortality.

The procedures for the elaboration of Codex Standards and Related Texts state that the Codex Alimentarius Commission "should have due regard to the purposes of the Codex Alimentarius concerning protection of the health of consumers and ensuring fair trade practices as well as the economic interests of the Member concerned." When elaborating standards, Codex may consider where appropriate "other legitimate factors" relevant for the health protection of consumers and for the promotion of fair practices in food trade. Regarding the general aspects of "other factors" in the decision process, the Codex Committee on General Principles is developing a general orientation for Codex work in the framework of risk analysis, with the understanding that other Codex committees responsible for risk analysis can provide specific clarification on the integration of such factors in their work.

The question of whether socioeconomic concerns such as animal welfare, the environment, and biodiversity should be addressed within, or separate from, the food safety regulatory system is more controversial. Some countries emphasize the importance of taking account of such factors in their food safety regulations. In these countries, these factors are included in the basis for selecting risk management measures but not in the assessment of health risks. Other countries express concern that the introduction of such factors may undermine the integrity and credibility of science-based food regulatory systems and could be used to impede trade unjustifiably in agricultural and food products. Efforts to discuss and agree on the legitimacy of such factors in food safety regulation are under way in a variety of international fora, including the Codex Alimentarius Commission.

Limits of Science

Although Article 5.3 of the SPS Agreement (and Article 2.2 of the TBT Agreement) mention economic assessment, such considerations only have a limited place in the settlement of sanitary and technical disputes, and economic considerations are far less central than risk assessment. While the reference to a "science-based, rules-based approach" is appropriate for most sanitary and phytosanitary issues, this approach may be less effective in solving those conflicts related to other aspects of food quality that are less easily measurable (Bureau and Marette 2000).

From a scientific point of view, what is safe in one country should also be considered safe in others. However, from an economic point of view, the issue is more complex. The same level of risk is not perceived the same way everywhere, and the relative weight given to the various attributes is different across countries (e.g., acceptance of unpasteurized cheese, which is considered a delicacy in some countries and a potential hazard in others). Moreover, science is not always conclusive. For example, uncertainty still surrounds the adequacy of standards for chemical residues (Antle 1995) and the maximum residue limit for bovine somatotropin (rBGH) in Codex.[7] Even if only a few respected scientists disagree with the majority of the profession, the jurisprudence of the SPS Agreement clearly indicates that such opinions should be taken into account in dispute settlement (Roberts 1998, Bureau and Doussin 2000). The willingness of several countries to give more scope to the precautionary principle is likely to make scientific considerations even more debated.

In practice, it is almost impossible to separate scientific considerations from economic and political ones. Ever since scientists' recommendations acquired the status of potentially mandatory standards with considerable economic interests at stake, it has been difficult for scientists to ignore economic considerations. Salter (1988) and Powell (1997) have given numerous examples of "mandated science" or "negotiated science." Manufacturers are also strongly represented in the committees of the various organizations that set international standards, and economic interactions with standard setting are more than likely.

Protocol on Biosafety

Parties to the Convention on Biological Diversity agreed on the Protocol on Biosafety in January 2000. Under the protocol, parties may take into account—consistent with their international obligations—socioeconomic considerations arising from the transboundary movement of living modified organisms (LMOs) resulting from modern biotechnology that may have an adverse effect on the conservation of biological diversity.

In relation to LMOs for direct use as food or feed or for processing, parties to the protocol making a decision regarding the domestic use, including placement on the market, of an LMO that may be subject to transboundary movement are required to notify other parties. The information that must accompany the notification is set out in the protocol and includes a risk assessment report. The objective of the risk assessment is to identify and evaluate the potential adverse effects of LMOs on the conservation and sustainable use of biological diversity in the potential receiving environment, also taking into account risks to human health. Where there is uncertainty regarding the level of risk, it may be addressed by requesting further information, implementing appropriate risk management strategies, and/or monitoring the receiving environment.

The protocol has a built-in agenda and calendar for work on issues that need further elaboration including the handling, transport, packaging, and identification of LMOs; procedures and mechanisms to facilitate decisionmaking; elaboration of international rules and procedures for liability and redress for damage resulting from transboundary movement of LMOs; cooperative procedures and institutional mechanisms for promoting compliance and handling noncompliance; and modalities and operations of the Biosafety Clearinghouse for information sharing.

Animal Welfare

Amid the broader public concern for food quality and production methods, animal welfare has emerged as an important issue in many countries. Increasingly, society looks to governments to adopt policies to ensure farm animal welfare, and legislation for animal welfare has evolved from simple anticruelty measures to more comprehensive rules and guidelines for the rearing, transport, and slaughter of farm animals. Most OECD countries have rules governing the transport and slaughter of farm animals; many also have regulations for the rearing of farm animals. Policy responses to animal welfare concerns differ according to cultural, social, and political values.

The key question in this area is how domestic objectives can be achieved without violating rules of the international trading system. Though no trade disputes have yet arisen, such conflicts could easily arise, given the economic importance of trade in animals and livestock products and as different regulations evolve among countries. When a country's domestic regulations for animal welfare standards are higher than those of their trading partners—and, by implication, its costs of production are higher too—domestic producers may find that they are priced out of export markets or even from their domestic market when imports are permitted. This makes it difficult for a country to raise animal welfare standards without regard to what is done in other countries.

Current interpretations of the WTO trade agreements are not likely to permit trade restrictions based on animal welfare production criteria. In particular, Article III of the GATT requires identical treatment for "like" products regardless of country of origin. Production measures that ensure animal welfare do not alter in any identifiable manner the final product; thus, production processes cannot be used to distinguish products, and such products may be considered "like" products. Restricting trade on the basis of production methods would be in conflict with this interpretation of Article III. The trade agreements do, however, provide for exceptions, although case law in some of these areas has not yet been established. For instance, it may be possible to appeal to Article XX(a), which permits trade restrictions for reasons of public morals, but current interpretations suggest it must be the effect of the product that is morally offensive and not its production method. Article XX(b) provides for trade restrictions to protect human, plant, or animal health, but farm animal welfare is not, strictly speaking, an issue of animal health.

Labeling products according to production standards may be an option, as it would at least permit consumers to make informed choices. It is uncertain whether required labeling of imports according to production methods is possible within the framework of the TBT Agreement, which ensures that labeling and other technical requirements do not create unnecessary obstacles to trade. This agreement applies to any food safety regulation that may fall outside the scope of the SPS Agreement, as well as to other food quality requirements such as nutritional standards, composition, grading, packaging, and labeling.

The TBT Agreement encourages WTO members to base their standards or technical regulations on internationally developed standards but does not explicitly identify the relevant standard-setting bodies. A government may choose not to base national requirements on an international standard if it considers this inappropriate to achievement of its particular objectives. These objectives may include the prevention of deceptive practices; protection of human, animal, or plant health or safety (if not covered by the SPS Agreement); or protection of the environment. The TBT Agreement requires notifications similar to those for sanitary or phytosanitary measures; it further requires notification of bilateral technical agreements and compliance by national standard-setting bodies with a Code of Good Practice for the Preparation, Adoption, and Application of Standards.

Protecting Quality and Authenticity

Some countries, especially in Europe, have developed regulations governing the use of certain geographical names in order to guarantee consumers the authenticity of these products or safeguard the typical character attached to the traditional production and processing methods. Some of these products, because of their quality or character, have indeed developed over time a reputation that has led to a strong price differentiation and the creation of market niches (e.g., Bordeaux, Champagne, Porto, and Xeres wines and Parma ham). Geographical labels do not necessarily correspond to patented know-how but to a particular practice that the government wants to regulate to achieve the above-mentioned objectives. Such technical specifications usually lead to higher costs of production, which producers may choose to follow with a view to the market premiums obtained for such "appellation" products.

Problems of intellectual property rights to a region's traditional products that demonstrate specific know-how but do not bring novelty to the product remain unsettled.[8] Wine appellations, for example, continue to be an area of contention between the EU and the United States (Chen 1996). Different positions also exist on the issue of restricting inputs. It is sometimes difficult to judge whether products made using other methods are fraudulent imitations. It is not always evident that the technical restrictions in question are necessary in order to obtain a particular quality.[9] Imposing such restrictions on other countries can create obstacles for their exporters. Conversely, imposing them on domestic producers alone can leave them at a competitive disadvantage.[10]

Legal, historical, and economic arguments lie behind these international disagreements (OECD 2001). Each country has its own legal system of protection for geographical names. Some have instituted a special protection scheme based on designations (or appellations) of origin. Others have preferred to use marks (trademarks, collective marks, or certification marks). Some names protected as designations of origin in the country of origin have been registered as marks elsewhere. But other names so protected cannot secure protection in another country, because a firm there has already registered them as trademarks. The result is a clash between the rights attaching to designations of origin and to trademarks. Then of course there are names that are deemed worthy of protection in some countries but deemed generic in others.

In many cases, there is a historical dimension to be taken into account. A number of European producers settled abroad in Australia, the United States, Canada, and South Africa, for instance, and began producing wine under the same names as in their country of origin. Over the years, numerous marks have been registered. Their proprietors also claim intellectual property rights.

The economic dimension was noted above. A protected geographical name can have a reputation that has been built up over time. Misappropriating that name means taking advantage of another producer's investment in goodwill by trading on its product's reputation among consumers and their good faith. In terms of trade flows, a geographical indication may be used to penetrate a new market (in which the name is registered and valued by consumers).

AN ECONOMIC FRAMEWORK FOR ANALYZING FOOD QUALITY AND TRADE ISSUES

International agreements approach the concept of product quality mainly on a scientific and technical basis, and economic aspects are second to risk assessment and conformity to technical standards. Roughly speaking, trade restrictions must be justified by sound science, and measures that are not supported by scientific evidence based on well-codified risk assessment are unlikely to be found in compliance with international agreements by WTO panels (OECD 1999; Roberts 1998; Bureau and Doussin 2000, who give details about the jurisprudence of the SPS panels). That is, even though some references are made to the economic cost of the measures (e.g., Article 5.3. of the SPS Agreement), far less attention is paid to the costs and benefits of the measures than to the scientific risk assessment.

Degree of risk, however, bears little relationship with the overall impact of that risk in the economy. That is, measuring risk gives no indication of the loss of utility for consumers. Although there may be a very slight risk that a product is dangerous, the mere fact of knowing this to be the case could result in a very high proportion of consumers refusing to buy the product, with associated high welfare costs (Josling 1998). In addition, product safety is one of many components of product quality, which is defined as a multi-attribute concept (Caswell and Mojduszka 1996). If consumers have genuine preferences for other characteristics of the products than the safety attribute, these characteristics affect their utility. A broad definition of product quality would include all characteristics that affect consumer utility, including safety, taste, integrity, etc. With such a concept of quality, consumer satisfaction or dissatisfaction depends not only on the product's characteristics but also on the way in which it has been produced.

Economic theory addresses product quality mainly in terms of differentiated products. The issue of product safety can best be addressed as a vertical differentiation problem. That is, if the price of all products were equal, consumers would unambiguously choose the highest quality. Horizontal differentiation (at equal prices, consumers would choose different products) refers to a concept of product variety rather than quality *stricto sensu* and is more appropriate to some other product attributes than safety, such as color, shape, or taste.

Since the early work of Krugman (1979), there has been considerable literature on trade of differentiated products. Overall, the introduction of product differentiation in the theory of international trade has not contradicted the traditional arguments for trade liberalization. The fact that country specialization according to comparative advantage leads to lower real prices has not been challenged. Hence, for a given level of expenditure, freer trade allows for the possibility of consuming the same amount, but a higher quality, of products (vertical differentiation). In other cases, trade liberalization reduces the cost of the consumer's preferred basket and increases welfare through increased product variety (horizontal differentiation). When markets are more open, economies of scale reduce production costs at constant quality. The increased competition resulting from trade liberalization encourages firms to offer a better quality-price mix. In the case of vertical differentiation, regulatory barriers to trade typically result in a restriction on consumer choice in the available quality segment. The market may not be covered as a result, and a proportion of the population may be deprived of the opportunity to consume a cheaper but lower quality product.

However, if the fundamental results of freer trade are not altered by the introduction of product differentiation, accounting for quality differences raises specific issues through the linkage with imperfect competition and imperfect information. As a result, freer trade may sometimes have a relatively ambiguous effect on welfare in the presence of heterogeneous quality of the products. This is particularly relevant with regard to food safety issues. Overall, the beneficial effects of trade liberalization may be attenuated by spontaneous market inefficiencies. The effects involved fall in the general category of cases particularly well described by Stiglitz (1994) where incomplete markets (including incomplete markets for risk), nonconvexities, and imperfect information limit the scope of the central welfare theorems, which are implicit in the standard legitimization of trade liberalization.

The following subsections focus on three economic issues linked to food quality and trade: imperfect competition, imperfect knowledge, and the presence of risk. By exposing some hypothetical situations where trade liberalization could have possible adverse effects on quality, the intention is to illustrate how to better take into account consumer concerns regarding trade liberalization. If some consumers oppose globalization on the basis of product quality, this implies that trade affects their welfare. These concerns can be addressed by the usual framework of normative economics.

Quality-Cutting Trade Liberalization

As a general case, imperfect competition does not necessarily provide incentives for supplying socially optimal quality (Krouse 1990). A monopoly firm will in general seek to limit the quantity on offer, but may in some cases set the quality on offer at an undesirable level for the collectivity in order to maximize the firm's private profit. Because social welfare depends on the sum of consumer willingness to pay, whereas a monopoly setting the quality of its output considers only the marginal consumer willingness to pay, the quality choice will be less than optimum from a social standpoint (Spence 1975). This is particularly true in the presence of fixed costs and entry barriers. This might be a self-reinforcing procedure since Shaked and Sutton (1983) have shown that vertical differentiation may lead to a natural oligopoly.

However, by increasing competition, trade liberalization may sometimes have a negative influence on the quality on offer. Greater competition may result in certain quality segments not being supplied at all or in an overall decline in quality on the market (Gal-Or 1989a). When firms have fixed costs, it has also been shown that greater competition can cause producers to set quality levels farther removed from the socially optimum level in order to limit a fall in profits (Reitzes 1992). *Ceteris paribus*, by increasing competition in an industry, freer trade could encourage quality-cutting or fictitious differentiation, especially if consumers track prices more readily than quality (Beales, Craswell, and Salop 1981), or when there is a negative correlation between the quantity of output and quality (e.g., in sectors where quality depends on restricting yields).

The hypothetical case in Box 1 illustrates a mechanism by which trade liberalization (and more generally increased competition) could affect producers' choice on quality and lower their incentive to enhance safety. It is not intended to describe a realistic situation, and it relies on extremely simplified assumptions (the negative effect resulting from the possible decrease in effort is lower when one considers a bilateral opening of borders, for example). In reality, markets are more competitive. However, the mechanism illustrated could occur in real life, since it is only an international extension of quality-cutting competition. For example, in many countries, domestic competition policy acknowledges that increased competition can result in lower quality. The regulator often permits barriers to entry, such as geographical barriers (e.g., areas of exclusive dealership to ensure that adequate maintenance service will be provided) or vertical contracts between processors and dealers. The purpose is to limit competition when it is acknowledged that this results in an increase of quality and an improvement in collective welfare.

In practice, it is difficult to imagine a situation where any adverse effects on quality caused by excessive competition leading to suboptimal product differentiation, as a result of the opening up of borders, would outweigh the benefits of trade liberalization. Provided that consumers are not being misled when a quality is claimed, quality-cutting competition is likely to be limited to very specific cases. Nevertheless, it is a point on which theory remains ambiguous, and cases where competition from foreign firms has an adverse effect on product quality cannot be ruled out. In addition, the problems of less-than-optimal quality supply can be exacerbated by imperfect information.

Imperfect Information

Broadly speaking, if consumers are not fully informed about product characteristics, they may consume a dangerous product, acquire a quality they do not wish to consume, or pay a price that does not reflect the real quality of the good in question. In all of these cases, the level of welfare in society may be lower than under perfect information. Relying on an expected quality rather than on a given certainty affects consumer behavior (adverse

Box 1. A Possible Case Where Trade Results in Lower Quality Supplied

The purpose of the following stylized model, which draws from Gozlan and Marette (2000), is to show a possible mechanism where trade liberalization lowers incentives for ensuring product quality. For the sake of simplicity, assume that trade liberalization results in a shift from a monopoly to an oligopoly. In a given country, consider a producer deciding upon a level of quality effort $\lambda \epsilon [0;1]$. Although the demonstration is more general, we focus here on a safety effort. Without loss of generality, this effort can be identified as the probability of getting safe products. Only safe products are on demand. The cost of the effort is $f\lambda^2/2$, which is independent of quantity produced. By assumption, the producer decides upon λ in a first step, on the basis of an expected price over the present and future periods (subgame perfect equilibrium). Consumers and suppliers are aware of the quality of the products on offer. Demand for high-quality (safe) products can be represented as $x = 1 - p/q_h$ (see Mussa and Rosen 1978).

This follows the assumption of a continuum of consumers with different preferences θ for quality, represented by a uniform unit distribution of a parameter $\theta \epsilon [0,1]$. The net utility of each consumer willing to buy a unit of the high-quality q_h for a price p is $U = \theta q_h - p$. The parameter $\theta_0 = p/q_h$ characterizes the consumer who is indifferent between acquiring the good or not, so that demand for high-quality goods is $x = 1 - \theta_0$. The profit of the monopolistic supplier is $\Pi = \lambda p(1 - p/q_h) - f\lambda^2/2$.

By backward induction, profit maximization leads to an equilibrium price $p^* = q_h/2$ and to a quality choice $\lambda^* = Min[1; q_h/(4f)]$. When the unit cost of quality effort f is low, the effort is maximal, i.e., $\lambda^* = 1$. This leads, by assumption, to production of safe products only. Overall welfare, the sum of consumer surplus and producer profit, is $W_A = \Pi_A + CS_A = 3q_h/8 - f/2$. If $f > q_h/4$, the effort is $\lambda^* = q_h/(4f) < 1$, resulting in the possible production of tainted products. The effort decreases when f increases, and welfare is $W_B = q_h^2/16f$.

Now, assume that the country opens its domestic market to imports. The foreign supplier (F) is similar to the domestic one (D). Assume that they compete in price, provided that they both produce safe products. This occurs with a probability $\lambda_D\lambda_F$. Price-cutting competition leads to a zero profit. Consumer surplus is $sc_c = \int_{\theta_0}^{1} \theta q_h d\theta = q_h/2$ with $\theta_0 = 0$ in that particular case where the market is covered. With a probability $\lambda_D(1 - \lambda_F)$, the domestic firm is the only one to offer safe products, and the foreign one faces no demand. The gross profit of the domestic producer is $q_h/4$, and consumer surplus is $sc_c' = \int_{1/2}^{1} (\theta q_h - p^*) d\theta = q_h/8$. In the first step, the expected profit of the domestic supplier is therefore $\Pi_D = \lambda_D(1 - \lambda_F)q_h/4 - \lambda_D^2/2$.

Maximization of the expected profit leads to a quality effort $\lambda^{**}_D = \lambda^{**}_F + q_h/4f + q_h < 1$ as soon as $f > 0$. That is, the effort in quality is lower under free trade than under autarky, since $\lambda^{**}D = \lambda^*$. The reduction in profit leads the domestic supplier to cut the quality effort. The resulting domestic welfare is $W_C = q^2_h(q_h + 3f)/2(q_h + 4f)^2$.

Denote f_1 as the unit cost of quality effort so that $W_A = W_C$. The welfare under autarky is larger than under free trade for the domestic country when $f \epsilon [f_1; q_h/2\sqrt{2})]$.

The negative effect on welfare caused by the decrease in effort dominates the positive effect caused by increased competition (i.e., the reduction in deadweight losses). As a result, freer trade results in both a decrease in product safety and in domestic welfare. Conversely, the welfare of the domestic country under autarky is lower than under free trade when f is close to zero or when f becomes very large—i.e., $f < f_1$ and $f > q_h/(2\sqrt{2})$—meaning that the effect of the fall in safety effort is offset by the reduction of deadweight losses. When f is close to zero, the effort of both firms is close to the effort of a firm under autarky (i.e., $\lambda^* = 1$).

selection effect). In addition, the workings of the market may cause vendors to offer an inadequate level of quality or safety when information is imperfect (moral hazard effect).

In all cases, imperfect information has a cost. The most widely known case is the classic "lemon" effect, described in Akerlof's famous example of poor quality chasing away high quality on the second-hand car market. When consumers are not able to distinguish the specific quality of different products, they are not willing to pay as high a price as they would if they were sure that the product was of high quality. Akerlof (1970) has shown that imperfect consumer information about product quality could even result in a total closedown of the market (absence of trade) if, because of a lack of information, buyer willingness to pay was insufficient to cover production costs. If buyer willingness to pay is less than the cost of producing high-quality goods, only low-quality goods (those less costly to produce) are traded, and high quality is frozen out of the market.

Bureau, Marette, and Schiavina (1998) have investigated the economic mechanisms linked to adverse selection in the case of the EU ban on hormone-treated beef (see Box 2 for a brief description of the analytical framework). The conclusions could be extended to imports containing GM material, or all kinds of credence goods where consumers cannot draw information on the product quality based on previous consumption. They show that it is theoretically possible for the welfare loss resulting from reduced consumer willingness to pay to outweigh the welfare gain resulting from cheaper imports. Under these circumstances, it is possible for trade liberalization to result in greater trade flows but a

Box 2. A Possible Case of Trade That Reduces Consumption

The purpose of this example, drawn from Bureau, Marette, and Schiavina (1998) is to illustrate a case where trade increases imperfect consumer information on quality, leading to a decrease in consumption and possibly to multiple equilibria. Consider a simple one-period framework under vertical differentiation, with two qualities for a single good and a competitive industry. Assume that good 2 (hormone-free beef) is perceived by European consumers as of higher quality than hormone-treated beef (denoted by subscript 1). Respective production costs are c_2 and c_1, with $c_1 < c_2$. The aggregate supply function $S_i(p)$ and aggregate surplus for producers of quality i products are $S_i(p) = p/c_i$, and $Ps_i = pq_i$ 2 $\frac{1}{2}c_i q_i^2$. Demand is represented by the classic framework introduced by Mussa and Rosen (1978). Consumers purchase one unit of the good and have different preferences for quality, represented by a uniform unit distribution of a parameter $\theta \in [0,1]$. Consumer willingness to pay for a quality k is given by uk, and increases with θ and k. The net utility of an individual buyer with a preference for quality θ is equal to $\theta k - p$. Aggregate demand depends on consumer belief about the relative quality of the two types of meat, but also on consumer information on the types of meat available on the market.

The parameter β measures the difference between the two perceptions of quality. That is, if β is close to zero, consumers see quality 1 as being much inferior to quality 2. If β is close to one, consumers perceive almost no difference between quality 1 and 2, i.e., between hormone-treated and hormone-free beef.

Under autarky, hormone prohibition is enforced in the domestic country. Consumers know with certainty the quality of the product. Their expected quality is therefore the perceived quality k_2. Demand is $D_2(p) = 1 - p_2/k_2$. Supply is $S_2(p) = p_2/c_2$, and equilibrium results in welfare $W^A = k_2^2/2(c_2 + k_2)$. Domestic producers benefit from the autarky situation, since they do not face competition from foreigners. Consumers suffer from the absence of choice between hormone-free goods and cheaper goods. Some consumers may prefer to buy quality 1 products at a lower price than quality 2 products, and under autarky the market is not covered.

Empirically, consumers who suffer from the ban are those who have little aversion to hormone-treated meat products and who would buy these if they were cheaper than the goods presently available in the EU. The lack of product diversity limits domestic welfare in the autarky situation. On the other hand, there is no uncertainty on quality, and therefore none of the problems linked to adverse selection.

Opening borders to products whose quality is perceived as low by EU consumers may result in market inefficiencies if buyers are unable to determine the actual quality of the products decline in collective welfare worldwide. It remains to be proved whether what is possible in theory will actually happen in practice. At a theoretical level, however, there is a substantial body of research to show that information effects may limit the welfare gains made possible by trade liberalization as a result of lower prices and greater product diversity (Thilmany and Barrett 1997, Grossman and Shapiro 1988).

To alleviate market inefficiencies due to imperfect information, vendors may signal the quality of their products. For an experience good (i.e., when consumers detect quality from past purchase decisions), this signal may be conveyed by price. Shapiro (1983) has shown that a higher price than the perfect information price could encourage producers to offer high quality on a lasting basis in order to preserve their reputations. This price supplement constitutes the information rent, which enables quality to be maintained over time and creates an incentive not to cheat on quality. It therefore informs consumers of the quality of the products. However, there is a cost to society in comparison with a situation of perfect information, since consumers have to pay the higher price needed to signal

they purchase. Consumers expect an average quality when both domestic and imported products are available on the market. Total supply $S(p)$ includes domestic supply $S_2(p)$ and imports $S_1(p)$. However, there is a single price clearing the market, at least if no label makes it possible to segment the market. Assuming rational expectation on quality, it is possible to determine the equilibrium price and derive producer and consumer surplus. One can show that trade liberalization has two opposite effects on overall welfare. The first is caused by imperfect information. Since consumers cannot differentiate between the two qualities, they expect an average quality $\bar{k} < k_2$. This results in a decrease both in price and demand for the domestic production. The second effect is a price decrease. One can show that if trade liberalization involves a large decrease in the quality expected by consumers, and if the difference in production costs of imported production relative to domestic products is small, trade liberalization can result in welfare losses for the domestic country. The parameter β, which determines perceived quality, plays a key role in the welfare changes resulting from trade liberalization.

As is often the case under imperfect information, trade may also result in multiple equilibria, as described by Wilson (1980). Bureau, Marette, and Schiavina (1998) provide an example, with a slight change in the demand function for hormone-free products, i.e., $S_2(p) = (p - H)/c_2$, where $H > 0$ is a given constant. Consumer demand is no longer linear in p, since it depends on the average quality $\bar{k}$ perceived by consumers. Market clearing under free trade may result in two possible equilibria, in the sense that for the same value of the exogenous parameters c_1, c_2, β, and H, there are two possible prices clearing the market. The determination of one equilibrium among many possible equilibria depends on many factors, and there is no reason for the optimal equilibrium to be selected. In this (theoretical) case, trade liberalization can result either in a loss or gain of welfare in a somewhat random way, compared to the autarky situation, depending on which equilibrium is selected.

Imperfect information therefore has important empirical implications. First, trade liberalization may result in a situation where goods perceived as low-quality products drive high-quality products out of the market. When consumers are reluctant to eat the only goods supplied on the market, this is hardly a situation that is satisfactory from the public point of view. For particular values of the parameters, the aggregate welfare of the two countries could even be lower under free trade than under autarky, since the welfare losses of the importing country could exceed the welfare gains of the exporter. Second, the possibility of multiple equilibria caused by asymmetric information could increase uncertainty on the market, and producers may not know which equilibrium price will prevail in the future. In theory, it is possible that trade liberalization involves either welfare gains or losses for a given country in a somewhat unpredictable way.

quality (see Box 3 for a brief presentation of the framework). This means that if, because of the existence of imports of less familiar products, consumers have doubts about the quality of the products available on the market, they may have to pay a higher price for recovering the information on quality. The information costs must be taken into account when assessing the overall impact of trade on welfare.

In addition, signaling mechanisms based on reputation building do not work with credence goods (i.e., when consumers do not detect quality even after consumption, a frequent case with quality dimensions that involve production methods). As consumers never detect the quality of the product, repeat purchases do not bring them any additional information and will not change their behavior, thus not providing any incentive to producers to offer higher quality. With credence goods, there is no spontaneous mechanism for market regulation, and it is more difficult to indicate quality in a credible way. It is also difficult to monitor the production process of imported credence goods, which is the sole means for acquiring information about their quality. Foreign firms are also less exposed to judicial sanctions (liability), which may encourage fraud when the consumer is unable to verify the quality of the good in question directly. The market failures highlighted by Akerlof may extend into the long term. If, for example, trade liberalization results in the presence of GM organisms in a country where consumers have a low willingness to pay for these products, market inefficiencies can be detrimental to welfare. Alleviating these inefficiencies may require public intervention, which also has a cost for society.[11]

Increased Risk Resulting from International Trade

By allowing the spread of pests and pathogens, international trade may increase sanitary and phytosanitary risk. The blocking of sewers in North American cities by exotic mollusks brought in on the hulls of cargo ships is one example of this phenomenon. Various outbreaks of food poisoning in the United States caused by imported foods provide another example (e.g., gastroenteritis—*Cyclospora*—apparently due to fruit from Guatemala, and epidemics linked to Peruvian carrots, Mexican strawberries, Thai coconut milk, Chinese mushrooms, Israeli snack foods, etc.). Food poisoning imposes costs on society, such as lower yields in the case of an epizootic or the spread of a plant pest, or health care costs. These costs may be considerable because of the externalities that exist where epidemics are concerned.

Trade liberalization therefore modifies the public good aspect of food safety. For example, a country's reputation as a producer of safe food may suffer when there is an outbreak of a foodborne disease, affecting all exporters through the misdeed of only one producer. By increasing the number of consumers of a given product, freer trade may also modify the economically optimal provision of food safety, since, as is generally the case with public goods, this provision is a function of the sum of the willingness to pay of all consumers.

Usually, when economic agents are risk-averse, they are willing to pay in order to eliminate risk (e.g., in the form of insurance), and the social cost of risk may be estimated as the difference between the anticipated welfare and the welfare of society that would prevail in a situation without uncertainty.[12] As far as food safety is concerned, however, consumer aversion to risk is complex. In some cases, consumers are willing to pay a very high premium for zero risk in comparison with very low risk (Magat and Viscusi 1992). In

Box 3. A Possible Case Where Trade Affects Incentives for Signaling Quality

The purpose of this example, inspired by Falvey (1989), is to illustrate a possible unwanted effect of trade liberalization should trade make it costlier to signal product quality. Consider an experience good such that consumers repeat their purchases over several periods, drawing lessons from the quality of the goods they bought in the previous period. Consider a vertical differentiation framework such that quality is a single attribute and consumers are willing to pay a higher price for higher quality. Producers of high-quality goods can signal their quality to imperfectly informed consumers. A convenient representation is the classical price distortion described by Shapiro (1983).

Assume a competitive industry, and that production cost $c(q)$ increases with the quality q. In period 1, firms set a price that is acceptable by consumers who are not aware of the quality of the product. That is, they set a price equal to the minimum quality that it is possible to market, given technology or a possible minimum quality standard q_o. A firm choosing to produce a quality $q > q_o$ therefore experiences a loss $c(q) - c(q_o)$ in the first period. This corresponds to the initial investment in reputation. The equilibrium price in the following period must therefore be high enough for the firm to sustain its quality effort. The price that provides a credible quality signal to the consumer is therefore $p(q) = c(q) + r[c(q) - c(q_o)]$. The term after the "+" sign is the information rent, r being a discount factor (all future time periods are assumed to be aggregated into a single "second" period). Incentives for maintaining a reputation, rather than milking it at a given point in time, require a positive price distortion in the second period. This distortion is the information rent. If a firm sold a low-quality product with a price signaling higher quality, buyers would not repeat their purchase from this particular firm. This mechanism describes a quality signal to consumers through the product price. However, it is widely used, since the initial investment in reputation can represent other forms of quality signal (investment in advertising, etc.).

In the context of international trade, consumers may have imperfect information on the origin of the goods sold on the domestic market. This case is developed by Falvey (1989). Assume that foreign producers benefit from a lower production cost for low-quality goods, while domestic producers are more competitive in the production of high-quality goods. Opening the market to imports would result in a decrease in price for the lower quality segment of the market. However, it will also affect the price distortion that is necessary to signal high quality. Indeed, sellers now have access to a cheaper low quality that they could sell at a high price if they milked their reputations. The incentives for maintaining their reputations are therefore different from those under autarky. The price that makes it possible to maintain a supply of quality q on the domestic market is now $N(q) = c(q) + r[c(q) - c^*(q_o)]$, where the asterisk denotes foreign production cost. The equilibrium price is not $Min[p^*(q), p(q)]$ as it would be under perfect information, but $Min[p^*(q), N(q)]$. Falvey shows that trade has, therefore, two opposite effects. The decrease in price on the low-quality segment increases welfare, but the increase in price in the high-quality segment—which is detrimental to welfare—can result in an overall decrease in welfare.

addition, consumers' behavior can be affected by what they imagine to be a risk, even if it is not backed up by scientific evidence, resulting in costs to society.[13] Trade liberalization, which exposes consumers to less familiar products, may increase the number of cases where consumers have an inappropriate evaluation of the risk level, raising some very difficult questions for economists. Pollak (1995, 1998) shows that the way imagined risks should be accounted for by economists, in particular in cost-benefit analysis, is still unclear.

It is not easy to assess the extent to which any increase in sanitary and phytosanitary risk is attributable to international trade rather than other factors such as tourism, and the previous subsections show that estimating the social costs of these extra risks is difficult.

However, the increased risk may limit the welfare gains from international trade and should, in any rigorous approach, be taken into consideration when assessing the gains resulting from trade liberalization.

Trade Liberalization and Welfare: A Case-by-Case Assessment

The examples developed by Falvey (Box 3) and Bureau, Marette, and Schiavina (Box 2) are very particular cases. They are presented as illustrations of possible economic mechanisms, not as empirical evidence that freer trade can have negative effects on product quality. In practice, however, it is conceivable that imperfect information on product quality raises problems that might limit the positive effect of trade liberalization.

A possible reason for consumer demand to be affected by the presence of less familiar imports is the perception that these products are less safe than the domestic ones. This case is typically the one that U.S. and European consumer organizations put forward when they claim that trade results in imports that are potentially less safe than domestic goods. Such worries can result in externalities even for domestic goods. The main reason for such market inefficiencies lies in the heterogeneous risk aversion across countries. The same raw milk cheese can be considered a delicacy in France or Italy, but potentially unsafe in the United States. The perception of risk is highly subjective, and the weight given to potential risks or to long-term risks is not the same in every country (Magat and Viscusi 1992).

Subjective considerations related to the heterogeneity of consumer preferences across countries go beyond the safety aspect. For example, if consumers know that foreign goods are produced under conditions of which they disapprove (e.g., child labor, destruction of rainforests, ethical considerations), they may reduce their consumption. If they experience difficulties in identifying those goods that are imported, this may affect the consumption of all products. This was observed, for example, in the case of fur products, since coats made from minks raised on farms were hard to distinguish from those made from animals caught with leghold traps. By affecting consumer perceptions about the average quality of the products on the market, trade liberalization may therefore contribute to a reduction in demand or in consumer willingness to pay.

If trade liberalization may have a negative overall effect on welfare, it is limited to specific cases. In the situations described above, the possible negative outcome was emphasized to stress the theoretical possibility of welfare reducing trade. In all cases, there were other outcomes depending on the assumptions, the value of the parameters, or the relative magnitude of opposite effects. For example, Bureau, Gozlan, and Marette (1999) show that even if a country with a high level of food safety opens its borders to imports from a country that lacks capacity for detecting unsafe products (typically a north-south problem), the pressure from imports of uncertain quality may result in a higher safety effort from domestic producers (so that they differentiate their products from imports). Overall, trade liberalization could result in a higher welfare in the importing country (see Box 4).

The various cases presented in Boxes 1 to 4 attempt to give some stylized economic interpretation to the observed fears that trade liberalization could affect the quality and safety of food products. It is noteworthy, however, that no general rule emerges. If consumers' unease with the idea of opening the domestic market to imports with which they are less familiar can be supported by market inefficiencies, the outcome always depends on the degree of competition, the level of consumer information, the cost of production, and the shape of demand. The central conclusion is that case-by-case analyses are necessary in order to assess the likely effect of trade liberalization on welfare.

AN ECONOMIC APPROACH TO INCORPORATING QUALITY ISSUES IN TRADE REGULATIONS

The previous section presented a theoretical framework that made it possible to account for observed consumer concerns about the possible effect of trade on the quality of food products. Even though there is still limited literature on this topic, it is theoretically possible that trade results in overall negative effects on welfare in particular cases. These cases can be assessed using standard welfare analysis. This section assesses how the normative economic framework developed above could contribute to defining rules for international trade. The idea is that the use of economic criteria may make it possible to account for the particular cases where trade liberalization results in a loss of utility for consumers, or, more generally, in a fall in welfare.

The Potential Role of Cost-Benefit Analysis

When cultures differ, economic analysis may perhaps help in finding a common playing field. This possibility has progressively been accepted in the area of environmental disputes, and it is progressing, albeit slowly, in the phytosanitary area and, to a lesser extent, in the sanitary area. Here we consider the possibility of a broader use of economic assessment in food quality regulations as well as in trade disputes over regulations as nontariff barriers.

Cost-benefit analysis is already used to enable public authorities to make decisions concerning national regulations (Grabowski and Vernon 1983). It is an important stage in the framing of regulations in the United States. Roberts (1998) explains how U.S. regulatory reform initiatives lead officials to base decisions on assessments of their benefits and costs, and how this has changed the parameters for regulating imports of agricultural products. U.S. domestic legislation, far more than the SPS Agreement, explicitly endorses the consideration of benefits associated with different risk mitigation measures. In most other countries, import restrictions are introduced on sanitary grounds, to avoid the spread of pests for example, without making any prior estimate of potential losses. These may sometimes be very small in comparison with the cost to consumers caused by such restrictions.

Arrow et al. (1996) recommend that cost-benefit analysis be used systematically, since they observed considerable differences between the cost of different public health measures and their real impact on health. For example, they give estimates where, within the same agency, the cost per life saved varies between $200,000 and $10 million, depending on the program, which means that more lives could be saved at the same cost to society. Even though society does not accept all risks in the same way and social choices cannot be reduced to the equalization of a statistical cost between programs, cost-benefit analysis should take a more important place in regulatory decisionmaking.

Cost-benefit analysis can also be of particular interest in regard to ethical or cultural values. If, for example, consumers place particular value on the fact that a good is produced without the use of biotechnology or irradiation techniques, estimating their willing-

Box 4. Welfare Effects of Trading with a Country That Lacks Safety Controls

The limited ability of some developing countries to detect and control the safety of their products has been used as a motivation to ban imports, especially by the European Union and the United States. Consumer organizations emphasize cases of sanitary problems caused by imports in order to demand strengthened border control and a revision of the provisions of the SPS Agreement that facilitate trade with developing countries (Silverglade 1998).

Bureau, Gozlan, and Marette (1999) have explored the case where a northern country trades with a country lacking infrastructure or skills for testing the safety of its exports. The framework is that of adverse selection with an exogenous sanitary risk. Imperfect competition is represented by the assumption of a single producer in each country. Producers in both countries have the same marginal cost c for the last unit of production. The level of risk is $(1 - \lambda)$ in both countries, but countries differ in their ability to get information on the actual safety of a particular product. The northern producer can inspect production and plants, and can signal to the consumers that its products are safe. The southern producer does not have the ability to do so. Assume that the product traded is an experience good. It is either of a high quality q_h (with a probability λ) or tainted (with a probability $1 - \lambda$). In the first period, only the northern producer has the information on the actual quality of its product. In the second period, all agents are informed, since it is assumed that quality is linked to the production process and that a low-quality producer in the first period will also supply tainted products in the second. In the second period, informed consumers will therefore only acquire safe products. Assuming a unit inelastic demand, consumer willingness to pay is λq_h for products of unknown quality (rational expectations). Willingness to pay is q_h for safe products, and it is equal to zero for tainted products.

Under autarky, the northern producer selects a strategy of signaling quality (separating equilibrium) or not (pooling equilibrium). If the separating strategy is chosen, the northern producer only offers high-quality products, sets a price lower than marginal cost in the first period in order to signal its quality, and sets a price equal to consumer willingness to pay in the second period, thus making a second period profit $\pi_r = (q_h - c)$. Buyers expect that this first period price cannot be mimicked by a low-quality producer.

If the northern producer selects the strategy of not signaling its quality, the price set in the first period is λq_h, which brings no information to the consumer, and the resulting profit is $\pi_d = \lambda q_h - c + (q_h - c)$ if goods are of high quality. This first period price can be set by a low-quality producer in the first period. The northern producer chooses the separating equilibrium only if $\pi_r > \pi_d$, that is, if the probability of supplying tainted products is high. Otherwise, by choosing not to signal its quality, the northern producer avoids the negative price distortion necessary for the signal to be credible. If the northern country opens its market to imports from the southern country, producers compete in price over both periods, by assumption. The profit of the southern producer is $\pi_e = \pi - c + \lambda(1 - \lambda)(q_h - c)$, if it is the only one to supply the market in the first period. The lowest price the southern producer can set in the first period is therefore $\bar{p} = c - \lambda(1 - \lambda)(q_h - c)$, resulting in $\pi_e = 0$. The northern producer must set a first period price lower than $\bar{p}$ in order to signal its quality. This leads to a profit $\bar{p} - c + (1 - \lambda)(q_h - c)$, which is strictly positive.

Under free trade, the northern producer will therefore signal its quality, even when the risk is low (λ high). This was not the case under autarky. That is, trade liberalization, by increasing the contestability of the market, provides incentive for signaling product quality. It creates conditions under which the northern producer has more incentive to position itself as a high-quality one, and to systematically inform consumers. Even in the case of trade liberalization with a country that has an informational handicap and that may unwillingly export tainted products, trade might have positive effects on domestic welfare because of informational aspects. Note, however, that this result only holds for experience goods (not for credence goods). Nor is it valid if the southern producer has a much lower marginal cost than the northern, which would offset the informational advantage.

ness to pay means that the variation in consumer satisfaction resulting from a regulation prohibiting the technique in question can be quantified in monetary terms (Viscusi, Vernon, and Harrington 1995; Magat and Viscusi 1992). One application could be the animal welfare issue, an awkward case where public opinion is being represented by vociferous consumer lobbies in Europe, and where scientists have been of little help. More economic assessment would make it possible to determine the real importance of this concern throughout the entire population.

Box 5 describes a few possible techniques for introducing more economic assessment into the setting of sanitary and phytosanitary regulations. There are clearly many technical difficulties. Measuring the benefits procured by regulations designed to guarantee certain ethical or cultural aspects of product quality is no easy matter, and the problem of the valuation of imagined risks is a difficult one (Pollak 1995, 1998). Estimates of cancer risk from pesticide residues contain a substantial degree of uncertainty as to the risk, making any economic estimate particularly difficult. In addition, it is not possible to calculate the probability of a risk that is too uncertain, making it difficult to carry out analysis with conventional tools. This may be the case, for example, with the risk of GM organisms propagating genes, the risk of long-term epidemics such as bovine spongiform encephalopathy and Creutzfeldt-Jakob disease, or environmental risks.

In addition, with an economic approach, it is possible to use approaches based on the measurement of changes in the consumer utility function when consumers have access to a product with attributes to which they are attached (Kopp, Krupnick, and Toman 1997). When human health is at stake, the topic is more sensitive, since giving a value to illness or even a human life saved is not always well accepted, especially in some EU countries. It is, however, worth noticing that in the same countries, transportation and energy departments use such calculations on a daily basis when they decide priorities for investment in road safety or thresholds in dam building. Economic assessment would simply make choices more explicit, although concepts such as the value of life (actually, the value of a life saved) can still be shocking to many people.

Up to a certain extent, willingness to pay is a defendable measure of people's concerns. Genuine consumer aversion to certain characteristics of the products, for sanitary as well as cultural reasons, is reflected in a willingness to pay in order to avoid the products. Although there are still some technical difficulties and conceptual obstacles, contingent valuation techniques or experimental economics may help people from different cultures find a common metric for more objectively defining how genuine the concerns of their consumers are, and for finding solutions to complex issues that largely reflect cultural differences. In this respect, microeconomics can be seen as a useful language for negotiation.

A Parallel with Competition Policy

The procedure for settling sanitary and technical disputes under the auspices of the WTO could draw on the competition policy example. Virtually all developed countries' competition policies are ultimately directed not at preserving and enhancing competition but at greater consumer welfare. Consequently, most competition agencies are prepared to make certain trade-offs (OECD 1996; Viscusi, Vernon, and Harrington 1995). For example, if a number of competing smaller grocers were to agree to pool their purchasing power, this could tend to reduce the degree of competition prevailing among them

Box 5. Methods for Estimating the Benefits of Sanitary and Technical Regulations

Where food safety and the spread of plant and animal diseases are concerned, cost-benefit analysis involves quantifying the level of risk and estimating its economic impact. This approach is widely used, though very unevenly from one country to another, not only to assess the rationale of a regulation but also to compare the advantages and disadvantages of several possible means of government intervention. In particular, it can be used to rationalize the strengthening of sanitary and phytosanitary controls in relation to the dissemination of information and the raising of consumer awareness, or to inform decisions about the introduction of regulatory standards (Kopp, Krupnick, and Toman 1997).

Although there are still some technical difficulties, there are few major obstacles to complementing classical risk analysis by cost-benefit analysis in the phytosanitary and animal health area. Things are more complex, however, when cultural values are at stake and when one deals with human health issues.

Several methods exist for estimating the cost of mortality and morbidity and evaluating in monetary terms the benefits of government action resulting in a reduction of sanitary risk. With the *human capital* method, a value is placed on the reduced risk of premature death based on an evaluation of discounted labor wage flow. For an individual of a given age, the value of the life prolonged (statistically) by a regulation corresponds to the discounted sum of the mathematical expectation of the person's revenues (Freeman 1993). Some extensions of this method have been proposed, in particular by integrating nonmerchant aspects and the value of the individual's descendants (Viscusi 1993). With the *cost of illness* method, a value is placed on the reduced morbidity resulting from sanitary or regulatory methods based on an estimate of medical costs and productivity losses due to illness (Buzby et al. 1996, Crutchfield et al. 1997). Opportunity costs from investing in activities that reduce risk are included in the value of reduced illness (Landelfeld and Seskin 1982). As with the human capital method, statistical methods have to be used to estimate the risk, especially dose-effect relationships.

Methods based on estimates of willingness to pay, although more difficult to apply, are wider reaching, since they make it possible to include quality-related aspects that cannot be

at least on the purchasing side. Common purchasing might nevertheless be tolerated by competition agencies if they were convinced that the arrangement reduces competition to the minimum necessary to enable smaller retailers to be more efficient, hence more effective competitors of larger chain grocers.

Another example could be found in the steps manufacturers might take to ensure that each of their dealers sells only in an assigned territory. Such exclusive territories virtually eliminate so-called intra-brand competition, but this might be necessary to facilitate a more than compensating increase in inter-brand competition. In general then, competition agencies keep their eye on the ultimate objective and are prepared to apply a kind of cost-benefit analysis to arrangements that may appear somewhat anticompetitive. Competition agencies tend to apply rigid rules only where experience has shown that a certain practice has almost no potential to generate net advantages to consumers.

From an economist's point of view, the main legitimacy of international trade agreements lies in the effectiveness of trade in increasing the well-being of citizens. International trade rules are necessary to avoid problems of free riding, which would result in retaliation, so that citizens can enjoy the benefits of specialization according to comparative advantage. The examples described previously where trade involved some negative effects that limit the positive consequences of trade liberalization deserve examination.

translated into identifiable short-term illness. The *preventive expenditure* method seeks to measure agents' willingness to pay by observing the efforts made to avoid illness. With this method, a monetary evaluation of the disutility of being ill is added to the estimated cost of illness, together with an estimate of the preventive expenditure that an individual is willing to commit according to a given pathogen level (Harrington and Portney 1987). *Contingent valuation* methods involve asking individuals directly about their willingness to pay to reduce the risk of an illness, or more generally to obtain higher quality in a good. By directly revealing willingness to pay, this method theoretically makes it possible to gain a monetary estimate of all the benefits arising from a given measure. Answers have to be corrected for statistical bias, however, due to respondents' incentives to over- or underestimate their willingness to pay (which depends in particular on whether they anticipate having to pay the disclosed sum or not). As these methods are widely applied to environmental issues, efforts have recently been made to harmonize survey methodologies

Another method being used increasingly widely at present is the *experimental economics* method, which involves getting a group of individuals in a situation where their real behavior is simulated to reveal their willingness to pay for particular qualities. Such methods are relatively onerous to put in place, but they make it possible to measure the value that a sample of individuals places on different sanitary thresholds, according to information received, for example (Hayes et al. 1995).

The methods described above are used to evaluate the benefits of drawing up a regulation to protect consumers' health or to ensure that they acquire the quality they desire. Methods for evaluating the cost of regulations are generally based on estimates of the welfare loss of the agents concerned when they have to comply with a regulation. This includes, for example, the cost to firms of acquiring suitable equipment and many other direct and indirect costs. Kopp, Krupnick, and Toman (1997) provide illustrations of such estimates. One method involves valuing them as opportunities that had to be foregone. This includes the diversion of resources, the value of specific inputs that become useless, the excess cost of substitution technologies, and the price differentials with replacement products borne by the consumer.

Clearly, if international trade disciplines result in imposing measures that increase trade flows but decrease welfare, such a discipline would have no economic legitimacy.

Baldwin (1970) proposed to define as nontariff barriers all nontariff policies that reduce potential world income. Such a definition of nontariff barriers is narrower than more general concepts under which a nontariff barrier is a policy that distorts trade flows. With Baldwin's criterion, palliative measures aimed at correcting market failures may have some protection effect without being classified as nontariff barriers. In the context of issues related to quality attributes, Mahé (1997) proposes to widen this definition to encompass nonmarket effects and to qualify as nontariff barriers those measures that decrease potential world welfare.

Economic analysis can provide a framework for assessing, on a case-by-case basis, whether a measure falls in the category defined by Baldwin and Mahé as nontariff barriers. Consider, for example, the case of adverse selection described in Box 2. This example focuses on hormone-treated beef, but the economic framework is valid for other credence goods, such as GM, organic, and irradiated foods; goods with an ethical content, such as compliance with animal welfare or environmental protection; etc. It is possible to define thresholds for the parameters that represent the perception of quality by consumers, and the cost of production of the various qualities, so that the world welfare would increase or decrease with trade (Bureau, Marette, and Schiavina 2000). That is, under a certain threshold, trade liberalization leads to a decrease in world welfare.

For this range of parameters, considering the ban on imports by the domestic country to be a nontariff barrier would be questionable, on the basis of the Baldwin-Mahé definition. In other cases, the positive effects of trade on welfare clearly provide a basis for promoting trade liberalization, even though the distribution of the welfare gains remains a problem. While the welfare criterion relies on the idea that there is a possibility for the gainers to compensate the losers, in practice such compensation is seldom observed, nor is compensation necessarily legitimate from a philosophical point of view.

SUMMARY AND CONCLUSIONS

Issues of food quality are rising on the policy agenda of many countries, driven by greater public awareness of foodborne diseases and increased concerns over the quality of food, how it is produced, the use of modern biotechnology, and the impacts on the environment. In response, many national governments are reforming their food safety institutional structures and regulatory frameworks. Such domestic reforms can have an impact on trade, although international trade agreements impose certain disciplines. A number of disputes related to sanitary and phytosanitary measures have already been brought before the WTO since the dispute settlement procedure was established in 1995. With the strengthening of international rules, increased trade in agro-food products, and growing domestic pressures to address consumer demands for quality, trade conflicts over food regulatory issues could become more common.

Some of the ensuing policy issues related to food quality that have implications for trade include the way in which countries establish the appropriate level of protection (acceptable level of risk) or apply precaution in circumstances of scientific uncertainty, regulate modern biotechnology in food production, and address socioeconomic concerns within the food safety regulatory system. Domestic decisions increasingly take into consideration international standards, guidelines, and recommendations, but continuing international dialog is required to ensure that governments address these public concerns without forgoing the substantial potential benefits of further technological developments, trade liberalization, and economic growth.

It is important that the rules governing trade at the international level be compatible with consumer demand for quality in order to avoid weakening support for trade liberalization. A major difficulty is that these demands vary across countries, with a different emphasis put on various quality attributes. This makes it difficult to define common rules acceptable to all WTO countries. This chapter attempts to examine some of these issues within a normative economic framework that considers the potential effects of freer trade on welfare. In some hypothetical cases, it is conceivable that trade liberalization could have unwanted effects on the quality perceived by consumers, the level of risk, or the quality effort of producers. However, the overall effect on welfare is, even in these particular cases, conditional on particular assumptions and to particular values of the parameters, calling for a case-by-case examination.

In assessing how this normative economic framework could contribute to defining rules for international trade, we suggest that the use of economic criteria may make it possible to account for the particular cases where trade liberalization results in a loss of utility for consumers, or, more generally, in a fall in welfare. For example, genuine consumer aversion to certain imported products for sanitary or cultural reasons is normally reflected in a willingness to pay to avoid the products. Giving this willingness to pay greater importance in the settlement of disputes by comparing it with the costs to other economic agents would help take account of consumer preferences and hence internalize hitherto diffuse fears about globalization (e.g., an obligation to consume products that do not correspond to consumer aspirations).

This would imply giving a broader role to cost-benefit analysis, which itself raises a number of technical difficulties. Estimates are controversial, and there is no agreement on methodology. In addition, there is a risk that the economic approach conflicts with some cultural values. The methodologies described in Box 5, however, have raised similar difficulties in the evaluation of environmental costs and benefits, and agreements on procedures have progressed (e.g., the use of contingent valuation for assessing environmental damages and calculating fines in a trial is now relatively well accepted). One may think that economic analysis in the food quality area is at a stage comparable to that of economics in the environmental area two decades ago. In many cases, cost-benefit analysis can already be a useful negotiation tool. Its potential contribution in the settlement of disputes within the WTO procedure deserves more careful consideration.

Since the 1994 SPS Agreement, the reference to a "science-based, rules-based approach," has helped in making food safety legislation more consistent across countries. However, scientific risk assessment does not account for the other legitimate concerns of consumers on food quality (i.e., economic, social, ethical, and environmental concerns), which are becoming a major area of contention in international trade (Baghwati and Hudec 1996). Defining criteria that are based on the economic impact of regulations—possibly from the point of view of global welfare—could help in distinguishing palliative measures aimed at correcting market inefficiencies from those that are designed to erect nontariff trade barriers and protect local interest groups.

The procedure for settling sanitary and technical disputes under the auspices of the WTO could perhaps draw on developments in competition policy. The principle aim of most competition policies is not to preserve competition but to achieve greater consumer welfare. From an economist's point of view, the main legitimacy of international trade agreements lies in the effectiveness of trade to increase the well-being of citizens. If nontariff barriers are defined as those measures that decrease potential world welfare, economic analysis can assess whether a given measure falls into this category. Situations where trade could involve some negative effects that could at least partially offset the positive consequences of trade liberalization deserve examination. It would be paradoxical if trade liberalization were to result in more trade but less welfare.

NOTES

1. The concept of quality adopted here is very general, covering all the attributes included in the consumer's utility function, i.e., all those factors that are likely to cause a consumer to prefer one good to another. Quality refers not only to safety-related and nutritional aspects but also to wholesomeness and product characteristics such as the

taste, integrity, and even authenticity of products. It also includes ethical factors, whereby the consumer's satisfaction or dissatisfaction is not with the characteristics of the product but with the way in which it has been produced (Mahé 1997). For example, a good produced in an environmentally harmful way or using child labor or in breach of the elementary rules of animal welfare may be of "low quality" for some consumers because it offends their personal values. This extensive definition of quality also includes individual sensibility to particular technologies, such as biotechnology or irradiation, and procedures (kosher or halal products) for cultural or religious reasons.

2. The Organisation for Economic Co-operation and Development has recently expanded its work in the area of biotechnology and other aspects of food safety at the request of member countries. Consultations were held in November 1999 with a wide range of nongovernmental organizations and industry, a conference was held in March 2000 on the safety of genetically modified food, and a new Ad Hoc Group on Food Safety was established to document what is being done at the national and international levels to address food safety issues. Much of the material in this section is based on the results of these activities. In addition, some of the material on regulating biotechnology and most of the discussion on animal welfare are taken from OECD 2000b (pp. 95–113, modern biotechnology; pp. 79–80, animal welfare).

3. The Appellate Body further stated that it appeared important

> to note some aspects of the relationship of the "precautionary principle" to the SPS Agreement. First, the principle has not been written into the SPS Agreement as a ground for justifying SPS measures that are otherwise inconsistent with the obligations of Members set out in particular provisions of that Agreement. Secondly, the "precautionary principle" indeed finds reflection in Article 5.7 of the SPS Agreement. We agree, at the same time, with the European Communities, that there is no need to assume that Article 5.7 exhausts the relevance of a "precautionary principle."

It is reflected also in the sixth paragraph of the preamble and in Article 3.3. These explicitly recognize the right of members to establish their own appropriate level of sanitary protection, which level may be higher (i.e., more cautious) than that implied in existing international standards, guidelines, and recommendations. Third, a panel charged with determining, for instance, whether "sufficient scientific evidence" exists to warrant the maintenance by a member of a particular SPS measure may, of course, and should, bear in mind that responsible, representative governments commonly act from perspectives of prudence and precaution where risks of irreversible, e.g., life-terminating, damage to human health are concerned. Last, however, the precautionary principle does not, by itself, and without a clear textual directive to that effect, relieve a panel from the duty of applying the normal (i.e., customary international law) principles of treaty interpretation in reading the provisions of the SPS Agreement.

4. SPS Article 5.7 provides that:

> In cases where relevant scientific evidence is insufficient, a Member may provisionally adopt sanitary or phytosanitary measures on the basis of available pertinent information, including that from the relevant international organizations as well as from sanitary or phytosanitary measures applied by other Members. In such circumstances Members shall seek to obtain additional information necessary for a more

objective assessment of risk and review the sanitary and phytosanitary measure accordingly within a reasonable period of time.

5. *The Chairman's Report* and the *Rapporteurs' Summary* from the OECD Edinburgh Conference on the Scientific and Health Aspects of Genetically Modified Food, "GM Food Safety: Facts, Uncertainties, and Assessment," are available at http://www.oecd.org/subject/biotech/edinburgh.htm.

6. In certain OECD countries, the approval process is generally based on a formal process of risk assessment in which the concept of "substantial equivalence" (developed by the Food and Agriculture Organization, the World Health Organization, and OECD) is a key element. The interpretation of substantial equivalence differs among regulatory authorities and stakeholders. For some, the concept incorporates an analysis of possible intended and unintended effects of genetic modification. For others, it focuses on the substantive quality and characteristics of the final product. Efforts are currently under way through the Codex Ad Hoc Intergovernmental Task Force on Foods Derived from Biotechnology and the OECD Task Force for the Safety of Novel Foods and Feeds to strengthen the existing common set of principles and information, including substantial equivalence, that can be applied to the safety assessment of novel foods.

7. Even though the international scientific committees found an absence of risk under normal rearing practices, some Canadian and European scientists raised questions regarding the collateral production of other hormones (such as the insulin growth factor). This, together with other considerations on animal welfare and some economic considerations, was invoked to ban the use of rBGH in Canada and the EU.

8. Such concerns have been brought up to the WTO. The Trade-Related Aspects of Intellectual Property Rights Agreement, which came into effect January 1995, includes geographical indications (Section 3, Article 22-24) in the area of intellectual property rights.

9. One example is restrictions on the shape of cheese (e.g., round cheese), which protects a tradition rather than any technical quality imperative.

10. Some foreign wines are produced using techniques that are not accepted by EU regulations (though at present they may be imported under the terms of temporary exceptions). Techniques that are not authorized in some European countries, such as adding oak chips to wine instead of aging in barrels, considerably reduce the production costs of wines from third countries, thus creating trade tensions. Countries that prohibit such practices argue that they have an adverse effect on quality, whereas others regard the prohibition as merely protection of traditions that bar the way to innovation.

11. Low introductory prices are not the only way in which quality can be signaled. Firms can spend heavily on advertising, for example, and consumers will anticipate that such expenditure can only be covered by an information rent, indicating that the product is of high quality (if it is an experience good). Warranties or substantial compensation in the event of problems are other types of signals (Gal-Or 1989b). Firms can also secure a reputation via a trademark or a quality signal such as a label. Governments can enhance the credibility of quality signals by certifying them. Conversely,

consumers may use intermediaries such as brokers or dealers which, being better informed, can give them credible information on the quality of the offered goods. In all these cases, however, imperfect information has a welfare cost to society.

12. A simple example is that of production in an uncertain world: to continue production in the presence of climate risk or price risk, firms demand a premium which is reflected in higher production prices. The price is paid by consumers, whose welfare is reduced by a corresponding amount. In comparison with a risk-free situation, the producers' welfare is unchanged, but the consumers' welfare has declined.

13. Magat and Viscusi (1992) have observed many cases where consumers seem to deviate from "rational" behavior, inasmuch as their behavior was inconsistent with the predictions of the anticipated subjective utility model. According to the authors, individuals accord excessive importance to low probabilities of risk. The questions raised by risk misperception are complex. Even when public fears are not shared by experts, these fears affect their economic behavior and, therefore, the state of an economy. Governmental regulations should account for unjustified public fears to a certain extent. In addition, in a democratic society, the government ought to respond to consumer worries, however remote and conservatively estimated the risk. However, spending money on expensive treatment of (clean) water, just because "people feel worried about some risk" would be clearly economically inefficient (Pollak 1998).

REFERENCES

Akerlof, G. A., 1970, The market for "lemons": Quality uncertainty and the market mechanism, *Q J Econ* **84**(3):488–500.

Antle, J. M., 1995, *Choice and Efficiency in Food Safety Policy*, AEI Press, American Enterprise Institute, Washington, DC.

Arrow, K. J., Cropper, M. L., Eads, G. C., Hahn, R. W., Lave, L. B., Noll, R. G, Portney, P. R., Russell, M., Schmalensee, R., Smith, V. K., and Stavins, R. N., 1996, Is there a role for benefit-cost analysis in environmental, health and safety regulation?, *Science* **272**:221–222.

Baghwati, J. N., and Hudec, R. E., eds., 1996, *Fair Trade and Harmonization, Prerequisites for Free Trade?*, MIT Press, Cambridge, MA.

Baldwin, R. E., 1970, *Non-Tariff Distortions in International Trade*, Brookings Institute, Washington, DC.

Beales, H., Craswell, R., and Salop, S., 1981, The efficient regulation of consumer information, *J Law Econ* **24**(Dec.):491–544.

Bureau, J. C., and Doussin, J. P., 2000, Sanitary and technical regulations: Issues for trade liberalization in the dairy sector, *Can J Agric Econ* **47**(5):149–157.

Bureau, J. C., and Marette, S., 2000, Accounting for consumers' preferences in international trade rules, in: *Incorporating Science, Economics, and Sociology in Developing Sanitary and Phytosanitary Standards in International Trade: Proceedings of a Conference*, Board on Agriculture and Natural Resources, ed., pp. 170–198, National Academy Press, Washington, DC.

Bureau, J. C., Gozlan E., and Marette, S., 1999, Quality Signaling and International Trade in Food Products, THEMA series, Working Paper 99-13, University of Paris X-Nanterre.

Bureau, J. C., Marette, S., and Schiavina, A., 1998, Non-tariff trade barriers and consumers' information: The case of the EU-US trade dispute over beef, *Eur Rev Agric Econ* **25**(4):437–462.

Buzby, J. C., Roberts, T., Lin, C.-T. J., and MacDonald, J. M., 1996, Bacterial Foodborne Disease: Medical Costs and Productivity Losses, Agricultural Economic Report 741, Economic Research Service, U.S. Department of Agriculture, Washington, DC.

Caswell, J. A., and Mojduszka, E. M., 1996, Using Informational Labeling to Influence the Market for Quality in Food Products, paper presented at American Association of Agricultural Economists meeting, Jul. 29, 1996, San Antonio.

Chen, J., 1996, A sober second look at appellations of origin: How the United States will crash France's wine and cheese party, *Minn J Global Trade* **5**(1):19–32.

Crutchfield, S., Buzby, J. C., Roberts, T., Ollinger, M., and Lin, C.-T. J., 1997, An Economic Assessment of Food Safety Regulations: The New Approach to Meat and Poultry Inspection, Agricultural Economic Report 755, Economic Research Service, U.S. Department of Agriculture, Washington, DC.

Falvey, R. E., 1989, The composition of trade within import restricted trade categories, *J Polit Econ* **87**:1105–1114.

Freeman, A. M., 1993, *Measuring Environmental and Resource Values: Theory and Methods*, Resources for the Future, Washington, DC.

Gal-Or, E., 1989a, Quality and quantity competition, *Bell J Econ* **16**:590–600.

———, 1989b, Warranties as a signal of quality, *Can J Econ* **22**(1):50–61.

Gozlan, E., and Marette, S., 2000, Commerce international et réglementation optimale de la qualité des produits, *Economie Internationale* **52**:54–61.

Grabowski, H. G., and Vernon, J. M., 1983, *The Regulation of Pharmaceuticals: Balancing the Benefits and Risks*, American Enterprise Institute, Washington, DC.

Grossman, G., and Shapiro, C., 1988, Counterfeit product trade, *Am Econ Rev* **75**:59–76.

Harrington, W., and Portney, P. R., 1987, Valuing the benefits of health and safety regulations, *J Urban Econ* **22**(1):101–112.

Hayes, D., Shogren, J., Shin, S., and Kliebenstein, J., 1995, Valuing food safety in experimental auctions markets, *Am J Agric Econ* **77**(1):40–53.

Hoban, T., 1998, Trends in consumer attitudes about agricultural biotechnology, *AgBioForum* **1**(1):3–7, http://www.agbioforum.org/vol1no1/hoban.html (accessed Jul. 27, 2001).

James, S., and Anderson, K., 1998., *On the Need for More Economic Assessment of Quarantine/SPS Policies*, CIES Seminar Paper 98-02, University of Adelaide.

Joly, P.-B., and Lemarié, S., 1998, Industry consolidation, public attitude and the future of plant biotechnology in Europe, *AgBioForum* **1**(2):85–90, http://www.agbioforum.org/vol1no2/joly.html (accessed Jul. 27, 2001).

Josling, T., 1998, EU-US Trade Conflicts over Food Safety Legislation: An Economist's Viewpoint on Legal Stress Points That Will Concern the Industry, paper presented at Forum for US-EU Legal-Economic Affairs, Sept. 16–19, Helsinki.

Kopp, R. J., Krupnick, A. J., and Toman, M., 1997, Cost Benefit Analysis and Regulatory Reform: An Assessment of the Science and the Art, Discussion Paper 97-19, Resources for the Future, Washington, DC.

Krouse, C. G., 1990, *Theory of Industrial Economics*, Basil Blackwell, Cambridge, MA.

Krugman, P., 1979, Increasing returns, monopolistic competition and international trade, *J Int Econ* **9**:469–479.

Landelfeld, J. S., and Seskin, E. P., 1982, The economic value of life: Linking theory and practice, *Am J Public Health* **6**:555–566.

Magat, W. A., and Viscusi, W. K., 1992, *Informational Approaches to Regulation*, MIT Press, Cambridge, MA.

Mahé, L. P., 1997, Environment and quality standards in the WTO: New protectionism in agricultural trade, *Eur Rev Agric Econ* **24**(3–4):480–503.

Mussa, M., and Rosen, S., 1978, Monopoly and product quality, *J Econ Theory* **18**:301–317.

Organisation for Economic Co-operation and Development (OECD), 1996, *Competition Policy and the Agro-Food Sector*, Paris.

———, 1999, *Food Safety and Quality: Trade Considerations*, Paris.

———, 2000a, Report of the Ad Hoc Group on Food Safety, Paris.

———, 2000b, *OECD Agricultural Outlook 2000–2005*, Paris.

———, 2001, Designations of Origin and Geographical Indicators in OECD Member Countries: Economic and Legal Implications, Paris.

Pollak, R. A., 1995, Regulating risks, *J Econ Lit* **33**(1):179–191.

———, 1998, Imagined risks and cost-benefit analysis, *Am Econ Rev, Papers and Proceedings* **88**(2):376–379.

Powell, M., 1997, *Science in Sanitary and Phytosanitary Dispute Resolution*, Discussion Paper 97-50, Resources for the Future, Washington, DC.

Reitzes, J. D., 1992, Quality choice, trade policy and firm incentives, *Int Econ Rev* **33**(4):817–835.

Roberts, D., 1998, The WTO SPS Agreement: Overview and Implications for Animal Health and Animal Product Decision Making, paper presented at the U.S. Department of Agriculture Workshop on Use of Economic Analysis in Evaluating Animal and Animal Product Import Request, Mar. 24–25, Riverdale, MD.

Salter, L., 1988, *Mandated Science: Science and Scientists in the Making of Standards*, Kluwer, Dordrecht, the Netherlands.

Shaked, A., and Sutton, J., 1983, Natural oligopolies, *Econometrica* **51**:1469–1484.

Shapiro, C., 1983, Premiums for high quality products as returns to reputations, *Q J Econ* **98**:659–679.

Silverglade, B., 1998, Should the SPS Agreement Be Amended? A Modest Proposal to Restore Public Support, paper presented at the Ceres Conference on Politicizing Science: What Price Public Policy?, Apr. 4, 1998, Georgetown University Public Policy Institute, Washington, DC.

Spence, M., 1975, Monopoly, quality, and regulation, *Bell J Econ* **6**(2):417–429.

Stiglitz, J., 1994, *Whither Socialism?*, MIT Press, Cambridge, MA.

Thilmany, D. D., and Barrett, C. B., 1997, Regulatory barriers in an integrating world food market, *Rev Agric Econ* **19**(1):91–107.

Viscusi, W. K., 1993, The value of risks to life and health, *J Econ Lit* **31**(Dec.):1912–1946.

Viscusi, W. K., Vernon, J. M., and Harrington, J. E., Jr., 1995, *Economics of Regulation and Antitrust*, MIT Press, Cambridge, MA.

Wilson, C., 1980, The nature of equilibrium with adverse selection, *Bell J Econ* **5**:275–284.

A GREAT TRANSFORMATION IN WORLD TRADE LAW

Can the WTO stay afloat?

David G. Victor and Rebecca U. Weiner*

MODERN MATURITY

Many international relations theorists argue that the rising flow of goods, services, and money is eroding state power. Businesses, nongovernmental organizations, and disaggregated states are now the key actors in the international arena. Transnational links between nonstate actors are supplanting the state and state-controlled international institutions.[1] We offer the alternative perspective that globalization requires more of states and intergovernmental fora, not less. States remain at the center of an evolving international arena; they continue to be the agents and enforcers of policy, and the most capable enforcement mechanisms are state-dominated intergovernmental fora. Yet governments must now exert their power in a far more complex and constraining environment. This new environment asks them to exercise unprecedented maturity and sophistication. It asks that they be accommodating and flexible, that they make subtler and more sophisticated policy decisions even as their leverage over their own national policy declines. Most important, it requires that governments pick their battles wisely.

Indeed, a great transformation is under way in international relations, and the influence of nonstate actions on policy is rising. But the driving force of this transformation is that traditional modes of international cooperation, which focus on coordinating government policies and on border measures such as tariffs, have been so successful that they deliver diminishing returns today. Deeper international cooperation is forcing governments to cross a new frontier to coordinate policy reform behind national borders; this need is

---

* The authors are at the Council on Foreign Relations—David G. Victor is Robert W. Johnson, Jr., Senior Fellow for Science and Technology, and Rebecca U. Weiner is a research associate. David Victor acknowledges a close collaboration with Kenneth A. Oye and Thomas Bernauer on a closely related issue, the difficulty of regulating highly controversial nontariff trade measures through the World Trade Organization. We also thank Stefan Tangermann for his comments on a draft of this chapter.

Global Food Trade and Consumer Demand for Quality, edited by Krissoff *et al.*
Kluwer Academic/Plenum Publishers, New York, 2002.

most evident where the great transformation is most advanced: international trade, in particular the efforts within the World Trade Organization (WTO) to manage nontariff barriers to trade. Our focus is the area where new international trade rules have been the most politically sensitive—rules that discipline how nations regulate food and environmental quality. The transformation will bring new and stronger storms to buffet the WTO. We ask: What can governments do to keep the WTO afloat?

TRADING WORLD TRANSFORMED

For centuries, international law has been concerned with the external conduct of states. It has sought to leverage and regulate how governments interact with other governments; it has been a tool that governments use to protect and control action at the borders. A separate domain—domestic politics—governed conduct behind borders. Often these two worlds of international law and domestic politics would interconnect. But the norm was separation, not unity.

From 1947 to the onset of the Uruguay Round in 1986, international trade law operated mainly in the normal interstate tradition of international law. Agreements focused on policies that distorted trade by protecting or promoting producers—protectionist tariffs, quotas, producer subsidies, and the like—implemented, for the most part, at the border. The trading system was built on the simple but compelling logic that, except for a few circumstances such as those outlined in the famous Article XX of the General Agreement on Tariffs and Trade (GATT), there was no justification for countries to maintain producer-protecting impediments to trade. The objective—remove them all—was clear and (in principle) widely accepted. Through rounds of negotiations, GATT members linked together thousands of bilateral agreements and tariff concessions. The GATT's requirement that all GATT member countries treat each other as "most favored" ensured that multilateral packages emerged from these bilateral deals. Because the ultimate goal was to eliminate essentially all trade impediments, the "round" approach was ideally suited to getting the best deal since it ensured as wide a terrain for deal-making as possible. Governments proposed concessions that they could deliver; if they failed to deliver, simple reciprocity could bring them into line. The system was largely self-enforcing because it focused almost entirely on border measures that governments controlled; the threat of retaliation kept each country in line.

Beyond the threat of retaliation, the GATT architecture offered weak formal mechanisms for handling violations or disputes. Definitive judgment on disputes required universal consent by GATT members—a nearly impossible standard to meet because few countries would agree to accept an adverse decision. The system was not completely hamstrung, but the ability to block consensus meant that, in essence, states could defer the most inconvenient commitments (Hudec 1993, Busch 2000).

For example, the longest standing and highest profile unresolved dispute began in the early 1970s as a European challenge to U.S. tax legislation for domestic international sales corporations, or DISCs, that, in effect, subsidized exports from U.S. firms. (The GATT bars most export subsidies, but in practice—as the DISC case showed—subsidies are often woven through complex but legitimate national tax measures.) The United States adjusted the tax law on DISCs to eliminate the most blatant violations of GATT rules, but the adjustment only went part of the way to alleviating European objections. In the end, the United States refused to make further adjustments; it also refused to accept GATT panel rulings against DISCs and lashed back at the Europeans with a counterdispute against European tax rules. Neither the original dispute nor the counterdispute was fully settled; together, they became glaring symbols of the GATT's inability to behave as a true judicial system capable of imposing its rules even when they are inconvenient for countries to follow. (Revisions to tax law on DISCs produced a new U.S. tax provision for foreign sales corporations [FSCs], and a new dispute under the WTO; we return to the FSC dispute below.)

Similarly, when European countries and then the European Community banned meat hormones in the early 1980s, the United States sought to dispute the measure as incompatible with the "Standards Code" on technical barriers to trade that was part of the round of negotiations that ended in 1979. When European governments refused to accept the jurisdiction of the Standards Code, which was separate from the core GATT commitments, there was little more that the United States could do to prosecute the case within the GATT legal system.

The combination of early exclusive focus on producer distortions, broad self-enforcement through reciprocity, and a weak dispute resolution mechanism explains the international trading system's initial momentum. As progress continued and options for tariff reductions waned, this momentum could have been expected to level off. The Uruguay Round launched in 1986 marked a turning point, however. Regulation expanded into areas previously privy to states alone: behind-the-border barriers to trade. Notably, international standards now affect not only producer measures but also consumer-oriented regulations. Examples include competition policy and the protection of intellectual property rights, as well as technical standards (e.g., labeling) and sanitary and phytosanitary (SPS) measures.

Because such commitments intrude into domestic politics, reaching and maintaining them is often much more complex than it has been in years past. Unlike producer-oriented trade distortions, there is no simple and assured rule that governs which consumer-oriented regulations are inappropriate. Rules motivated by fears of health and safety risks are widely viewed as acceptable; merely protectionist rules are not. But sifting protectionism from genuine safety concerns is extremely difficult and politically sensitive in these instances.

In addition to facilitating the transition from border measures to behind-the-border trade barriers, from producer- to consumer-endorsed price distortions, the Uruguay Round changed the face of international trade by establishing a strong enforcement mechanism—the Dispute Settlement Body—that marches according to strict time tables and delivers impartial and definitive judgments. Countries may no longer use the GATT requirement for universal consent as a shield to protect noncompliant behavior.

The Uruguay Round therefore caused a sea-change in international trade law. Since the round concluded in 1994, nearly the entire world economy has shifted to trade rules of dramatically greater scope. The new areas of discipline are no longer simple border measures that governments may trade away to zero, but instead include nonborder measures that touch on the core legitimate functions of national government, such as protection of consumer safety and taxation. Moreover, although many of these new disciplines are likely to be inconvenient, a strong enforcement mechanism severely constrains the ability of countries to skirt inconvenient rules. In essence, the old system was stable because it remained in shallow water. The Uruguay Round has moved the trading system into deeper, more turbulent seas that threaten its ability to stay upright.

CONSEQUENCES OF THE TRANSFORMATION

Three consequences logically follow the transformation of international trade law from a system that focused on the coordination of border measures to one that acts behind borders. First, the transformation creates vast new potential for reducing trade barriers, which is good news for promoters of free trade.

Second, instances of noncompliance with international legal commitments will increase. These episodes are a consequence not only of willful disregard for the law but also massive expansion of international trade rules into arenas where governments are often unable to adjust policy to conform to international disciplines. Previously, when international trade negotiations focused on border measures that governments controlled themselves, agent and principal were nearly one. After a round of negotiations and adoption of unified tariff schedules, implementing legislation was a relatively straightforward matter. Certainly there were battles over interpretation, and certainly interest groups that lost cherished protectionism were aggrieved and opposed. But it was nonetheless relatively easy for governments to ensure compliance. Today that is no longer true. Under the Uruguay Round agreements, governments must implement reforms to their patent systems, technical regulations, and sundry other areas of policy. The level of reform that is required to pass muster is unknown in many cases. If analysts actually attempted to measure the level of compliance with a strict interpretation of WTO rules, they would probably find a very low level—even, perhaps, in the United States, which crafted WTO rules in its own image and therefore already applies key provisions.

Food safety illustrates the problem. The SPS Agreement declares that countries are in compliance if they adopt international standards. Elsewhere, however, Victor (2000) has shown that implementation of those standards is extremely low. When countries don't apply international standards, the SPS Agreement requires that countries base their SPS measures on risk assessment. Yet countries apply risk assessment in different, inconsistent ways—if they apply it at all. Six years ago, governments did not need to worry much about trade disputes caused by inconsistency in how they applied risk assessment; today they must.

Third, the use of enforcement provisions will increase. This is not merely the consequence of decreased compliance, since the international trading system has always had a large overhang of unprosecuted cases. Rather, the greater use of enforcement provisions is the product of an enforcement system that can deliver assured results. Tiny Ecuador can now bring a case against the European Union's (EU's) discriminatory banana import regime and win. With 137 members in the WTO (and growing), the number of Ecuadors is rising, and they are becoming aware of their power. The WTO's enforcement system has not eliminated the importance of might—Ecuador is still fearful of harming itself if it actually implements the retaliatory sanctions it won against Europe—but effective legal systems often operate in the shadow of power.

Increased enforcement also is the consequence of a legal culture emerging in the WTO that prizes enforcement as evidence that the law is taken seriously. Today the WTO system is celebrating its 200th enforcement action; previously, enforcement actions such as the GATT's DISC case symbolized lameness rather than strength.

The good news is that these consequences are the growing pains of a legal system under transformation. The U.S. Supreme Court experienced similar pains—for seven decades starting in the late 18th century, state courts and politicians often undercut central authority by blatantly disregarding central judgments. Only after the Civil War were the Court's decisions (even those that were inconvenient for state and local authorities) truly the law of the land (Movsesian 1999).

The bad news is that the characteristics and consequences of the transformation—more intrusive international law; decreased compliance; and stronger, more automatic enforcement—create complex "problem cases" that threaten to arrest the dynamism of the international trading system. WTO rules are forcing policy changes in areas where governments find it extremely difficult to dismantle offending measures because they are endorsed by consumers; therefore, public support for the offenses is deep. And because these measures can serve legitimate (e.g., food safety) as well as illegitimate (e.g., protectionist) purposes, the emergence of powerful "Baptist-bootlegger" coalitions is more likely.

The WTO looks to scientific risk assessment as an impartial and decisive arbiter of legitimate and illegitimate measures. For example, Article 5 of the SPS Agreement requires that countries base SPS measures on available scientific evidence of risk to plants, animals, or humans. Often, however, consumer regulations can't meet this test because they are the product of democratic policy processes that politicize some issues while ignoring others, making it impossible to apply risk assessment in an even-handed manner. Worse, as a dispute over the measures unfolds and becomes more salient, political pressure to defend popular trade barriers grows—as with the beef hormones case today. In democratic countries especially, there are strong incentives for countries to paint themselves into a corner by encouraging public support for an offending measure.[2]

In the past, these problem cases in which science and consumer sentiment diverge have caused bruises but not open wounds for the international trading system; offending governments could simply defer inconvenient trade rules and disputes. Today, however, the existence of an automatic enforcement mechanism magnifies the risks to the trading system by ensuring that states will be held accountable. Once a problem case is formally launched, the system marches inexorably toward final judgment and penalties. Keeping the transformation on track will require that states work hard to either avoid or defuse these frequently thorny, sometimes intractable, problem cases. The hormones case is an existing example; others, such as those involving genetically modified organisms (GMOs), loom on the horizon. The problem for policymakers, however, is that there is no easy way to institutionalize a mechanism for resolving or preventing these problem cases.

THE PATHOLOGY OF PROBLEM CASES

Problem cases tend to have particular characteristics that make them difficult to avoid and difficult to settle once they are formalized. First, they tend to emerge among democratic countries, whose governments must be especially responsive to mass public intent, even when public pressure is not aligned with international rules. They tend to involve mainly consumer-endorsed price distortions that evolve through Baptist-bootlegger coalitions.

Second, problem cases are often characterized by "phantom risks," which are chronic, cumulative, low dose, uncertain, and irreversible. Examples include beef hormones and GMOs. Because they are so difficult to measure, phantom risks mandate inconsistent behavior. The combination of powerful constituencies and phantom risks yields a "culture of concern" that is wary of reforming behavior in the absence of conclusive evidence. Yet what constitutes proper risk assessment in these cases is difficult to determine and harder to universalize. This ambiguity makes consumer regulations ripe for Baptist-bootlegger coalitions, not least because bootleggers are less able to use traditional measures—such as tariffs and quotas—to achieve protectionism.

Third, problem cases generally have low financial stakes; the more money at stake in a dispute, the more likely the dangers will be spotted early—and the more likely that the highest levels of government will be engaged to dampen the dispute. The recent progress made toward settling the FSC dispute brought by the EU against the United States illustrates this phenomenon. Faced with the knowledge that the FSC issue is a tinderbox stoked with billions of dollars of tax consequences, the United States is starting to back down and working to find a way to conform to WTO rules on export subsidies.

Problem cases are important because they create festering wounds that weaken the legal system at the core of the transformation. Though they probably account for only a small fraction of the total number of potential trade disputes—and it is unclear exactly how many such wounds a robust legal system can tolerate—they are disproportionately damaging because they become unstoppable once they start. Once the WTO's legal machinery is in motion, the outcome is Kabuki-like: unambiguous judgment, a clear obligation to reform offending behavior, and retaliation if compliance does not follow swiftly. Yet the offender won't budge because its national policy is at stake, and it has built democratic credibility on the defense of the offending measure. The prospect of retaliation further entrenches both sides. The system can do little to soften the blow because the law is aligned with scientific risk assessment rather than the political winds. Again, the beef hormones case offers a clear example: European support for the hormones ban has grown as the public has become aware of the issue; a clear ruling from the WTO has not made it easier for Europe to comply; the United States has exercised its right to retaliate and redoubled the stakes with the threat to rotate (carousel) its retaliation sanctions every six months. What was a small-stakes problem in economic terms has managed to assume enormous proportions.

REMEDIES

Five possible remedies for problem cases present themselves. First, international agreements could allow countries simply to opt out of inconvenient commitments. That, in essence, was the approach taken earlier, when there were few international disciplines on behind-the-border measures and when inconvenient enforcement actions could be ignored. The obvious flaw in that approach is that it does not solve the underlying problem—trade barriers that are disguised as or interwoven with legitimate policies. An alternative is a limited escape hatch such as Article 5.7 of the SPS Agreement, which allows countries to impose strict (temporary) SPS measures without a full risk assessment in cases where scientific information is incomplete. By another name, Article 5.7 is the "precautionary principle." Already, governments have figured out that this is one of the best ways to protect dubious measures, and it is particularly well suited for cases characterized by phantom risks. All three of the first SPS-related disputes were decided, in part, by the fact that governments had put final measures into place; had the measures been temporary, they might have been easier to defend under Article 5.7. Now, especially controversial measures—such as bans and tight restrictions on GMOs—are carefully described as interim and precautionary. This strategy is a way to avoid some disputes; the open question, of course, is how elastic the precautionary principle will become.

Second, governments could devise an impartial test to determine which measures are valid. That is the approach already attempted in the SPS Agreement with the requirement that risk assessment be the arbiter of valid and invalid measures; the Technical Barriers to Trade Agreement has similar requirements. The risk assessment test is probably as clear and robust as possible; yet obviously it is not a contraption into which scientists plug numbers and bureaucrats turn a crank that produces policy. In some cases, risk assessment is not used at all; in most others, it is merely one factor among many that determines policy outcomes. There might be a convergence under way toward the use of risk assessment as part of "good policy"; the SPS Agreement is probably helping to accelerate that convergence, but the process is a slow one.

Third, offending governments could simply offer compensation. When a politically popular but dubious trade measure causes harm and is declared invalid, the offending government could avoid the extremely difficult task of dismantling the offending measure by simply compensating the losers. Next to removal of the illegal measure, compensation is the remedy most often envisioned in the international trading system. But compensation may be extremely difficult to supply. For governments that are under strong domestic pressure not to admit error, compensation remains politically difficult; few parties blatantly disregard the law, agree with judgments that declare them scofflaws, and then willingly compensate the harm. Moreover, the traditional form of compensation is to offer countervailing relief by reducing border measures—which is hard to do when tariffs and other border measures are already approaching zero. Other forms of compensation, such as cash payments, might work, but politically they are difficult to deliver because they are so transparent and are visible on government budgets.

Fourth, a political body could interpose itself between the technical and legal process of delivering a judgment and the politically problematic act of compliance. This approach too has been tried already and is a limited feature of the current system. Under the old GATT system, unanimous consent was needed to convene a dispute panel and decision—which ensured strong political input as well as gridlock. The WTO system requires unanimous consent to *block* enforcement decisions, which also offers an opportunity for political intervention—but it probably never will be deployed because governments will not be unified in their views. The problem with interposing a political body is that it is difficult to design the rules that would govern that body's operation; by design, the body would become highly politicized and perhaps a lightning rod for dissent. A better approach is to empower a body that can masquerade as an objective, technical entity but insert political judgments about what is good for the system as a whole where necessary. The Appellate Body, in part, fulfills that function today, but it is limited in how far it can and should stretch the law to accommodate political winds. Its decision in the shrimp-turtle cases illustrates the critical importance of its sensitivity: as a matter of politics, its approval (in principle) of the use of trade sanctions for protecting endangered species helped to blunt some of the WTO's severest critics from the environmental community. The Appellate Body must stick to its mandate, which is mainly to create a coherent body of law that is faithful to the WTO agreements.

Fifth, governments can exert restraint. The miracle of the WTO is not that the system is celebrating its 200th dispute but rather that there aren't more. Perhaps that is because governments are overwhelmed and unable to bring more disputes; more likely, it reflects a measure of caution and restraint. Restraint in bringing problem cases is mandatory to the survival of the WTO. Because the problems are political rather than legal, strategies for dispute settlement must also be political rather than legal. Primed to the typical characteristics of problem cases, however, governments can look ahead and envision the train wreck that would result if they dragged more cases like the hormones dispute through the system.

Ironically, responsibility for exercising restraint lies with the aggrieved state rather than the offending state; the hands of the offending state are already tied by domestic consumers. How will aggrieved governments know when to exercise restraint? As a general rule, when the offending behavior poses small trade effects but large political consequences. Aggrieved states initially underestimate these political consequences, which occur both within the offending state and between the disputants. However, the danger lies in the fact that the consequences necessarily grow as the dispute proceeds.

In particular, governments should attend carefully to the strength of consumer preferences and the context in which these preferences operate. First, they should avoid cases where consumer preferences are most at odds with scientific risk assessment. This advice may be especially difficult to follow; it suggests that governments should be most cautious about bringing the cases that their legal advisors will declare most ripe for victory. Second, they should avoid cases where the offending measure is backed by passionate democratic support. Such cases are probably growing in number as consumer groups become better organized and more influential; they also involve situations where democratically elected governments will find it most difficult to align with the WTO and against their constituencies. Third, restraint will be hardest (but most important) when consumer preferences vary internationally. In those cases, the aggrieved country will be under the strongest public pressure to prosecute a case, and its public will be least likely to understand the need for restraint. That remains the situation today in the hormones dispute; and there is also a strong transatlantic divergence on GMOs. (Today, perhaps, GMO-phobia is spreading to America as well, which will narrow the divergence.)

The danger of restraint as a solution to problem cases is that, like the precautionary principle or honor code, it invites abuse. Under the assumption that the aggrieved party will use more restraint in more extreme cases, the temptation for offending governments is to exaggerate their predicament when their dubious policies come into the cross hairs. Incidences of Baptist-bootlegger coalitions might increase as offending governments bank on the fact that others will get the message and back off.

In essence, the criteria for exercising restraint require governments to behave as unitary strategic actors that pay close attention to the preferences of both domestic and international consumers. That is a tall order for democratic governments—perhaps especially for the United States, where power is often divided between warring parties. Nonetheless, this may be the only way to keep the WTO afloat as it transfers international law to discipline behind-the-border consumer safety regulations. A functional WTO therefore depends on, rather than supercedes, the self-discipline of the nation-state.

CONCLUSION

The beefed-up international trading system offers states more leverage over one another's behavior: the new trade rules are more intrusive, and enforcement is more effective. However, the transformation of trade law also grants states the power to destroy the institutions by using this leverage to the wrong ends and on the wrong issues. As advocates of free trade, we are sanguine about the potential gains for further reducing trade barriers that the recent transformation may grant. We are also aware of the power of consumer preferences—and the need for democratic countries to respond to these. When the goal of freer trade conflicts with consumer preferences, problem cases will arise and threaten the transformation. We have offered some remedies, but none is a silver bullet. To some degree, the WTO can snuff out some of these problem cases as they arise, but its capacity is limited. Ultimately, careful restraint in avoiding unsolvable disputes may be the only way to keep the WTO's new powerful legal machinery from grinding itself into political destruction.

NOTES

1. In particular, see Mathews (1997) and Slaughter (1995, 1997).
2. This was hypothesized as a general strategy by Fearon (1997) and confirmed by Busch (2000).

REFERENCES

Busch, M. L., 2000, Democracy, consultation, and the paneling of disputes under GATT, *J Conflict Resolut* **44**(4):425–446.

Fearon, J., 1997, Signaling foreign policy interests: Tying hands versus sinking costs, *J Conflict Resolut* **41**(1):68–90.

Hudec, R. E., 1993, *Enforcing International Trade Law: The Evolution of the Modern GATT Legal System*, Butterworth Legal Publishers, Salem, NH.

Mathews, J., 1997, Power shift, *Foreign Aff* **76**(1):50–67.

Movsesian, M. L., 1999, Sovereignty, compliance, and the World Trade Organization: Lessons from the history of the Supreme Court, *Mich J Int Law* **20**(4):775–818.

Slaughter, A.-M., 1995, International law in a world of liberal states, *Eur J Int Law* **6**(4):503–538.

———, 1997, The real new order, *Foreign Aff* **76**(5):183–197.

Victor, D. G., 2000, Risk management and the world trading system: Regulating international trade distortions caused by national sanitary and phytosanitary policies, in: *Incorporating Science, Economics, and Sociology in Developing Sanitary and Phytosanitary Standards in International Trade: Proceedings of a Conference*, Board on Agricultural and Natural Resources, ed., pp. 118–169, National Academy Press, Washington, DC.

UNIFYING TWO FRAMEWORKS FOR ANALYZING QUALITY AND QUALITY ASSURANCE FOR FOOD PRODUCTS

Julie A. Caswell, Corinna M. Noelke, and Eliza M. Mojduszka*

It is clear that quality and quality assurance have become more central features of international and domestic markets for food products. It is also clear that quality and quality assurance are nebulous terms and that a unified approach to analyzing them has not yet emerged. On the one hand, economic models emphasize the role of consumers' ability to perceive quality in influencing how markets for quality work. On the other hand, marketing models emphasize a broader range of information and communication available to consumers in making quality judgments and purchase decisions. Here we propose to outline these two frameworks and then unify them in a model of quality and quality assurance that reaches from farm to table.

We refer to the set of economic models that focus on consumer information and knowledge as the consumer interface framework. These models are useful in a period when consumers appear to be changing their attitudes toward quality and toward the definition of quality. When judging an apple, for example, today's consumers may care about its taste, freshness, pesticide residue content, nutritional value, growing conditions as they affect worker safety, and country of origin, among other attributes. This stronger consumer focus on quality is affecting demand for food products, especially in the industrialized, high-income countries but also among higher income consumers in less wealthy countries.

The consumer interface models seek to explain under which conditions firms offer high or low quality. They also focus on how companies communicate (signal) quality to consumers and the truthfulness of their claims. These models have had difficulties in ad-

* Julie A. Caswell is a professor and Corinna M. Noelke is a former research assistant in the Department of Resource Economics, University of Massachusetts Amherst. Eliza M. Mojduszka is an assistant professor in the Department of Agricultural, Food, and Resource Economics at Rutgers University. This research was funded by USDA National Research Initiative Competitive Grant #98-35400-6113 and a USDA Cooperative State Research, Education, and Extension Service Special Grant to the Food Marketing Policy Center, University of Connecticut, and by subcontract at the University of Massachusetts.

dressing quality attributes that are important but are not easily observable and are costly to test for and measure. For example, *Salmonella enteritidis* in eggs is expensive to test for, but its absence, depending on cooking methods, can be crucial to consumer health.

We refer to the second framework for analyzing quality and quality assurance as the perceived quality approach. These models were developed in the applied psychology, consumer behavior, and marketing areas. They were built to explain what consumers take into account when they judge the quality of a product. Using the results from these models and experiments based on them, firms can adjust the attributes of a product so that consumers perceive it as being of high quality.

As Westgren (1999) noted:

> Quality is most typically associated with use characteristics: intrinsic attributes associated with nutritive, organoleptic, or other biochemical and biophysical values to users. Food safety, the assurance of safety, or the absence of foodborne pathogens might be considered quality characteristics in use. So might the "green" attributes of the product or the process. This does not appear to be fully codified yet.

This chapter moves that codification forward by exploring two alternative frameworks and then proposing a simple, unified framework. The value of this unification is in its comprehensiveness. Each of the two alternative frameworks focuses on a particular view of the quality story, leaving out important subplots. The insights offered by each alone are insufficient to understand the complex concepts of quality and quality assurance. The result has been a disjoint set of empirical results that are difficult to relate to each other. The unified framework will also offer a clear link between quality and quality assurance systems in the supply chain, especially in the case of attributes that are difficult or costly to verify.

A clear conceptual approach to quality and quality assurance is especially important in the context of the expanding global trade in food products that are increasingly differentiated. A central question in comparing consumer demand for quality across countries is which product quality attributes are differentiated, in what way, and to what degree. We make use of the distinction between vertical and horizontal differentiation (see Sutton 1991 for an extensive discussion). If quality is vertically differentiated, all consumers share the same quality ranking. If alternative products with different levels of a quality attribute were offered for sale at the same price, all would buy the same product with the level of quality they view as superior. If quality is horizontally differentiated, consumers would have different quality rankings and would choose different products with different quality attributes if they were all offered at the same price. For example, the level of pesticide residues in an apple may be vertically differentiated (less residue is always better), while the variety of apple (McCoun, Granny Smith, Gala) may be horizontally differentiated. The operative word here is "may," since whether a product attribute is horizontally or vertically differentiated depends on how consumers view it, which may vary across countries. We discuss if and how the different frameworks handle the distinction between vertical and horizontal differentiation.

THE CONSUMER INTERFACE FRAMEWORK

The economic literature on quality focuses on the interface between the consumer and the manufacturer or seller of the product. The models often revolve around what levels and types of quality information consumers have when they make purchase decisions and what level of quality firms will offer in the market. Thus, our designation of this model as the consumer interface framework. Thinking most generally, consumer interface models can have at least three major dimensions based on the following:

- Is quality vertically or horizontally differentiated?
- Is quality one-dimensional or multidimensional?
- What is the information environment for consumers? In other words, how much quality information do they have when making purchase decisions?

The possible mixes between these dimensions are numerous. Modeling efforts to date have only addressed a very small subset of the possibilities.

In a majority of these models, quality is assumed to be vertically differentiated and one-dimensional. Quality is objectively quantifiable. A product is either of good or bad quality or of high or low quality, and every actor in the marketplace agrees on this ranking. This implies that quality is one-dimensional. Either there is only one product attribute, all attributes of a product are at a similar level on the quality scale, or the quality of one attribute dominates the overall quality evaluation of a product. These assumptions are the simplest possible but clearly limiting. Everyone may agree that an apple free of mold is of good quality, and a moldy apple is of bad quality. However, to agree whether an organic Red Delicious apple grown in Washington State is of high or low quality is more difficult.

The consumer interface models that address vertical differentiation focus on the economics of information by emphasizing the different ways that market players find out about the quality of a product. The models acknowledge that every good consists of many characteristics. However, not every consumer of a good is capable of knowing and identifying all of these characteristics. Take as an example a consumer who buys apples in a grocery store. Some characteristics of apples are easily identifiable by examination: price, color, variety, size, smell, softness, and blemishes. Other characteristics can only be judged after buying and consuming the product, such as taste, freshness, texture, perishability, and convenience of preparation. Additionally, the consumer cannot directly judge other characteristics even after purchase and consumption, such as pesticide residues, nutritional value, and whether the apple was produced organically. Product labeling may aid consumers in their choices by, for example, providing information on nutritional content or production practices. This now familiar categorization of the level of information available to the consumer is based on early work by Stigler, Nelson, and Darby and Karni.

Stigler (1961, 1962) labeled the first category of characteristics as search attributes. Nelson (1970) then more narrowly defined these attributes as those that the consumer can know by inspecting the product prior to purchase. He also extended this approach to allow for experience characteristics that can only be judged after purchase and consumption. Finally, Darby and Karni (1973) introduced the category of credence attributes that cannot be judged independently by the buyer even after consumption. At most, the consumer can have a belief about these characteristics. Thus, as shown in Figure 1, a product's quality is dependent on a mix of search, experience, and credence characteristics (Caswell and Mojduszka 1996).

For food products, different search, experience, and credence attributes have been grouped as food safety, nutritional, sensory/organoleptic, value/function, and process characteristics (see e.g., Hooker and Caswell 1995). In general, there is no one-to-one mapping between a particular attribute and whether it is a search, experience, or credence

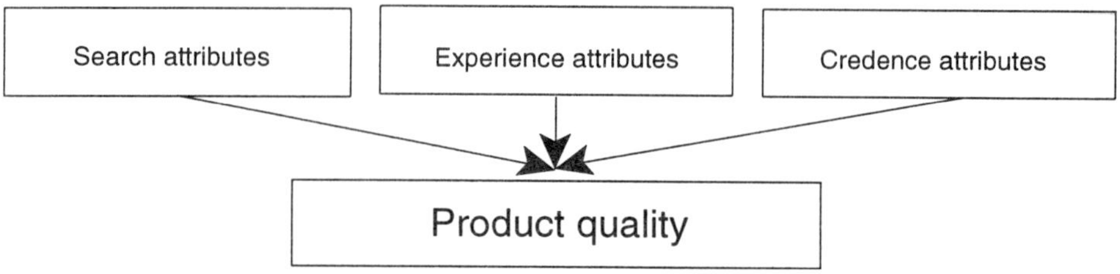

Figure 1. The consumer interface framework emphasizes the economics of information.

characteristic. For example, contamination of a food product with foodborne pathogens may be an experience attribute if the consumer becomes ill, but a credence attribute if he or she does not. It is also important to emphasize that which category an attribute falls into depends on the ease or difficulty (i.e., the costliness) of obtaining information, which can be altered by changes such as new technology or labeling.

Economists have modeled the relationship between firms and consumers when the product in question is vertically differentiated, quality is one-dimensional, and the information environment is predominantly search, experience, or credence in nature. In other words, they assume that a good consists mostly of search, experience, or credence characteristics. One subgroup of these models asks under what circumstances firms produce high- or low-quality products (see Tirole 1988). Another group is concerned with when a firm should signal the high or low quality of a product and how signaling influences the consumer's decision to buy the product when the good itself is a search, experience, or credence good.

Using the assumption that consumers have incomplete information and quality is a search characteristic, Spence (1975, 1976) and Sheshinski (1976) developed a model where a single-product monopolist chooses price and quality and where costs increase with rising quality. They found that the incentive to provide quality is related to the marginal willingness to pay for quality, for the marginal consumer in the case of a monopolist and for the average consumer in the case of a social planner.

Most of the models of vertical differentiation focus on the case where the product is an experience good. These models find that in a market where consumers buy an experience good only once—that is, they only know the true quality of the product after purchase and consumption and are not likely to purchase it again—there is a high probability that producers will offer only low-quality products. The seminal paper presenting this finding was by Akerlof (1970) on the market for used cars.

As an approach to analyzing quality and quality assurance for food products, vertical differentiation models can be criticized because they have had limited success in providing insights into the operation of markets for credence goods. For these products, consumer information remains imperfect even after purchase, although warranties, reputation, repeat purchases, and signaling through brand or store names may ease the information problem. Private incentives for companies to provide high quality may be weak, and government regulation may be the most likely way to ensure that minimum quality standards are met. Work by Segerson (1999) and Auriol and Schilizzi (2000) are exceptions to the lack of modeling in this area. Segerson found that where the quality/safety of a product is mainly dependent on credence characteristics, consumers are likely to underestimate or ignore the potential damages from an unsafe product. An example is the quality of a hamburger, which is dependent on whether it is contaminated with *E. coli* O157:H7. In these circumstances, firms may—depending on the liability system—have little incentive to invest in high quality/product safety. However, a credible threat of government regulatory action may induce firms to produce higher safety levels voluntarily, under the assumption that the implementation of government regulation will be more expensive for them than voluntary implementation.

Auriol and Schilizzi considered the role of product quality certification in markets where consumers have significant difficulty or cannot assess quality even after consumption. All consumers prefer high over low quality at given prices; thus, quality is viewed as vertically differentiated. Their model explores dependencies between demand for certification, the affluence of the population, certification costs, and market structure. On the demand side, the price elasticity decreases with wealth, so it depends on wealth and at the same time is independent of consumer tastes. On the other hand, the demand elasticity with respect to quality is independent of both wealth and tastes and is equal to one. The only problem that exists in the market is the quality-signaling problem for a credence attribute. On the supply side, it is assumed that, originally, the market is competitive and that any existing imperfections in the market are related to the signaling problem.

The main predictions of the Auriol-Schilizzi model are that when quality is unobservable, only the minimum quality is supplied and there is a decrease in variety offered. Certification is the only way to solve this problem. When firms self-certify, at equilibrium, the market structure depends on certification costs, demand size, and consumer wealth. The rich purchase high quality and the poor buy low quality. Therefore, certification is more prevalent in developed than developing countries. Also in the model, it is suboptimal for firms to self-certify because certification involves large fixed costs and there are increasing returns to scale. Self-certification might lead to wasteful duplication of certification costs among downstream firms. Government intervention can eliminate this problem, and certification can be financed by private or public funds. For poor countries, it is better to use public funds to pay for certification; for rich countries, it is better to use private funds. The optimal choice depends on the value of the shadow cost of public funding. The authors' concentration on only vertical aspects of quality limits the model's results and its applicability.

Even if quality attributes are vertically differentiated, the vertical differentiation models of the consumer interface can also be generally criticized for their treatment of quality as one-dimensional and, consequently, of the information environment as one-dimensional as well. A product may have several attributes that are of interest to consumers, each of which may have an information environment that is search, experience, and credence. The framework may grossly simplify the process through which consumers form expectations of and ultimately experience quality.

As noted earlier, many of the consumer interface models assume that the market for a product is vertically differentiated. In contrast are models that assume that quality is horizontally differentiated. Here product characteristics can signal different levels of quality to different consumers depending on their perceptions. For many attributes, horizontal differentiation may be more realistic because there is no established rank order and quality rankings differ across consumers. Like vertical differentiation models, horizontal models until recently have tended to treat quality as one-dimensional. Unlike vertical models, they assume perfect information for all market players, thus ignoring issues related to how much information consumers have when making purchase decisions.

With horizontal differentiation models, quality rankings depend on varying consumer tastes, but quality is still viewed as one-dimensional (e.g., linear in the case of Hotelling 1929 or circular in the case of Salop 1979). In his study of the economic impact of space, Hotelling proposed a simple model of horizontal differentiation. He assumed that consumers were located evenly over space along a straight finite line. Each consumer was assumed to purchase one unit of the good at the lowest price, thus demand had to be proportional to the length of the market served. Instead of physical distance, Hotelling said, one could consider the line to represent product characteristics, for example, sweetness of cider or fatness of meat. Then, at one end of the line are those consumers who like the sweetest cider and, at the other, those who like tart cider. Consumers incur utility loss from not consuming their preferred product. Also, firms can produce at various points on the line, and relocation (producing products with a different content of characteristics) is costless. The most important conclusion Hotelling made is that predictions about spatial effects can be extended to cover product differentiation and that firms locate where the demand is (near the center of the line). Several researchers have extended Hotelling's work. Eaton and Lipsey (1976) explored the assumption of fixed location and found it to be appropriate when more than half of a firm's costs were "location specific." Schmalensee (1978) argued that relocation (repositioning) costs might be substantial in a product development context. The limitation of these horizontal differentiation approaches—in addition to the assumption of perfect information—is that attributes (e.g., sweetness or fat content) are only considered one at a time, so quality is viewed as one-dimensional.

In his characteristics approach, Lancaster (1966) extended economic modeling of quality to include multiple dimensions. He suggested that consumers' preference orderings could be defined on bundles of characteristics rather than on bundles of goods. Here quality is horizontally differentiated because consumers have heterogeneous preferences over product characteristics. In the vertical and horizontal differentiation models discussed above, it was assumed that consumers purchase only one product and that they do not get extra utility from consuming a variety of products. For Lancaster, consumers are also producers and act as their own middlemen. Goods do not possess final consumption attributes, but rather are purchased as inputs into self-production functions for ultimate characteristics. Consumers ultimately care only about the characteristics of the bundle of goods, i.e., the sum of the characteristics of the goods in the bundle. The key to this approach is to be able to sum up the characteristics. In some cases, where there are indivisibilities of consumption, this does not seem to be possible. As Rosen (1974) noted, "two six-foot cars are not equivalent to one twelve feet in length, because they cannot be driven simultaneously."

Rosen departed from the Lancasterian framework on the assumption of divisibility. He also introduced a market between buyers and sellers. In his scenario, producers themselves tailor their goods to embody final characteristics desired by consumers and receive returns for performing this intermediary function. These returns arise from the economics of production that are achieved by specialization and division of labor through market transactions not available outside of organized markets with self-production. Rosen's approach assumes perfect competition on the supply side of the market. The limitation of the

Lancasterian approach is the frequent assumption of perfect information so that the information environment does not enter into the model.

More recently, Perloff and Salop (1985), Deneckere and Rothschild (1986), and Anderson, de Palma, and Thisse (1989) have proposed multidimensional models of vertical and horizontal product differentiation that consider oligopoly markets. The authors built probability models in which consumer tastes may differ and, in addition, are random. This approach is reminiscent of the discrete choice theory developed in econometrics (see, e.g., Amemiya 1981 and McFadden 1984). In this theory, individuals face mutually exclusive choices of brands or products and are assumed to maximize a stochastic utility function. As a result, each individual has a positive probability defined on each choice. Randomness in observed consumer behavior lies partially in the unobserved product attributes that determine consumer choices.

These models resemble other horizontal and vertical models in that each consumer consumes only one brand in the differentiated products market. An important difference, however, is that products are differentiated in multiple dimensions and that consumers' valuations for the various brands are random. In addition, with one-dimensional models—whether vertical, linear, or circular—each firm and product competes directly only with its two neighbors, one on either side. Thus, competition is local, and, with local competition, cross elasticities are equal to zero. In contrast, in multidimensional models, firms and products compete along several dimensions and competition is global. With global competition, all cross elasticities are non-zero and need not be equal. Like horizontal differentiation models, these models assume perfect information on the demand and supply sides of the economy.

Economic models of product differentiation at the consumer interface make contributions to the understanding of markets for quality by delineating important dimensions of these markets and isolating particular cases to explore their implications. Overall, the models seem able to address at one time only two of the three relevant dimensions of markets for quality (vertical or horizontal differentiation; one- or multidimensional quality; and search, experience, or credence information environment). This limits their usefulness for understanding quality and quality assurance throughout the supply chain. In the food industry, this supply chain reaches from the farm input supplier, to the farmer, through several processors and storage and handling locations, and via transportation systems to the retailer or restaurant, and finally to the consumer. The quality of a good can be influenced at each of these links. Product quality is multidimensional, and these dimensions are vertically and horizontally differentiated. Recent research shows that, within the supply chain, firms do not decide whether to deliver high or low quality but whether to deliver goods with agreed-upon or contracted-for quality indicators (e.g., Westgren 1999). The amount of quality information available and whether it is of a search, experience, or credence nature varies by attribute and can be influenced by market participants.

THE QUALITY PERCEPTION FRAMEWORK

The alternative quality perception framework was developed within the literature of applied psychology, consumer behavior, and marketing. The goal of this literature is to understand how consumers perceive quality. That is, which cues do consumers use to judge the quality of a product before and after buying it? This knowledge helps firms determine which product characteristics should be enhanced. In addition, companies may find that consumers need more information about specific characteristics that are good indicators of a product's quality but are not currently used by consumers to evaluate quality. Here we discuss representative work in the quality perception area.

Jacoby, Olson, and Haddock (1971) conducted one of the first experiments to test the characteristics that consumers use to perceive product quality. Perceived quality was defined as "the perceived ability of a product to provide satisfaction relative to the available alternatives" (Monroe and Krishnan 1985, p. 212). Jacoby, Olson, and Haddock looked at three characteristics of different beers: price, brand name, and composition. They found that brand name and composition are more important in determining perceived quality than price. This finding was contrary to studies and models developed earlier that presumed that price is the most important factor in the perception of quality. The attributes included in the analysis may be considered search characteristics because they are evaluated by examining label information. However, an attribute such as composition may also be an experience or credence characteristic. Jacoby, Olson, and Haddock do not explicitly address this type of distinction. The approach also focuses on how individual consumers combine various cues in evaluating product quality. This effectively incorporates the multidimensionality of product differentiation but does not address differences between consumers in their perceptions of specific quality attributes. Therefore, it does not distinguish between attributes that are vertically and horizontally differentiated.

Olson and Jacoby (1972) partially addressed this issue by introducing two terms: intrinsic and extrinsic cues. An intrinsic cue is defined as "a product attribute that cannot be changed or experimentally manipulated without also changing the physical characteristics of the product itself" (Olson and Jacoby 1972, p. 169). An extrinsic cue is one that if experimentally changed, "the physical characteristics of the product need not necessarily change." Examples of intrinsic cues are taste, color, nutritional content, and food additives and preservatives. Extrinsic cues are, for example, price, brand name, store name, or presence of nutritional labeling. Extrinsic cues can be influenced by marketing efforts. The distinction between the two types of cues implies that cues are product specific and may be consumer specific. Olson and Jacoby found that consumers prefer to use intrinsic cues. If these cues are not easily available, however, they refer to extrinsic cues to judge the quality of a product. Szybillo and Jacoby (1972, 1974) replicated these results.

The Olson-Jacoby approach classifies the product characteristics that influence quality perception on their physical basis, rather than on the bases used in the consumer interface framework such as whether the characteristic is vertically or horizontally differentiated and the information environment. There is no straightforward connection between the two frameworks because physical attributes may be vertically or horizontally differentiated and be search, experience, or credence in nature. For example, in terms of the information environment, pesticide residues are physical characteristics of a product that may be—but probably are not—detectable by the consumer either before or after purchase.

Steenkamp and Meulenberg (1986) further defined the notion of intrinsic versus extrinsic cues in order to incorporate the distinction between a product's search, experience, and credence characteristics. First, they divided the intrinsic category in two. They referred to the intrinsic characteristics of a product that the consumer can search for as intrinsic cues, and to the intrinsic characteristics that are experience or credence in nature as intrinsic attributes. Second, they specified that a product's extrinsic cues are always searchable.

Steenkamp (1989, 1990) used these definitions to develop a model of quality perception in which consumers go through three stages to form a judgment on the perceived quality of a product (see Figure 2). He argued that, given a consumer's personal background, there are certain cues in the environment that influence intrinsic and extrinsic quality cue beliefs. "Quality cues are defined as informational stimuli that are, according to the consumer, related to the quality of the product, and can be ascertained by the consumer through the senses prior to consumption" (Steenkamp 1990, p. 312). In Stage 1 of the model, the consumer acquires and categorizes intrinsic and extrinsic cues. In Stage 2, quality attribute beliefs are formed. The prior (intrinsic and extrinsic) quality cues influence beliefs about quality attributes that are unobservable prior to consumption. These beliefs are defined as "what the product is perceived as doing or providing for the consumer" (Steenkamp 1990, p. 313). Using quality cues, a consumer can infer the quality attributes (experience and credence) of a product prior to purchase. Finally, in Stage 3, consumers integrate their quality attribute beliefs. These beliefs feed into their perception of the product's quality. Perceived quality is defined as "an idiosyncratic value judgment with respect to the fitness for consumption, which is based upon the conscious and/or unconscious processing of quality cues in relation to relevant quality attributes within the context of significant personal and situational variables" (Steenkamp 1990, p. 317). Thus

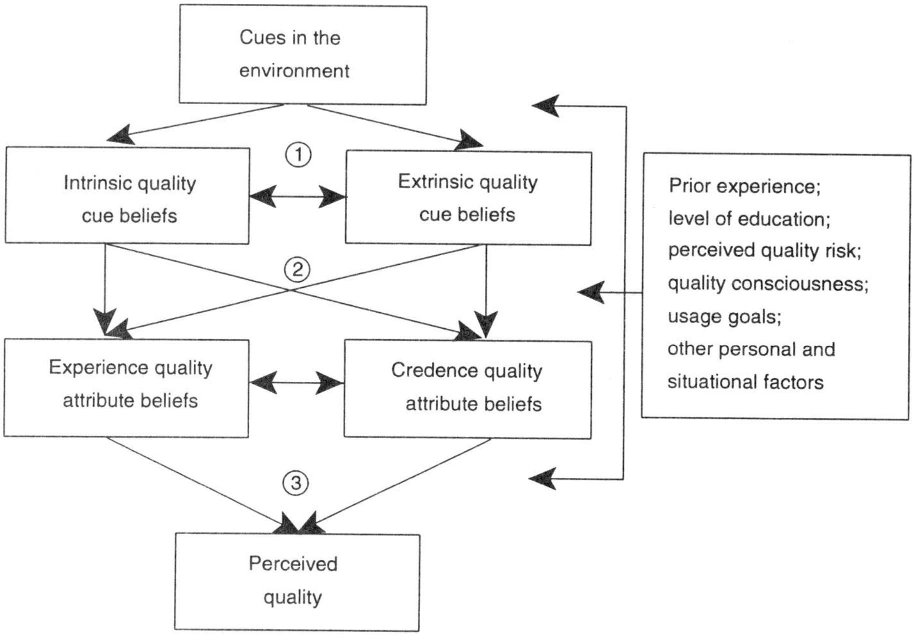

Figure 2. Steenkamp's model focuses on how consumers' quality perceptions are formed. Note: Stage 1 is cue acquisition and categorization, Stage 2 is quality attribute belief formation, and Stage 3 is integration of quality attribute beliefs (Steenkamp 1989).

the model focuses on horizontal product differentiation, although vertical differentiation could also be present if all the individual consumers agree on the rankings of particular quality attributes.

Steenkamp and van Trijp (1996) added two more steps to the above model. Rather than reproduce their figure (Steenkamp and van Trijp 1996, p. 199), we incorporate the additions into Figure 2 and show the complete framework in Figure 3. First, they introduced a term called physical product characteristics. These characteristics determine the composition of a product and thus affect its intrinsic cues as well as its intrinsic attributes. They also influence extrinsic cues. For example, a product's nutritional content is a physical characteristic that influences its intrinsic quality and the extrinsic cue of nutritional labeling. The second term introduced is quality expectation. This concept hinges on the idea that, after looking at extrinsic and intrinsic cues, a consumer expects a certain level of quality. These quality expectations influence the consumer's decision to buy the product. They also alter the consumer's quality perceptions. An example is the perceived quality of restaurant food. Assume that a cheap diner and a two-star restaurant use the same supplier for ice cream. Consumers are likely to assume that the food in the two-star restaurant is of very high quality. They are then likely to perceive the quality of ice cream in the restaurant to be higher than the quality of the same ice cream in a neighborhood diner. We also

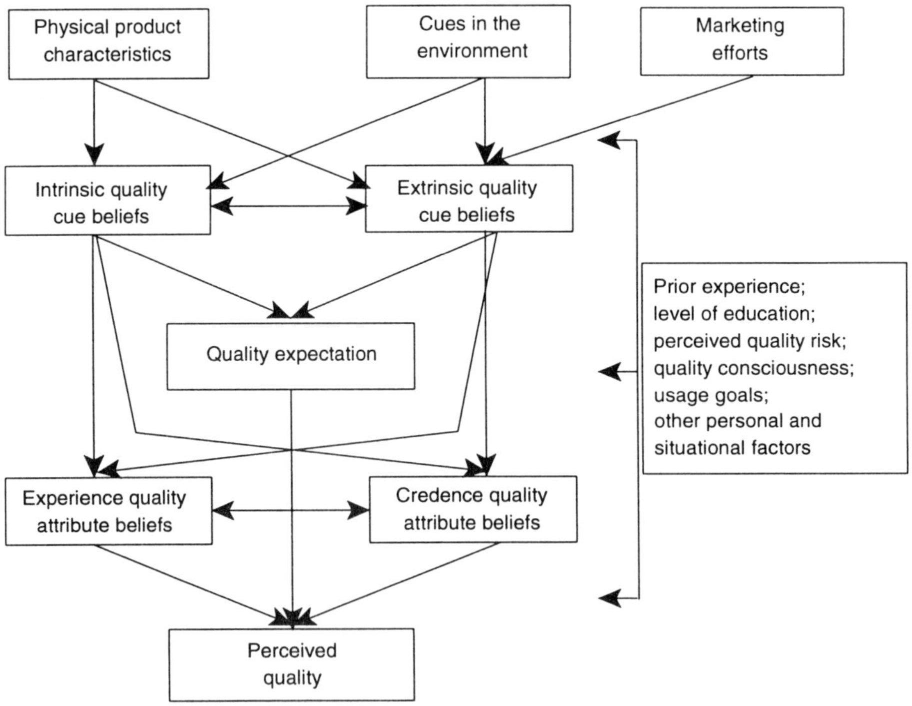

Figure 3. Expanded model of how consumers' quality perceptions are formed. Adapted from Steenkamp (1989, 1990), Steenkamp and van Trijp (1996), and Figure 2.

include the term marketing efforts in Figure 3. Steenkamp and van Trijp described these as influencing extrinsic cues but did not include them in their figure.

Steenkamp and van Trijp applied this model to the formation of quality judgments with respect to blade steak. They asked 192 Dutch consumers who regularly purchased blade steak to evaluate freshly cut and cooked blade steak. They found a significant relationship between the different steps of their model. Physical product characteristics, as determined a priori by scientists (color, fatness, pH, water binding capacity, shear force, and sarcomere length) were found to influence the consumers' intrinsic quality cue beliefs (freshness, visible fat, and appearance), which in turn significantly influenced quality expectations. Although the researchers found that physical product characteristics significantly influenced quality attribute beliefs (tenderness, leanness, flavor), which in turn significantly influenced (except for flavor) quality expectations, they did not find a significant relationship between quality expectation and perceived quality. In this context, comparisons across consumers would allow for identification of attributes, and possibly products, that are vertically or horizontally differentiated in the market.

Grunert et al. (1996) developed an even more comprehensive model than Steenkamp's, while incorporating many of his ideas. Bredahl, Grunert, and Fertin (1998) then tested this total food quality model (see Figure 4). The model distinguishes between extrinsic and intrinsic quality cues and between expected and perceived quality (they refer to perceived quality as "experience quality"). They broadened the model by allowing for cost cues and explicitly modeling the intention to buy. Cost cues influence perceived cost cues, which in turn influence perceived costs. Perceived costs are, together with expected quality, the major influences on intention to buy. Additionally, the model allows for methods of meal preparation to influence perceived quality. The new term technical product specifications includes what Steenkamp called physical product characteristics; sensory characteristics are similar to experience attributes; and purchase motives are such things as family well-being, social relationships, enjoyment, and pleasure.

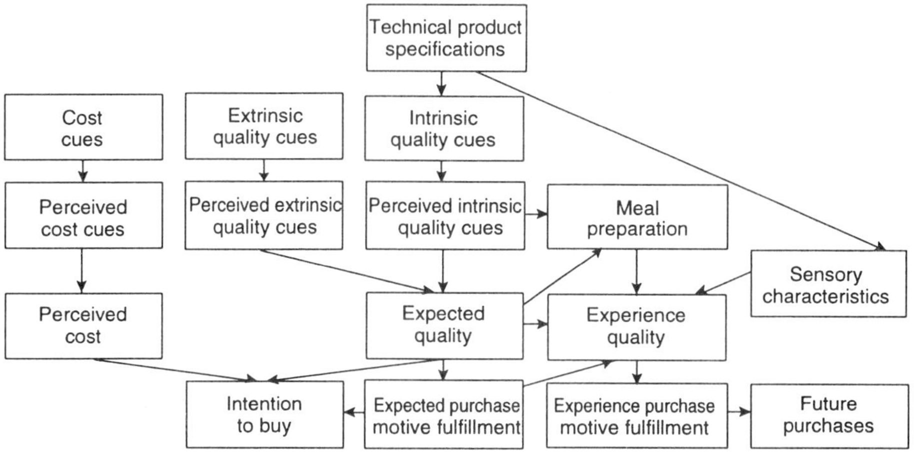

Figure 4. The total food quality model (Bredahl, Grunert, and Fertin 1998, p. 2).

Bredahl, Grunert, and Fertin tested only a small part of this model related to intrinsic quality cues. Their experiment included 200 German consumers who regularly bought pork chops. The experiment was set up in a manner similar to that used by Steenkamp and van Trijp. They measured six technical product specifications/physical product characteristics (color, intramuscular fat, pH value, PSE, halothane, and blood splashes) and estimated their influence on four intrinsic quality cues (color, share of fat, fat marbling, and meat juice) and seven expected quality criteria (tenderness, nutritional value, wholesomeness, freshness, leanness, juiciness, and taste). As did Steenkamp and van Trijp, they found that the perception of intrinsic quality cues influences expected quality criteria. However, contrary to Steenkamp and van Trijp, they could not satisfactorily explain consumer perceptions with the physiological characteristics of the product. Instead, they found a significant relationship between quality expectation and experienced quality.

In the previous section, we discussed several critiques of economic models within the consumer interface framework based on their lack of comprehensiveness. We noted that the vertical differentiation models had limited success in providing insights into the operation of markets for credence goods, while the horizontal differentiation models tend to ignore the information environment entirely by assuming perfect information. Both types of models pay limited attention to the multidimensionality of product differentiation. The perceived quality framework has some success in addressing these critiques. Its distinction between intrinsic and extrinsic cues allows modeling of the different steps consumers go through in evaluating a product. Intrinsic and extrinsic cues allow consumers a first impression of the product that leads to the purchase decision. Intrinsic attributes add to the picture after purchase and influence the experienced quality. Additionally, attributes that cannot be assessed even after purchase—credence attributes—can at least be partly made known through extrinsic cues. For example, the label "organic" on a food product, which is an extrinsic cue, tells consumers how the product was produced and may give them information about possible levels of pesticide residues in the product. The perceived quality framework has been much less specific in distinguishing between elements of vertical and horizontal differentiation for food products. It does offer an approach for addressing supply chain issues by providing a menu of means through which companies can affect the quality perceptions of consumers.

On the other hand, the perceived quality framework can itself be critiqued. The Steenkamp and van Trijp model (Figure 3) is most straightforward in incorporating the information environment into the formation of quality perceptions. The Bredahl, Grunert, and Fertin model (Figure 4) can in some ways be viewed as a step backward because it does not maintain the distinction between experience and credence attributes that is a central part of the earlier model. In both cases, the definitions used lack sharpness. For example, "physical product characteristics" or, alternatively, "technical product specifications" are ambiguous terms. These could include only those physical product characteristics that are searchable by the consumer but might additionally include all physical characteristics, including experience and credence attributes. Thus, the information environment for attributes is not fully used in the perceived quality framework. Finally, while the framework could incorporate the concepts of vertical and horizontal differentiation, the examples we have discussed have not done so explicitly.

A UNIFIED FRAMEWORK

Our goal is to bring together the strengths of the consumer interface and perceived quality approaches in a unified framework that facilitates the analysis of quality control and communication throughout the supply chain. Steenkamp (1989) already incorporated the distinction between search, experience, and credence attributes into his model (see Figure 3). Here we simplify and adapt his framework.

In adapting Steenkamp's model, we assume that a product has an array of intrinsic quality attributes that, in terms of the buyer's information environment, may be search, experience, or credence attributes (see Figure 5). This array of attributes includes the physical characteristics of the product plus other attributes that define the quality of a product (for an extensive list of attributes, see the left side of Figure 6). These attributes can relate to food safety, nutrition, sensory/organoleptic, value/function, and process characteristics. A

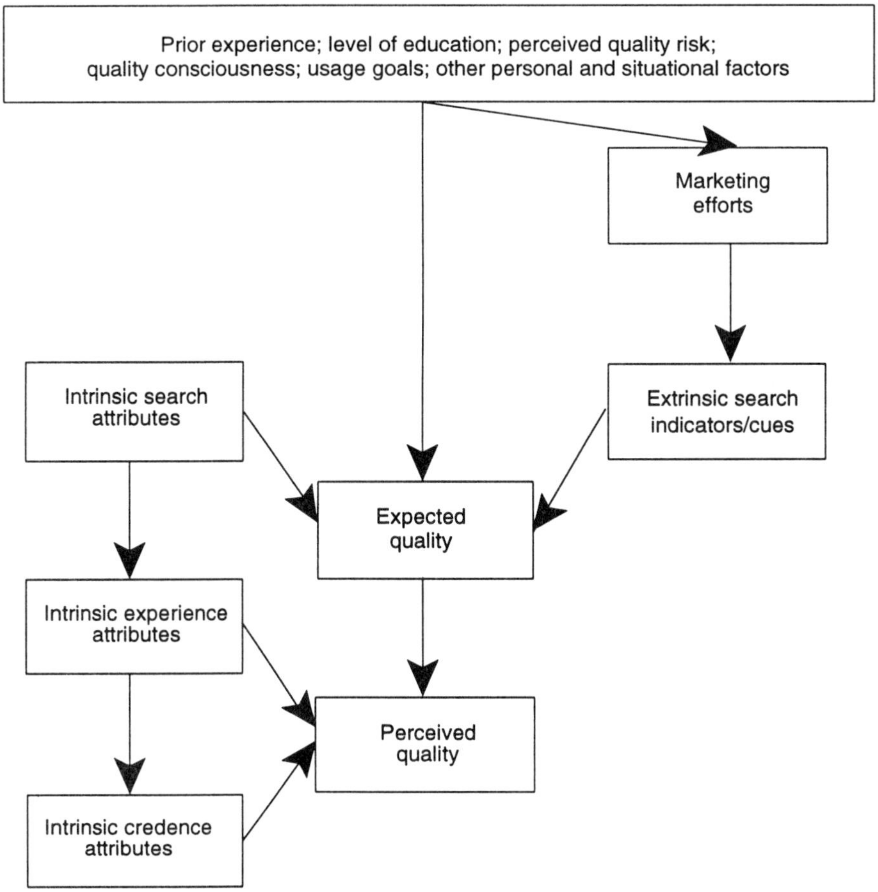

Figure 5. A unified quality framework.

key point is that there is no one-to-one mapping of specific attributes into the categories of search, experience, or credence attributes. Whether a specific attribute (e.g., presence of foodborne pathogens) falls into one or the other of these categories depends on the benefits and costs to the buyer of acquiring and using information on the attribute in decision-making. These benefits and costs can, in turn, be affected by technology (e.g., testing techniques) and mandatory and voluntary information provision by sellers. A second key point is that there is no one-to-one mapping between a specific attribute and its vertical and/or horizontal differentiation. This model is generic in that it represents the quality perception process for buyers as well as sellers at any level in the supply chain, including consumers. Which attributes are search, experience, and credence and which are vertically or horizontally differentiated is likely to differ at different levels in the supply chain.

In addition to intrinsic attributes, products offer extrinsic indicators and cues to buyers. By definition, these are searchable and are closely related to the marketing and differentiation efforts of companies (see right side of Figure 6). Extrinsic indicators and cues help to determine expected quality and the quality performance, or perceived quality, of the product. They are especially important for credence attributes. If successful (e.g., a reliable certification system), they can transform intrinsic credence attributes into extrinsic search indicators or cues, thus facilitating quality evaluation by both the buyer and seller. Intrinsic search attributes and extrinsic search indicators/cues influence a buyer's expectation of quality. Intrinsic experience and credence attributes, together with quality expectations, influence perceived quality. Overall, this process is influenced by such things as prior experience, level of education, usage goals, and quality consciousness.

Ben and Jerry's ice cream offers an example illustrating how consumers use extrinsic quality indicators and cues. As is true for all food sold in the United States, Ben and Jerry's products carry an extrinsic indicator of quality in the form of a label indicating the levels of nutritional attributes such as calories, fat, cholesterol, protein, carbohydrates, fiber, sodium, vitamins, and minerals. Additionally, the Ben and Jerry's brand name gives cues to consumers regarding the ice cream's taste, compositional integrity, and place of origin (Vermont). The company uses advertising and reputation as other cues of the ice cream's quality, including its record of social responsibility. Some ice cream attributes are vertically differentiated. For example, the less likely the product is contaminated with *Listeria monocytongenes* the better. Other attributes are horizontally differentiated. Although consumers may prefer tastier ice cream, when taste is connected to butterfat content, some may prefer less taste and lower fat. In the supply chain, the implementation of quality management systems acts as an extrinsic indicator that allows Ben and Jerry's to certify to its buyers—for example, supermarkets—that its ice cream meets an array of quality standards.

This framework can be used to analyze buyer and seller behavior along the supply chain. Like consumers, companies look at intrinsic attributes to determine a product's quality. However, it is very costly to find out about some attributes, especially credence attributes. Thus firms, like consumers, use extrinsic indicators and cues to determine the quality of these attributes. Consumers are likely to use such cues as price, brand name, warranties, and advertisements; firms are likely to examine the level of quality management systems adopted by their suppliers, look at supplier records, and check whether the supplier is certified by a third party to adhere to specific quality standards. For example, Hazard Analysis Critical Control Points adoption or ISO (International Organization for Standardization) 9000 certification are strong signals to buyers that the supplier closely

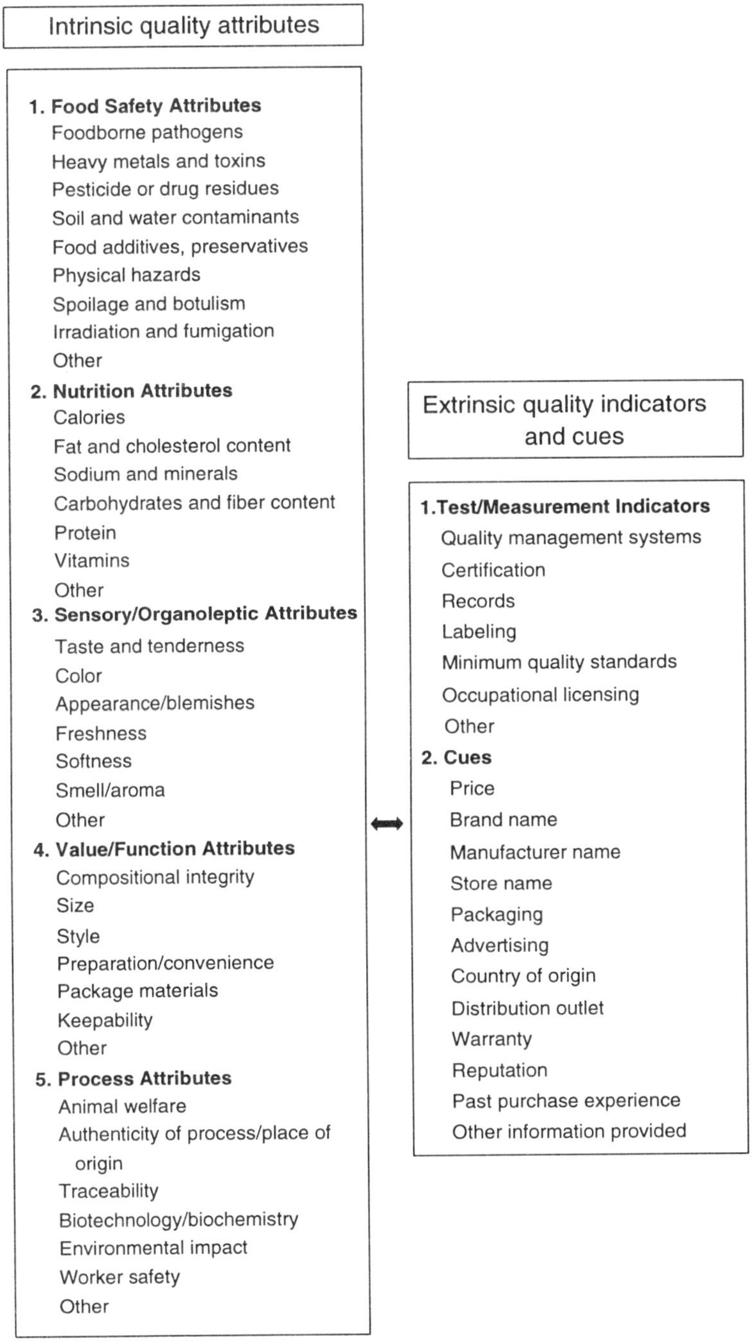

Figure 6. Intrinsic attributes and extrinsic indicators and cues.

monitors product quality and will be able to deliver the agreed-upon quality. Additionally, the use of extrinsic indicators and cues makes it easier to verify when quality standards have been met.

An important difference between the unified quality model presented here and the consumer interface framework presented earlier regards how quality is defined. The economic models simplify the definition of quality. As discussed earlier, quality is usually one-dimensional and vertically or horizontally differentiated. In the unified quality model, quality is multidimensional and both vertically and horizontally differentiated. Within the supply chain, having quality is often defined as consistently meeting or exceeding defined sets of standards for extrinsic indicators and cues. For example, a firm uses a set of extrinsic indicators, possibly combined with its own tests of intrinsic experience and credence attributes, to judge whether a supplier is likely to deliver the contracted level of quality. Consumers are much less likely to find the effort worthwhile to specify closely the quality attributes of the food products they buy. Thus they will rely on less formal information in evaluating quality, with the result that more attributes are credence at the consumer level than within the supply chain. Consumers will tend to rely on simple indicators such as brand name, retailer reputation, and labeling in their evaluations.

As an application, Noelke and Caswell (2000) used the unified quality framework to develop a model of quality assurance for credence attributes. The model takes into account the relationship between firms in the supply chain as well as the interface with the consumer. It highlights the practice of companies to employ extrinsic indicators and cues to transform intrinsic credence attributes into extrinsic search indicators. This enables firms to monitor the quality of their suppliers' goods as well as their own product's quality level. Additionally, they find that the level of quality assurance practiced by companies at one level of the supply chain influences the quality assurance–related investment decisions of their suppliers and buyers. This effect is stronger the closer the company is to consumers who demand high levels of quality.

The unified quality framework offers two main advantages. First, it allows for the distinction between search, experience, and credence attributes and the fact that this distinction will vary across circumstances and among individuals and firms. Second, it distinguishes between intrinsic attributes and their extrinsic indicators and cues. This mirrors the language used by companies and the way they contract for quality. The unified framework will make it easier to model why and how firms employ extrinsic indicators such as quality management systems and how consumers' perceptions of quality influence companies' decisions.

THE UNIFIED QUALITY FRAMEWORK AND TRADE

Quality perception and quality assurance are gaining in importance as international trade in food products increases. Companies must understand consumer demand for quality attributes across countries and continents. They must also design systems that successfully control and communicate quality levels along the supply chain and at the consumer level. Governments must understand quality attributes, indicators, and cues in designing regulatory programs and in negotiating agreements and settling disputes with their trading partners. Ultimately, understanding trends in quality perception and assurance is central to evaluating the welfare impacts on consumers of global trade in food products.

The unified quality framework raises several key questions that need to be understood better regarding consumer demand for quality and global food trade:

- How does quality perception vary across buyers within and across countries? Which intrinsic quality attributes and extrinsic quality indicators and cues are important?
- Which intrinsic attributes and extrinsic indicators/cues are vertically differentiated among which buyers? How much does the scale of vertical differentiation differ among various buyers? For example, if cheese is vertically differentiated in France, is it vertically differentiated but less so in the United States, and along which dimensions?
- If we see different patterns of demand in different countries, is the underlying pattern of vertical differentiation the same, and do differences reflect price and ability to pay? For example, do all consumers view quality about the same way but, since higher quality comes at a higher price, they buy what they can afford given their income?
- What is the level of horizontal differentiation across buyers and countries for intrinsic attributes and extrinsic indicators/cues?
- How do we distinguish between vertical and horizontal differentiation? For example, is the presence of genetically modified organisms a vertically or horizontally differentiated attribute of food products?
- What determines whether an intrinsic attribute is search, experience, or credence for the buyer? How do technology and information programs affect this classification? How does it vary by level in the supply chain?
- How universal or standardized is or can be the use of extrinsic indicators/cues in the supply chain? Can companies develop multinational strategies for quality assurance and communication? Is this more possible in the supply chain and less feasible at the consumer level?
- As trade increases, how do governments reengineer their regulation of intrinsic attributes and extrinsic indicators/cues for food products? If increased coordination is desirable, how do governments deal with basic disagreements about the level of quality attributes they want to assure in food products?
- What are the welfare implications of increased trade in food products? Will trade facilitate vertical and horizontal differentiation that more closely meets the needs of buyers or will it have a tendency to level differentiation?

The unified quality framework offers a systematic means of analyzing quality and quality assurance. This is particularly important in a trade environment where the dimensionality of the issues is growing rapidly. We must consider distinctions between search, experience, and credence intrinsic attributes, and extrinsic indicators and cues. We must also recognize variation in how these attributes, indicators, and cues are vertically and horizontally differentiated among different buyers and in different countries.

REFERENCES

Akerlof, G. A., 1970, The market for "lemons": Quality uncertainty and the market mechanism, *Q J Econ* **84**(3):488–500.

Amemiya, T., 1981, Qualitative response models: A survey, *J Econ Lit* **19**:481–536.

Anderson, S. P., de Palma, A., and Thisse, J.-F., 1989, Demand for differentiated products, discrete choice models, and the characteristics approach, *Rev Econ Stud* **56**:21–35.

Auriol, E., and Schilizzi, S. G., 2000, Quality Signaling through Certification, paper presented at the Fourth Conference on Industrial Organization and the Food Processing Industry, Jun. 22–23, Toulouse, France.

Bredahl, L., Grunert, K. G., and Fertin, C., 1998, Relating Consumer Perceptions of Pork Quality to Physical Product Characteristics, Working Paper No. 53, Centre for Market Surveillance, Research, and Strategy for the Food Sector, Aarhus School of Business, Aarhus, Denmark.

Caswell, J. A., and Mojduszka, E. M., 1996, Using informational labeling to influence the market for quality in food products, *Am J Agric Econ* **78**(5):1248–1253.

Darby, M. R., and Karni, E., 1973, Free competition and the optimal amount of fraud, *J Law Econ* **16**(1):67–88.

Deneckere, R., and Rothschild, M., 1986, Monopolistic Competition and Preference Diversity, Discussion Paper 684, Center for Mathematical Studies in Economics and Management Science, Northwestern University, Evanston, IL.

Eaton, B. C., and Lipsey, R. G., 1976, The non-uniqueness of equilibrium in the Loschian location model, *Am Econ Rev* **66**:77–93.

Grunert, K. G., Larsen, H. H., Madsen, T. K., and Baadsgaard, A., 1996, *Market Orientation in Food and Agriculture*, Kluwer Academic/Plenum Publishers, New York.

Hooker, N. H., and Caswell, J. A., 1995, Trends in food quality regulation: Implications for processed food trade and foreign direct investment, *Agribusiness* **12**(5):411–419.

Hotelling, H., 1929, Stability in competition, *Econ J* **39**: 41–57.

Jacoby, J., Olson, J. C., and Haddock, R. A., 1971, Price, brand name, and product composition characteristics as determinants of perceived quality, *J Appl Psych* **55**(6):570–579.

Lancaster, K. J., 1966, A new approach to consumer theory, *J Polit Econ* **74**:132–157.

McFadden, D., 1984, Econometric analysis of qualitative response models, in: *Handbook of Econometrics*, vol. 2., Z. Griliches and M. Intriligator, eds., North Holland, Amsterdam.

Monroe, K. B., and Krishnan, R., 1985, The effect of price and subjective product evaluations, in: *Perceived Quality*, J. Jacoby and J. C. Olson, eds., Lexington Books, Lexington, MA.

Nelson, P., 1970, Information and consumer behavior, *J Polit Econ* **78**(2):311–329.

Noelke, C. M., and Caswell, J. A., 2000, A Model of the Implementation of Quality Management Systems for Credence Attributes, paper presented at the AAEA Annual Meeting, Aug. 1, Tampa, FL.

Olson, J. C., and Jacoby, J., 1972, Cue utilization of the quality perception process, in: *Proceedings of the Third Annual Conference of the Association for Consumer Research*, M. Venkatesan, ed., Association for Consumer Research, University of Iowa, Iowa City.

Perloff, J., and Salop, S., 1985, Equilibrium with product differentiation, *Rev Econ Stud* **52**:107–120.

Rosen, S., 1974, Hedonic prices and implicit markets: Product differentiation in pure competition, *J Polit Econ* **82**:34–56.

Salop, S., 1979, Monopolistic competition with outside goods, *Bell J Econ* **10**:141–156.

Schmalensee, R., 1978, Entry deterrence in the ready-to-eat breakfast cereal industry, *Bell J Econ* **9**:305–327.

Segerson, K., 1999, Mandatory versus voluntary approaches to food safety, *Agribusiness* **15**(1):53–70.

Sheshinski, E., 1976, Price, quality and quantity regulation in monopoly, *Econometrica* **43**:127–137.

Spence, M., 1975, Monopoly, quality, and regulation, *Bell J Econ* **6**(2):417–429.

———, 1976, Product differentiation and welfare, *Am Econ Rev* **66**:407–414.

Steenkamp, J.-B. E. M., 1989, *Product Quality: An Investigation into the Concept and How It Is Perceived by Consumers*, Van Gorcum, Assen/Maastricht, the Netherlands.

———, 1990, Conceptual model of the quality perception process, *J Bus Res* **21**(4):309–333.

Steenkamp, J.-B., and Meulenberg, M. T. G., 1986, Perceived Quality and Its Relationship to Preference: An Application to Margarine and Butter, paper presented at Contemporary Research in Marketing, XVth Annual Conference of the European Marketing Association, Helsinki.

Steenkamp, J.-B. E. M., and van Trijp, H. C. M., 1996, Quality guidance: A consumer-based approach to food quality improvement using partial least squares, *Eur Rev Agric Econ* **23**(2):195–215.

Stigler, G. J., 1961, The economics of information, *J Polit Econ* **69**(3):213–225.

———, 1962, Information in the labor market, *J Polit Econ* **70**(5):94–105.

Sutton, J., 1991, *Sunk Costs and Market Structure*, MIT Press, Cambridge, MA.

Szybillo, G. J., and Jacoby, J., 1972, The relative effects of price, store image, and intrinsic product differences on product quality evaluation, in: *Proceedings of the Third Annual Conference of the Association for Consumer Research*, M. Venkatesan, ed., Association for Consumer Research, University of Iowa, Iowa City.

———, 1974, Intrinsic versus extrinsic cues as determinants of perceived product quality, *J Appl Psych* **59**(1):74–78.
Tirole, J., 1988, *The Theory of Industrial Organization*, MIT Press, Cambridge, MA.
Westgren, R. E., 1999, Delivering Food Safety, Food Quality, and Sustainable Production Practices: The Label Rouge Poultry System in France, Working Paper, Department of Agricultural and Consumer Economics, University of Illinois at Urbana-Champaign.

LDC FOOD EXPORTS AND FOOD SAFETY STANDARDS IN HIGH-INCOME COUNTRIES

What role for the public sector in overcoming barriers to trade?

Laurian J. Unnevehr*

Food safety standards may pose a barrier to expanded food exports from less developed countries (LDCs) (Thilmany and Barrett 1997, Henson et al. 2000). The importance of such barriers may be growing as traditional trade barriers in the agricultural sector are reduced, as new hazards are identified and regulated in high-income countries, and as LDCs seek more open and export-oriented growth for their agricultural sectors. These trends converge to make food safety standards an important potential barrier to trade.

This chapter starts from the premise that there are economic gains to be captured from expanded LDC food exports and, therefore, that overcoming market failure in the provision of food safety is a desirable economic goal. LDCs benefit from expanded food exports in terms of enhanced foreign exchange and potential rural income generation. High-income countries benefit from expanded variety and availability and reduced cost of food supplies. Benefits to high-income consumers and to low-income producers will not be realized, however, if food exports from LDCs do not meet food safety standards in high-income markets.

How these standards will be met, whether meeting them will have benefits beyond simple export income generation, and the role for public sector interventions are the issues explored in this chapter. The chapter begins with a brief overview of the export market environment for LDCs, including how high-income markets are changing their quality assurance management and their regulation of food safety. Next, some examples of private and public activities to address this potential trade barrier are presented. Public activities include interventions by LDC governments and donors/importers. Next, a framework for evaluating the public role in this particular market failure is examined, including issues of

---

* The author is a professor in the Department of Agricultural and Consumer Economics, University of Illinois at Urbana-Champaign.

Global Food Trade and Consumer Demand for Quality, edited by Krissoff *et al.*
Kluwer Academic/Plenum Publishers, New York, 2002.

regulating quality and safety, achieving domestic public health goals, and choosing interventions when public capacity is limited. Finally, some case examples where public intervention has fostered export market development are discussed.

FRESH FOOD EXPORT MARKETS FOR LDCS

The LDCs were predicted to benefit as a group from the 1994 General Agreement on iffs and Trade Agreement on Agriculture (Tyers and Anderson 1992). Many developing countries have seen substantial growth in nontraditional agricultural exports of specialty food products such as fruits, vegetables, seafood, and meats. In developed countries, these fresh food products have a high income elasticity of demand, and, in many cases, they have not been protected by traditional agricultural trade barriers. Trade in these products has been expanding rapidly in high-income markets, and the fresh product share of agricultural trade has increased in many developing regions (Thrupp 1995).

Fresh food products—including fruits, vegetables, seafood, and meats—accounted for half of the value of total food and agricultural exports from all LDCs in the mid-1990s (Unnevehr 2000a). These exports go in roughly equal shares to three high-income markets: North America, the European Union (EU), and Japan. Exports of fresh food are particularly important for Latin America and East Asia, where middle-income countries have well-developed market channels. Among the four fresh product categories, fish is most important, followed by fruits, vegetables, and meats. How food safety standards may affect these products is considered next.

Food Safety

Food safety issues are more likely to be a concern in fresh food product trade than in other kinds of agricultural product trade. First, fresh products are shipped and consumed in fresh form, so handling at all points of the food chain can influence food safety and quality. Manufactured or processed food products have more widely established and recognized standards, and may not deteriorate during shipping and handling. Second, standards in developing country markets are based on sanitation and good agricultural practices/good manufacturing practices (GAPs/GMPs) that may not exist in LDCs. Meeting such standards may require that LDCs make greater initial investments in quality control and sanitation. Third, these fresh commodities are subject to increasing scrutiny and regulation in developed economies as food safety hazards are better understood and more often traced to their sources. Examples of new standards in the United States include regulations in the 1990s to address microbial hazards in seafood, meat, and poultry. Another example is the specification of GAP guidelines to address potential microbial contamination in fruits and vegetables by the U.S. Food and Drug Administration (FDA). These guidelines are used by importers as a basis for private certification of exporter practices.[1]

The Food and Agriculture Organization (FAO) of the United Nations summarized FDA import detention data by reason for detention and region of the world for 1996–97. Most detentions were for contamination of food with insects and rodent filth, followed by microbiological contamination and pesticide residue violations. More than half of the rejections are attributable to lack of basic food hygiene and failure to meet labeling requirements (FAO 1999). Pesticide residue violations were relatively important for Latin America; microbiological contamination was more important in violations from Africa or Asia. These patterns reflect the relative importance of fruits and vegetables in Latin American exports compared to exports of seafood and fishery products from Asia and Africa (Unnevehr 2000a). The case studies later in this chapter provide examples: pesticide residues on snow pea exports from Guatemala and microbial contamination of shrimp exports from Bangladesh. Overall, the FDA data confirm that sanitary and phytosanitary standards are important challenges to fresh food product exports from LDCs.

Farm-to-Table Management

Management paradigms are changing, which also places new demands on LDC exporters. There is growing recognition that food safety hazards are best controlled through adoption of GAPs or GMPs in food production and processing. Many hazards are expensive to test for and may enter food products at several points in the production process. Therefore, an emphasis on prevention and control of hazards through documented production practices is becoming accepted as the most cost-effective means of reducing food safety hazards.

Management of food safety hazards is part of a trend toward greater quality management to meet increasingly specialized product specifications and niche market demands. Such approaches—sometimes characterized as total quality management —provide quality assurance that products will meet complex specifications (Mazzocco 1996). Internationally recognized certification, often through the International Organization for Standardization (ISO), is increasingly applied to food production and processing (Caswell, Bredahl, and Hooker 1998). The ISO provides a "standard for standards" through application of a framework for verifying the elements of a firm's production process that assure quality. This type of quality and safety management is increasingly in demand in high-income markets, and new institutions are evolving to certify production practices for meats and horticultural products (Unnevehr, Miller, and Gomez 1999).

In addition to private sector use of farm-to-table production management, the public sector has also embraced the concept of process control and hazard prevention. Farm-to-table risk assessment has been recognized as the operating principle for new regulation by the United States and the EU, even though in practice this approach is still in its infancy (U.S. GAO 1999). A related trend is the mandated use of the Hazard Analysis Critical Control Points (HACCP) system by government regulation for some part of the food system in the EU, Australia, New Zealand, Canada, and the United States (Unnevehr and Jensen 1999). The World Trade Organization's Sanitary and Phytosanitary Standards (SPS) Agreement also recognizes risk assessment as the appropriate means to determine whether equivalent risk outcomes have been achieved among countries (Hathaway and Cook 1997).

The movement toward farm-to-table process control has implications for LDC exporters of fresh food products. First, there are market incentives for LDC exporters to adapt these management practices and to coordinate safety and quality management more closely with importers. However, exporters must receive enough value to cover the costs of these practices. When the costs of meeting safety standards are higher than the value received in export markets, these standards will prevent trade. Furthermore, even when such costs do not prevent trade, they may influence the distribution of benefits from trade.

Studies in the United States and Europe have demonstrated that there are economies of scale in food safety management (Unnevehr 2000b). It is possible that meeting safety standards will favor large-scale producers in export industries.

Second, the growing use of HACCP in public regulation means that LDC exporters must demonstrate equivalent safety outcomes for differing production practices. In other words, they will need to be able to demonstrate that their hazard preventions and controls lead to equivalent risk outcomes (Hathaway and Cook 1997). To do so, the public sector in LDCs will need to demonstrate equivalent regulatory capacity in order to be recognized as meeting importers' food safety standards (FAO 1999).

EXAMPLES OF PUBLIC AND PRIVATE ACTIONS TO MEET FOOD SAFETY STANDARDS

To meet differing food safety standards, the private sector must vertically coordinate from the import market back to export production. Many examples of successful vertical coordination to meet quality and safety standards can be found in LDCs. Production in an LDC could be tightly controlled by a multinational firm for export to a high-income market, e.g., Kenya vegetables for the UK market (Unnevehr and Hirschhorn 2000). An exporting firm might own the production process or might contract with small producers. Local growers may be coordinated through an exporting firm that provides guidance on quality standards and assurances to importers, e.g., Ivory Coast fruits for the EU market (Unnevehr and Hirschhorn 2000). Jaffee (1992) found that the private sector in LDCs played the dominant or exclusive role in successful export market development, and a high degree of vertical integration was an important feature of successful export production.

In addition to private vertical coordination, there are several potential public activities to support improved food safety in exports. These activities fall into four categories: policymaking, provision of information, prevention and control of hazards, and investments in infrastructure and research.

Policymaking refers to actions at the national level to establish food safety–related policies. Policymaking includes (1) establishing a legal and regulatory framework that will be recognized by importing countries, (2) participating in the three international standard-setting organizations recognized by the SPS Agreement to ensure that internationally agreed-upon standards reflect production conditions particular to an LDC, and (3) developing capacity for monitoring and evaluation of risks to demonstrate equivalence of risk outcomes to importers.

Provision of information often is the most direct means of addressing the market failure in food safety. In this case, it would mean (1) providing exporters with information about import market requirements; (2) negotiating precertification by an importing country government, such as that carried out by the U.S. Department of Agriculture's (USDA's) Food Safety and Inspection Service for exporting meat plants; (3) negotiating recognition of equivalent outcomes by importing country governments; and (4) facilitating certification of product quality and safety by authorizing testing agencies or auditing producer group records.

Direct efforts to prevent and control hazards can be useful when hazard control is a public good. Limited public capacity might limit the scope of such actions in LDCs. Such measures include (1) programs to control single-source hazards, which are likely to be easier to implement than controls for hazards with multiple vectors; (2) targeted infrastructure investments to facilitate better handling and processing, such as cold storage facilities in ports; and (3) training programs to help small producers and processors improve hazard prevention and control.

Investments in infrastructure and research obviously carry large spillover benefits for domestic public health and food system performance. As such investments are made as part of overall development of the food system, they will improve the ability of export industries to meet standards in high-income markets at lower cost. Such investments include (1) sanitation and water supply infrastructure that support better hygiene throughout the food chain; (2) marketing infrastructure that improves the performance of the system in terms of timeliness, freshness, cleanliness, and quality; and (3) applied research to find or adapt new methods of control for important hazards—e.g., when research is undertaken to find aflatoxin-resistant varieties.

High-income importer governments and multilateral donors can also facilitate improved food safety. Importers can provide precertification or in-country inspection for exporters at the importing country's expense. Importers—as required now by the SPS Agreement—can also provide information about standards and requirements, as well as technical assistance in meeting standards. Bilateral and multilateral donors can fund all of the kinds of activities discussed above.

EVALUATING PUBLIC INVESTMENTS IN FOOD SAFETY FOR EXPORT MARKETS

The justification for public intervention to ensure food safety is market failure arising from imperfect information (Unnevehr and Jensen 1996, Antle 1995). Food producers cannot always guarantee a particular level of safety, and consumers cannot always effectively demand safety. Thus, improved food safety is not always rewarded in the marketplace.

Public actions can address this market failure through a variety of means, as discussed above. To evaluate such activities in simple cost-benefit terms, the benefits of food safety investments for export promotion can be measured as the value of additional exports gained through access to new markets or the value of avoiding loss of reputation in existing markets. These benefits can be compared to the costs of public investments to improve food safety and certify that a standard is met.

But evaluating whether and how to intervene is not quite this simple. Private actions may be sufficient to meet export standards, so the degree of market failure or the public goods component in hazard control will be important. Public activities are unnecessary when they displace private activities. Furthermore, most food safety interventions are not discrete, but are usually part of larger initiatives in market development or public health. In particular, there will be a strong relationship between public interventions to address export quality or domestic public health and public interventions to improve food safety of exports. The following section discusses how these three issues may influence public sector involvement.

DEGREE OF MARKET FAILURE

The degree of information failure in food safety varies among products, hazards, and market institutions. The market failure may be more acute in international trade due to differences among countries in the existence of potential hazards, as well as in methods of production and consumption. For example, some food products may be prepared so as to destroy hazards in one country's cuisine but not in another's. An example is fish, which is cooked in western countries and often eaten raw in Japan. However, exports also may be more easily identified as the source of an exotic hazard or foodborne illness outbreak. If so, exporting countries and industries have strong incentives to avoid food safety incidents and the resulting loss of market access and product reputation.

An argument in favor of public involvement arises from the public goods nature of certain kinds of hazard control and of negotiating with foreign governments. Individual producers or firms may not be able to control an environmental food safety hazard adequately without cooperative effort, and the public sector may be needed to enforce controls. Negotiating access, demonstrating equivalence in standards, and participating in international trade negotiations are clearly public functions.

An argument against public involvement is the limited public capacity and the move toward deregulation of agricultural markets in LDCs. A World Bank review of agricultural sector reform loans stated: "Residual market controls applied in the name of public objectives...serve to protect established interests, restrict the activities of certain ethnic groups, and supplement the salaries of public officials" (Meerman 1997). In many LDCs, removing government intervention has been crucial to improving export competitiveness and reducing disincentives to trade. When food safety regulations or controls run counter to those deregulation efforts, they could interfere with the ability of private firms to meet export standards.

Quality and Safety

Food safety can be confused with quality. Quality includes all product attributes that influence a product's value to consumers. This can include positive attributes, such as flavor or pleasing appearance, and negative attributes, such as spoilage or safety hazards. Safety refers only to hazards to human health in food.

Market failures can occur for both quality and safety attributes that are difficult to detect. Industry might lobby for public quality certification to secure product reputation. This reputation may be considered a public good, and regulation is called for to prevent "free riders" from supplying bad quality in the market. This is the argument for a public role in setting quality grades and standards, and in certifying that products meet those grades and standards.

Interventions to improve food safety are motivated by the public role in protecting consumers and promoting public health, rather than by industry development. Thus, it may make sense to address food safety separately from more general quality issues. Public efforts can focus on health hazards and consumer protection, and quality issues can be left to private industry management. Public intervention can mandate a minimum level of safety and facilitate quality control and certification for nonsafety attributes.

If improving food safety for exports is primarily an issue of ensuring market access, then safety in this case is like other quality attributes. In export markets, the appropriate public role might be to facilitate certification and provide information about foreign standards. The consumer protection motivation for public action relates only to foods consumed domestically.

Domestic Public Health

All countries share similar concerns about food safety hazards, but the relative importance of risks differs with climate, food habits, levels of income, and public infrastructure. Thus, food safety risks differ both between LDCs and high-income countries and among LDCs in their incidence and severity.

Some risks are greater in developing countries. Poor sanitation and inadequate drinking water supplies pose a much greater hazard to health in developing countries than in developed ones. Diarrheal disease accounts for most illness and death in children under age five, and contaminated food contributes to 70 percent of these deaths (Motarjemi et al. 1993). Mycotoxins are more prevalent in the subtropics and tropics, and pose greater risks where diets are concentrated in foods with higher mycotoxin levels (Ghat and Vasanthi 1999). Parasites are also more common. For example, cysticercosis is endemic in rural areas of Latin America, Asia, and Africa, infecting between 2 and 15 percent of the population, compared with an infected population of less than 0.01 percent in the United States (Roberts, Murrell, and Marks 1994).

These differences in source and incidence of foodborne illness mean that public interventions to address public health in LDCs would differ from those that would address export barriers. At low levels of income, investments in water and sanitation, as well as targeted interventions to reduce child malnutrition, are the kinds of investments with the greatest public health benefits (Unnevehr and Hirschhorn 2000). Such investments are not specifically for food safety, but address the multiple environmental health hazards that affect low-income populations. As the food system develops, targeted programs to control single-source food safety hazards become feasible. Such interventions are unlikely to improve export product quality directly.

A related question is whether investments to meet export market standards will have spillover benefits for domestic food safety. Positive spillovers for domestic markets can be expected when the product is consumed domestically and the investments affect a large portion of production. In such cases, investments in infrastructure or regulations for processing hygiene have the potential to benefit domestic consumers.

Jaffee (1992) reviewed LDC food export success stories and found that there was often a strong interaction with the domestic market. Domestic demand for a product provided producers with experience and an assured fallback market. Often, however, the domestic market consumed a lower quality (although not necessarily less safe) product. Alternatively, certain kinds of export products may be produced almost entirely for export (as in the Guatemalan snow pea example discussed below). In this case, investments to meet high standards for quality and safety in exports will have little or no direct spillovers for domestic food safety.

Is it desirable for an LDC to have a dual standard for food safety? New export markets provide income generation and may be expected to improve health and well-being primarily by increasing household income. Furthermore, the relative importance of food safety risks and market mechanisms for determining who bears risk will differ between developing and industrial countries. Thus, it may or may not be beneficial for export standards to apply to domestic production even when the commodity is widely consumed locally.

What Factors Favor Public Intervention?

Table 1 summarizes the factors favoring and not favoring public sector involvement in improving export food safety. These factors point to a case for public intervention when there is a lack of private information, hazard control is a public good, or there are large spillover benefits for domestic consumers.

Table 1. Issues influencing LDC public sector involvement in helping exporters meet food safety standards in high-income countries

Favoring involvement	Not favoring involvement
Lack of information may be a more binding constraint to private action in export markets	Clear private incentives to meet standards in order to maintain market access
Spillover benefits for domestic public health	No clear benefits to domestic public health
Joint production of public goods in product quality and safety (e.g., certification programs) competitiveness	Would interfere with reducing government control of markets, which may be needed to foster export
	Limited public capacity and potential for corruption
Type of hazard makes control a public good	Limited public funds with other, higher priority uses
Negotiating trade access and recognition is a public good	

SPECIFIC CASES OF PUBLIC ACTIONS IN EXPORT MARKETS TO ADDRESS FOOD SAFETY STANDARDS

The following cases demonstrate the importance of managing safety throughout the production process and show how certain kinds of public action have facilitated export market access.

Public Research to Reduce Phytosanitary Barriers for Snow Pea Exports from Guatemala

Snow peas are an important nontraditional export from Guatemala, but insect and disease infestations have led to excessive reliance on chemical control measures (Julian, Sullivan, and Sanchez 2000). During 1984–94, more than 3,000 Guatemalan shipments valued at more than $18 million were detained and/or rejected at U.S. ports of entry for chemical residue violations. Case studies in Guatemala found that chemical overuse or use of pesticides not allowed in the United States were the primary factors contributing to these high detention and rejection rates. A 1995 outbreak of the leaf miner plant pest resulted in a USDA plant protection quarantine for all Guatemalan snow pea shipments. Research sponsored by the government of Guatemala and the U.S. Agency for International Development identified the leaf miner species as not exotic to the United States—

and therefore not a threat to U.S. producers—and recommended control strategies to reduce chemical residues. Research also demonstrated that snow peas cultivated under integrated pest management had reduced pesticide applications and lower product rejection rates. The quarantine was removed in 1997, reestablishing a $35 million annual market for Guatemala. Imports from Guatemala remain under automatic detention by FDA because of frequent pesticide violations. This is an example of how public research can address unfamiliar hazards and develop new practices to reduce food safety risks. In this case, the research was facilitated by donor assistance.

Public Investments to Reduce Microbial Hazards in Frozen Shrimp and Prawns from Bangladesh

Bangladesh exports frozen shrimp and prawns to the EU, the United States, and Japan; the total value of exports in 1996 was $288 million (Cato and Dos Santos 2000). In July 1997, the EU banned imports of fishery products from Bangladesh. EU inspections of Bangladesh processing plants determined that deficiencies in infrastructure and hygiene resulted in a potentially high risk to public health. In the U.S. market, Bangladesh seafood was placed under automatic detention, so that each shipment is tested (at the expense of the importer) and allowed to enter only if it meets safety standards. In 1997, 143 shipments of frozen shrimp from Bangladesh to the United States were detained, usually for microbial contamination with *Salmonella*. To overcome these problems, both industry and government in Bangladesh made major investments in more modern plants and laboratories and in personnel trained in HACCP procedures. HACCP was implemented as a nationwide program in December 1997. This quality assurance legislation was recognized as acceptable to the EU, and the EU import ban was lifted for six approved establishments in December 1997. In this case, several kinds of public activities were undertaken, including establishing a legal framework, investing in infrastructure, and providing training. FAO provided technical assistance.

Integrated Food Safety Investments in Mexico for Fruit and Vegetable Exports

Horticultural crops (fruits, vegetables, and flowers) account for about one-third of the value of agricultural production in Mexico and about half of the value of Mexico's exports to the United States (Almonte 1999). During the 1990s, exports to the United States grew rapidly, as new opportunities arose under the North American Free Trade Agreement. To facilitate meeting food safety standards in the U.S. market, the Mexican federal government established the Technical Working Group on Food Safety, which includes the 15 states that account for most horticultural production within Mexico. This working group, in collaboration with USDA and FDA, will carry out an integrated program to improve food safety. The program intends to include training, establishment of GAPs and HACCP, and certification programs to address basic issues of quality and safety. Complementary investments are planned in water quality, research, rural infrastructure, and assistance to agricultural workers. This is an example of public intervention of a broad scope that seeks to capture spillover benefits for domestic public health and food system performance. The size of the subsector and of the export market justify large investments in the entire production chain in this case.

CONCLUSIONS

Capturing new opportunities to export high-value food products will require LDC exporters to manage safety from farm to table and meet increasingly stringent food safety standards in import markets. Successful market performance has the potential to allow substantial gains from trade, as well as rural sector income generation in LDCs, but will require new and different kinds of export market coordination. The cases discussed above demonstrate how private and public efforts, as well as donor assistance, can address these challenges.

Public sector interventions to facilitate meeting food safety standards in export markets include establishing policies, providing information, carrying out prevention and control programs, and making investments in infrastructure and food safety research. Given the limited public funds and capacity in LDCs, however, such interventions must be evaluated carefully. Such evaluation includes considering the extent of the market failure, the public goods nature of hazard control or trade negotiations, and the interface with promoting quality and improving domestic public health. The complexity of these issues means that the role for the public sector is likely to vary with the nature of the export market and the food safety issues in question.

NOTE

1. Personal communication from Harold Machias, Agricultural Marketing Service, U.S. Department of Agriculture, May 13, 1999.

REFERENCES

Almonte, J., 1999, Food Safety: Mexican Strategy, in: *Food Safety in International Agricultural Trade,* Proceedings of the World Bank-EMBRAPA-IICA Conference on Future Food Safety Strategies, Aug. 26-27, 1999, San Jose, Costa Rica.

Antle, J. M., 1995, *Choice and Efficiency in Food Safety Policy*, AEI Press, American Enterprise Institute, Washington, DC.

Caswell, J., Bredahl, M. E., and Hooker, N. H., 1998, How quality management metasystems are affecting the food industry, *Rev Agric Econ* **20**(2):547–557.

Cato, J. C., and Dos Santos, C. A. L., 2000, Costs to upgrade the Bangladesh frozen shrimp processing sector to adequate technical and sanitary standards, in: *The Economics of HACCP*, L. J. Unnevehr, ed., Eagan Press, St. Paul.

Food and Agriculture Organization (FAO), 1999, The Importance of Food Quality and Safety for Developing Countries, Committee on World Food Security, 25th Session, May 31–Jun. 3, Rome, http://www.fao.org/docrep/meeting/x1845e.htm (accessed Jun. 1999).

Ghat, R. V., and Vasanthi, S., 1999, Mycotoxin Contamination of Foods and Feeds, Third Joint FAO/WHO/UNEP International Conference on Mycotoxins, Mar. 3–6, Tunisia, http://www.fao.org/waicent/faoinfo/economic/ESN/mycoto/papers/myco4a.pdf (accessed Jun. 1999).

Hathaway, S. C., and Cook, R. L., 1997, A regulatory perspective on the potential uses of microbial risk assessment in international trade, *Int J Food Microbiol* **36**:127–133.

Henson, S., Loader, R., Swinbank, A., Bredahl, M., and Lux, N., 2000, *Impact of Sanitary and Phytosanitary Measures on Developing Countries*, Centre for Food Economics Research Report, Reading, UK.

Jaffee, S., 1992, Exporting High-Value Food Commodities: Success Stories from Developing Countries, World Bank Discussion Paper No. 198, Washington, DC.

Julian, J. W., Sullivan, G. H., and Sanchez, G. E., 2000, Future market development issues impacting Central America's nontraditional agricultural export sector: Guatemala case study, *Am J Agric Econ* **82**(5):1177–1183.

Mazzocco, M., 1996, HACCP as a business management tool, *Am J Agric Econ* **78**(3):770–774.

Meerman, J., 1997, *Reforming Agriculture: The World Bank Goes to Market*, World Bank, Washington, DC.

Motarjemi, Y., Kaferstein, F., Moy, G., and Quevedo, F., 1993, Contaminated weaning food: A major risk factor for diarrhoea and associated malnutrition, *B World Health Org* **71**(1):79–92.

Roberts, T., Murrell, K. D., and Marks, S., 1994, Economic losses caused by foodborne parasitic diseases, *Parasitol Today* **10**(11):419–423.

Thilmany, D. D., and Barrett, C. B., 1997, Regulatory barriers in an integrating world food market, *Rev Agric Econ* **19**:91–107.

Thrupp, L., 1995, *Bittersweet Harvests for Global Supermarkets: Challenges in Latin America's Agricultural Export Boom*, World Resources Institute, Washington, DC.

Tyers, R., and Anderson, K., 1992, *Disarray in World Food Markets*, Cambridge University Press, Cambridge, UK.

Unnevehr, L. J., 2000a, Food safety issues and fresh food product exports from LDCs, *Agric Econ* **23**:231–240.

———, ed., 2000b, *The Economics of HACCP: Costs and Benefits*, Eagan Press, St. Paul.

Unnevehr, L. J., and Hirschhorn, N., 2000, Food Safety Issues in the Developing World, World Bank Technical Paper No. 469, Washington, DC.

Unnevehr, L. J., and Jensen, H. H., 1996, HACCP as a regulatory innovation to improve food safety in the meat industry, *Am J Agric Econ* **78**(3):764–769.

———, 1999, The economic implications of using HACCP as a food safety regulatory standard, *Food Policy* **24**:625–635.

Unnevehr, L. J., Miller, G. Y., and Gomez, M. I., 1999, Ensuring quality and safety in farm level production: Emerging lessons from the pork industry, *Am J Agric Econ* **71**(5):1096–1011.

U.S. General Accounting Office (U.S. GAO), 1999, *Food Safety: Experiences of Four Countries in Consolidating Their Food Safety Systems,* GAO/RCED-99-80, Washington, DC.

SECTION II

CASE STUDIES

POTENTIAL IMPLICATIONS OF ANIMAL WELFARE CONCERNS AND PUBLIC POLICIES IN INDUSTRIALIZED COUNTRIES FOR INTERNATIONAL TRADE

David Blandford, Jean-Christophe Bureau, Linda Fulponi, and Spencer Henson*

The intensification of systems of agricultural production has generated increasing concern in some countries about the treatment of farm animals. Perhaps nowhere are these concerns more apparent than in Europe. Wide-ranging legislation governing the treatment of farm animals exists in many European countries and at the multinational level through the European Union (EU). Private initiatives on the development of standards for the production and marketing of food products have emerged in some countries in response to public concerns over animal welfare. The EU accounts for roughly 50 percent of the trade in live animals, meat, and livestock products by the members of the Organisation for Economic Co-operation and Development (OECD).[1] Private and public actions relating to animal welfare have potentially broad-reaching implications for agricultural practices in the countries concerned, and beyond their borders through effects on international competition and trade.

This case study examines the current status of animal welfare measures, both private and public, in the European Union. We do not address animal rights issues, since most proponents of animal rights would not accept the use of animals in agricultural production in the first place. We also do not attempt to address philosophical issues about whether society's preferences for animal welfare can be expressed through markets and the role of public policy in correcting market failure; these issues have been dealt with elsewhere (Blandford and Fulponi 1999). Our focus instead is on the nature of public concerns about

* David Blandford is a professor in the Department of Agricultural Economics and Rural Sociology at the Pennsylvania State University; Jean-Christophe Bureau is a professor at the Institut National Agronomique, Paris-Grignon, France; Linda Fulponi is an economist with the Organisation for Economic Co-operation and Development (OECD) in Paris; and Spencer Henson is a reader at the University of Reading, UK. The opinions expressed do not necessarily correspond to those of OECD or its member governments.

Global Food Trade and Consumer Demand for Quality, edited by Krissoff *et al.*
Kluwer Academic/Plenum Publishers, New York, 2002.

animal welfare in the EU and the way that these are being reflected in private initiatives and public policy. We examine the implications of the actions being taken for international competition and trade. Finally, we offer some suggestions on ways in which animal welfare preferences might be accommodated at the multinational level, particularly through the World Trade Organization (WTO).

NATURE AND IMPLICATIONS OF ANIMAL WELFARE CONCERNS: WHAT IS ANIMAL WELFARE?

There are several approaches to defining animal welfare. A widely used definition holds that "welfare" refers to the state of a being in relation to its environment (Broom 1991). This definition implies that it is possible to measure animal welfare by assessing an animal's ability to cope with its environment and that failures to cope, or difficulties in coping, indicate poor welfare. Approaches to the measurement of welfare using science-based principles have emerged with the increase in social concern about the quality of life of farm animals (see Box 1). However, it is difficult to decide what should be measured and how these measurements should be weighted, since there is no universally agreed-

Box 1. Measuring Animal Welfare

There are three main science-based approaches to defining "animal welfare":

1. **Subjective experience of animals.** This approach rests on the belief that animals can experience affective states (have feelings or emotions). Thus, animals can suffer if their living conditions are poor and enjoy if conditions are good. A number of indicators are used to assess an animal's welfare status: behavioral (indicators of stereotyped behavior for pain, hunger, frustration, and boredom); vocalized; and physiological (heart rate, secretion of stress hormones). The challenge is to link the unobserved affective experience of the animal to a set of observed phenomena.
2. **Biological functioning of animals.** This approach assesses the extent to which biological systems are functioning normally with respect to animal growth, reproduction, and longevity. Also examined are the physiological and neurophysiological responses of animals to different environments, as revealed by endocrine responses and abnormal behavior. The connection between biological functions and animal welfare is not always clear. For example, the fact that a cow is producing more milk may not reflect an increase in its well-being, though clearly an animal that ceases to reproduce at normal intervals is experiencing poor animal welfare.
3. **The nature of animals.** This approach assumes that animals should be able to express the full range of movements compatible with their natural state and thus compares animals in the wild state to their counterparts in confinement to assess deficiencies. An attempt is made to compare animal behavior under different environments to assess the implications of confinement. Animal behavior in the wild is frequently an expression of adaptation for survival in a difficult environment and its usefulness in assessing welfare can be questioned. However, the prohibition of conditional behavior in response to specific circumstances may indicate poor welfare.

Source: Adapted from Duncan and Fraser (1997).

upon definition of what constitutes higher versus lower levels of welfare. Consequently, it is typical to use a range of science-based indicators.

To the extent that the welfare of farm animals is dependent on human care, this raises the ethical issue of what the duties of humans are to animals, given generally accepted moral principles in a society. The usual premise is that while animals can be used for the benefit of humans, such use carries certain obligations (Sandoe, Crisp, and Holtug 1997; Tannenbaum 1991), namely, the provision of essential food, water, and shelter; health care and maintenance; alleviation of pain and suffering; and the ability to enjoy minimal movement. Such obligations are reflected in the "five freedoms" elaborated by the Brambell Committee of the UK Parliament in 1965[2] and in subsequent conventions on animal welfare agreed in the Council of Europe.[3] These conventions have been extremely important in guiding legislation on animal welfare in the EU.

In Europe, animal welfare concerns are frequently engendered by modern methods of intensive agriculture, which confine animals in specialized housing with limited space for movement, often necessitating prolonged antibiotic treatment to avoid the spread of disease. Other welfare concerns arise regarding the transportation of animals over long distances as the result of the concentration of production and processing facilities. The conditions under which animals are slaughtered pose another issue.

PUBLIC CONCERNS ABOUT ANIMAL WELFARE

Level of Concern

It is widely contended that consumers in the EU have high levels of concern about the welfare of farm animals. The evidence used to support this assertion includes the results of national and pan-European consumer surveys and the growth in demand for so-called "animal-friendly" food products (e.g., free-range eggs). Studies conducted in individual EU member states (Association of Consumer Research 1998; Becker, Benner, and Glitsch 1997; Bord Bia 1995; Harper and Henson 1999a,b, 2000a,b; INRA-CORELA 1998; Issanchou 1996; Meat and Livestock Commission 1997, 1999; Noelle-Nuemann and Kocher 1997; Richardson, Shepherd, and Elliman 1993; and Ziehlberg and von Alvensleben 1998) generally indicate a high level of concern in the population as a whole. Few rigorous studies of consumer concerns about animal welfare exist; nor are there many that assess the level of concern across EU member states in a consistent manner. Consequently, our understanding of such concerns is limited.

Figure 1 reports the results of a pan-European survey of primary food purchasers undertaken in 1996 and 1997 that aimed to assess consumer attitudes toward meat. As part of this survey, respondents were asked to indicate the extent to which they agreed with the statement, "I worry about the welfare of animals used for meat production." In all but one of the 11 EU member states covered by the survey, over 70 percent of respondents agreed with this statement.

The results of the survey appear to contradict a commonly held belief that there is greater concern about animal welfare in the northern member states (e.g., Germany and the United Kingdom) than southern states (e.g., Greece and Spain). Indeed, the survey suggests that the level of concern is *greater* in southern member states. In a second study

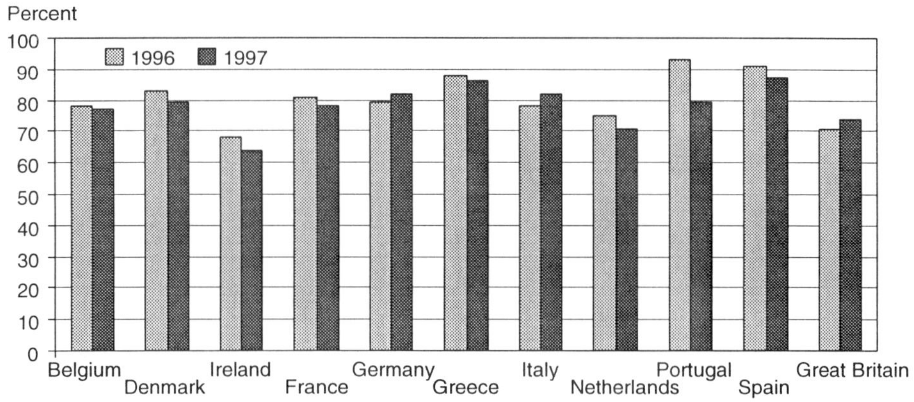

Figure 1. A significant proportion of EU consumers agree (either "strongly" or "slightly") with the statement "I worry about the welfare of animals used for meat production" (Meat and Livestock Commission 1997).

of consumer concerns about animal welfare in France, Germany, Ireland, Italy, and the United Kingdom (Harper and Henson 1999a,b), results suggest that the level of consumer concern is comparable across EU countries. Consumers expressed greater concern over chemical residues and hormones in meat (Figure 2), indicating that safety rather than animal welfare is a more important issue for EU consumers.

Although replies to specific questions about animal welfare suggest high levels of concern among EU consumers, this is not borne out by replies to general questions about

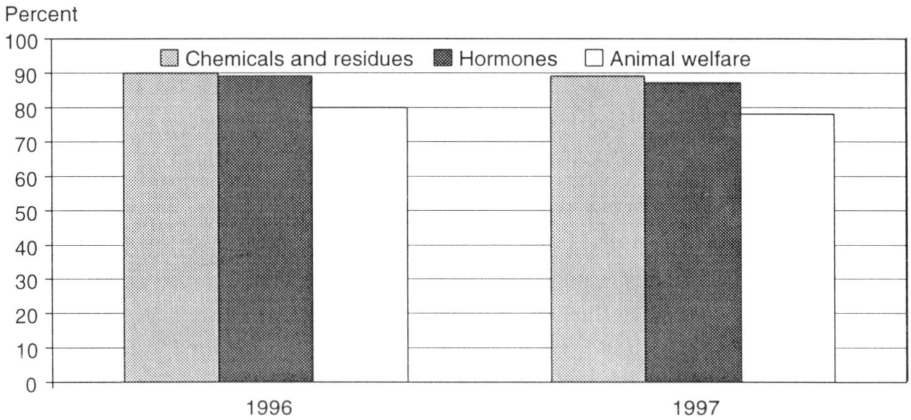

Figure 2. The proportion of EU consumers agreeing that animal welfare concerns are important is less than for other sources of concern about meat (Meat and Livestock Commission 1997).

issues associated with animal products. For example, Figure 3 details the unprompted responses of respondents in the survey reported above. Across all the study countries, the proportion of respondents who spontaneously mentioned animal welfare as a concern was less than 10 percent, and in all but one case was 5 percent or less. Similarly, Harper and Henson (1999b) report that, while animal welfare is mentioned spontaneously by consumers, it is far outweighed by responses associated with food safety and human health, for example, bovine spongiform encephalopathy (BSE), hormones, and genetically modified organisms.

In summary, the evidence suggests that EU consumers are concerned about the welfare of animals in the context of food production, but that such concerns are not at the forefront of their minds. There is evidence that concern about animal welfare in food production is closely related to—and indeed may be confused with—issues such as animal experimentation and pet ownership (Harper and Henson 1999a,b). This clearly has implications for the degree to which consumers take their concerns about animal welfare into account in their decisions on food purchases.

Research on consumer concerns about animal welfare demonstrates the importance of information and awareness in the development of attitudes toward animal agriculture (Harper and Henson 1999a,b). On the one hand, greater awareness is generally associated with greater levels of concern. On the other hand, consumers actively use avoidance of information as a strategy to deal with their concerns about animal welfare, as is evident in comments such as "I try not to think about it" by survey participants.

Nature of Consumer Concerns about Animal Welfare

The available evidence suggests that concerns about the treatment of farm animals are real in the European Union, but that our understanding of the motivation and nature of such concerns is weak. There are two possible interpretations of the concerns:

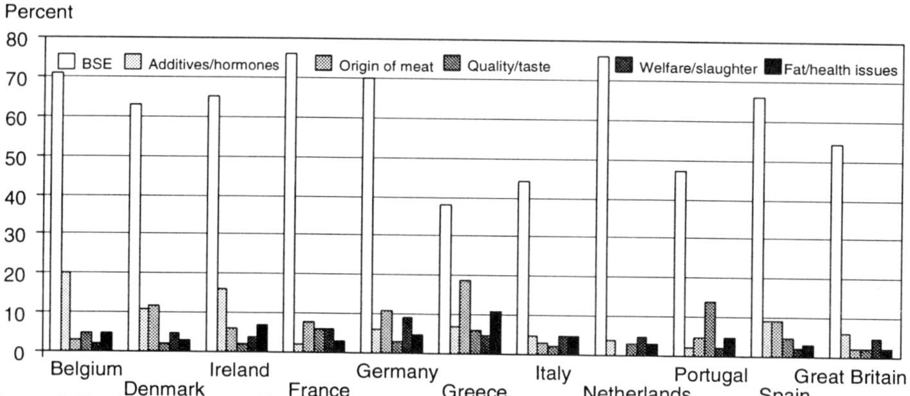

Figure 3. Few EU consumers identify animal welfare spontaneously as a source of concern about meat (Meat and Livestock Commission 1997).

- Consumers have moral objections to the ways in which animals are treated.
- Consumers view farm animal welfare to be associated with particular characteristics of animal products, for example, safety and taste.

Survey results suggest that both of these interpretations are valid and that the concerns of individuals will reflect either or both factors. However, recent research (Harper and Henson 1999a,b) indicates that the second interpretation seems to be most applicable to EU consumers as a whole. Although consumers may feel a moral obligation to avoid cruelty to animals and/or to care for animals, they are more likely to perceive a number of personal benefits from high levels of animal welfare in terms of quality and/or safety of the end product. Thus, animal welfare (which is itself a credence characteristic) is used as an indicator of credence characteristics associated with the end product. Further evidence of this is provided by a study by Becker (1999) of several EU countries (Germany, Ireland, Italy, Spain, and the United Kingdom). That study concluded that consumers view "free range" as an important indicator of safety when purchasing chicken.

Very little research has been conducted on the relationship between consumer concerns about farm animal welfare and methods of production. The studies that have been undertaken (e.g., Cowan and Mannion 1997; Harper and Henson 1999a,b) suggest that concerns relate primarily to intensive methods of production, including lack of space and freedom of movement (encapsulated in images of battery cages for hens) and the use of hormones and antibiotics. Consumers seem to assess animal welfare in terms of their own well-being. That is, they put themselves in the animals' place in judging the acceptability of production practices. Reference is frequently made to concepts of "natural" or "humane." Consumers may deem certain practices unacceptable that scientists do not consider as posing a major animal welfare issue.

Responsibility for Animal Welfare

An important issue is whom consumers view to be responsible for ensuring that the treatment of animals in food production is acceptable. This has important implications for the extent to which consumer concerns about animal welfare will influence their food purchase decisions. Consumers will only make choices between products that are associated with different levels of animal welfare if they feel a personal responsibility for ensuring that animals are well treated in the production process and/or that their choices will make a difference. In the European Union, minimum standards for animal welfare are determined by legislation; beyond those, however, there are gradations of welfare levels (e.g., in the production of eggs) that are left to consumer choice, backed up by labeling, underpinned by domestic legislation.

Harper and Henson (1999a,b) suggest that consumers frequently attribute the responsibility for ensuring "acceptable" levels of animal welfare to government through legislation and/or to producers and retailers. Consumers are not prepared to take responsibility for the welfare of animals on an individual basis but instead consider this to be a collective responsibility. The implication is that many consumers consider it unacceptable that any products offered for sale may have been produced with "unacceptable" levels of welfare. Similarly, consumers do not accept that they should be required to pay more for products associated with enhanced levels of welfare, although they often do this in practice by choosing to purchase products that are perceived to have more "animal-friendly" characteristics.

Consumer concerns about animal welfare can manifest themselves in two ways: (1) through the demand for government regulation, and (2) through demand for food products perceived to have different characteristics in terms of the welfare of animals in the production process. These effects have important implications for the way in which consumer concerns about animal welfare are evaluated. The use of "willingness to pay" measurements through product price (see, e.g., Table 1) may be unreliable because nonconsumers may still demand regulation of the production practices employed in the supply of such products.

Due to the credence nature of animal welfare, trust in the information provided about the ways in which animal-based foods are produced is a major factor influencing consumer behavior. A key factor in the level of trust is the perceived credibility of the source of information and the means of verification/traceability employed by that source to ensure that the product complies with the standards of animal welfare claimed. There is evidence that EU consumers are cynical about labels on food products and that this cynicism may act as a barrier to changes in their food purchasing behavior (Harper and Henson 1999a,b). However, consumers may also use mistrust in information as an *ex post* rationalization of their reluctance to change their purchasing behavior in accordance with their professed concerns.

Table 1. Willingness of UK consumers to pay for legislation to ban battery cages through higher prices for eggs

Increase in price of dozen eggs (pence)	% Respondents
0	14
0 to 20	10
20 to 40	32
40 to 60	18
60 to 80	11
80 to 100	7
100 to 120	6
More than 120	3

Note: 1 UK penny = 1.6 U.S. cents.
Source: Bennett (1998).

Impact on Purchasing Behavior

Consumers may respond to concerns about animal welfare in a number of ways. First, they may cease to consume some or all animal-based food products. Thus, for example, many consumers in the United Kingdom and Ireland refuse to consume veal or foie gras because of concerns about the welfare of the animal in the production process. They may become vegetarians. Data for 1995 suggest that less than 1 percent of the population was vegetarian in France, compared to roughly 5 percent in both Germany and the United Kingdom (Mintel Market Intelligence 1996; personal communication from the Federacion Naturista Vegetariana). Evidence indicates, moreover, that the number of vegetarians is increasing across the Union. Survey results suggest that this reflects not only concerns about animal rights and animal welfare, but also attitudes to food safety, nutrition and health, and the environment (Harper and Henson 1999a,b).

Second, consumers may choose product variants that are perceived to be associated with higher levels of animal welfare. These may include products that are explicitly labeled as being produced with higher levels of welfare or products for which the consumer perceives this to be the case; for example, organic products or those having a particular geographic origin. In certain cases, specific product descriptions allied with systems of production are defined legally. In the European Union, for example, this applies to eggs and chickens for which terms such as "free range" can only be used if systems of production comply with specified standards. The market for such products is attractive to economists because it provides a means to determine the implied value of animal welfare. However, consistent data on the price and market demand for such products across EU member states are difficult to obtain.

Within the European Union, eggs are the product for which variants associated with different standards of animal welfare are presented most explicitly to consumers. In general, three product variants are available, according to the methods of production employed (as defined by the EU): (1) conventional battery production, (2) barn production, and (3) free-range production. Eggs produced by each of these methods can be labeled accordingly. In many member states all three variants are available side by side in retail food outlets. Table 2 reports the market share of free-range eggs—those with the highest animal welfare standards—in selected member states. The market for free-range eggs is well established, and demand is growing at a rapid rate.

Table 2. Market share of free-range eggs across EU member states

Member state	Year	Market share (%)
Austria	1996	40
Denmark	1996	25
France	1996	8
Germany	1996	11
Italy	1997	3
Netherlands	1996	22
United Kingdom	1998	20

Source: Leatherhead Food Research Association (1999).

More generally, a number of surveys indicate that consumers are willing to pay a price premium to secure higher standards of animal welfare. For example, INRA-CORELA (1998) reports that 45 percent of French consumers would be willing to pay more for enhanced animal welfare standards, particularly for an increase in living space for battery chickens, pigs, and veal calves. Similarly, Schulz (1997) reports that 88 percent of German consumers would be willing to pay a higher price for food products associated with higher levels of animal welfare.

Finally, consumers may not change their food purchase behavior, even though they may be concerned about animal welfare. There may be many reasons for this. First, they may not perceive that their purchase decisions will have any significant impact on how food is produced. Second, they may mistrust information provided on the manner in which food is produced. Third, they may not be able to afford the price premium associated with products perceived to be associated with higher levels of animal welfare.

Political Action

Concerns about animal welfare have motivated political activities aimed at implementing stricter standards for the treatment of farm animals at both the EU and member state levels. These activities take two forms. First, individuals have taken direct action to prevent practices they consider cruel. Examples include protesting against live animal exports, freeing animals from production facilities, and even making attacks on producers. Radical groups have made it very difficult, for example, to market veal in the United Kingdom. Second, animal welfare groups are active in lobbying government at both the member state and EU levels. Within the European Union, for example, national animal welfare groups are represented by the Eurogroup for Animal Welfare, which is officially recognized by the European Commission as a lobbying organization and meets with EU officials on a regular basis; it is also active in broader European institutions. National and pan-national lobbying groups are well organized and highly influential in the debate on animal welfare policy in the EU.

ANIMAL WELFARE LEGISLATION[4]

The Treaty of Rome, which established the European Economic Community (EEC) in 1957, did not include any provisions on animal welfare. Much of the subsequent discussion of such issues took place in the Council of Europe, of which the EEC was a member. In 1968, the council drew up a convention on the protection of animals during international transport; in 1976, it agreed to a further convention on the protection of animals kept for farming purposes. A convention on the protection of animals for slaughter was concluded in 1979.

The convention on animals kept for farming purposes was an extremely significant document for subsequent European legislation. Approved in 1978, the convention was designed to apply "to the keeping of animals, and in particular to animals in modern intensive stock-farming systems." Such animals are defined as those bred or kept for the production of food, wool, skin, or fur or other farming purposes; the systems covered are those that "predominantly employ technical installations operated principally by means of automatic processes."

The convention specifies that animals must be housed, fed, and cared for in a manner that "is appropriate to their physiological and ethological needs in accordance with established experience and scientific knowledge." The convention calls for the provision of appropriate freedom of movement; space; environmental conditions (lighting, temperature, air circulation, ventilation, gas concentration, and noise intensity); food and liquids; inspection of the state of the animals' health; and inspection and maintenance of any equipment affecting the welfare of the animals. It also calls for the establishment of a standing committee to develop recommendations on detailed provisions for the implementation of these principles based on scientific knowledge of various animal species.

In approving the convention, the Council of the European Communities noted that its provisions covered areas for which the EEC did not have common rules and that the protection of animals was not an EEC objective. It also noted that disparities between national laws on the protection of farm animals could affect competition between member states in agricultural markets. Given the potential implications for the common agricultural policy of any competitive effects, the council decided that it was necessary to participate in the convention. The idea that animal welfare regulations can affect the competitive position of EU member states has been a recurring theme in subsequent legislation. The principal animals affected by EU legislation covering minimum welfare standards are laying hens, pigs, and veal calves.

In 1980, a council resolution indicated that minimum standards should be developed for the protection of laying hens kept in cages; the council requested that the European Commission develop these standards. In 1985, the commission established regulations for the production standards that must be met for eggs to be labeled as "free range," "semi-intensive," "deep litter," or "perchery (barn)" eggs. In the following year, the council approved mandatory standards for the protection of laying hens kept in intensive caged systems. The European Court of Justice subsequently annulled these on procedural grounds, and a revised set of standards was approved in 1988. The standards called for the provision of 450 square centimeters of cage area per bird, a feed trough of 10 centimeters per bird, and a height of at least 40 centimeters over 65 percent of the cage area, with not less than 35 centimeters at any point. The floor of the cage must be constructed so as to support adequately each of the forward-facing claws of each foot; the slope cannot exceed 14 percent.

In 1999, the Council approved a new set of standards for birds kept in intensive caged systems. These provide for 550 square centimeters of space per bird by 2003. From 2002 onward, all newly constructed systems must satisfy a broader set of standards, including the provision of nesting space, perches, and a littered area. Regulations are also specified for systems that involve multiple levels and access to open runs. A maximum stocking density of nine laying hens per square meter of available area is to be introduced into all non-intensive cage systems by 2007. Most important, the rearing of birds in intensive caged systems will be prohibited as of 2012.

Minimum standards for the welfare of pigs came into effect in 1994. These prohibit the use of tethers in units constructed from 1996 onward and require the conversion of existing units by 2006. Standards are specified for the construction and maintenance of stalls and equipment; heating and ventilation; lighting; and inspection, feeding, and veterinary treatment of the animals. The animals must be able to see other pigs. Minimum floor space requirements are specified for weaners and rearing pigs depending on their weight. The requirements must be satisfied by 2006.

Minimum standards for the protection of veal calves were announced in 1991. These prohibit the use of tethers in units built from 1994 onward. They also require a minimum crate size that allows calves to turn around, groom themselves, and rest. The animals must be able to see other calves. Existing units must conform by 2003. The directive permits calves to be fed on a diet devoid of roughage or iron, to keep veal pale in color. In 1997, a further council directive prohibited the confinement of calves in individual pens after eight weeks of age unless required to do so by a veterinarian, and specified precise space requirements. These came into force for all holdings brought into use from 1998 onward.

Another area of legislation in the EU relating to animal welfare is the use of bovine somatotropin (rBst) in dairy cattle. The use of this hormone has been prohibited in the European Union since 1990. Whereas the initial rationale for the ban was its potential impact on the dairy market, the well-being of dairy cattle was presented as the rationale in 1994 when the ban was extended until the end of 1999. The factors cited were the impact of the use of the hormone on the incidence of mastitis and associated metabolic disorders.

In summary, then, minimum animal welfare standards for the husbandry of laying hens, veal calves, and pigs have been implemented by the EU. The standards have targeted production practices, such as intensive egg production, that have generated the greatest public concern. It is important to note, however, that the practices concerned are not necessarily associated with large and intensive production systems—the use of veal crates being a case in point—and that the legislation specifically exempts small producers in many cases. The scope and level of the standards have been increasing. Standards are under development for other farm animals, in particular, broilers and turkeys. Since considerable controversy is associated with the traditional production method for foie gras, which involves forced feeding of geese, it is possible that standards may be developed for these animals. Beef and dairy cattle are other animals for which production standards may be established. EU standards also exist for the transport of farm animals and for slaughter.

Some European countries have adopted more stringent production regulations for animal welfare than those of the European Union. For example, Switzerland prohibits the use of intensive cage systems for laying hens; the cage requirements are such that they constitute an effective ban on traditional cages.[5] In 1988, Sweden banned the keeping of laying hens in battery cages from January 1, 1999; beak trimming of hens is also not permitted. In a number of Austrian *lander,* the use of cages for laying hens will be forbidden; in Finland, a ban on battery hen production will be effective as of 2005. In Denmark, the minimum space allowance is 600 square centimeters per hen; in Belgium and the United Kingdom, the required space for single-bird cages is 1,000 square centimeters per bird or 750 square centimeters per bird for two-bird cages. These figures may be compared to the 550 square centimeters per bird requirement for the European Union. Austria and Finland provide some financial support for conversion of cage systems. Thus, current EU legislation should be considered as providing minimum standards for animal welfare in many European countries. It is unlikely to represent the final development of animal welfare legislation in Europe as a whole.

It is important to note that such legislation focuses on setting production standards that are believed to enhance animal welfare. There is only a loose linkage between these standards and any science-based indicators of welfare. The production standards adopted are a function of scientific evidence, public perceptions of what constitutes a welfare-improving production environment, and political acceptability. An additional issue is that fixed production standards can become outdated, since legislation takes a long time to implement and the phase-in period is often prolonged. Furthermore, genetic modification of animals can make standards obsolete. For example, it is now possible to breed congenitally blind chickens. The EU's current lighting standard for poultry houses could be made obsolete by this development.

PRIVATE SECTOR RESPONSES

Concerns about animal welfare have generated private sector responses, in addition to legislative responses. The supply chain for animal products within the European Union has become progressively more concentrated at all levels, but in particular in processing and distribution. Major food suppliers have attempted to minimize the risk posed to their brand capital though failure to satisfy consumer concerns about animal welfare. One mechanism through which this has been achieved is the development of private animal welfare standards. In many cases, these have been a component of general attempts to improve product quality management and to provide traceability of final products back to the producer. These initiatives, in turn, reflect public concern about the efficacy of public regulation to ensure product safety and quality in the wake of scares associated with BSE and chemical contamination (e.g., with dioxin).

Private animal welfare standards have been implemented in two main ways. In most cases, animal welfare requirements have been specified as part of broader end-product quality standards. These have largely been promulgated by private businesses, either individually or through a trade organization. Examples of such private standards are Carne con Amore in Italy and the Scottish Pig Industry Initiative (discussed as Case 1 below). Elsewhere, standards have been the initiative of public bodies, as with the Label Rouge quality assurance scheme in France.

In a limited number of cases, private animal welfare standards have been implemented. These are linked to explicit animal welfare labels or brands. One example, which is of particular interest in view of the fact that it involves the largest animal welfare organization in the United Kingdom, is Freedom Food (see Case 2 below).

Although private animal welfare standards are, by nature, voluntary, in certain EU member states (e.g., Ireland and the United Kingdom), the level and nature of consumer concerns are such that compliance with these standards has become the industry norm. Thus, major retailers and/or processors typically require that producers implement these standards and that a third party certify compliance.

The development of private animal welfare standards raises a number of issues regarding the future role of public regulation. Given that private standards typically exceed the requirements of public regulation and can be changed with relative ease, it might be expected that in contexts where private standards become the norm, public regulation could largely become obsolete. Further, private standards can act as a mechanism to overcome trade distortions between countries. For example, while Denmark applies lower standards of welfare in pig production than the United Kingdom, Danish producers of pork and bacon have implemented private standards that certify that they satisfy UK regulatory requirements, as required by major retailers.

Case 1. Scottish Pig Industry Initiative

The Scottish Pig Industry Initiative was established by the Scottish pig industry in 1990 as a quality assurance scheme for pork and bacon. The scheme sets standards for animal welfare and establishes controls on the use of veterinary medicines, hygiene, and end-product quality. Although these standards are based on legal requirements, they impose additional demands on members. Scottish Food Quality Certification Ltd. independently audits producers to ensure that they meet the standards.

Since the initiative's launch, membership has grown significantly (Figure 4). Currently, the scheme covers over 300 farms, which collectively account for 92 percent of the Scottish pig herd. The scheme also encompasses eight approved processors that slaughter and process meat from member farms.

Case 2. Freedom Food

Freedom Food Ltd. is a not-for-profit scheme established in 1994 by the Royal Society for the Prevention of Cruelty to Animals (RSPCA), the United Kingdom's largest animal welfare organization. Members of Freedom Food are required to comply with animal welfare standards established by the RSPCA. Producers are inspected annually to ensure that they comply; additional random checks are also undertaken.

Table 3 details the membership of Freedom Food in July 1994, when the scheme was established, and the current membership. The scheme now has 4,000 members, including producers, livestock transporters, and abattoirs. The end product is labeled with the Freedom Food logo. Roughly 6,000 food stores, including some of the major supermarket chains, carry these products. The most successful product is free-range eggs, annual sales of which are currently 72 million units.

Table 3. Freedom Food membership, 1994–2000

	July 1994	April 2000
Members	119	4,000
Retailers stocking Freedom Food Products	400	6,000
Animals	1 million	19 million

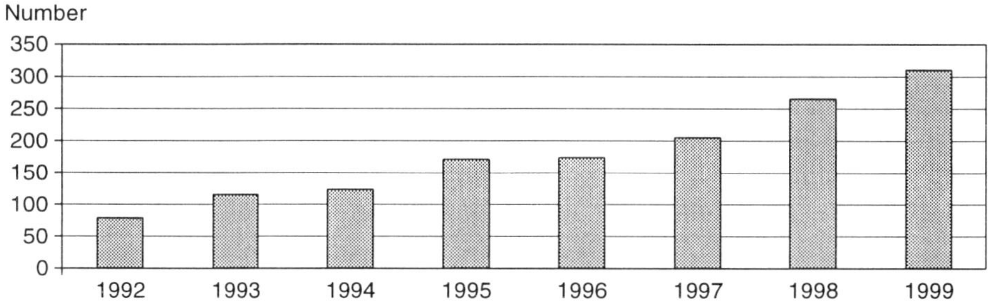

Figure 4. The number of farms that are members of the Scottish Pig Industry Initiative has increased substantially in recent years.

ECONOMIC IMPACTS

The application of higher standards for animal welfare is likely to increase the fixed and variable costs of production, at least in the short run. Evidence suggests that feed costs increase through reduced conversion rates; other variable costs, such as energy and labor, are higher. Since the standards generally require new investments in buildings and equipment, fixed costs are likely to rise. Cost increases are affected by a number of factors, including the divergence between existing production practices and the new standard and the availability of technical expertise and technologies to meet the standard. The impact will also be affected by the amount of time allowed to achieve compliance. Costs may increase in other parts of the supply chain, due to the requirement for product traceability. Such costs are likely to be lower with simpler supply chains and more concentrated production.

On the positive side, health and mortality costs may go down with more animal-friendly systems. It should also be borne in mind that the social costs associated with positive or negative externalities from animal agriculture might also be affected by changes in production systems. For example, pollution could increase or decrease depending on the nature of the change in systems.

How Much Will Production Costs Increase?

The UK Ministry of Agriculture has estimated that the recently announced EU standards for laying hens will cost existing producers roughly £10 ($14) per bird.[6] For a 10-year-old unit with 50,000 birds and five birds per cage, the nonrecurring costs of compliance will amount to £833,000 ($1.2 million). Additional production costs for this type of unit are estimated to be over £36,000 ($50,000). The ministry has also estimated that the nonrecurring costs of complying with the standards for stalls and tethers and space requirements for pigs would cost between £39,000 and £65,000 ($55,000 and $90,000), depending on the type of operation. Annual production costs would increase by 3 to 11 percent of total turnover.

According to the European Commission, egg production costs could be expected to increase by 5 to 7.5 percent when 600 square centimeters cage area per bird is required, and by about 10 to 15 percent at 800 square centimeters per bird.[7] Assuming that not more than 80 percent of all eggs produced are sold as table eggs and that there is no change in the price of processing eggs, the farm price of table eggs is expected to increase by 12 to 18 percent. Eggs produced in aviary, perchery, deep litter, or free-range systems command a premium price in certain areas, but it is not certain that the premium will be maintained if most of the production is undertaken in more "welfare-friendly" alternative systems. In addition, the commission's report notes that the additional expenditure for consumers is very small, estimated at 1.12 to 1.56 Euros ($0.95 to $1.33) per head per year with the higher space requirement (800 square centimeters).

In Italy, the adoption of EU regulations for laying hens will increase costs of production by an estimated 12 to 15 percent.[8] This includes increased feed consumption, greater losses (number of broken eggs), increases in other variable costs, and depreciation of additional fixed costs. Another implication of the EU regulations is an estimated reduction of output of 20 percent, which translates into a loss of 6,000 jobs. A study on animal welfare measures for pigs, commissioned by the Italian Ministry of Agriculture, finds that the costs of new pig units would increase by 18 to 22 percent. The cost of adapting existing units to conform to the greater area requirements would be about 500 million lira ($220,000) per firm. Where the firm decreases the number of animals to conform to the space requirements, a substantial loss of productivity is envisaged due to the smaller number of pigs over which costs must be distributed.[9]

All the available studies indicate that substantial costs are likely to be imposed on producers, under existing technology, as a result of the imposition of higher animal welfare standards; this would influence their competitive position. In a closed economy, the increased costs would eventually be passed on to consumers in the form of higher prices for final products. However, induced innovation may eventually lead to some reduction in additional costs, as new technologies and production practices are developed. Demand for the product would be expected to fall, particularly if the own and cross-price elasticities are high. There could be some offsetting effects in that consumers who have ceased eating meat because of animal welfare concerns could re-enter the market. If the welfare standards for all animal agriculture were increased, the costs of animal products as a whole could rise. This would reduce the amount of switching of consumer demand among products that would be associated with the application of higher standards to only certain parts of the system.

Implications for EU Trade

The European Union's trade in the poultry sector is likely to be most affected by higher animal welfare standards in the foreseeable future. The impact will depend on the type of standard imposed, as well as upon technological change and structural adjustment.

As indicated above, the imposition of a higher standard on the number of chickens that can be kept per square meter can have a large effect on production costs. Economists from INRA, France, have examined the impact of a general shift in poultry production standards to those applied in less intensive production. They examined a reduction in stocking density from between 21 and 23 to 18 birds per square meter. Using data for 1998, they estimated an increase in production costs of 17 percent, through extra heating, building space (since the standard allows only 4.7 rather than 6.2 successive flock rotations per year), feeding, and labor costs. Mahé and his colleagues at INRA, Rennes, introduced a 17 percent reduction in productivity into their economic model of commodity markets. With export subsidies at their 1998 level, this results in a predicted decrease of 70 percent in EU poultry exports (Jolly 1998). These results suggest that higher animal welfare standards in Europe could have a dramatic effect on trade flows.

The limited empirical evidence that exists tends to suggest that the impact of compliance with EU animal welfare legislation is likely to be substantial and that this will have a significant impact on the competitiveness of agricultural producers and processors in the European Union. In fact, there is some evidence that suppliers, particularly those oriented to export markets, are already responding in such a way as to minimize their exposure to these costs by developing a supply base in countries outside Europe. France is a major player in the world market of poultry meat, and two large companies—Doux and Tilly-Sabco—produce mainly for export. Competition is severe in world markets, and margins are thin. In 1999, the largest French producer, Doux, purchased Frangosul, a large Brazilian producer. This diversification has been partly driven by currency fluctuations, the need to adapt to General Agreement on Tariffs and Trade (GATT) constraints on exports, and stricter environmental regulations; changes in animal welfare regulations, however, are also playing a part in influencing the location decisions of an industry that employs roughly 50,000 people.

The impact of higher standards on competitiveness could be less dramatic once possible adjustments due to changes in technology and husbandry practices are taken into account. Although there are no direct estimates of how important such adjustments might be, related work provides some insight. Porin (2000) examined the impact of two types of standards on production costs. The first was a reduction in stocking density in terms of kilos of chicken per square meter; the second was a mandatory reduction in daily growth rate (increase in the feed-out period). Porin concluded that cost savings due to such factors as decreased mortality rate and changes in feed requirements could reduce the impact of such higher standards. He found that a reduction in the current stocking density of 38 kilograms per square meter to 25 kilograms per square meter would increase production costs by 8 to 10 percent in the intensive systems in Europe rather than the 17 percent assumed in the study discussed above.[10] With an increase in the feed-out period from 41 to 50 days (corresponding to an intermediate step between regular chicken and gourmet, or premium, chicken), Porin calculates that the increase in production costs could be as low as 2 to 5 percent. These results suggest that technological change and changes in husbandry practices could reduce the impact of higher standards on production costs and competitiveness, particularly over time.

DOMESTIC AND INTERNATIONAL POLICY RESPONSES

With no trade restrictions and no differentiated product effect, higher cost domestic production is likely to be replaced by competing supplies in both domestic and international markets. Domestically, the only damper might be the natural protection provided by transport costs. Country of origin labeling could provide some protection if consumers interpret this to signify that certain foreign countries do not meet the higher welfare standard. The domestic industry would be likely to introduce labeling and to try to differentiate its product. There would be substantial incentives to do this.

With labeling, the impact on the domestic industry would depend on the increases in production costs brought about by the higher standard, and the proportion of the population prepared to pay a premium for products that meet the standard. With no way to impose the domestic standard on foreign suppliers, there would be problems, particularly in the processed product market and in food delivery, since it would be difficult to maintain the identity of the original product and to communicate this to consumers. There are also practical difficulties with labeling in terms of what to indicate to consumers, for example, that certain products meet the standard or that some do not. In any event, with an open market the final effect of the higher standard would eventually revolve around the willingness of consumers to pay for the conforming product. Given the difficulties with labeling and ensuring compliance by foreign suppliers, the temptation will be to resort to import prohibition for products that do not meet the standard.

One possibility might be to use direct payments to offset the higher costs imposed on domestic producers from animal welfare standards. If one were to take the view that the public as a whole (consumers and nonconsumers of animal products) benefits from improved methods of production, direct payments could compensate producers for the higher costs of achieving conforming production. There would be the issue of whether such payments should be transitional or permanent and whether they should be linked primarily to the higher fixed costs involved or should also cover higher variable costs. Payments of this type would probably not qualify under existing green box criteria in the GATT, but their status could be addressed in future negotiations. In Europe, at least, the use of such payments might be seen as being consistent with the concept of "multifunctionality" or the pursuit of a European model of agriculture.

Another option might be to use the existing tariff structure to offset the competitive disadvantage faced by domestic producers as a result of the higher welfare standard. For example, differential tariffs might be defined with rates inversely proportional to the conformity of foreign products with the domestic standard. Such a tariff structure could also be applied within a tariff rate quota system, with preferential rates that are based on product conformity. To be consistent with international obligations, the highest tariff rate applied would have to be at the bound (maximum agreed) rate or below. Alternatively, country-specific tariffs could be used to favor imports from conforming countries, providing these are below the bound tariffs. There could be challenges to such an approach on the basis that it violates the most favored nation principle. Substantial reductions in bound tariffs in any upcoming round of trade negotiations could make unworkable the use of tariffs to offset the competitive disadvantage created by higher welfare standards.

With respect to exports, export refunds could be used to overcome the competitive disadvantage created by the higher standard, particularly if it is not possible to extract a consumer premium in foreign markets for the conforming product. In practice, the use of such refunds would be limited by the constraints imposed on the use of subsidies agreed in the Uruguay Round and by any further negotiated reductions. Furthermore, the use of subsidies may limit the incentive to develop a market for the differentiated product internationally.

Any attempt to redress the competitive disadvantage created by the adoption of higher standards would have implications for third countries and would create the possibility for trade diversion. Understandably, a number of countries that are in the process of joining the European Union (e.g., Czech Republic and Poland) are developing animal welfare standards that conform to EU standards; some countries outside Europe are also taking similar action to protect their export markets.

The most interesting case is New Zealand. Roughly 40 percent of New Zealand's meat and livestock exports go to the European Union. In recognition of the growing importance that animal welfare concerns may have for New Zealand's animal-based export agriculture, the country passed the Animal Welfare Act in 1999. The act provides for the development of detailed codes based on the five freedoms, covering farm practices and management procedures for livestock producers to meet minimum standards for animal welfare and to promote best practices. Breaches of the code can result in legal action. It is now an offense to export a live animal without a certificate provided by the Ministry of Agriculture. This certificate guarantees that appropriate conditions are provided for animals during transport.

Richer exporting countries may be able to adjust relatively easily to the requirements of higher welfare standards in importing countries. It is not clear how such standards would affect the competitive position of developing country exporters.

Finally, multinational food corporations, which may have a lot to lose from negative consumer reaction to animal welfare concerns, are taking steps to protect their position. McDonald's Corporation has instituted animal welfare programs for its suppliers that require them to meet or exceed applicable laws, regulations, and industry standards for animal welfare. Regular audits of meat packing plants are conducted to ensure that standards for humane treatment are met. It is interesting to note that the company advertises its commitment to animal welfare as part of its "commitment to quality," thus positioning animal welfare in terms of consumer concerns about product quality. McDonald's appears to be having an impact on standards in countries where these are not as wide-ranging as in Europe. The company has announced that its U.S. egg suppliers will be required to increase the size of cages for laying hens from 320 to 465 centimeters. It will also require producers to abandon the practices of forced moulting and beak trimming.

MULTILATERAL ISSUES

An important question is whether unilateral restrictions on nonconforming imports are permissible under the GATT. Animal welfare standards are not included as a reason for banning imports under Article XX or in the Technical Barriers to Trade (TBT) or Sanitary and Phytosanitary (SPS) Agreements. GATT panels have ruled that Article XX is not applicable to environmental protection (e.g., the dolphin-tuna and shrimp-turtle cases). Article III would seem to prohibit the use of import charges or restrictions on like products. It is difficult to argue that products that are derived from production systems employing differing standards of animal welfare differ in any objective sense, even though they may be viewed as such by some consumers.

Under current interpretations of the GATT agreements, the scope for applying import restrictions for noncompliance with domestic animal welfare production standards appears quite limited. Import prohibitions or restrictions on imports would constitute a violation of GATT Article XI.1. The reason for this is largely due to the limitations on trade restrictions for like products under Article III.4 (1994): "The products of the territory of any contracting party imported into the territory of any other contracting party shall be accorded treatment no less favorable than that accorded to like products of national origin in respect of all laws, regulations requirements affecting their internal sale, offering for sale, purchase..."

While it might be reasonable to interpret Article III as permitting production requirements/regulations if applied in an even manner to both domestic and foreign producers, a key issue is the interpretation of the like product for purposes of comparing domestic and imported goods. The likeness issue has been interpreted within the context of the aim and effect of the measure and whether de facto it offers protection to the domestic product (Scott 1999, Noltkaemper 1996).[11] Article III requires comparison between products and not between production processes or policies of importing and exporting countries. In commenting on the shrimp-turtle panel report, Scott suggests that a crucial point in attempting to distinguish products by production processes is that it prejudices the imported product and hence the national treatment principle. Legal opinion has consistently interpreted the concept of national treatment as permitting only the application of domestic product standards to imported goods (Scott 1999). Animal welfare production measures do not, in general, alter the physical characteristics of the final product; the implication is that final products produced under animal welfare measures are like products and fall under Articles III and XI.1.

The GATT does permit exceptions to these rules, for reasons specified under Article XX:

> Subject to the requirement that such measures are not applied in a manner that would constitute a means of arbitrary or unjustifiable discrimination between countries where the same conditions prevail or a disguised restriction on international trade, nothing in this Agreement shall be construed to prevent the adoption or enforcement of measures
>
> (a) Necessary for the protection of public morals
>
> (b) Necessary for the protection of human, animal and plant health.

In the past, a restrictive interpretation has been applied to the scope of this article. However, production processes should not necessarily be assumed to be excluded from Article XX, since XX(e) refers to methods of production by including goods produced with prison labor. It is also the case that common legal and academic interpretation has been against the use of trade measures to influence policies in third countries. The GATT/WTO has avoided approval of widespread use of Article XX exceptions to avoid the possibility of undermining the international trading system by permitting each country to apply its own specific production standards to traded goods. The proliferation of differing standards could hamper the development of the trading system.

To permit appeal to any clause of Article XX, the first part of the article cited above would need to be satisfied. A country would have to have attempted to reach a multilateral or bilateral agreement on standards or procedures before taking unilateral action, such as imposing an import ban or restriction. In fact, according to Perkins, in both the U.S. shrimp-turtle and tuna-dolphin cases, the GATT/WTO panels suggested that the U.S. import bans might be justified if they were based on animal protection standards embodied in a multilateral agreement (which they were not). The leghold trap ban in the European Union is similar to the animal welfare production standards case, in that both attempt to provide higher levels of animal welfare through regulation. In the leghold trap case, an import ban has been passed, but only after the failure of the International Organization for Standardization (ISO) to develop a set of humane trapping standards. It was also understood that the ban would not be enforced on individual nations with which the European Union had negotiated or was negotiating an agreement on humane trapping standards (Perkins 1998).

Note that in the U.S. shrimp-turtle case, the panel allowed, by its choice of illustration, that the legitimacy of applying domestic process standards to imported goods was not excluded but would need to be treated on a batch-by-batch basis, rather than a country-wide one. Thus, the production process for a particular product could be prohibited, but not all products from a given country. If each case were judged individually as to its conformity to the importing country's production standard, it might be possible to restrict imports (Scott 1999).

If the overall requirements of Article XX could be met, it would be possible to examine conformity with one of the specific clauses, in particular (a) or (b). It is highly unlikely that animal welfare could fall under the protection of the human, animal, or plant health clause since animal welfare production standards are not, strictly speaking, an issue of animal health. Animal welfare measures could possibly fall under the exemption on moral grounds; however, there is no case law relating to that clause. Furthermore, the use of the clause would require an acceptance of the argument that certain farm animal production methods are offensive to public morals. The wording, if not interpretation, of Article XX is ambiguous and could result in controversy if it were invoked to justify trade restrictions for animal welfare reasons. Nevertheless, the texts are sufficiently ambiguous that it is not certain that production and process methods relating to animal welfare would have no possibility of justification. In any event, WTO members always have the option of using trade restrictions and paying compensation to affected parties.

While multilateral harmonization of differing production standards would be highly desirable to avoid trade conflicts, this may not be feasible. The challenge remains one of reconciling different standards in an open trading environment. Many of the issues relating to differences in product or process standards are similar, whether they pertain to animal welfare, food safety, or environmental quality. Labeling, which allows consumers to distinguish differences among goods, is usually recommended as a practical solution.

Could labeling be required under current international law? The TBT Agreement covers technical regulations and standards, including packaging, marking, and labeling. Article 2 provides for the use of regulations and standards to achieve certain objectives "inter alia, national security requirements; the prevention of deceptive practices; protection of human health or safety, animal or plant life or health, or the environment."

Animal welfare is not specifically mentioned, but the words "inter alia" would seem to imply that other objectives that are not explicitly identified might be allowed. In addition, Annex 1 of the agreement defines technical regulation as a "document which lays down product characteristics or their related processes and production methods, including the applicable administrative provisions with which compliance is mandatory. It may also include or deal exclusively with...labeling requirements as they apply to a product, process or production method."

Any regulations applied should not create unnecessary impediments to trade. Where appropriate, technical regulations are supposed to apply to the performance of products rather than the design of a product. There is a requirement to accord treatment no less favorable to like products of national origin and to like products originating in any other country and to notify other countries before introducing a standard. There is an obligation to accept equivalent technical regulations in other countries, even if these differ, provided that they fulfill the objectives of the domestic regulations. The agreement also calls for the participation of international bodies in developing and harmonizing standards.

One such international body is the Codex Alimentarius Commission. Although this body has mainly focused on safety, its deliberations on the use of rBst have an animal welfare dimension. Codex has been trying to set standards for the use of this hormone in milk production. The EU and Canadian bans on the use of rBst were justified (at least partially) on animal welfare grounds. It is possible that Codex, or some other international mechanism, for example, the ISO, could be used to establish minimum production standards that could be reviewed and updated as necessary, but it would be difficult to base such standards solely on scientific principles in the case of animal welfare. The establishment of minimum standards would not preclude the adoption of higher standards by some countries and their promotion through private labeling schemes. If, in the future, the ability to sell products to increasingly demanding and discriminating consumers is affected by the production methods used, the private sector will find ways to implement the higher standards in any case.

CONCLUDING COMMENTS

In a submission to the WTO on animal welfare and trade in agriculture, the European Commission has proposed that multilateral agreements should be developed to deal with the protection of animal welfare, compulsory or voluntary labeling of products should be used to inform consumer choice, and producer compensation should be permitted to offset the higher costs of meeting welfare standards. The commission would like these mechanisms to be sanctioned as part of the current round of negotiations on agriculture.

In the absence of multilateral action, the imposition of higher animal welfare standards seems likely to put EU exporters at a competitive disadvantage, unless improvements in husbandry practices and new technologies can offset the higher fixed and variable costs that will likely result. It is difficult to assess whether EU exporters can develop a profitable market for "animal-friendly" exports.

As far as imports are concerned, consumers and food retailers in Europe will largely determine the importance of animal welfare standards in influencing EU trade in livestock products. Recent experiences with genetically modified foods seem to suggest that if exporters cannot meet the demands of retailers and consumers with respect to key product attributes (including animal welfare), they will likely have fewer and fewer possibilities for selling their products in the European Union. Some exporting countries, most notably New Zealand, are already taking steps to protect their position in European markets by addressing animal welfare standards. Multinational corporations in the food industry, such as McDonald's, are doing the same. In the final analysis, it will probably be the trend toward the implementation of private standards for animal welfare, within an increasingly vertically coordinated food system, that will drive the future of international trade in animal products.

NOTES

1. Data for 1998 are from the OECD Foreign Trade Statistics database, excluding intra-EU trade.
2. The five freedoms for animals are the freedom to turn around, groom themselves, get up, lie down, and stretch their limbs.
3. The Council of Europe is one of the oldest pan-European intergovernmental institutions, founded in 1949. It focuses on issues such as human rights, education, culture, and environment and currently has a membership of 40 countries, including the 15

member states of the European Union. The council draws up conventions that, once signed and ratified by its members, become legally binding through national legislation.

4. The legislative process in the EU has evolved as its membership has grown and its institutions have developed. The European Commission draws up proposals for directives or regulations. Directives are binding on member states in terms of the results to be achieved; national authorities implement legislation. Regulations are binding in their entirety and are directly applicable to the member states. Proposals are subject to scrutiny and amendment in the Council of Ministers and the European Parliament.

5. The requirements address perches (at least 14 centimeters per hen); nests (darkened, protected with soft floor or litter); and stocking density (up to 10 hens, at least 1,400 square centimeters per hen; 11 to 20 hens, 1,200 square centimeters per hen; more than 40 hens, 800 square centimeters per hen).

6. Personal communication. The exchange rates used here and subsequently are as of May 2001.

7. Communication from the European Commission.

8. Estimates provided by Unione Nazionale dell'Avicoltura.

9. Summarized from personal communication.

10. In some countries, such as Spain, production costs would not be affected because of low stocking density.

11. Scott notes that, according to Schoenbaum (1997), "mutual exclusivity of the two articles, XI and III often presents difficult and can be understood only in the context of correct methodologies for applying the tests of the two articles. The measure in question should first be analyzed as to whether it is protected by Article III." See also Farber and Hudec (1996).

REFERENCES

Association of Consumer Research, 1998, *Choosing the Meat You Eat*, London.

Becker, T., 1999, *Quality Policy and Consumer Behaviour in the European Union*, Wissenschaftsverlag Vauk Kiel, Kiel, Germany.

Becker, T., Benner, E., and Glitsch, K., 1997, Wandel des Verbraucherverhaltens bei Fleisch, *Agrarwirtschaft* **45**(7):267–277.

Bennett, R., 1998, Measuring public support for animal welfare legislation: A case study of cage egg production, *Anim Welf* **7**(1):1–11.

Blandford, D., and Fulponi, L., 1999, Emerging public concerns in agriculture: Domestic policies and international trade commitments, *Eur Rev Agric Econ* **26**(3):409–424.

Bord Bia, 1995, *European Attitudes to Meat*, Dublin.

Broom, D. M., 1991, Animal welfare: Concepts and measurement, *J Anim Sci* **69**:4167–4175.

Cowan, C., and Mannion, M., 1997, *Consumer Perceptions of Meat Quality in Ireland*, National Food Centre, Dublin.

Duncan, I. J. H., and Fraser, D., 1997, Understanding animal welfare, in: *Animal Welfare*, M. Appleby and B. Hughes, eds., CAB International, Wallingford Oxon, UK.

Farber, W., and Hudec, R., 1996, GATT legal restraints on domestic environmental regulations, in: *Fair Trade and Harmonization: Prerequisites for Free Trade?*, vol. 2, J. Bhagwati and R. Hudec, eds., MIT Press, Cambridge, MA.

Harper, G., and Henson, S. J., 1998, *Consumer Concerns about Animal Welfare and the Impact on Food Choice: Overview of the Literature in the UK, Ireland, Italy, France and Germany*, Department of Agricultural and Food Economics, University of Reading, UK.

———, 1999a, *Consumer Concerns about Animal Welfare and the Impact on Food Choice: Report of UK Focus Groups*, Department of Agricultural and Food Economics, University of Reading, UK.

———, 1999b, *Consumer Concerns about Animal Welfare and the Impact on Food Choice: Overview of Focus Groups in the UK, Ireland, Italy, France and Germany*, Department of Agricultural and Food Economics, University of Reading, UK.

———, 2000a, *Consumer Values and Concern about Animal Welfare*, Department of Agricultural and Food Economics, University of Reading, UK.

———, 2000b, *Consumer Values and Concern about Animal Welfare: Comparative Report*, Department of Agricultural and Food Economics, University of Reading, UK.

INRA-CORELA, 1998, *Consumer Concerns about Animal Welfare*, Paris.

Issanchou, S., 1996, *Consumer Expectations and Perceptions of Meat*, INRA, Dijon, France.

Jolly, C., 1998, Réglementation et commerce international des produits agro-alimentaires, M.S. thesis, DEA Economie internationale, Institut d'Etudes Politiques, Paris.

Leatherhead Food Research Association, 1999, FOMAD database, Leatherhead, UK.

Meat and Livestock Commission, 1997, *European Attitudes to Meat*, Milton Keynes, UK.

———, 1999, *European Attitudes to Meat*, Milton Keynes, UK.

Mintel Market Intelligence, 1996, *Red Meat*, London.

Noelle-Neumann, E., and Kocher, R., 1997, *Allensbacher Jahrbuch der Deomoskopie 1993–1997*, Allensbach am Bodensee, K. G. Saur, New York.

Noltkaemper, A., 1996, The legality of moral crusades disguised in trade laws: An analysis of the EC "ban" on furs from animals taken by leghold traps, *J Environ Law* **8**(2):237–256.

Perkins, N. L., 1998, Introductory note, *Int Legal Materials* **37**(3), http://www.asil.org/ilm/PERKINS.htm (accessed May 31, 2001).

Porin, F., 2000, *The Welfare of Chickens Kept for Meat Production (Broilers)*, Report of the Scientific Committee on Animal Health and Animal Welfare, European Commission, Health & Consumer Protection Directorate-General, Brussels.

Richardson, N. J., Shepherd, R., and Elliman, N. A., 1993, Current attitudes and future influences on meat consumption in the UK, *Appetite* **21**(10):41–51.

Sandoe, P., Crisp, R., and Holtug, N., 1997, Ethics in animal welfare, in: *Animal Welfare*, M. Appleby and B. Hughes, eds., CAB International, Wallingford Oxon, UK.

Schoenbaum, T. J., 1997, International trade and protection of the environment: The continuing search for reconciliation, *Am J Int Law* **268**:271, quoted in: On Kith and Kine (and Crustaceans): Trade and Environment in the EU and WTO, J. Scott, Harvard Jean Monnet Working Paper 3/99, http://www.jeanmonnetprogram.org/papers/99/990301.html (accessed May 31, 2001).

Scott, J., 1999, On Kith and Kine (and Crustaceans): Trade and Environment in the EU and WTO, Harvard Jean Monnet Working Paper 3/99, http://www.jeanmonnetprogram.org/papers/99/990301.html (accessed May 31, 2001).

Schulz, F., 1997, *Der Beitrag des Involvementkonstrukts zur Erlarung des Konsumentenverhaltens beim Kauf von Rind fleisch*, Reihe V Volks und Betriebswirtschaft, Frankfurt.

Tannenbaum, M., 1991, Ethics and animal welfare: The inextricable connection, *J Am Vet Med Assoc* **198**:1360–1376.

Ziehlberg, R., and von Alvensleben, R., 1998, Die Bedeuteng Ethischer Motive beim Kauf von Lebensmitteln am Beispiel fair Gehandelten Kaffeess, in: *Jahrbuch der Absatz- und Verbrauchsforschung*, Jahrgana, Duncker & Humblot, Berlin.

RESPONSE TO A FOOD SAFETY PROBLEM IN PRODUCE

A case study of a cyclosporiasis outbreak

Linda Calvin, William Foster, Luis Solorzano, J. Daniel Mooney, Luis Flores, and Veronica Barrios*

Imports play an increasingly important role in produce consumption in the United States. In 1996, imports accounted for 38 percent of fresh fruit consumption and 14 percent of fresh vegetable consumption (Lucier, Pollack, and Perez 1997). Although infrequent, food contamination problems, traced to both domestic and imported produce, have raised consumer concerns about food safety generally and about the sources of fresh produce specifically (Tauxe 1997). Although researchers have not found clear evidence that imported produce poses more health risks than domestic produce (Zepp, Kuchler, and Lucier 1998), a small number of well-publicized incidents of contamination implicating foreign producers has increased consumer awareness of the possible role imports might have in food safety problems. In the global economy for fresh produce, a food safety problem in an exporting country has important effects on producers and consumers in the importing country and on producers in other countries competing in the same market.

---

* Linda Calvin is an agricultural economist with the Specialty Crops Branch, Market and Trade Economics Division, Economic Research Service, U.S. Department of Agriculture. William Foster is a professor of agricultural economics at the Pontifical Catholic University, Santiago, Chile. Luis Solorzano is a consumer safety officer with the Office of Regulatory Affairs, U.S. Food and Drug Administration. J. Daniel Mooney is a raspberry producer, executive director of the High-Level Commission for Food Safety, and vice president of the Guatemalan Berry Commission, Guatemala. Luis Flores is the chief of inspectors with the Integral Program for Agricultural and Environmental Protection, Guatemala. Veronica Barrios is the subdirector of the Nontraditional Markets Identification and Promotion Board, Secretariat of Agriculture, Livestock, and Rural Development, Mexico. The views expressed here do not necessarily reflect those of the authors' institutions. The authors would like to acknowledge support provided by the Farm Foundation, the Economic Research Service's Mexico Emerging Market Program, and an Economic Research Service cooperative agreement. Note that this study was completed in early June 2000 and does not reflect later events.

Global Food Trade and Consumer Demand for Quality, edited by Krissoff *et al.*
Kluwer Academic/Plenum Publishers, New York, 2002.

In the United States, responsibility for food safety of imported foods resides with the U.S. Department of Agriculture's (USDA's) Food Safety and Inspection Service (FSIS) and the U.S. Food and Drug Administration (FDA). FSIS deals with meat, poultry, and some egg products; FDA covers all other food products, including produce. FSIS allows only imports from countries with food safety systems deemed to be equivalent to those in the United States. Unlike FSIS, FDA does not require equivalence and instead relies on inspections at the port of entry to ensure product safety. Produce imports must meet the same standards as domestic goods for pesticide residues and food safety but are not required to use the same production standards. Generally, FDA collects random samples at the border, preventing entry of products that fail inspection. The agency can also detain a product without physical examination if the shipper has failed previous FDA port inspections or if FDA has other information indicating that the product might violate standards. When FDA identifies a source of a public health concern, it blocks shipments only from those firms with a problem.

Former President Clinton's Produce and Imported Food Safety Initiative, announced in October 1997, called for additional resources to improve domestic standards and ensure that imports are equally safe (Crutchfield 1999). Three broad areas of action were identified. First, the president directed FDA to seek new legal authority to require equivalence in food safety systems in foreign countries. Today, although FDA still has no legal authority to require equivalence before allowing imports into the United States, it can enter into voluntary agreements with other countries to establish equivalent inspection systems. An equivalence agreement between the United States and another country would provide FDA with reasonable confidence that the country grows produce under an equivalent food safety system. While FDA would still need to continue standard monitoring of imports from a country with an equivalence agreement, it could redirect some of its limited resources to more problematic imports.

Second, the initiative targeted more resources at improving inspection activities abroad by providing technical assistance. Third, it focused on providing guidance to both domestic and foreign producers on good agricultural practices (GAPs) and good manufacturing practices (GMPs). National-level guidelines on GAPs and GMPs enhance the consistency and scientific basis of food safety standards developed by public and private institutions; these guidelines were published in late 1998 (U.S. FDA 1998).

While the U.S. government is involved in ensuring food safety of imports, individual producers, producer and retail organizations, and other governments are also actively engaged in efforts to maintain food safety standards. This case study investigates one food safety outbreak and traces the efforts by all involved parties to resolve the food safety problem. In 1996, the United States and Canada experienced a widespread outbreak of cyclosporiasis, a type of gastroenteritis, which the Centers for Disease Control and Prevention (CDC) linked epidemiologically to fresh Guatemalan raspberries contaminated with the parasite *Cyclospora*. Developing food safety measures to reduce the risk of *Cyclospora* contamination took several years. Although economists know that producers provide food safety when it is profitable or when they are required to provide it (Caswell and Mojduszka 1996), our understanding of the details of this process is often incomplete. This chapter illuminates the complicated process of resolving a food safety problem. The Guatemalan *Cyclospora* contamination problem provides the first example of FDA's expanded role under the Food Safety Initiative.

This chapter begins with a brief review of the literature regarding the market for food safety and response to food safety problems. As background, we describe the U.S. raspberry market and imports from Latin America, the parasite *Cyclospora*, and the first U.S.-Canadian outbreak of cyclosporiasis in 1996 that was epidemiologically associated with Guatemalan raspberries. Then we address two broad issues. First, what was the Guatemalan and international response to the *Cyclospora* food safety problem? We examine efforts by individual producers, producer and other organizations, and governments to establish a reputation for food safety. Since food safety is a public good, the existence of free riders will tend to favor mandatory programs with oversight provisions. Second, in an international market, food safety problems in Guatemala had spillover effects on producers of other crops in Guatemala and raspberry producers in other countries. We examine the impact of the food safety problem on Guatemala, producers and consumers in the United States, and other Latin American suppliers of raspberries to the U.S. market. Much of the information regarding the impact of the cyclosporiasis outbreak on markets comes from personal interviews with raspberry producers and shippers. A concluding section highlights our findings.

MARKETS FOR FOOD SAFETY

Food quality attributes are commonly defined as size, ripeness, condition, etc. Food safety attributes are also important food quality attributes. Consumers select products with varying levels of food safety and other quality attributes to maximize their utility. Under conditions of full information prior to purchase regarding the characteristics of a product, one would expect markets efficiently to offer a range of product qualities at different prices according to various consumer demands (e.g., Bockstael 1984, and Caswell and Mojduszka 1996). When there is uncertainty about the quality of a product, one would expect that markets would function less successfully (Akerlof 1970). If the quality characteristic were in fact measurable prior to purchase—that is, if it were a search attribute—consumers could determine the quality of the product by observation or research, and adjust their willingness to pay accordingly. Market prices could serve to signal to producers the relative benefits of providing products of various qualities. But in many situations, as in the specific case of food safety for produce, quality is likely to be an experience characteristic, which consumers can identify only after they consume the product.

The reduction or elimination of consumer uncertainty regarding a product's quality would be a source of benefits that, potentially, producers or others could internalize. Some costs, however, are required somewhere in the marketing chain to transform an experience characteristic into a search attribute, either by the use of certification, investing in the development of a reputable brand name, or by other means of credibly signaling quality. In the case of agricultural products, the degree of the credibility of signaling quality often depends both on overcoming the free-rider problem and on the success of coordinating the actions of many producers and decisionmakers in the marketing chain. The private transaction costs associated with the organization of firms and markets that could internalize all the social benefits of transforming an experience characteristic into a search attribute may be prohibitive. In the case of a perceived quality problem, the existence of apparently prohibitive private costs or insurmountable free-rider problems offers a rationale for government action to resolve the problem and to provide information about a product to mitigate consumer uncertainty.

Food safety problems have several possible solutions. First, an individual producer can address the problem directly by improving production processes or adopting GAPs or some other means of enhanced process control. A producer can use third-party food safety certification to signal to buyers and consumers that vigilance is real and effective. The response of individual firms will be most successful when buyers and consumers can identify the source using better food safety standards and are willing to pay for the additional precautions. Low consumer awareness of individual producers or low credibility of certification reduces the effectiveness of individual responses.

A second strategy is for grower organizations to adopt voluntary or mandatory standards for an industry. If voluntary, distributors and consumers may still be unable to identify products with higher food safety standards and so may be unwilling to pay for the additional effort. Mandatory grower organization programs may be difficult to organize, but they do lower the cost of credibly signaling consistent product quality through the elimination of free riders in the provision of what is often a public good for all producers that benefit from enhanced consumer confidence.

A third method is voluntary or mandatory government intervention. With imported produce, action from several governments may be required to signal product safety effectively. Government intervention may be particularly effective in resolving negative externalities when a food safety problem for one crop threatens to spill over and damage the reputation of other crops grown in the same country. In some cases, all three types of intervention may be used sequentially or simultaneously to resolve a food safety problem.

Of course, individual consumers and retail and wholesale buyers may also pursue actions to reduce uncertainty. They may decide to limit purchases from regions with food safety concerns. Retail and wholesale buyers may require third-party food safety certification. Shippers that buy or market products from other producers may try to increase food standards by vertically integrating back into production, either through direct control or some form of contractual arrangement (Hennessy 1996).

The actions taken by growers and shippers of fresh produce in attempting to offer credible claims of food safety will depend on the audiences that effectively determine the demand for their product. Final consumers in the grocery store will respond to a variety of signals in a different manner than buyers for the grocery store and shippers. The reputation of a grocery chain, or a shipper with a recognizable brand name, for supplying safe produce, for example, is likely to be far more relevant to consumer purchases than esoteric information regarding the specific production practices of producers in a particular country. A foreign produce shipper will find its safety claims aimed at many final consumers relatively ineffective without establishing the reputation of a brand name. A large grocery chain, on the other hand, seeking to maintain the value of its reputation, has both the negotiating power and the incentive to make its purchases contingent on third-party certification of the safety of grower production practices. A foreign shipper using certification can more easily establish and maintain its reputation with respect to an audience of buyers for grocery stores than with respect to an audience of final consumers. The "public" consumer, a government taking on the responsibility to ensure food safety, has the power to affect the demand facing growers and shippers. When a question of safety arises in the political realm, as in the case of Guatemalan raspberries, producers must target their safety claims to government agencies, which may require far more technical assurances and information than shippers or final consumers under normal circumstances.

U.S. RASPBERRY MARKET AND LATIN AMERICAN IMPORTS

Fresh raspberries, once consumed only during the summer, are now available in the United States year round. Commercial fresh raspberry production is concentrated in California, with smaller amounts in Oregon and Washington State. Although California produces fresh raspberries throughout the year, most shipments come from central California between late May and early November (Figure 1), with less volume from southern California during the winter. The U.S. fresh raspberry industry grew rapidly in the last decade, increasing production approximately 52 percent from 1990 to 1999 (Table 1). Fresh raspberries are fragile, with a limited shelf life. As a result, much of the small-scale fresh

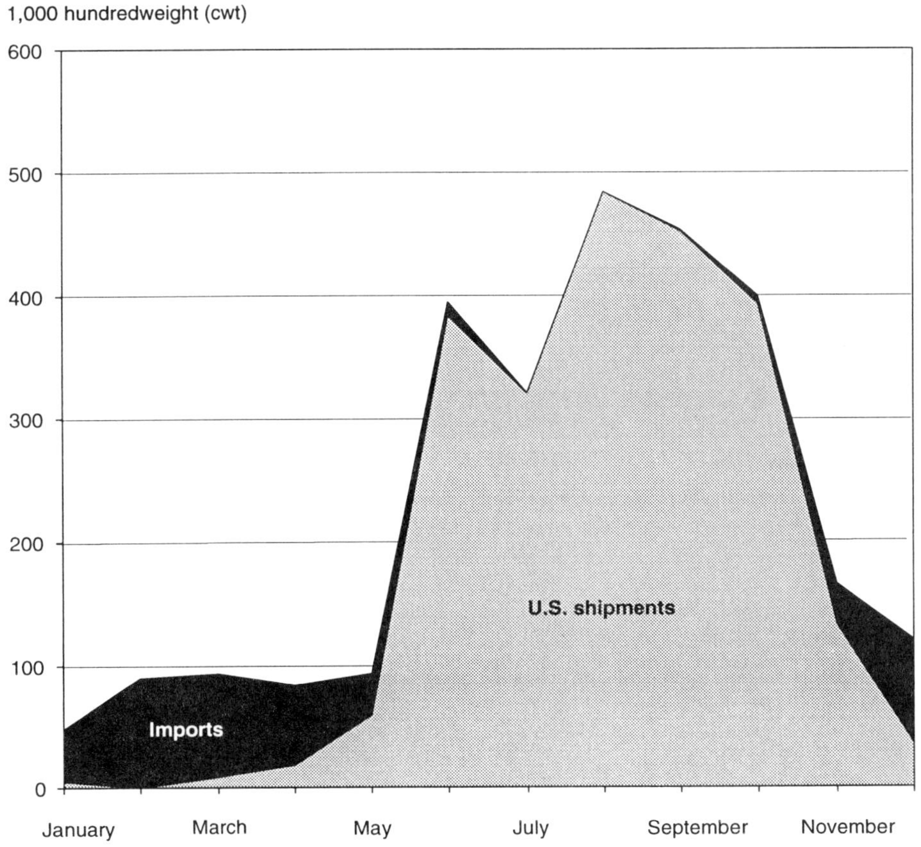

Figure 1. In 1999, U.S. raspberry shipments dominate the summer season and imports the winter season.

raspberry production in other states is sold at roadside stands, farmers markets, and pick-your-own operations, a fact that would imply that production and consumption statistics are biased downward.

Table 1. U.S. fresh raspberries: supply and utilization

Year	Production[a]	Imports[b]	Supply (million lbs)	Exports[c]	Con-sumption	Per capita consumption (lbs)
1990	16.58	3.50	20.10	0.80	19.40	0.08
1991	n.a.	2.50	n.a.	1.40	n.a.	n.a.
1992	28.24	2.10	30.30	1.50	28.80	0.11
1993	28.44	2.30	30.70	1.00	29.70	0.12
1994	23.84	3.40	27.30	2.20	25.00	0.10
1995	17.01	4.40	21.40	2.20	19.20	0.07
1996	17.65	4.40	22.10	3.90	18.20	0.07
1997	18.00	4.40	22.40	2.90	19.50	0.07
1998	17.90	3.80	21.70	5.30	16.40	0.06
1999	25.20	5.10	30.30	7.10	23.20	0.08

n.a. = not available

[a] Only includes production from California, Oregon, and Washington; and assumes that all California production goes to the fresh market. Data do not include fresh black raspberries.

[b] Includes only 5 percent of U.S. fresh raspberry imports from Canada as going to the fresh market. The rest are fresh but are not packed for the fresh market and are sent directly to cold storage or processing.

[c] Does not include any exports to Canada. Again, much of the U.S.-Canadian trade is assumed to be destined for processing. Canada does import fresh raspberries for the fresh market. The statistics here undercount exports to Canada and overcount U.S. consumption. Data for raspberry exports also include blackberry, mulberry, and loganberry exports.

Sources: National Agricultural Statistics Service, USDA; Economic Research Service, USDA; and U.S. Department of Commerce.

The United States imports raspberries from Chile, Mexico, Guatemala, and several smaller suppliers during the winter, which augments seasonally lower quantities supplied by domestic sources. During the winter months, California producers generally supply the west, and imports supply the east. During the height of the U.S. summer raspberry season, western production is also shipped to eastern markets. In 1999, overall imports were only 20 percent of domestic supply, but they represented 84 percent of the January to April and December shipments. Paralleling the growth of domestic production, total imports increased 46 percent from 1990 to 1999.

Table 2 shows imports by source and the changing patterns of trade during the 1990s. In the 1989/90 winter season, Chile provided 98 percent of the imports, because of the counterseasonal nature of the Chilean growing season, which generally runs from late November through May. Table 3 indicates import seasons in 1999. Seasons shift somewhat from year to year based on weather and market conditions. Mexico began exporting raspberries to the United States in 1993, and volume grew rapidly thereafter. By the 1998/99 season, Chile's share of winter imports had decreased to 49 percent, and Mexico had become the largest supplier with a 51 percent share. Some Californian, Chilean, and Guatemalan shippers source from Mexico for the U.S. market. Although the Mexican season runs from September to June, Mexican sources of imported raspberries dominate in November and March to April.

Table 2. U.S. fresh raspberry imports

Season[a]	Mexico	Chile	Guatemala	Others[b]	World[c]
			(metric tons)		
1989/90	0	1,370.2	0	24.9	1,395.1
1990/91	0	925.6	3.7	38.6	967.9
1991/92	0	643.9	1.4	13.9	659.2
1992/93	4.9	590.3	22.9	9.7	627.8
1993/94	52.6	894.6	34.6	73.4	1,055.2
1994/95	173.4	1,013.0	147.1	238.8	1,572.3
1995/96	284.2	1,096.6	313.7	146.0	1,840.5
1996/97	267.0	1,387.2	196.8	6.9	1,857.9
1997/98	470.9	959.3	44.8	16.3	1,491.4
1998/99	1,047.0	942.1	1.6	62.6	2,053.4

[a]Defined from September through August of the following year.
[b]Not including Canadian imports of fresh berries, which are often technically still fresh berries but destined immediately for processing facilities.
Source: U.S. Department of Commerce.

Table 3. U.S., Guatemalan, Mexican, and Chilean raspberry shipping seasons, 1999

	Jan	Feb	Mar	Apr	May	Jun	Jul	Aug	Sep	Oct	Nov	Dec
United States	x		x	x	x	X	X	X	X	X	x	x
Guatemala			x	X	X	X	x	x	x	x	x	
Mexico	x	X	X	X	x	x			x	x	x	X
Chile	X	X	X	X	x	x					x	X

Note: x indicates volume less than 10 percent of a country's annual shipments; X indicates higher volume.
Sources: Agricultural Marketing Service, USDA; and Guatemalan Berry Commission.

The Guatemalan raspberry industry began in the late 1980s as part of the U.S. Agency for International Development's efforts to expand nontraditional agricultural exports. U.S. Department of Commerce trade data show U.S. imports of Guatemalan raspberries in 1989 and then from 1991 to the present. The country provided an excellent source of raspberries, having an ideal climate and located just two hours away from Miami by air. Although Guatemalan labor costs are low, labor is not as efficient as in other countries as it is hampered by a lack of infrastructure—the legacy of years of guerilla warfare. By spring 1996, the Guatemalan raspberry industry was at peak production, exporting 314 metric tons of raspberries to the United States during the 1995/96 season, up 113 percent from the previous season. Guatemalan-owned firms dominated the industry, although there was some foreign involvement, most notably a large Chilean firm. Guatemala's share of raspberry imports in the winter months peaked at 17 percent in the 1995/96 season; the country also dominated import supplies in the May–June and October–November periods, which is to say, just after and before the main Chilean season. By 1999, the *Cyclospora* contamination problem had changed trade patterns, and Guatemala lost its dominant market position in the spring and fall months (Figure 2). The U.S. Department of Commerce does not report trade statistics when a very small number of firms are involved, so U.S. statistics show very low volume of imports from Guatemala in the 1998/99 season. According to Guatemalan statistics, raspberry exports to all countries totaled 107 metric tons in calendar year 1999.

Currently, two firms account for a large part of the U.S. raspberry market—a large California shipper, which supplies raspberries and other berries year round; and a large Chilean company, which supplies raspberries and other berries to the United States almost year round. The Californian firm ships raspberries only from the United States and Mexico. The Chilean firm uses raspberry sources in Chile and Mexico.

CYCLOSPORA

Cyclospora cayentanensis is a protozoan parasite that causes cyclosporiasis, a potentially debilitating diarrhea that can last for three weeks or more (Jackson et al. 1999). Transmission is via the fecal/oral route; humans contract cyclosporiasis after eating food or drinking water contaminated with fecal matter containing *Cyclospora* oocysts. An oocyst is the cyst stage of the parasite; it needs to mature in the environment before becoming infectious. The disease is treatable and is only considered potentially life threatening to those with compromised immune systems; even without treatment, most individuals eventually recover.

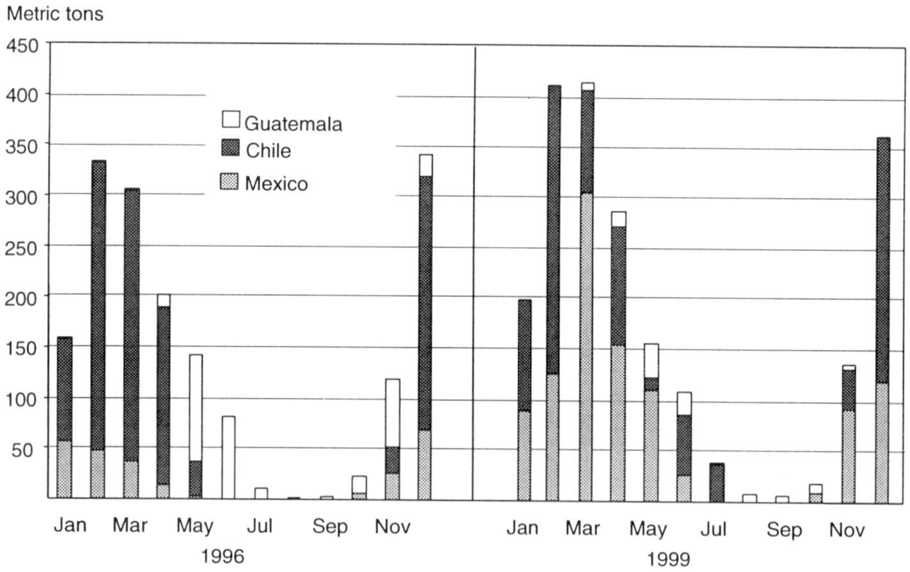

Figure 2. U.S. monthly raspberry imports show the decline between 1996 and 1999 in Guatemalan imports during the spring and fall months.

The first human cases of cyclosporiasis were reported in Papua New Guinea in 1979 (Ashford 1979), and *Cyclospora* itself was described definitively only in 1994 as a new species of the genus *Cyclospora* (Ortega, Gilman, and Sterling 1994). Until recently, *Cyclospora* was only occasionally seen in the United States, primarily in tourists returning from abroad. The distribution of this emerging parasite is not known, but, as more cases are identified around the world, it appears that a more widespread distribution is possible than was previously thought (Sterling and Ortega 1999).

Table 4 lists some of the documented outbreaks of cyclosporiasis in the United States and Canada in the 1990s. Scientists estimate that on an annual basis, cyclosporiasis cases account for 0.1 percent of illnesses caused by known foodborne pathogens (Mead et al. 1999). The first known cyclosporiasis outbreak in the United States occurred in Chicago in 1990 and was attributed to tap water that may have been contaminated with stagnant water from a rooftop reservoir.[1] For some cyclosporiasis outbreaks, it is not possible to identify either the contaminated product or country of origin. CDC has identified only three produce items linked with outbreaks in the United States—raspberries (1996, 1997), basil (1997, 1999), and mesclun lettuce (1997). Canada had cyclosporiasis outbreaks associated with Guatemalan raspberries in 1996 through 1998. Canadian officials also linked Guatemalan blackberries to an outbreak in 1999.

Table 4. Partial list of U.S. and Canadian cyclosporiasis outbreaks, 1990–99

Year	Location	Product epidemiologically associated with outbreak	Source of origin for contamination	References
1999	Florida	Unknown	Unknown	
1999	Missouri	Basil[a]	Unknown	
1999	York, Canada	Blackberries	Guatemala	Health & Social Services Comm. 2000
1998	Canada	Raspberries	Guatemala	CDC 1998
1997	U.S. & Canada	Raspberries	Guatemala	Herwaldt & Beach 1999
1997	U.S.	Basil	Unknown	CDC 1997a
1997	U.S.	Mesclun lettuce	Unknown	CDC 1997b
1996	U.S. & Canada	Raspberries	Guatemala	Herwaldt & Ackers 1997
1995	Florida	Unknown	Unknown	Koumans et al. 1998
1990	Chicago	Tap water, possibly contaminated with stagnant water in a rooftop reservoir	U.S.	Sterling & Ortega 1999

[a] First case where product identification was based on actual observation of *Cyclospora*, not only on epidemiology.

With the exception of the 1999 basil outbreak, all links between particular products and *Cyclospora* have been based on epidemiological evidence alone. Methods to test produce for *Cyclospora* are relatively insensitive for detecting low levels of the parasite. The probability of detecting *Cyclospora* with random sampling of all shipments, as opposed to sampling an implicated lot, is quite low. Oocysts are probably not evenly distributed in a shipment, further reducing the probability of detection. Since cyclosporiasis may not develop for up to 14 days after consuming a contaminated product, a perishable product is rarely available for testing when CDC investigates. In the basil case, some of the product had been frozen and investigators found *Cyclospora* when testing the implicated product.

Of the cyclosporiasis outbreaks attributable to produce, only in the case of Guatemalan raspberries did CDC definitively identify the country of origin. Although the origin of the mesclun lettuce and basil is not clear, they did not come from Guatemala.

The spring 1996 cyclosporiasis outbreak was the largest to date in the United States and Canada. In 1996, *Cyclospora* was a little-known parasite never before associated with raspberries. Researchers, however, now wonder if the 1995 Florida cyclosporiasis outbreak might have been related to Guatemalan raspberries (Koumans et al. 1998). To date, *Cyclospora* has never been found on Guatemalan raspberries by FDA or CDC laboratory analysis using either microscopy or DNA testing. This is a common outcome of investigations into *Cyclospora* contamination, however, because of the low probability of detecting the parasite in any sample. Basing the link between Guatemalan raspberries and the cyclosporiasis outbreak on epidemiology alone was initially a controversial and unpopular decision in Guatemala.

No one knew which raspberries were contaminated, how they became contaminated, or what was required to solve the problem. Neither growers nor buyers could assess the safety of the berries. Antle (1998) describes this as a state of symmetric imperfect information, as opposed to a state of asymmetric information where producers know more about the safety of their product than the buyers. There is no recognized method of cleaning potentially contaminated fresh berries to remove a food safety threat (Dixon 1999). Washing raspberries is not effective in removing the parasite. Although commercial freezing may kill the *Cyclospora* parasite, it transforms the fresh berries into a less profitable product.

The method of contamination in Guatemala has never been definitively determined. Suspicions have centered on contaminated water mixed with pesticides and fungicides, and on lax field sanitation (Herwaldt and Beach 1999). Because raspberries tend to deteriorate after contact with water, drip irrigation was and is the method generally used; therefore, irrigation water was not a likely source of contamination since it does not come into contact with the fruit. Food safety programs have focused on improving water quality, field sanitation standards, and inspection measures.

1996 CYCLOSPORIASIS OUTBREAK LINKED TO GUATEMALAN RASPBERRIES

In the spring and early summer of 1996, CDC and Health Canada (HC) received reports of more than 1,465 cases of cyclosporiasis in the United States and Canada, with no fatalities. Except for a small number in Colorado, all the cyclosporiasis cases occurred in the eastern United States and Canada, areas generally supplied by Guatemala. The true number of cases was probably underreported in the past because the medical profession did not routinely test for *Cyclospora* as it did for some other foodborne pathogens. On June 8, 1996, the Texas Department of Health issued a health warning that identified the source of the problem as California strawberries and recommended that consumers avoid them. The warning was lifted on June 27; on the same day, the New York Public Health Department announced that raspberries were suspected as a source of the outbreak in New York.

Once CDC or state or local health departments identify a product as the vehicle of a foodborne outbreak, FDA becomes involved and tries to trace the contaminated product to its origin. CDC studied 55 events such as wedding receptions or banquets that were linked to a cluster of cyclosporiasis cases. For the 29 events where the source of the raspberries could be traced, analysts definitely connected 21 events to raspberries from Guatemala and concluded that, for the remaining 8, the raspberries may have come from Guatemala (Herwaldt and Ackers 1997). On July 18, 1996, CDC and the Ontario Ministry of Health issued a statement reporting that Guatemalan raspberries were the most likely source of the outbreaks. By that time, the Guatemalan spring season was over, so no immediate regulatory action was taken. However, FDA and CDC sent a team of investigators to Guatemala in 1996 to observe growing conditions and to better understand the berry industry there. Table 5 shows a chronology of events as the *Cyclospora* contamination problem evolved.

Table 5. Chronology of events related to the Guatemalan *Cyclospora* contamination

	1996	1997	1998	1999	2000
United States					
Trade	✓	✓		✓	✓
Outbreaks	✓	✓			
Guatemalan suspension		✓			
U.S. import alert			✓		
Canada					
Trade	✓	✓	✓		
Outbreaks	✓	✓	✓		
Guatemalan suspension			✓		
Canada import alert				✓	✓

Despite the facts that Guatemalan blackberry exports to the United States have always exceeded raspberry exports and that, in some locations, both berries are grown on the same farms, no 1996 cases of cyclosporiasis in the United States were definitely associated with Guatemalan blackberries. One potential explanation for this difference in contamination is that blackberries have a much smoother surface than raspberries. The latter are covered with fine hairs and crevices that may affect adherence of the parasite or provide places for it to hide. For one event in Canada in 1996, no Guatemalan raspberries were involved, but Guatemalan blackberries were served in a fruit mixture (Herwaldt and Ackers 1997).

POLICY RESPONSES TO THE CYCLOSPORIASIS OUTBREAK

In the first year after Guatemalan raspberries were implicated, individual raspberry growers, the Guatemalan Berry Commission (GBC), and the Association of Exporters of Non-Traditional Products (AGEXPRONT) attempted to determine the source of potential contamination and solve the problem. GBC is a grower organization composed of owners of raspberry, blackberry, and strawberry farms. It and other associations, such as the Exporters of Snow Peas, belong to AGEXPRONT, a private sector organization.

CDC concluded, after considering the many differences in various aspects of the distribution systems for the implicated raspberries, that simultaneous and persistent contamination on multiple farms was the most likely explanation for the outbreak (Herwaldt and Ackers 1997). Research based on the events for which well-documented traceback data about the sources of the raspberries were available, indicated that the 1996 outbreak could have been accounted for by as few as six farms (Herwaldt and Beach 1999).

FDA provided advice and technical assistance in developing a food safety plan. Since the methods of detecting *Cyclospora* are insensitive to low levels of contamination, testing was not an option, leaving process controls as the only realistic possibility. Guatemala proposed a type of Hazard Analysis Critical Control Points (HACCP) program. An HACCP program identifies points in production where preventative control measures are introduced into a process to reduce or eliminate food safety hazards that are likely to occur. Since the exact method of contamination and complete biology of the parasite are not known, precise preventative measures cannot be applied. Therefore, such a program would be more correctly identified as an HACCP-like program. The United States does not require HACCP programs for fresh fruit and vegetable producers. FDA views GAPS as more appropriate for field-grown commodities. For Guatemala, FDA recommended the use of GAPs, GMPs, and sanitation standard operating procedures (SSOPs). In the United States, GAPs are voluntary guidelines for producers, and GMPs are strongly encouraged.

Because *Cyclospora* was an emerging parasite, both FDA and CDC were more active in helping the Guatemalans develop a response to the problem than if the food safety problem involved a more common pathogen. In addition to gains to consumers from safe raspberry imports and gains to scientific knowledge, FDA and CDC had incentives to solve the food safety problem in order to reduce the labor and cost of investigating cyclosporiasis outbreaks. In 1997, FDA spent 6,274 hours investigating the cyclosporiasis outbreak (U.S. GAO 1998).

Due to the public-good nature of the industry's reputation for food safety, the analysis of the problem seemed to suggest a solution requiring a mandatory, industrywide program that would bar free riders. For the 1997 spring season, GBC developed a system to characterize farms according to risk. A classification of low, medium, or high risk was based on four factors: water quality; infrastructure (the use of drip irrigation, for example); use of HACCP, GAPs, GMPs, and SSOPs; and maintenance of records. High-risk farms were not allowed to export at all. Low-risk farms were allowed to export anytime, including the spring season, which was considered to be the period with the highest risk for *Cyclospora* contamination. Medium-risk farms could export anytime except the spring season. This plan had no enforcement mechanism for the 1997 season, which yielded predictable results.

No cases of cyclosporiasis were detected in the United States during Guatemala's 1996 fall and winter raspberry export season. Indeed, there have never been any outbreaks of cyclosporiasis in the United States epidemiologically linked to Guatemala's fall and winter raspberries. Guatemalan growers started to see lower prices for raspberries and blackberries beginning that fall, however. Since raspberries are generally sold in plastic clamshells labeled with the country of origin, consumers in grocery stores—in addition to importers and retailers—could identify berries from Guatemala.[2]

Despite efforts to assess risk and reduce the likelihood of contamination, a new outbreak of cyclosporiasis (again, with no fatalities) traced to Guatemalan raspberries occurred in the United States and Canada during the 1997 spring season. For events with well-documented traceback data, all but two were associated with raspberries from Guatemala. In most cases, the berries were from lots composed of products from several Guatemalan berry farms, making it difficult to determine which farms produced the contaminated berries. According to CDC, the 1997 outbreak could have been associated with as few as four farms and outbreaks over the two years by as few as seven farms (Herwaldt and Beach 1999). In 1997, traceback data for two events led to only non-Guatemalan sources—Chile and California. With respect to the Chilean berries, however, the produce distribution center also had Guatemalan berries in stock at the same time, and Guatemalan blackberries were served with the raspberries. In the case of the Californian berries, the investigator thought there was a possibility of commingled berries (Herwaldt and Beach 1999). The possibility of *Cyclospora*-contaminated blackberries for one event in Canada was raised, but the number of people interviewed regarding the event was so small no conclusions could be made and good traceback information was not available (Herwaldt and Beach 1999).

Either the new practices developed for the 1997 spring season were not completely implemented, were ineffective, or were not directed at the true source of contamination (Herwaldt and Beach 1999). After consulting with FDA, on May 30, 1997, GBC voluntarily stopped raspberry exports to the United States until August 14, 1997. No more U.S. cases of cyclosporiasis developed after Guatemala stopped its exports. Exports, however, continued to Canada, although there were no new cases of cyclosporiasis attributed to Guatemalan raspberries. Exports also continued to Europe, which has never reported a case of cyclosporiasis linked to Guatemalan raspberries. After losing their largest fresh market, many growers sent their raspberries to freezing plants. Commercially frozen Guatemalan raspberries and blackberries have never been implicated in a cyclosporiasis outbreak. Guatemala estimated that stopping exports in the middle of the spring season resulted in a loss of $10 million in income (Powell 1998).

The evidence suggests that, through spring 1997, individual actions to improve food safety were inadequate and GBC efforts at joint action had failed. When basic scientific research was required to understand the nature of the contamination problem, individual grower action to resolve the issue appeared particularly improbable. An individual would incur all costs for research but might have difficulty retaining the exclusive rights to the benefits. Moreover, it was unlikely that U.S. consumers could be induced to identify individual Guatemalan producers or brands as safer than the rest, particularly when all clamshells were identified as a product of Guatemala so producers would only succeed or fail as a group. Compounding the difficulty in coordination was the doubt in some producers' minds that there was a contamination problem (particularly when no physical evidence had ever been found) and that drastic action was required. Scientific uncertainty regarding the source of the contamination and the remedies adequate to resolve the problem contributed further to confusion and delay. After a second season with *Cyclospora* contamination problems, both GBC and the government of Guatemala realized that more stringent controls and enforcement were required to resolve the problem.

GBC asked the Guatemalan government for help, and, in November 1997, the government created the High-Level Commission for Food Safety, which included the participation of the Guatemalan Ministries of Agriculture, Food, and Livestock; Health; and Economy. The commission has five working groups: science and epidemiology, post-harvest issues, certification, public relations to promote Guatemalan products, and a World Trade Organization (WTO) commercial practices group, which documents any potential trade barriers. The certification process with enforcement power was critical to making any export plan manageable. GBC also sought help from the Food Marketing Institute (FMI) in Washington, D.C., which serves U.S. retail buyers and has expertise in setting up HACCP plans. FMI agreed to help Guatemala develop better field standards because its members strongly favored resolving the problem with Guatemalan berries, an otherwise high-quality and profitable item in the spring and fall seasons. FMI had played such a role only once before—in Chile after the controversial incident involving two cyanide-laced grapes found in Philadelphia in 1989.

In December 1997, FDA—not yet convinced that Guatemala had adequately addressed the *Cyclospora* contamination problem—issued an import alert for Guatemala for the following spring season, March 15 to August 15, 1998. Under an import alert, FDA puts all shipments from the country under detention and denies imports entry into the United States without physical examination. Denying all imports of raspberries based on country of origin rather than rejecting products from specific shippers was an unusual response, and one used only after all other means of resolving the problem were exhausted. Furthermore, to deny imports without physical evidence is very rare: in this case, the import alert was based only on epidemiological evidence about past outbreaks and FDA observations on current production procedures. However, under the WTO Sanitary and Phytosanitary Standards Agreement, the United States can restrict imports to protect human health. Raspberries in other seasons and blackberries were not restricted. FDA, HC, the Canadian Food Inspection Agency (CFIA), and Guatemalan officials consulted to consider improved intervention strategies for raspberry production. FDA later used this experience in Guatemala when developing guidelines for GAPs as part of the Food Safety Initiative.

The United States did not import raspberries from Guatemala in spring 1998, and there were no cases of cyclosporiasis due to raspberries. The United States did import 132 metric tons of blackberries during the March–August period with no reported health problems. Canada, however, decided that limiting exports to low-risk farms was an adequate precaution against a cyclosporiasis outbreak and continued to import raspberries. The different U.S. and Canadian decisions on imports further fueled suspicions of those Guatemalan producers that thought the U.S. decision to deny imports was due to protectionism and not food safety. The debate regarding risk and risk-mitigating measures frequently leads to discord among scientists, government officials, and trading partners (Buzby and Roberts 1999). Unfortunately, another outbreak linked to Guatemalan raspberries occurred in May in Canada. CFIA reported that a traceback investigation indicated that Guatemalan raspberries from farms classified as medium risk had been shipped to Canada (Health and Social Services Committee 2000). In June, Canada asked the Guatemalan authorities to stop shipping raspberries voluntarily due to the outbreak. That September, a formal restriction was imposed on Guatemalan raspberries. The Canadian public and press were vociferous in their blame of public health officials (Powell 1998). Scientific uncertainly played a role in this controversy. With an emerging parasite and an unknown transmission method, it is difficult to determine if safeguards are adequate.

Europe continued to import raspberries with no observed ill effects, but only a small portion (estimated at less than 15 percent) of Guatemalan raspberries were exported to that market. Beginning in 1998, Guatemala allowed only blackberry exports from low-risk farms to reduce the spillover effects of the raspberry *Cyclospora* contamination problem to the blackberry industry.

THE MODEL PLAN OF EXCELLENCE

Beginning in the spring 1999 season, the United States allowed entry of raspberries produced under the Model Plan of Excellence (MPE), which had been in development for over a year. GBC and the Guatemalan government presented their new MPE safety program for raspberry exports to the United States in February 1998. FDA, HC, CFIA, and FMI all helped revise the plan.

Only growers in the MPE program may export raspberries to the United States during the period March 15 to August 15. Nonparticipating growers may export to other markets during the spring/summer season and to any market during the rest of the year if they are considered low or medium risk. High-risk farmers are not allowed to export. Growers and shippers join the MPE by complying with a detailed program of food safety precautions and successfully passing Guatemalan government inspections and FDA audits.

Economists generally believe that performance standards are more efficient than process standards (Antle 1996). All firms incur costs to comply with performance standards regardless of whether their produce has the potential to be contaminated with *Cyclospora* or they have a cheaper way to reach the same quality standard. The MPE relies on a process control standard, since a performance standard is unenforceable in this case. This program is intended to provide a credible signal that consumers can use to identify raspberries produced under high food safety standards—an attempt to turn the absence of *Cyclospora* on raspberries from a potentially noisome experience characteristic to a search attribute.

Farmers must use microbiological water filters to reduce risk of contamination. In 1999, the MPE for exports to the United States required a nominal 1 micron filter used as a prefilter to remove particulate matter and an absolute 0.45 micron filter for water used on plants and for employee hygiene. Manufacturers guarantee the specified diameter of an absolute filter but not of a nominal filter; an absolute filter is also more expensive than a nominal filter. For 2000, the MPE for the United States requires an absolute 1 micron filter instead of the absolute 0.45 micron filter, which is less expensive but still provides protection. Under the WTO, sanitary technical barriers must be the least trade-distorting possible to achieve a national safety goal.

The MPE requires growers to improve handling conditions. Raspberries are hand-harvested, and the harvested fruit is not washed because it deteriorates rapidly after contact with water. Gloves are not a realistic option, because they interfere with the harvesters' ability to detect ripeness. Hand-washing stations with filtered water and better toilet facilities are required to reduce the threat of contamination via handling. Toilet use and hand washing are also monitored. In addition, the MPE requires testing of employees for *Cyclospora* before hiring and a random testing of 10 percent of the employees during harvest. In spring 1999, no workers tested positive for *Cyclospora* on any MPE-participating farms.

The MPE also requires use of a code applied to each clamshell of raspberries that allows traceback to an individual grower. Traceback and traceforward capabilities are critical in the event of a food safety problem. These tools can be used to revoke the export authority of any firms associated with a food safety problem in order to maintain the integrity of the MPE. The United States has no regulations regarding record maintenance for tracebacks, but many firms have excellent systems for their own benefit and marketing advantage.

The success of the MPE program is largely due to the surveillance provided by the Integral Program of Agricultural and Environmental Protection (known by its Spanish acronym, PIPAA). PIPAA is a quasi-public organization which receives both its authority to enforce the MPE program and part of its funding from the Ministry of Agriculture, Food, and Livestock. PIPAA also receives partial funding from the private AGEXPRONT. The organization was created in 1991 to deal with a pesticide residue problem with snow peas. In general, PIPAA conducts food safety programs for growers of any nontraditional export to help them comply with sanitary and phytosanitary requirements of countries buying Guatemalan produce. In the raspberry case, PIPAA monitors and certifies MPE program participants for the Guatemalan government to provide proof that the program satisfies food safety requirements. PIPAA inspects farms and warehouses almost daily during the spring season to ensure compliance with the MPE. Warehouses of shippers participating in the MPE program are monitored to ensure that MPE and non-MPE berries are not commingled (Jackson et al. 1999). During the rest of the year, the level of inspections decreases but other practices remain in place. PIPAA employees, trained by FDA, monitor the MPE program.

To support the MPE program, GBC currently assesses producers $0.08 (up from $0.04 in 1999) on each flat of exported raspberries and blackberries. The funds collected cover the costs of lobbying and advocacy, management support, research projects for new varieties, inspection, and other miscellaneous projects. The government of Guatemala contributes by paying salaries of PIPAA executives and inspectors. The Inter-American Development Bank also supports the program by providing technical consultants.

Although the method of potential contamination has never been conclusively determined, FDA decided that, based on current scientific knowledge, Guatemalan producers had done everything possible to ensure food safety with the MPE program. In spring 1999, FDA officials went to Guatemala to audit the eight farms that the Guatemalan government, GBC, and PIPAA determined were in compliance with the MPE. By the time FDA arrived, only five farms planned to export: one firm decided to get out of the raspberry business, and two others had production problems. FDA gave permission for the five farms to export to the United States for the 1999 spring season, although two decided later not to export due to production problems. Shippers were also approved for export. All shippers were Guatemalan companies. FDA also audited testing laboratories.

FDA revised its import alert to allow the approved firms to export raspberries to the United States. The product must still be inspected but now is not rejected outright at the port of entry. FDA audits farms and tests exports for *Cyclospora* at the beginning of the spring season to ensure that the program continues to meet U.S. food safety requirements. FDA's visit to Guatemala in spring 2000 was primarily to audit the MPE, participating MPE farms, and PIPAA. If the 2000 season succeeds, Guatemala hopes to engage FDA in discussions to begin the equivalent agreement process. If such an agreement were in effect, PIPAA alone would audit the program. This would provide Guatemala with an additional tool to signal food safety of its raspberries to potential buyers. The equivalent agreement process is part of the Food Safety Initiative and seeks to assure FDA that products produced abroad meet U.S. levels of public health protection (U.S. FDA 1999).

In spring 1999, the United States imported raspberries from farms participating in the MPE. Raspberry sales were quite low in the spring 1999 season, because few farms exported and those that did experienced problems in the marketplace stemming from safety concerns of U.S. importers, retail and wholesale buyers, and consumers. No cases of cyclosporiasis were traced to Guatemalan raspberries in 1999. Outbreaks of the disease in both the United States and Canada caused concern, however. In the Florida outbreak, GBC could show, using its traceback and traceforward capabilities, that Guatemalan raspberries were not served at the event. Guatemalan producers believe that for each cyclosporiasis outbreak, the common assumption is that the problem must be due to their berries. If another product turns out to be the culprit, the producers think there is little effort by the media to correct the story. Producers need traceback information to protect themselves against new suspicions or allegations.

In December 1999, Canada authorized imports of Guatemalan fall and winter raspberries which had been banned since the previous year. The raspberries must be produced under the MPE. The ban on spring season raspberries will remain in effect until CFIA and HC officials develop a policy for that season.

Canada has continuing concern about the possibility of *Cyclospora* contamination of blackberries. In 1999, there was a cyclosporiasis outbreak in York, Canada, and HC implicated Guatemalan blackberries (Health and Social Services Committee 2000). Guatemala feels that Canada's finding linking blackberries to cyclosporiasis outbreaks is unreasonable since only 6 out of 176,240 flats of blackberries exported by Guatemala in 1999 were involved. In response to the implications of the Canadian investigation, Guatemala developed a new MPE for exports of blackberries that took effect at the end of March 2000. With such a program, Guatemala will be able to provide a defense of its food safety standards for blackberries if there are any future concerns. This program is proactive: Guatemala requires its use, even though no country currently requires it for entry of the product. The program is similar to the MPE for raspberries except for the inspections. There are so many blackberry farms compared to raspberry farms that it is not now possible to inspect them in the same manner.

In 2000, all raspberry producers participated in the MPE program. As of this writing, Canada had not yet developed a spring import plan, so no raspberries have been shipped to Canada during the spring season. On April 7, 2000, Canada announced that it would not allow blackberry imports from Guatemala until a new import plan had been developed.

IMPACT OF CYCLOSPORIASIS OUTBREAKS ON THE GUATEMALAN RASPBERRY INDUSTRY

Although Guatemalan producers started seeing some discount for their raspberries and blackberries in the fall of 1996, the real impact began May 30, 1997, when GBC stopped exports for the rest of the spring at the height of the season. Growers faced large financial losses with the closure of their major market. The FDA 1998 import alert was a further blow. In 2000, there were only six raspberry farmers left in Guatemala, down from an estimated 85 farmers in 1996 before the first *Cyclospora* contamination problem (Table

6). Many growers decided to leave the raspberry industry, more because of the losses they had already incurred than because of the costs of implementing a food safety program. Some farmers shifted to blackberry production, since they had experience with berries and that market was not as severely affected. Some farmers went back to the crops they grew previously or adopted new crops. The large U.S. firm that marketed blackberries for one Guatemalan farm decided to stop shipping from Guatemala. The food safety problem was only one of several factors that influenced this company in its decision to stop sourcing blackberries from Guatemala. The large Chilean firm that grew raspberries and blackberries in Guatemala dropped raspberries completely. It still ships blackberries from Guatemala, however. Foreign firms that only used Guatemalan berries to fill out their season had more to lose than Guatemalan firms if any problems in that country spilled over to affect their reputation for their main production in their home countries. At least one Guatemalan firm moved all operations to Mexico.

Table 6. Guatemalan raspberry industry: number of producers and hectares

	Spring 1996[a]	Spring 1998	August 1998	August 1999	Spring 2000
Producers	85	46	37	12	6
Producers w/ at least 10 hectares	n.a.	14	11	2	2
Hectares	n.a.	369	310	115	77

[a]Rough estimate.
Source: PIPAA.

In addition to the decrease in Guatemalan supply, demand for Guatemalan berries decreased. While some retail and other buyers are comfortable with Guatemalan raspberries, others adopted policies of not buying Guatemalan berries. Industry experts say that, beginning in 1997, buyers generally preferred raspberries from other sources, and Guatemalan berries sold at a discount below other suppliers' prices. Anecdotal evidence suggests that the discount may be decreasing or at least that buyers are somewhat less likely to ask for non-Guatemalan raspberries. Guatemalan officials report that in no case have Guatemalan berries been observed selling at a premium because of the MPE. Although the consumer may not pay much attention to reports of *Cyclospora*, retail and other commercial buyers do. GBC, with FMI coordination, paid for major U.S. retailers and other large buyers to visit their production and see the new food safety standards in practice. GBC plans to repeat what it regards as a successful program to promote Guatemalan produce. The decline in demand for Guatemalan raspberries appears across all seasons even though fall and winter raspberries have never been associated with *Cyclospora* contamination problems. Although blackberries were never cited as a definitive cause of cyclosporiasis in any outbreak in the United States, they have also faced decreased demand and lower prices in export markets. In addition to possible food safety concerns, blackberries faced decreased demand because retailers prefer to buy a bundle of berries. When Guatemala could only provide blackberries, many buyers purchased berries from other regions that could provide the desired mix of berries. Figure 3 shows the decline in U.S. imports of Guatemalan raspberries and blackberries.

Some U.S. retail chains reportedly do not buy any Guatemalan produce. Guatemala plans to expand the MPE program to other nonberry crops, such as snow peas, mangoes, and melons. No country has asked for an MPE for other crops, so this is a proactive program to bolster the perception of product safety. Guatemala is investigating new sources of funding to support MPE expansion. To remain competitive, the country needs produce with a reputation for top quality and food safety. The food safety efforts are not targeted exclusively at export crops destined for more developed-country markets. Guatemala is expanding the program to crops grown for export to other Central American countries and eventually hopes to apply the MPE to production for domestic consumption also.

Guatemala went from no raspberry exports in the 1989/90 season to being a major supplier in 1995/96 to being a very minor supplier in 1998/99. Any country with a food safety problem might face a similar situation. While Guatemala worked to increase food safety standards, other competitors made inroads into its spring and fall raspberry markets. Mexico now supplies much of the spring and fall seasons that Guatemala previously dominated. In 1998, Spain and Portugal began shipping raspberries to other European countries. These suppliers took over much of Guatemala's spring market in Europe.

IMPACT ON THE UNITED STATES

In 1996, the cyclosporiasis outbreak affected U.S. strawberries more than raspberries. The publicity about the outbreak, and the suspicion that California strawberries were the source of the contamination, hit during the height of the strawberry season. The California Strawberry Commission estimates that the false alarm caused a loss of $16 million in

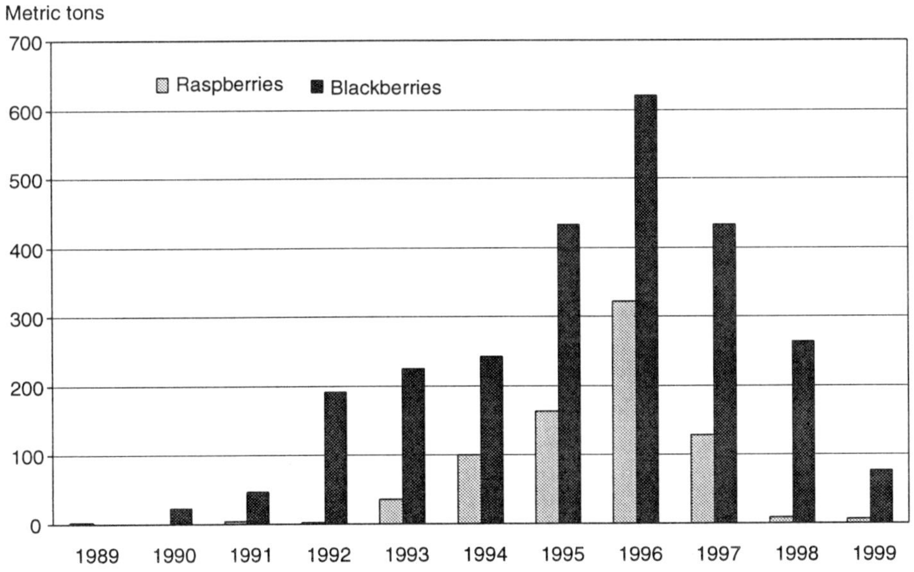

Figure 3. U.S. imports of Guatemalan raspberries and blackberries declined after 1996 *Cyclospora* contamination.

revenue to growers in the central coast of California during the month of June (Mischen 1996). Industry experts say that although the initial negative publicity focused on strawberries, all berries suffered a decline in demand by association.[3] Spring raspberries were affected, but, by the time the summer raspberry season began with higher volumes, CDC had decided that the contaminated fruit was Guatemalan raspberries. As a result, many consumers were eager to buy domestic fruit, which gave a boost to domestic producers. However, since all California raspberry shippers also ship strawberries, they experienced financial losses in that market.

The cyclosporiasis outbreak has increased the awareness of raspberry and strawberry producers regarding their vulnerability to food safety problems. Concerns about potential problems of liability in a food safety outbreak affect U.S. suppliers as well as foreign suppliers. U.S. industry insiders report that general concern over field sanitation is higher than before the outbreak. Costs increased for all producers of raspberries in the United States and Latin America, not just for Guatemala. The California Strawberry Commission developed the voluntary Quality Assurance Food Safety Program for producers. California standards for production practices and documentation were already fairly rigorous, but the plan strengthens documentation of practices. The California Strawberry Commission wants to be prepared should a similar food safety scare or problem occur. Like their Guatemalan counterparts, California producers realize that they must be proactive and ready to explain their practices in case of a problem.

After the cyclosporiasis outbreak, the leading California raspberry firm developed a new food safety program that increased water testing and standards for field sanitation and employee hygiene. FDA already required producers to use safe water for produce, following the U.S. Environmental Protection Agency's potable water standard. This standard generally involves testing for the presence of both *Escherichia coli* and fecal coliforms. The California firm now employs a third-party testing firm to sample water before and during the season and if it suspects a problem. This same program is used for all raspberries sold by the company whether grown in California or Mexico. For such a large firm, the cost of additional water testing is likely quite small compared to the losses associated with a potential food safety problem. If consumers and large-scale buyers recognize the brand name, this firm may be able to maintain consumer confidence even if other firms' reputations suffer from a potential food safety problem.

Smaller U.S. raspberry producers may have adopted similar programs either because of their own experiences with the *Cyclospora* scare or to keep up with the industry leader. An additional force that may increase efforts to implement food safety programs comes from U.S. retailers. Several large U.S. retail chains have recently begun to require that their suppliers have third-party food safety audits to ensure that they comply with GAPs and other food safety programs. As in Guatemala, this is a process standard given the low probability that random testing would detect food contamination problems. Large retailers account for an increasingly large percentage of total retail buying because of continuing consolidation in the U.S. grocery retail sector.

If raspberries from Guatemala are now safe, consumers are losing welfare from not having a larger supply of berries available at lower prices in particular seasons. The impact of the reduction in Guatemalan production is evident in 1999 New York wholesale market prices. During the spring market window that Guatemala once dominated, the price shot up to about double the price in the surrounding time periods. In the fall, the price also increased, but because Mexican production has taken over much of the Guatemalan market window, the price increase was smaller. If Mexican production had not expanded to fill some of the Guatemalan market windows, U.S. consumers would have felt more effect. Several U.S. raspberry firms source berries from Mexico, clearly indicating a level of consumer confidence in that product.

IMPACT ON CHILE

Although not implicated directly in *Cyclospora* outbreaks, the incidents related to Guatemala did affect the behavior of the Chilean berry industry. After initial concerns raised in 1996, Chile faced a short-lived dip in demand and price in 1996 when U.S. consumers were leery of any foreign raspberries. More enduring has been the behavior of the Chilean industry leader with respect to its use of non-Chilean sources and its strategies of quality control over Chilean sources. Prior to the initial outbreak, Guatemala represented an important source of berries for the Chilean industry as part of a competitive plan for a year-round supply, important in its rivalry with the California industry leader. This latter firm has a year-round supply from California and has also turned to Mexico as an important source of berries. Since the problems in Guatemala, the Chilean leader has shifted more investment into Mexico. Part of the motivation for shifting investment to Mexico was the ability to ship berries to the U.S. market via trucks with controlled cooling systems—a significant cost savings over air transport. However, the investment there was greater than if the Guatemalan raspberry industry had not been associated with the cyclosporiasis outbreak.

Shifting emphasis on supply sources away from Guatemalan producers to Mexican and Chilean sources afforded the Chilean industry leader an immediate means of sidestepping marketing problems associated directly with consumer concerns over contamination specifically originating in Guatemala. The issues of potential *Cyclospora* contamination from Chilean producers, and the increased apprehension of the safety of foreign produce in general, provoked a series of responses involving longer term changes requiring modification of production methods in the Chilean berry industry. In contrast to Guatemala's adoption of mandatory, centrally coordinated safety measures aimed at a particular problem, changes in quality control in Chile were initiated mainly at the level of industry associations and individual firms to avoid a wide range of possible troubles related to consumer confidence. In this respect, Chilean firms acted in a manner similar to those in California, responding to a generally heightened awareness of their vulnerability to a loss of consumer trust.

An initial industry reaction to the cyclosporiasis outbreak was to distribute testing kits by an association of exporters. The berry industry quickly perceived the long-term futility of what was considered primarily a cosmetic response meant to bolster consumer confidence related to a specific contamination problem. In light of the failure to identify *Cyclospora* directly in suspected sources of contamination, Chilean firms recognized the difficulty of using testing to credibly screen produce quality and assure consumers in the long term. Moreover, Chilean industry experts gave little credence to the belief that the parasite presented a potential problem in Chile, due to the country's climate and geography. Therefore, the focus of concern shifted from *Cyclospora* specifically to how firms and the industry might credibly assure the public of their products' safety more generally. Chilean quality control specialists describe the consumer anxiety over *Cyclospora* in the United States and Canada as an "alert" that clarified incentives to the industry to direct more resources to safety assurance for all berry products, not simply raspberries. The problem especially served to sensitize directors of the largest berry-exporting firm to the potential net benefits of making investments to market credibly reliable berry products.

In the case of Guatemala, the implementation of more stringent standards for quality control of exports to the United States was supported and coordinated by a producer association, reinforced and underwritten by the national government and U.S. agencies, and made mandatory by law. In the case of Chile, changes in production practices aimed at improved food safety were initiated at the firm level, primarily as a result of the incentives faced by the largest Chilean exporter, and have been voluntary in nature. Agricultural groups and institutions have, in part, financially supported private initiatives both to study the dissemination of improved production techniques to producers and to design stricter methods of quality control throughout the marketing chain. Chilean government agencies have primarily accepted the responsibility of heightening awareness and assisting communications and interaction in the industry, and, to date, mandatory regulations have played only a minor role in the adoption of safety standards to meet the concerns of foreign consumers of Chilean produce.

The desire to address foreign consumer concerns regarding biological contamination, mainly arising in North America, also coincided with an awareness of the potential gains to meeting greater demands for "chemically safe" and "labor-friendly" produce mainly by buyers in the United Kingdom. This led to the consideration of a more general approach to product quality than one simply designed to avoid contamination similar in nature to that associated with *Cyclospora*. Presently, the leading Chilean berry exporter considers Great Britain to be the most demanding importing country in terms of quality assurance. The firm seeks to persuade importers of the safety of its production practices through periodic visits by British importers and the adoption of third-party certification. Although British concerns focus mainly on the production environment and management of pesticides and chemical use generally, the leading Chilean exporter considers the British standards a target that, if met, might also allay concerns elsewhere regarding berry-borne diseases.

In terms of altering production practices, the leading Chilean exporter began a program of more stringent quality control with an attempt to adopt an HACCP approach both for its own production (approximately 50 percent of its raspberry supply from Chile) and for its independent Chilean suppliers. After an initial expenditure of effort and time, the firm's quality control specialists concluded that reliance on an intensive HACCP approach was a mistaken emphasis on details meant to address the hazards related to specific threats rather than an overall approach to product safety better suited to the general concerns of its customers and the realities of berry production. Regardless of whether the specialists' opinion is correct or can be generalized to all berry exporters-producers, the firm concluded that the most economically efficient method primarily involved the adoption of practices and performance standards based on GMPs, GAPs, and SSOPs already developed and formalized in the United States. A strategy of continuous training programs for agricultural workers and periodic inspections of suppliers supplemented these standards. The firm's enhanced quality control program only recently has been implemented in Chile, and, once fully established, the firm plans to carry the training program to its suppliers in Mexico to strengthen its standards there.

One benefit of the initial HACCP approach was to provide quality control specialists with a detailed catalog of workers' activities that structured the design of training manuals. Training programs for field workers, primarily oriented toward sanitation, are subsidized by the exporter. The firm is aware of the potential free-rider problem of investing in the human capital of independent suppliers that may take their safer product to other exporters, although no explicit changes in exporter-producer business relations to avoid the problem have been apparent. Through its prominence in the market, by establishing implicit long-term relationships with independent producers, and by absorbing the costs of the continuous training of workers prone to high turnover rates, the largest Chilean firm may mitigate this free-rider problem, but the program is still evolving.

In Guatemala, the credibility of efforts to ensure berry quality has been supported by the mandatory nature of the process standards aimed at eliminating the threat of *Cyclospora* contamination and by the participation of agencies such as FDA, which reviews those standards and audits the program. In contrast, Chile's leading exporter has sought credibility for its efforts at general safety control both through importer review of formalized production standards and inspection and, recently, through the use of third-party certification. The incentives for third-party certification not only derive from a self-initiated marketing strategy but also from the explicit demands of large buyers. For example, Safeway in the United States—a large buyer of Chilean berries—indicated to the exporter that it will require certification in the next year. Although they have not indicated certification as a requirement, large British buyers will also use the certification process as an indicator of the quality of the Chilean exporter's production practices, perhaps substituting certification in the future for buyer review of the firm's policy and buyer inspections. In addition to providing a credible *ex post* test of a firm's final production methods, the interactive nature of the certification process in the Chilean case has allowed incorporation of the expertise of a certifying firm in the *ex ante* development of control strategies.

The experience in Chile demonstrates the extent to which a large exporter-producer will invest by its own initiative in quality control measures and certification, applied both at its own production facilities and the facilities of its suppliers, to credibly signal the safety of its fresh produce. The contrast with the Guatemalan experience raises the question of what peculiar factors determine the differences in emphasis on private initiatives versus industrywide standards coordinated by producer organizations or enforced by governmental agencies. In Chile, the largest exporter sought separately to respond to, and in part to anticipate, the strengthened standards of its major buyers—a behavior consistent with the hypothesis that the firm perceived it could internalize a sufficiently large portion of the benefits of greater consumer confidence. That the firm retreated from Guatemalan suppliers after the initial cyclosporiasis alarm and initiated policy changes first in Chile with plans to apply those changes uniformly to Mexican suppliers suggests that the private net benefits of establishing credibility of produce safety depend on specific characteristics of the product's source.

It is an open question whether Guatemalan environmental conditions increase costs, relative to those in Chile, associated with the technical aspects of quality control. Perhaps instead, or in addition, Guatemalan institutions or producer attitudes and incentives decrease the expected benefits that an individual exporter can obtain first from investing in the production processes and human capital of its suppliers, and then from establishing the credibility of those investments. The Chilean export leader's size and reputation with large buyers would explain how it might internalize the benefits of the perceived enhanced safety of its branded berries due to its investments in quality control, but that leaves unexplained why the firm concentrated those investments on Chilean sources. The likely reason is that there are relatively lower costs in Chile of implementing quality control measures at the field level and of preventing the benefits of those measures from being shared among suppliers to other firms. The firm has direct control in Chile over the production of a large portion of its total shipments, allowing it to coordinate production changes directly and to avoid much of the free-rider problem of investing in quality control at the field level. Its historical importance in the Chilean market and the relatively lower cost of establishing long-term relations with its independent Chilean suppliers also likely reduce the free-rider problem and thus internalize a major portion of the benefits associated with improved consumer confidence in its branded berries.

IMPACT ON MEXICO

The Mexican raspberry industry began exporting raspberries to the United States in the 1992/93 season and grew rapidly to become the largest source of U.S. winter imports. Exports to the United States grew 268 percent from the 1995/96 to 1998/99 seasons. Exports through March of the 1999/2000 season were 16 percent higher than the same time last season. Much of this new production in Mexico competes with that of Chile and Guatemala. Since Mexico's exports to the United States had started to expand before 1996, it is not clear whether Guatemala would have lost some market share to Mexico even without the food safety problem. Mexico is the only country that supplies the U.S. raspberry market during the winter months that can rely on truck transport instead of airfreight, which is an important cost saving. Less competition from Guatemala meant higher prices, which provided a big boost for the Mexican industry.

As has been the case in the United States and Chile, Guatemala's experience makes Mexico's producers more careful about water quality and field sanitation. Most raspberry producers sell to the large Californian and Chilean firms, although there are several smaller shippers operating in Mexico. These two firms have private standards for production and food safety. The U.S. firm applies these standards to its producers in Mexico since it sells the Mexican product under their own labels in the U.S. market. The Chilean firm plans to replace as soon as possible its current food safety program in Mexico with the new program it has developed for its production in Chile. At least one Guatemalan firm now ships raspberries from Mexico. Interviews with Mexican berry producers indicate that growers distinguish different levels of food safety requirements for the various buyers.

Currently, the Mexican government is implementing a program of new food safety guidelines with particular emphasis on exported crops. The Secretariat of Agriculture, Livestock, and Rural Development is considering the use of GAPs and GMPs to ensure safety.

CONCLUSIONS

This case study has illustrated the difficulty of resolving a food safety problem once a grave question of confidence arises. CDC implicated Guatemalan raspberries in the cyclosporiasis outbreak in spring 1996. Not until spring 1999 did Guatemala export to the United States without a single case of cyclosporiasis attributed to its raspberries. And as of this writing, consumer confidence had apparently not been completely restored. Changing the attitudes of U.S. retail and wholesale buyers will be crucial to establishing the Guatemalan food safety program, MPE, as an economic as well as technical success.

The cost and years devoted to dealing with *Cyclospora* contamination have had a serious impact on the Guatemalan raspberry industry. Problems in the industry have also had important negative spillover effects on blackberries. There are only six Guatemalan raspberry producers still in business, and they have very few marketing options since other suppliers have partially filled their U.S. market windows. Rebuilding the raspberry industry will be difficult because buyers and consumers appear to be concerned about Guatemalan products despite FDA approval of the MPE process standard. If buyer and consumer opinion changes as slowly as it appears to have done in the Guatemalan case, producers must be prepared to incur the costs to improve food safety but not necessarily expect to see immediate benefits in the marketplace. As noted by Richards and Patterson (1999), negative news about a food safety problem for a product affects price more than good news.

A large number of individuals and organizations participated in resolving the *Cyclospora* contamination problem in Guatemala. Besides Guatemalan entities (individual growers, GBC, government agencies, the High-Level Commission, and PIPAA), FDA, CDC, and FMI were involved from the United States. FDA's involvement in the Guatemala food safety problem has been greater than in any previous case. Canada's CFIA and HC were also involved. The divergent responses of FDA and CFIA in denying imports underlines the level of scientific uncertainty in this case.

FDA's role in Guatemala was unique. Only once before had the agency gone abroad to look at farms and packing houses—in 1989 to Chile in the aftermath of the cyanide-laced grape problem. Under the Food Safety Initiative, FDA, as well as CDC and USDA, is becoming more involved in foreign technical assistance. Most of FDA's activities revolve around presenting information about GAPs and sending technical experts to help foreign producers resolve their food safety problems. Guatemala was also different in the level of FDA involvement. Because *Cyclospora* is an emerging pathogen, and the food safety problem was complex and long lasting, FDA committed more resources to this problem.

The Guatemalan experience with *Cyclospora* demonstrates that, with an internationally traded commodity, food safety problems in one country affect all producers trading in the market. Industry experts report that during the initial cyclosporiasis outbreak in 1996, demand for all berries declined until Guatemalan raspberries were implicated. Since the cost of a food safety problem is so high, raspberry producers in other countries developed improved food safety programs even though no cyclosporiasis outbreaks were traced to any country but Guatemala. With the exception of Guatemala, food safety programs for raspberries are voluntary, not mandatory. Individual shippers or retail/wholesale buyers often develop these food safety programs, leading to a wide range of standards. In contrast to Guatemalan producers and institutions, which sought to appease an audience of concerned government agencies in North America, the large shippers in the United States and

Chile instituted programs to bolster their claims of food safety aimed primarily at large buyers. These large buyers in turn sought to gain from heightened consumer confidence in their products on the grocery shelf.

Private standards augment government standards. When food safety problems can affect demand for berries from any source (even if temporarily) and production costs increase with additional food safety provisions, there is some incentive for international cooperation between producers to develop food safety guidelines (Richards and Patterson 1999). This type of collaboration is, however, more likely to occur when the impact on demand of all berries due to a contamination problem is relatively large and shipping seasons do not overlap. When seasons do overlap, one country's misfortune may be another's gain.

NOTES

1. In the early 1990s, there were several isolated cases of cyclosporiasis in the United States involving lake water, sewage backup possibly contaminated with runoff from a dairy, and well water (Sterling and Ortega 1999).
2. The Tariff Act of 1930, as amended, requires that containers holding imported fresh produce be labeled upon entering the country. County-of-origin labeling informs the ultimate U.S. purchasers of the product, generally the last person who receives the article in the form in which it was imported. A retailer buys produce in a box marked with the country-of-origin label, but, if the produce is taken out of the container and displayed loose in an open bin, each individual piece of produce does not have to be labeled. In this case, the retailer is the ultimate purchaser. In any case, raspberries are not sold in open bins, and the consumer in the grocery store is the ultimate purchaser, receiving the product in the form it was imported (U.S. GAO 1999).
3. Richards and Patterson (1999) show that news reports of disease outbreaks associated with strawberries in 1996 and 1997 (an outbreak of hepatitis A) did not reduce demand for nonberry fruit.

REFERENCES

Akerlof, G. A., 1970, The market for "lemons": Quality uncertainty and the market mechanism, *Q J Econ* **84**(3):488–500.

Antle, J. M., 1996, Efficient food safety regulation in the food manufacturing sector, *Am J Agric Econ* **78**(5):1242–1247.

———, 1998, Economic Analysis of Food Safety, Research Discussion Paper No. 20, Trade Research Center, Montana State University, Bozeman.

Ashford, R. W., 1979, Occurrence of an undescribed coccidian in man in Papua New Guinea, *Ann Trop Med Parasit* **73**(5):497–500.

Bockstael, N. E., 1984, The welfare implications of minimum quality standards, *Am J Agric Econ* **66**(4):466–471.

Buzby, J., and Roberts, D., 1999, Food safety and international trade in the twenty-first century, *Choices* 4th qtr:23–27.

Caswell, J. A., and Mojduszka, E. M., 1996, Using informational labeling to influence the market for quality in food products, *Am J Agric Econ* **78**(5):1248–1253.

Centers for Disease Control and Prevention (CDC), 1997a, Outbreak of cyclosporiasis—Northern Virginia–Washington, D.C.–Baltimore, Maryland, metropolitan area, *Morbidity and Mortality Weekly Report* **46**(30):689–691.

———, 1997b, Update: Outbreaks of cyclosporiasis—United States and Canada, 1997, *Morbidity and Mortality Weekly Report* **46**(23):521–523.

———, 1998, Outbreak of cyclosporiasis—Ontario Canada, May 1998, *Morbidity and Mortality Weekly Report* **47**(38):806–809.

Crutchfield, S., 1999, New federal policies and programs for food safety, *Food Rev* **22**(2):2–5.

Dixon, B., 1999, *Isolation and Identification of Cyclospora Oocysts from Berries*, Polyscience Publications, Laval, Quebec.

Health and Social Services Committee, Regional Municipality of York, 2000, The 1999 Outbreak of *Cyclospora* in York Region, Report of the Commissioner of Health Services and Medical Officer of Health, York, Canada.

Hennessy, D., 1996, Information asymmetry as a reason for food industry vertical integration, *Am J Agric Econ* **78**(4):1034–1043.

Herwaldt, B., Ackers, M.-L., and the *Cyclospora* Working Group, 1997, An outbreak in 1996 of cyclosporiasis associated with imported raspberries, *New Engl J Med* **336**(22):1548–1556.

Herwaldt, B., Beach, M., and the *Cyclospora* Working Group, 1999, The return of *Cyclospora* in 1997: Another outbreak of cyclosporiasis in North America associated with imported raspberries, *Ann Intern Med* **130**(3):210–220.

Jackson, G., Solorzano, L., Kvenberg, J., Flores, L., Mooney, J. D., and Castaneda, R., 1999, Routes by which *Cyclospora cayetanensis* may contaminate food, in: *Food Microbiology and Food Safety into the Next Millennium: Proceedings of the Seventeenth International Conference of the International Committee on Food Microbiology and Hygiene*, A. Tuijtelaars, R. Samson, F. Rombouts, and S. Notermans, eds., TNO Nutrition and Food Research Institute, Zeist, the Netherlands, pp. 49–51.

Koumans, E., Katz, D., Malecki, J., Wahlquist, S., and Arrowood, M., 1998, An outbreak of cyclosporiasis in Florida in 1995: A harbinger of multistate outbreaks in 1996 and 1997, *Am J Trop Med Hyg* **59**(2):235–242.

Lucier, G., Pollack, S., and Perez, A., 1997, Import penetration in the U.S. fruit and vegetable industry, in: *Vegetable and Specialties Situation and Outlook Report*, VGS-273, Economic Research Service, U.S. Department of Agriculture, Washington, DC.

Mead, P. S., Slutsker, L., Dietz, V., McCaig, L. F., Bresel, J. S., Shapiro, C., Griffin, P. M., and Tauxe, R. V., 1999, Food-related illness and death in the United States, *Emerg Infect Dis* **5**(5):607–625.

Mischen, P., 1996, Strawberry Update: $16 Million Loss due to *Cyclospora*, National Food and Agricultural Policy Project, Arizona State University, Tempe.

Ortega, Y. R., Gilman, R. H., and Sterling, C. R., 1994, A new coccidian parasite (Apicomplexa: Eimeriidae) from humans, *J Parasitol* **80**(4):625–629.

Powell, D., 1998, Risk-Based Regulatory Responses in Global Food Trade: Guatemalan Raspberry Imports into the U.S. and Canada, 1996–1998, paper presented at the Conference on Science, Government and Global Markets: The State of Canada's Science-Based Regulatory Institutions, Oct. 1–2, 1998, Ottawa.

Richards, T., and Patterson, P., 1999, The economic value of public relations expenditures: Food safety and the strawberry case, *J Agric Resour Econ* **24**(2):440–462.

Sterling, C., and Ortega, Y., 1999, *Cyclospora*: An enigma worth unraveling, *Emerg Infect Dis* **5**(1):48–53.

Tauxe, R. V., 1997, Emerging foodborne diseases: An evolving public health challenge, *Emerg Infect Dis* **3**(4):425–434.

U.S. Food and Drug Administration (U.S. FDA), 1998, *Guide to Minimize Microbial Food Safety Hazards for Fresh Fruits and Vegetables*, Washington, DC.

———, 1999, Notice of availability: Center for Food Safety and Applied Nutrition's Affirmative Agenda for International Activities, *Fed Reg* **64**(243):71145–71147.

U.S. General Accounting Office (U.S. GAO), 1998, *Food Safety: Federal Efforts to Ensure the Safety of Imported Foods Are Inconsistent and Unreliable*, GAO/RCED-98-103, Washington, DC.

———, 1999, *Fresh Produce: Potential Consequences of Country-of-Origin Labeling*, GAO/RCED-99-112, Washington, DC.

Zepp, G., Kuchler, F., and Lucier, G., 1998, Food safety and fresh fruits and vegetables: Is there a difference between imported and domestically produced products?, in: *Vegetables and Specialties Situation and Outlook Report*, VGS-274, Economic Research Service, U.S. Department of Agriculture, Washington, DC.

A CASE STUDY OF BEEF PRODUCTION AND EXPORT IN URUGUAY

María I. Marshall, Michael Boland, Daniel Conforte, and Deborah Cesar*

Uruguay has the world's highest per capita consumption of beef and exports approximately 60 percent of its production. Therefore, it is important for this small country to respond to international consumer tastes and preferences. Uruguay's ability to comply with regulations passed by the European Union (EU) on beef hormones and traceability has made it competitive in various markets. Uruguay also saw the opening of new markets previously unavailable to it when the country was declared free of foot-and-mouth disease (FMD) by the World Organization for Animal Health in 1995. Uruguayan beef is produced under pasture grazing systems rather than feedlot operations such as those found in North America and the EU.

In this chapter, we show how Uruguay has responded to consumer concerns about sanitary problems, growth hormones, and traceability issues. First, we provide an overview of Uruguay's beef industry. Second, we show how the public and private sectors mandated the Dicose system, which favorably positioned Uruguay to take advantage of the EU ban on imports of beef produced with hormones and requirements for traceability. Third, we describe how a producer-owned cooperative met the needs of export markets with respect to quality attributes (hormone-free beef and increased traceability). This cooperative also provided economic incentives in the form of a value-based marketing program linked to a traceability program that is more sophisticated than the Dicose and increased its export market share from lowest to highest quantity exporter.

* María I. Marshall and Michael Boland are a Ph.D. graduate research student and associate professor, respectively, in the Department of Agricultural Economics at Kansas State University. Daniel Conforte is area coordinator and associate professor at Universidad ORT, Montevideo, Uruguay. Deborah Cesar is a veterinarian at Instituto Plan Agropecuario, Montevideo, Uruguay. We acknowledge the assistance of the Farm Foundation in providing funding for the travel associated with the personal interviews. We also thank the Royal Agricultural College for assistance in locating European Union meat brokers, the managers of the six Uruguayan slaughterhouses for visiting with us, and the producers in attendance who answered our questions after the Mercedes meeting. We acknowledge the support of the Kansas Agricultural Experimental Station, Contribution No. 00-345-A. Finally, we thank Tu Jarvis for providing us with copies of several papers on the meat industry.

Global Food Trade and Consumer Demand for Quality, edited by Krissoff *et al.*
Kluwer Academic/Plenum Publishers, New York, 2002.

The chapter's findings are based on extensive personal interviews with the chief executive officers of Uruguay's six largest slaughterhouses—Canelones, Tacuarembó, San Jacinto, Carrasco, Las Piedras, and Productores Unidos Cooperativa Agraria Ltda. (PUL). In addition, we interviewed two PUL directors, and industry and university scientists in Uruguay and spoke with a group of beef producers after an extension seminar given by the authors in Mercedes, Uruguay. Telephone interviews and written surveys were also conducted with 16 leading meat brokerage firms that import Uruguayan beef into the EU.

ORGANIZATION OF THE URUGUAYAN BEEF INDUSTRY

Background

Uruguay is a small, beef-exporting country. Most of its population (about 50 percent) lives in Montevideo, the capital, although there are some medium-sized cities with approximately 30,000 to 60,000 inhabitants such as Salto, Paysandu, and Colonia. It has an extensive pastoral system with excellent sanitary conditions. The import of live animals and/or genetic material from countries affected by FMD or other exotic diseases is strictly prohibited. Live animal exports are allowed; animals are exported to countries including Argentina, Brazil, Paraguay, and Mexico.

Uruguay has approximately 29,000 ranchers as of the 1998 census (IPA 1998). Of these ranchers, 19,000 have farms that are solely for breeding; 4,000 have farms for finishing; and 6,000 have cow-calf farms (Figure 1). Fifty-one percent of the country's 29,000 farms are family farms of approximately 82 hectares or less; 26 percent are transitional farms of approximately 362 hectares; 18 percent are medium-sized farms of about 1,100 hectares; the remaining 5 percent are big farms consisting of about 3,500 hectares (INIA

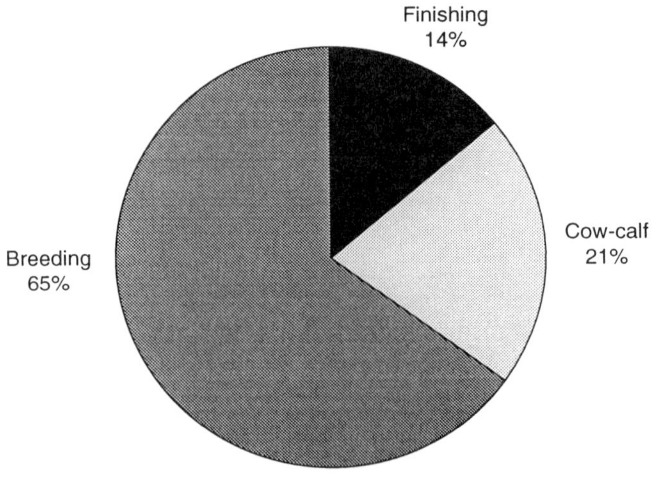

Figure 1. There are three main types of farming operations in Uruguay (IPA 1998).

1998). Figure 2 shows the proportions of the different farms in Uruguay. Figure 3 presents a map of Uruguay with the key grazing areas shaded.

The beef slaughter and processing industry (*frigorífico*) in Uruguay was under heavy government control until the late 1970s. A prime example of this control was the fact that the government allocated certain quotas for trade in the domestic market. The publicly owned Frigorífico Nacional had a monopoly in the Montevideo market, and privately owned firms were excluded from competing in the domestic market. By the early 1970s, however, the monopoly enjoyed by Frigorífico Nacional ended with the reduction of its domestic trade quota and the entrance of smaller privately owned plants that were technologically more advanced (Jarvis and Medero 1988). By 1980, the government was completely out of this industry, and there was free entry. Since the mid-1980s, more privately owned firms have entered the industry and compete not only in the export market but also in the domestic.

Industry Analysis

The standard industry analysis framework of Porter (1980) is used to describe competition in Uruguayan beef production, slaughter, and processing (called "the beef industry"). We begin with a discussion of the industry's economic traits, followed by information on drivers of change and level of competition in the industry. We then look at key factors of success and overall industry attractiveness.

Economic Traits

Uruguay's beef industry has several dominant economic traits. Uruguay is located between Argentina, the largest beef producer in the area, and Brazil, the largest poultry producer in the area. Uruguay has the world's highest per capita beef consumption at 63.8 kilograms, followed by Argentina (56 kilograms) and the United States (44.8 kilograms).

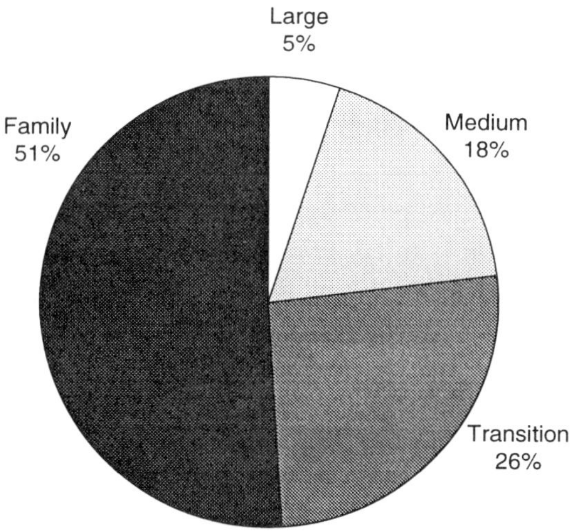

Figure 2. There are four main sizes of farm enterprises in Uruguay (IPA 1998).

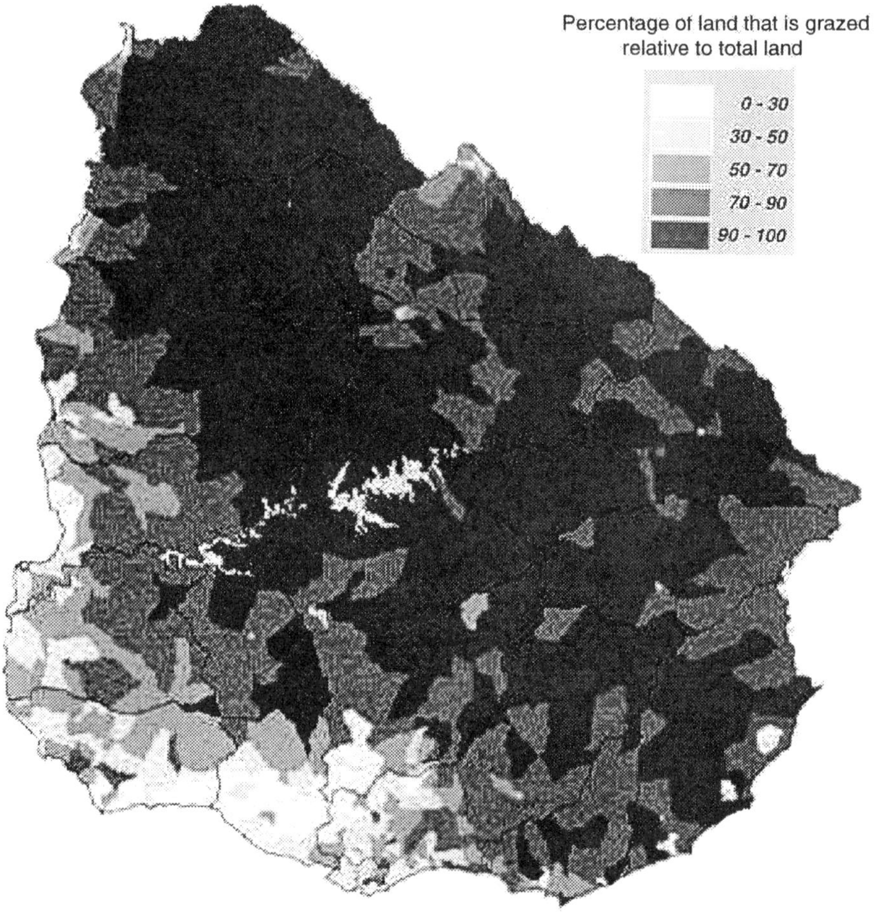

Figure 3. Grazing pasture is divided into five main categories which are expressed as percentage of total land in Uruguay (U.S. CIA 2000).

Per capita beef consumption in Uruguay has remained somewhat stable over the 1980–99 time period. Concurrently, Argentine per capita beef consumption decreased from 71 kilograms in 1990; and Brazilian per capita beef consumption increased from 34.9 kilograms in 1990 to 37.6 kilograms in 1997. Uruguayan per capita poultry consumption increased from 8 kilograms in 1990 to 16 kilograms in 1997. Poultry per capita consumption increased in Brazil and Argentina from 10 kilograms in 1986 to 30 kilograms and 25 kilograms, respectively, in 1998.

In 1994, the price ratio between poultry and beef was 0.92 in Uruguay; this fell to 0.57 in 1998.[1] Overall, meat consumption has increased over time. Figure 4 presents trends in meat consumption over the 1980–99 time period. Because there are no published per capita data (except for beef, as reported by the U.S. Department of Agriculture's Foreign Agricultural Service), we have shown total consumption of beef, chicken, pork, and lamb and mutton using the United Nations Food and Agriculture Organization's most recent data. The majority of beef is consumed in urban markets, while mutton is sold primarily in rural markets. In 1998, total stocks reached a record level of 11 million head of cattle. On average, approximately 1.5 million head of cattle are slaughtered annually, with a record level in 1997 of 2.1 million. The most common breed in Uruguay is a Hereford cross.

Beef production in Uruguay is expanding as a result of improved sanitary conditions due to the complete elimination of FMD in 1995, the decrease in sheep stocks leaving more room for cow-calf operations, the deregulation of the beef industry, and the ability to export live animals to Argentina, which is also due to the elimination of FMD (Figure 5). Uruguayan beef exports grew by approximately 300 percent in volume and 250 percent in value from 1991 to 1998, primarily because of better quality and entrance into new export markets; notwithstanding this growth, Uruguay supplies no more than 4 percent of the total beef traded internationally (Jarvis and Medero 1988). The ability to export to the United States opened other export markets previously closed to the country. Today, approximately 60 percent of beef production is destined for export, and 40 percent for the domestic market; this is a reversal of the historical ratio.

Annual seeding of pastures has increased from approximately 160,000 hectares in 1985 to over 700,000 in 1998. Natural pastures produce approximately 60 kilograms of beef per hectare, compared to seeded pastures that have a production of almost 300 kilograms per hectare. Some of this increase is due to pasture rotations with rice, wheat, grain sorghum, maize, and sunflower production. In addition, sheep stocks have declined from 23 million in 1985 to 15 million in 1998. This decline was a result of a sharp decrease in demand for wool due to the increased production of synthetic fibers. The pasture consumption of five sheep is equivalent to that of one cow.

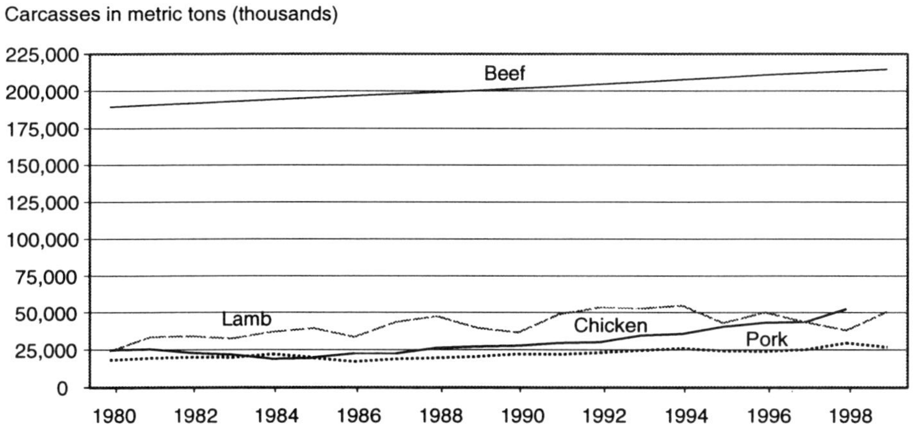

Figure 4. Meat consumption in Uruguay is measured by the number of carcasses processed annually, 1980–99 (FAO).

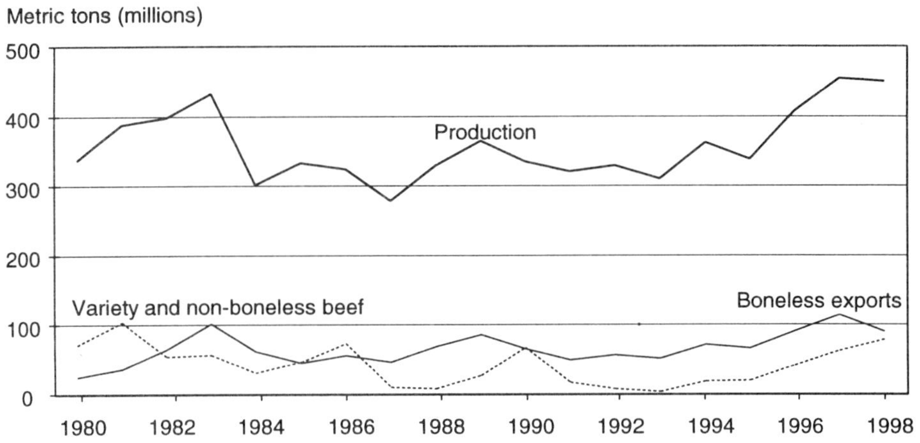

Figure 5. Uruguayan beef production was driven by consumption and exports over 1980–98 (FAO).

The Hilton quota is an import quota established by the EU. The EU gives a total of 55,000 metric tons per year of Hilton quota import permits; Uruguay has only 6,300 metric tons for the whole country, whereas Argentina has 28,000. Beef can still be exported to the EU beyond the 55,000 metric ton limit, but with a tariff of between 85 and 100 percent.

The import permits are given to the Uruguayan government to distribute. Approximately 97.5 percent of the quota is allocated based on a three-year average of exports. The remaining 2.5 percent is used for new entrants that have upgraded to meet EU specifications. The slaughterhouse with the largest amount of quotas is Frigorifico Canelones M. Ameglio S.A., with 850 metric tons per year. Uruguay has 39 major slaughterhouses, 30 of which are authorized to export beef. Only 16 of the 30 authorized export slaughterhouses have been given a portion of the Hilton quota. On average, these 16 plants send between 40 and 80 metric tons of beef per month to the EU, of which 95 percent are rump and loin cuts. Exporting rump and loin cuts under the Hilton quota adds a value of $3,500 per metric ton to the price of the cuts. Uruguay is guaranteed 20,000 metric tons of tariff-free beef imports into the United States. The value of these exports is $2,300 per metric ton.

In some instances, the slaughterhouses are forced to work together to fill export sales that require a large volume. For example, the six firms we interviewed sell to the same Italian baby food company. The slaughterhouses do compete against each other, however, when they sell within MERCOSUR (Mercado Común del Sur—Common Market of the South), North America, and Israel (U.S. CIA 2000). Israel imports most of its beef from Uruguay and has become its most stable and steady buyer. Its main purchase is the forequarter from animals that have been slaughtered according to kosher requirements.

MERCOSUR has been the primary destination of Uruguayan beef. It is in the process of becoming a common market (similar to the EU), where customs barriers in many industries have been reduced or eliminated. MERCOSUR members are Argentina, Brazil, Paraguay, and Uruguay; Chile and Bolivia are associate members. In describing Uruguay's advantages in belonging to MERCOSUR, Ekboir et al. (1998) state:

> Uruguay has a comparative advantage in cattle breeding with respect to Argentina, and could specialize in providing young steers for finishing in Argentina with mutual benefit to both countries. Alternatively, Uruguay could import cheap Argentine grain to establish a feedlot industry aimed at external markets. Uruguay may sell higher priced cuts to FMD-free developed countries and be able to sell lower priced cuts to Brazil, selling its beef for higher prices in both markets.

Plant capacity has not expanded greatly since the mid-1980s, which suggests that there was excess capacity in the Uruguayan slaughtering and processing industry. Excess capacity also likely accounts for the lack of new entrants in this industry due to low profitability. Plants that are not able to sell in export markets are in a weaker financial position.

Labor productivity in slaughterhouses has increased due primarily to reduction of excess labor.[2] Apparently no major technological improvements in grading have occurred, although officials at one plant did mention that they hope to have a new meat grading system in place within two years that will provide a number of carcass measurements which will then be linked to a value-based marketing program for producers. Until fairly recently, animals were priced strictly on live weight. Consequently, carcasses were much heavier, because it was more profitable to continue feeding animals for a longer period of time than to market them at lighter weights. The meat from these older and heavier grass-fed animals was less tender. Many major export markets desire boneless, tender cuts within certain weight categories. The industry has thus begun to provide discounts on heavier animals to induce producers to market younger animals with lighter weight carcasses. In addition, PUL introduced a value-based marketing program based on carcass pricing. The rest of the industry has since moved to carcass pricing, and, last year, almost 70 percent of the animals were priced on carcass weight.

Figure 6 shows changes in the composition of breeding herds since 1980. Despite having about the same number of animals in breeding herds as in 1980, beef production has increased due to better management (an increase from 52 kilograms of beef grazed per hectare in 1992 to 57 kilograms in 1999 and a 7 percent increase in reproductive efficiency). Thus, the discounts are working: production has increased while the number of breeding stock has remained constant and younger animals are being marketed.

Table 1 provides an overview of how the firms we interviewed advertise and promote their beef products. These promotional themes are aimed not only at import brokers but also at hotels, restaurants, and supermarkets in Europe, Asia, and North America. Many of these companies sell their products directly to hotels and restaurants. We obtained copies of all their advertising and promotional materials (brochures, labels, packaging, etc.) and listed how each firm marketed its beef quality attributes. The emphasis the companies put on "natural meat" is more for the benefit of the EU and Asia than for North America, where sanitary conditions are more important. Firms promote their meat as produced with the best breeds in a pollution-free environment or state that their animals are grass-fed and "roaming free," and use the traceability system as a way to differentiate their products from competition from other countries.

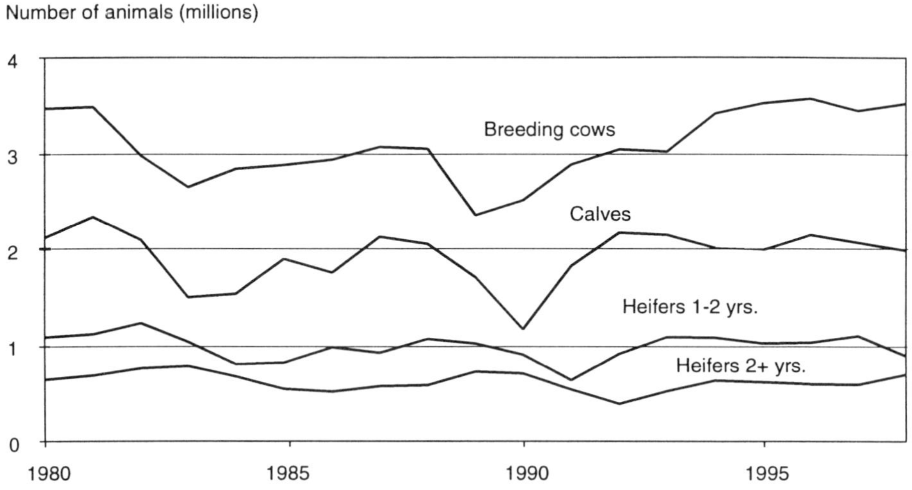

Figure 6. The breeding herd composition in Uruguay is cyclical (IPA 1998).

Table 1. Promotional themes used by different processors to differentiate Uruguayan beef

Processor	Sanitary conditions	Hormone-free	Natural meat	Breed	Environ-ment	Grass-fed	Trace-ability
Canelones			X				
Las Piedras	X						
San Jacinto		X	X	X	X	X	X
PUL	X	X	X		X	X	X
Tacuarembó	X	X	X		X	X	X

Drivers of Change

Drivers of change are variables that are hypothesized to affect industry profitability over the next three to five years. The personal interviews with processors showed some widespread consensus about these variables:

- Increased regulations on traceability and food safety that will continue to be demanded in export markets and, to a much lesser extent, in domestic markets;
- Increased consolidation of farms and ranches that likely will result in several feedlots being developed to help increase weight gain in young steers to meet the demand for tender beef and continued movement toward a value-based marketing program (hormone use will still be prohibited);
- Possible development of more branded beef products due to the opening of the country's first hypermarket, operated by a French multinational supermarket company (San Jacinto has recently developed a branded product in a retail supermarket chain);

- Increased promotion of the "natural beef" (no synthetic growth hormones, pastoral grazing systems, family farm operations) label for exported beef (if feedlot use increases, the promotion will have to shift to emphasize natural beef as beef bred without growth hormones instead of pastoral grazing or family farm size);
- Some investment by firms from Argentina and the United States in beef slaughter and processing plants through joint ventures or acquisitions (an Argentine firm recently bought a Uruguayan plant, and McDonald's has a venture with several plants for frozen hamburger patties);
- Increased exports due to the success of the MERCOSUR trading bloc; and
- Increased educational programs by processors to provide information to producers about domestic and international trends (these programs utilize Instituto Nacional de Investigación Agropécuaria staff).

Industry Competition

The Five Forces model of Porter (1980) suggests the following about competition between beef slaughter and processing plants:

- Weak to medium barriers to entry due to excess capacity;
- Strong market power exhibited by countries that import beef (increased demand for beef produced under some type of traceability system);
- Presence of strong substitutes (increased economic incentives in export markets will likely increase the price of domestic beef, which will likely increase domestic chicken consumption);
- Weak suppliers (producers) due to large numbers and large beef supply; and
- Firms compete on price, but there is an increased movement toward a value-based marketing program as evidenced by the carcass pricing system.

Key Success Factors

Based on the preceding discussion, there are several key success factors that would enable a firm to compete profitably in this industry. First, plants will likely increase their use of price-related economic incentives to coordinate production with producers (e.g., a grid pricing system with incentives based on carcass weight, muscling, or some other quality features; incentives for adoption of a cattle passport system). Second, increasing capacity utilization reduces a plant's average costs. Higher utilization would require a firm to increase exports or domestic market share through development of a relationship with a domestic retailer. Third, continued improvement in a plant's sanitation and production practices helps enhance its reputation for quality. Fourth, marketing and production contracts also help ensure a plant's ability to provide quality products all year. Finally, continued improvement of the traceability system contributes to success.

Overall Industry Attractiveness

This industry will continue to be attractive because of growing export markets including MERCOSUR countries, the ability to take advantage of natural beef production if the

EU continues to ban the use of growth hormones, and continued coordination with producers on traceability and value-based marketing.

HOW SUCCESSFUL ARE URUGUAYAN BEEF EXPORT FIRMS?

With the cooperation of the U.S. Meat Export Federation and the Royal Agricultural College, we developed a database of beef importers and wholesalers in the EU. Forty meat brokers that import beef from various countries into the EU were contacted by fax to determine which were active importers of Uruguayan beef. The faxed form allowed them to check off appropriate boxes and fax it back to us. Of the 32 brokers that responded (we had to fax some more than once), 16 had imported beef from Uruguay within the past three years. Twelve agreed to be interviewed over the telephone; the average interview length was about 30 minutes. The other four were too busy or not interested in helping us. The general results regarding how the brokers viewed Uruguayan beef are presented in Figure 7.

The brokers were quite complimentary about Uruguay and its beef products. When asked which country probably had the highest reputation (i.e., name recognition) among its buyers, Argentina was cited most often. However, almost all the brokers indicated that they saw very little difference between the two countries. The "natural beef" (that lacking synthetic growth hormones) was ranked as the most important attribute. They indicated that most EU plants couldn't meet the proposed traceability standard, so they did not see it affecting their business soon. The following comments stood out with respect to Uruguayan beef:

- The beef is high quality.
- Hotels and restaurants are primary retail markets.
- Several Italian baby food manufacturers are major customers.
- Argentina's traceability system (date of slaughter and lot number) is more effective than the Uruguayan approach.
- Because of its small volume, Uruguay cannot ship large containers at once, as can Argentina; this limits its markets.

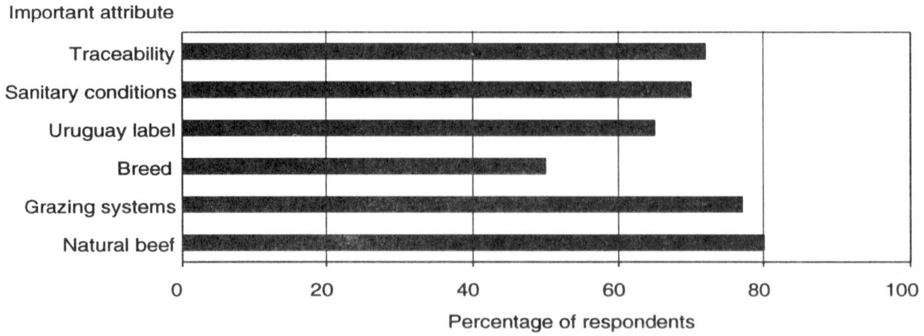

Figure 7. EU meat brokers have favorable attitudes about Uruguayan beef.

The ability to have a traceability system in place, coupled with no growth hormones and FMD-free status, has helped Uruguayan exports increase in recent years. Clearly, beef firms have responded to concerns over these quality attributes. Given that price and quality matter to the success of Uruguayan firms that are exporting beef, one would expect these firms to use similar promotion methods, which is clearly the case.

Eradication of Foot-and-Mouth Disease

The eradication of foot-and-mouth disease (also called hoof-and-mouth disease) has been important to the Uruguayan beef industry. FMD is a contagious viral disease found in cloven-hoofed animals such as cattle, swine, sheep, and goats. It is present on most continents except for North America and Australia. The disease can spread not only through the movement of infected animals, products, and people, but also by winds carrying the virus over widespread areas.

Cattle are infected mainly by inhalation, although feeding of waste products has also been associated with outbreaks of the disease. It causes a sudden fever and a decrease in milk production, followed by blisters in soft tissue areas such as the mouth and feet. Eventually the blisters burst and expose raw surfaces. Eating becomes difficult, and the soft tissue under the hoof becomes inflamed, laming the animal. Lameness is the predominant sign of FMD. The average incubation period of three to eight days is usually over by the time cattle show any signs of the disease, although recovered cattle can be carriers of the disease for approximately two years. The disease is eradicated through the slaughter of infected animals and vaccination.

Uruguay became free of FMD through the use of vaccination and by putting in place a system called Dicose. This system enabled the government to ensure that all farmers and slaughterhouses were complying with stricter sanitary requirements. A more detailed description of the Dicose system is given in the following section.

Uruguay had its last outbreak of the disease in 1989 and stopped vaccinating cattle in 1994. The United States recognized the declaration of Uruguay as free of FMD in October 1995, allowing Uruguay to begin shipping fresh, chilled, and frozen beef to the United States. In 1997, Japan and South Korea also recognized the International Office of Epizootics's declaration of Uruguay as free of FMD.

Although FMD is not considered to be a public health problem, there is a discrepancy in the price bid for beef from FMD-infected countries and that of countries declared free of the disease (Ekboir et al. 1998). The FMD-free countries are paid a higher price for their beef than those that are not free of the disease. They also have entry into higher processed consumption markets. Uruguay became an FMD-free country and, consequently, received these economic incentives.[3]

Dicose Traceability System

In 1973, the Uruguayan government created a division, today known as Dicose, with the objective of accounting for domestic animal stocks and movements in order to curtail smuggling and help with the eradication of FMD. Dicose required producers to indicate whether an animal had FMD. This system not only helped to eradicate FMD and improve overall sanitary conditions but also to provide animal traceability. Every year, each farmer is required to account for his herd. Farmers are given a code that consists of a region number, a police station number, and a farm number. Every time an animal is moved, bought, or sold, it must be accounted for and accompanied with its paperwork. The system is very similar to having a passport. The police must sign all sale documentation, and copies of the sale go to the seller; the buyer; the Ministry of Livestock, Agriculture, and Fisheries; and the police. The ministry checks all trucks and documentation at each slaughterhouse before unloading. Farmers are audited at random every year.

The Dicose system enables the government to ensure that farmers and slaughterhouses are complying with sanitary requirements. It allows the Ministry of Livestock, Agriculture, and Fisheries to trace any animal thought to have a problem back to its origin. The system has stayed in place because it curtails smuggling, helps improve sanitary conditions through accountability, and provides an excellent traceability system; in fact, Uruguay was one of the first countries in the world to be able to trace animals back to their origin.

Once the animals reach the carcass disassembly stage, however, it is virtually impossible to track each cut because of multiple cutting lines in most plants. An individual cut cannot be traced back to an individual animal, but it can be traced to a specific lot number. It is through this lot number, which includes the code given to the farmer, that animals can be traced to their origin. Some countries, such as Argentina, maintain an inventory number and date of slaughter on each shipment of beef. Today, Uruguay can account for the total number of animals slaughtered in each plant by lot number and the number of animals per lot.

Uruguay and the EU

Traceability

On January 1, 2000, Regulation 830-97 was to go into effect in the EU, which mandated that all beef should be traceable from the table to the producer. This regulation cannot go into effect, however, until all EU nations can comply. The World Trade Organization has established rules that prohibit a country from demanding anything of importers that they cannot comply with themselves. The Dicose system allows the Ministry of Livestock, Agriculture, and Fisheries to trace the beef back to its producer and has enabled Uruguay to be the first country to get its traceability system accepted by the EU. Each of the plants we interviewed indicated that a system that would maintain identity on each animal as it moves through the carcass disassembly stage would be costly to implement in any country and that there are currently no economic incentives for such a system.

Growth Hormones

In 1981, the EU began discussing Directive 81/602, which made the use of growth hormones in beef illegal except for therapeutic purposes. The directive banned the import of animals and the meat of animals that had been produced with growth hormones. This regulation effectively cut off all imports from the United States, Canada, Australia, and New Zealand. Although the European Commission Working Group stated in 1982 that no harm would come to consumers from hormone-treated beef and the Codex Alimentarius Commission supported the findings in 1987, Directive 81/602 went into effect on January 1, 1989 (for a summary of the beef hormone issue, see FAS 2000).

The use of growth hormones is strictly prohibited in Uruguay, which has an extensive pastoral production system. Its cattle are fed on pasture alone, although some supplemental grain-based feed is used. In the United States, however, 90 percent of cattle go through a feedlot system of production. In this type of production, growth hormones are necessary to lower the costs of production. Because Uruguay is too small a country to be able to influence world price, it has focused on selling into a niche market by promoting its natural meat produced without hormones.

CASE STUDY OF PRODUCTORES UNIDOS COOPERATIVA AGRARIA LTDA.

PUL is owned by a group of 260 producers which paid $18,000 each to purchase the plant in 1991 and reorganized it as a producer-owned cooperative. It has five members on its board of directors. The producers bought PUL not as an investment tool that would give them a return above the market rate, but so that they could gain price transparency and decrease the risk of marketing their production. Producers have always felt that they have received less than fair market value for their beef under the carcass weight pricing system. With PUL, they are able to identify exactly how the slaughterhouse arrives at the price they receive. PUL is the only vertically integrated plant in Uruguay, and its capacity is higher than that of most other plants.

PUL is the only plant in the Cerro Largo area, which is the same distance from the Brazilian border as it is from Montevideo. It has a competitive advantage over other plants for exporting to Brazil because it is closest to the Brazilian-Uruguay border. Because of its location, PUL is able to market much of its beef in the large urban city of Porto Alegre, Brazil. It slaughtered approximately 160,000 head in 1999, of which 80 percent came from its own members (Figure 8).

PUL had no trouble finding producers that would sell animals to it because it was a vertically integrated company; it did, however, have a hard time selling its product. It had many problems at first trying to find import brokers and freight forwarders that would work with it. As of 2000, 80 percent of its total sales were for export, including to the EU, Israel, United States, Brazil, and Japan. In 2000, PUL began exporting beef to Korea. Overall, PUL's annual growth rate has averaged 20 percent and is at 30 percent for the first six months of 2000. The annual value of these exports has averaged $40 million in the past three years. The manager indicated that the plant is running at full capacity and that other producers have expressed a desire to purchase stock in PUL.

Value-Based Marketing and Economic Incentives

PUL instituted several new practices in 1991 that were later adopted by the rest of the beef industry. The first was payment by carcass weight rather than live weight. Producers were willing to accept the change in payment method because they owned the plant and therefore received more price transparency. It was interesting to note from the interviews at other plants that many producers outside the cooperative dislike this carcass pricing system. The main reason for their dislike is that the system is less transparent than live pricing. The live pricing system pays the producer solely on the weight of the live animal,

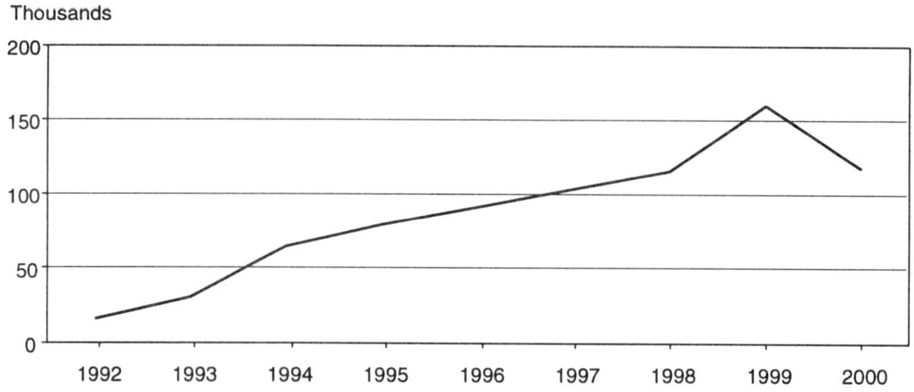

Figure 8. Number of beef carcasses processed by PUL, by year (2000 reflects first six months) (PUL 2000, unpublished data).

while the carcass pricing system rewards and discounts depending on the quality of the beef as related to external fat thickness and carcass weight.

Second, PUL started the practice of slaughtering younger animals. Its management knew that younger animals weighing from 420 to 430 kilos were worth more than heavy older ones because they had more valuable and tender rump and loin meat (Jarvis 1974). The use of economic incentives to increase the animal's marginal value enabled producers to bring in lighter animals. The plant receives incentives from export markets for lighter carcasses and primal cuts.

Third, PUL developed a "slotting system" to smooth out cattle marketing. By providing economic incentives to producers to market their cattle at various times during the year (called "slotting" in the United States), PUL has been able to smooth out the annual cycle of cattle marketing. November through April is the time when most producers bring their cattle to market due to the breeding cycle of a pasture system.

Fourth, PUL's vertically integrated structure helped it manage supply. Because most Uruguayan ranchers market their animals to more than one plant depending upon the time of year, weight of animals, and price (different plants have different carcass weight requirements), beef slaughter and processing firms have made attempts to enter into supply agreements (exports did not become a large factor until the past several years). PUL's vertically integrated structure and value-based marketing program have allowed it to become a low-cost leader in the industry.

More Sophisticated Traceability

In the late 1990s, PUL began development of a traceability program that would be more sophisticated than Dicose. The producer-owners knew that they could help develop such a system—and they had incentives to do so. When cattle come in for slaughtering, they are given a lot number that is associated with the producer. The animal then receives an individual number that follows it throughout the plant until it enters the carcass disassembly line. At this point, the primal cuts are separated according to lot number and boxed for export, and the slaughter date is stamped on the box. This traceability system is more sophisticated than the Argentine system, because it includes producer identity. The meat is not traceable by individual animal, but it is traceable by producer lot. Economic incentives to institute this system came from an Italian baby food company and other firms. PUL sells beef to the Italian company by placing one animal in one or two boxes and providing the producer number.

CONCLUSION

Uruguay has been expanding its beef exports since the government successfully eradicated FMD in 1995. In addition, the acceptance of the Dicose system by the EU and entrance into the U.S. market enabled Uruguay to increase its exports in the late 1990s. However, Uruguay has a small amount of Hilton quota, which affects its ability to supply more beef to the EU. Thus, other countries such as Israel have become important export markets.

A producer-owned cooperative has been able to take advantage of key success factors through the development of a value-based marketing program that provides economic incentives to producers to control supply (in terms of carcass weight, timing of marketing, volume, etc.); improves traceability efforts; and increases volume to help reduce the plant's average costs. Uruguay's beef industry will remain attractive for investors because of growing export markets including MERCOSUR countries, an ability to take advantage of "natural beef" production if the EU continues to ban the use of growth hormones, and continued coordination with producers on traceability and value-based marketing.

NOTES

1. Unpublished data from the Instituto Nacional de Estadìsticas (INE).
2. Unpublished data from INE.
3. After this chapter was completed, an outbreak of FMD occurred in October 2000 near the Brazilian-Uruguayan border and Uruguay's FMD-free status was set aside for 90 days until January 2001. If no new animals are found with FMD, Uruguay will be able to continue to export beef.

REFERENCES

Ekboir, J., Jarvis, L. S., Sumner, D. A., and Sutton, W. R., 1998, Changing World Beef Markets: Implications for Low Income Countries, unpublished report, University of California, Davis.

Food and Agriculture Organization (FAO), 1980–1998, *FAOSTAT: Trade Yearbook*, Rome.

Foreign Agricultural Service (FAS), U.S. Department of Agriculture, 2000, The U.S. – EU Hormone Dispute, http://www.fas.usda.gov/itp/policy/hormone.html (accessed Apr. 28, 2001).

Instituto Nacional de Investigación Agropécuaria (INIA), 1998, Producción de Carne de Calidad Para Distintos Mercados de Exportación, unpublished study, Montevideo, Uruguay.

Instituto Plan Agropecuario (IPA), 1998, La Importancia de la Integración en la Cadena Cárnica, unpublished report, Montevideo, Uruguay.

Jarvis, L. S., 1974, Cattle as capital goods and ranchers as portfolio managers: An application to the Argentine cattle sector, *J Polit Econ* **82**(3):489–520.

Jarvis, L. S., and Medero, M. d. R., 1988, The Effect of External Constraints When Policy Making Is Endogenous: Beef Export Taxes, Exchange Rates, and Other Policy-Induced Distortions in Uruguay, 1961–1986, unpublished report, University of California, Davis.

Porter, M., 1980, *Competitive Strategy*, The Free Press, New York.

U.S. Central Intelligence Agency (U.S. CIA), 2000, *The World Factbook 2000*, http://www.odci.gov/cia/publications/factbook/geos/uy.html (accessed Apr. 28, 2001).

SECTION III

SPECIFIC ISSUES AND METHODOLOGICAL CHALLENGES

PRODUCT DIFFERENTIATION, SANITARY BARRIERS, AND ARBITRAGE IN WORLD POULTRY MARKETS

David Orden, Timothy Josling, and Donna Roberts*

World poultry markets are one of the most rapidly growing sectors of the food industry. Poultry production rose from 11 million tons in 1965 to over 63 million tons in 1999. Consumption increases have exceeded population growth, with world per capita supplies of poultry meat tripling from 3.3 kilograms in 1965 to 9.9 kilograms in 1997. International trade has more than kept pace with this industry growth. World exports of poultry meat rose from 375,000 tons in 1965 to 6.4 million tons in 1999. Trade now accounts for about 10 percent of world consumption.

The objective of this chapter is to evaluate the effects of sanitary barriers to trade related to avian and human health in the context of the broader set of economic factors and policy decisions that determine product flows in international poultry markets. Poultry flocks are susceptible to diseases that can spread domestically and across borders. Microbial contamination of poultry for human consumption is also a serious problem in the sector, as with other meats, and is addressed by health regulations in exporting and importing countries. In addition, intensive poultry production can cause local environmental problems through pollution of groundwater, and the conditions under which chickens are kept have been subject to criticism from health and animal-welfare advocates. Thus, poultry markets are subject to a complex mix of national and trade regulations, together with traditional (nontechnical) tariff and nontariff barriers. The 1995 Uruguay Round Agreements on Agriculture and on the Application of Sanitary and Phytosanitary (SPS) Mea-

---

* David Orden is a professor in the Department of Agricultural and Applied Economics at Virginia Tech; Timothy Josling is a professor in Stanford University's Institute for International Studies; Donna Roberts is a senior economist with the Economic Research Service of the U.S. Department of Agriculture. The views expressed in this chapter are not to be attributed to any of the institutions with which the authors are affiliated. We thank Mark Gehlhar of the Economic Research Service for data access and advice and Dale Colyer for comments on the draft chapter.

Global Food Trade and Consumer Demand for Quality, edited by Krissoff *et al.*
Kluwer Academic/Plenum Publishers, New York, 2002.

sures have, to some extent, affected this mix, reducing or freezing levels of producer support while tightening the rules for sanitary measures.

To evaluate some of the policy effects on world poultry trade, an equilibrium model is constructed that simulates the trade flows among six key exporting and importing countries and two aggregate rest-of-world regions. Removal or modification of restrictions based on tariffs, tariff-rate quotas (TRQs), or sanitary regulations can potentially alter trade flows. For sanitary barriers, this does not necessarily imply that such regulations are unnecessary or protectionist in intent. Fuller evaluations of the impact of alternative sanitary regulations and the consequences of their modification are needed to complete judgments about whether a particular regulatory barrier is an efficient and effective way of controlling health risks. But the first steps in this process are to catalog those regulations that are in place and to identify their trade impacts.

A challenge faced in modeling global poultry trade is to choose a set of countries, products, trade barriers, and health regulations that encapsulates the essential features of the market but does not impose an unrealistic data requirement. We focus on six countries that account for the bulk of world production, consumption, and trade. The countries chosen include two of the largest exporters—the United States and Brazil—two of the most significant importers—Japan and Russia—and two countries that are both exporters and importers—China (including Hong Kong) and the European Union (EU).[1] The problem of the wide range of traded poultry products is simplified by focusing on one particular product grouping, poultry cuts and offals (other than liver) (Standard Industrial Trade Classification—SITC—code 01235), which accounts for nearly 70 percent of total world poultry trade value. Even within this category there is considerable heterogeneity. We model trade outcomes maintaining a distinction between "high-value" poultry products, going into Japan and the EU and elsewhere, and "low-value" poultry products, which are imported primarily into China, Russia, and other countries. The high-value trade includes primarily white meat (breasts and wings) of chicken and turkey together with de-boned meat and specialty items. The low-value trade includes mainly dark meat (drumsticks and thighs) of chicken and turkey. White and dark meat are produced in essentially fixed proportions.

The chapter is organized as follows. The next section provides a market and policy overview focused on the six countries chosen for our analysis. Production, consumption, and trade of poultry are summarized and nontechnical and technical trade barriers discussed. The empirical model of poultry trade is presented in the following section. The bilateral trade flows in high-value and low-value poultry products are described in some depth, a base model developed, and results presented for several counterfactual policy simulations. Among nontechnical barriers, we find that TRQs imposed on high-value poultry products by the EU result in somewhat lower world prices and trade than would prevail in their absence. Among sanitary regulations, we derive the result that there are often sufficient arbitrage possibilities in world markets for low-value and high-value products to mitigate an imposition of bilateral sanitary restrictions by one or more importers. We examine the effects of a hypothetical sanitary barrier by Russia against low-value U.S. poultry exports, and of an increase in the technical barriers imposed against high-value exports from Brazil. We find that the direction of impact on various importers and other exporters depends on how widespread such restrictions are assumed to become. Our conclusions about the importance of product differentiation and arbitrage opportunities in evaluating policy effects in world poultry markets are presented at the end of the chapter.

MARKET AND POLICY OVERVIEW

The dramatic growth in the poultry sector during the past 35 years is both demand- and supply-driven.[2] Income and price elasticities of demand for poultry are relatively high compared to those for other foodstuffs. Tastes have also shifted over time, as health considerations have contributed to a switch away from red meats in the developed world. Consumers in developing countries have responded to the ready availability of chicken, which offers an affordable form of animal protein to supplement a diet of cereals, beans, or root crops. The combination of these factors has led to a significant increase in demand both in those countries that are growing rapidly and in more mature economies. As a result, poultry's share of total world meat consumption rose from 20 percent in 1985 to 28 percent in 1998 and now exceeds that of beef.

Supply growth has accommodated the expansion in poultry consumption. There have been rapid changes in the method of poultry meat production, allowing real prices to decline relative to those for red meats. The production structure in the United States, Europe, Brazil, and Thailand—as well as in many other areas—has become highly concentrated, with a few large firms producing a high proportion of the poultry for a particular market. Traditional small-scale poultry production still exists side by side with modern industry in developing countries, but it has largely disappeared in industrial countries.

Basic statistics for the poultry sectors of the six countries on which this study focuses are shown in Table 1. World production of poultry, converted to a "ready-to-cook" equivalent, is about 53 million tons. The United States is the largest producer (15.1 million tons), followed by China (11.0 million tons) and the EU (8.4 million tons). Brazil and Japan also have substantial production, as do Thailand, South Africa, and Mexico (not included in the table). The same countries dominate consumption, since the bulk of poultry production is still consumed domestically despite the growing importance of trade. China (1.1 million tons), Russia (891,000 tons), and Japan (507,000 tons) are the largest import markets; the EU (mainly Germany) also purchases substantial quantities of poultry products. Mexico, Saudi Arabia, and the United Arab Emirates are major importers among those countries not shown in Table 1. The United States (2.5 million tons) dominates the exporters, while the EU (919,000 tons, mostly from France and the Netherlands), Brazil (628,000 tons),

Table 1. Basic statistics on the poultry sector in six countries, 1998

	Production	Consumption	Imports	Exports
	(thousand tons, ready-to-consume equivalent)			
Brazil	4,597	3,969	0	628
China (inc. Hong Kong)	10,978	11,762	1,118	366
EU-15	8,375	7,588	268	919
Japan	1,190	1,697	507	3
Russia	640	1,516	891	15
United States	15,131	12,623	2	2,514
Other countries (key markets)	12,148	11,925	1,737	1,233
Total	53,059	51,060	4,523	5,678

Note: EU figures exclude intra-EU trade. Hong Kong sales to China have been subtracted from China's trade to avoid double-counting.

Source: Commodity and Marketing Programs, Foreign Agricultural Service, U.S. Department of Agriculture.

and China (366,000 tons) have substantial export shares. Thailand and Hungary (not shown) are also major exporters, and exports from Canada have risen in recent years. The six countries shown in Table 1 account for 77 percent of world poultry production and similar shares of consumption and exports. Poultry imports are somewhat less concentrated: the six countries account for 62 percent of world imports.

International trade flows reflect policy decisions as well as consumer tastes and comparative advantage in production. Access to the markets of most of the major importing countries tends to be over tariffs that are typically 10 to 30 percent. This is high enough to keep internal prices above world market levels but not to discourage trade altogether. The different trade regimes of the six countries are shown in Table 2. The Japanese import market is relatively open, with modest tariffs; China and Russia maintain state trading structures and higher tariffs, which they have agreed to lower when they are admitted to the World Trade Organization (WTO). The EU retains protective TRQs and high over-quota tariffs, while Brazil and the United States have tariffs only.

Table 2. Summary of the trade regimes of the six countries

Country	Trade regime
Brazil	Tariffs bound in the WTO at 35 percent on all poultry products. Poultry included in free trade agreement with Argentina and other MERCOSUR members.
China	Tariffs of 45 percent will be reduced to 20 percent under U.S.-China Agreement if China joins the WTO, with further reduction to 10 percent by 2004.
EU	Tariff of 299 ECU per metric ton on whole chicken and 358 ECU per metric ton on parts (18 to 60 percent ad valorem); TRQs established with quantities allocated to Brazil and to Central and Eastern Europe. Export subsidies constrained under the WTO, used for lower value exports to Russia.
Japan	Tariffs of 11.9 percent on whole chicken and 8.5 percent on parts; no TRQs.
Russia	Tariffs of 30 percent on chicken and 15 percent on turkey; tariffs could be reduced on eventual WTO membership to 10 percent over 10 years. Trade agreement with EU gives no special access to European imports. Restrictions on transshipment through Baltic countries have been announced.
United States	Tariffs bound at 8.8 cents per kilogram for whole chicken and 17.6 cents per kilogram for parts (18 to 36 percent ad valorem). Poultry eligible for Export Enhancement Program payments (about $650 per ton).

Sources: U.S. International Trade Commission, U.S. Department of Agriculture, and WTO schedules.

International poultry trade is also affected by avian health problems, which are widespread and generally contained by strict regulations domestically and at international borders. The International Office of Epizootics (OIE) has designated two infectious avian diseases—exotic Newcastle disease (END) and highly pathogenic avian influenza (HPAI)—on its List A of those that have the potential for very serious and rapid spread, irrespective of national borders, which are of serious socioeconomic or public health consequence. Both END and HPAI pose significant threats to poultry production. International coordination of the response to outbreaks of these diseases attempts to inhibit the spread of infections across borders and to promote energetic eradication measures by exporters. Bans on poultry exports from a country or region afflicted with either of these two diseases by a country free of them have rarely been questioned.[3] Vaccination and/or mandatory process controls are generally regarded as sufficient safeguards against 10 other poultry diseases included on OIE's List B of those less harmful which are considered to be of socioeconomic and/or public health importance within countries. Control of these diseases adds to costs but does not necessarily preclude international trade.

Potential hazards to human health from poultry consumption are also of concern both within countries and with respect to trade. Consumer health issues include pathogens (e.g., bacteria, fungi, parasites, and viruses); zoonoses; environmental toxins such as persistent organic pollutants (e.g., dioxin) and metals (e.g., mercury and lead); and animal husbandry practices such as adding low levels of antibiotics to animal feed and the use of veterinary drugs (WHO 2000). The most significant foodborne pathogens associated with poultry products are bacteria—particularly, *Salmonella enteriditis*, *Campylobacter jejuni*, *Staphylococcus aureus*, and *Listeria monocytogenes* (FSIS 1995).

International harmonization of sanitary regulations related to food safety measures is coordinated by the Codex Alimentarius Commission. Relevant Codex texts include guidelines, recommended practices, and maximum levels for residues that specifically reference poultry products, as well as "horizontal" texts that span commodity categories. An example of the latter includes the General Principles of Food Hygiene which (among other things) establishes a template for a system of process controls (Hazard Analysis and Critical Control Points, or HACCP) to minimize contamination by foodborne pathogens. Other relevant texts describe general regulatory procedures for import/export inspection, certification, laboratory accreditation, and other processes that can affect poultry trade.

Nearly 10 percent (131 of 1,405) of all notifications of SPS regulatory decisions affecting trade that were submitted by member countries to the WTO in the first five years under the mandate of the SPS Agreement referenced measures addressing poultry products. In some cases, regulations were being rewritten in recognition of the fact that national standards had been developed without an explicit assessment of meat (rather than live animals) as an avian disease vector. To comply with new multilateral obligations, regulations were also modified to allow imports from regions *within* an exporting country, if animal health authorities could verify that the area was either free or nearly free of quarantine diseases. In other cases, food safety regulations were being changed, largely attributed to shifts from an emphasis on ante- and post-mortem inspection to HACCP systems.

Divergent sanitary measures among countries can be a serious impediment to trade for poultry and other animal products. Widespread adoption of international standards can therefore yield large benefits to exporters. Importers may benefit as well if the elimination of regulatory heterogeneity lowers prices and expands product choice while maintaining an appropriate level of protection for animal and human health. Yet international harmonization of poultry regulations appears to be infrequent, despite its potential advantages. Nearly two-thirds of the SPS notifications on poultry have indicated that an international standard did not exist for the measure(s) at issue. Given the absence of international standards for traded poultry products, it is not surprising that a number of disputes over different SPS policy regimes have emerged in this sector. During the first five years of the SPS Agreement, 10 of the 124 total "cross notifications" (complaints) raised within the WTO SPS Committee referenced poultry products (see Table 3).

Table 3. Complaints against poultry measures raised in the WTO SPS Committee, 1995–99

Respondent	Complaint	Complainant	Additional complainants	Date raised
United States	The United States does not yet recognize Argentina's claim that it is free of Newcastle disease, and therefore prohibits imports	Argentina		Jul 99
Australia	Australia's time/temperature regime to prevent the introduction of infectious bursal disease precludes imports of raw poultry meat	Thailand	European Community	Sept 98
Czech Republic	A maximum residue level of 0.1 parts per million for arsenic is not scientifically justified and effectively embargoes Thai exports to Czech Republic	Thailand		Sept 98
Switzerland	Proposed Swiss regulations that restrict the importation of meat from animals and poultry fed with hormones, antibiotics, and similar agents as growth promoters are unscientific because they are not based on a risk assessment and apply only to meat imported under Swiss TRQs (i.e., the regulations do not apply to over-quota meat imports)	United States	Australia, Canada, Israel, Hungary, Chile, Brazil, India, and New Zealand	Sept 98
Korea	Requirement that all imported poultry meat (including meat intended for further processing) of *Listeria monocytogenes* disregards the recommendations of the International Commission on Microbiological Specification for Foods	Thailand		Mar 98 be free
United States[a]	Poultry imports from European Community were suspended without specifying grounds upon which its poultry suddenly became ineligible for entry into the United States	European Community		Aug 97

The avian and human health issues associated with poultry trade have led, in some cases, to sharp segregation by country of origin by importers and potential importers among suppliers and potential suppliers. The United States, for example, has strict rules on which countries can export poultry products to its market. Only 13 countries are deemed by the U.S. Department of Agriculture (USDA) to be free of END, and only five countries are considered to meet HACCP requirements for poultry products. Only two countries, Canada and Great Britain, in addition to one region in northwestern Mexico, satisfy all USDA criteria for gaining access to the U.S. poultry market.[4]

The pattern of sanitary barriers on poultry trade among the six countries in our model is shown in Table 4. It might be expected that these countries would divide sharply into one group whose members mutually recognize each other as meeting adequate sanitary standards, and a group not recognized as meeting these standards, and that trade would occur within each group but not across the group boundary. This is not the case, however. Two importers, Japan and Russia, accept imports from all four exporters, the United States, Brazil, the EU, and China. Imports from the three other exporters are allowed by China as well, but given recurrent domestic outbreaks of Newcastle disease, China has not objected to restrictions on its exports by the United States, Brazil, and the EU.

Table 3. (continued)

Respondent	Complaint	Complainant	Additional complainants	Date raised
Venezuela	U.S. poultry was unjustifiably banned in 1993 because of the outbreak of nonpathogenic avian influenza in some backyard flocks and markets in the northeastern United States	United States		Jul 97
Honduras	"Zero-tolerance" standards for *Salmonella* in imported poultry meat exceed requirements for domestic meat	United States		Oct 96
Slovak Republic	"Zero-tolerance" standards for *Salmonella* in imported poultry meat exceed requirements for domestic meat	United States		Oct 96
El Salvador	"Zero-tolerance" standards for *Salmonella* in imported poultry meat exceed requirements for domestic meat	United States		Oct 96
Czech Republic	"Zero-tolerance" standards for *Salmonella* in imported poultry meat exceed requirements for domestic meat	United States		Oct 96
Chile	"Zero-tolerance" standards for *Salmonella* in imported poultry meat exceed requirements for domestic meat	United States		Oct 96

[a]The European Community's complaint against the U.S. measure is the only one that materialized as a request for formal consultations under the terms of the Dispute Settlement Understanding, rather than in the SPS Committee. Technically, the matter is still pending, as the parties have not notified the WTO that they have reached a mutually acceptable agreement; but, as a practical matter, the United States has withdrawn the restrictions and the European Community is now allowed to export poultry meat to the United States.
Sources: WTO (1997) and WTO (1995–2000).

Sanitary barriers on poultry meat exports from the United States to Russia were subject to a high-profile dispute that erupted in 1996, when an embargo on U.S. products threatened $600 million in annual sales (see Ames 1998 and Kahrs 1996). This dispute raised awareness of the potential for SPS measures to disrupt agricultural markets. A March 1996 agreement resolving the dispute included requirements on U.S. products for more systematic disease certification, *Salmonella* and residue standards, and a detailed regime for plant inspections. A side agreement required the U.S. poultry industry to convert a failed Russian poultry operation into a state-of-the-art production facility. Subsequent to these agreements, U.S. shipments to Russia quickly resumed.

Table 4. Poultry trade or potential trade allowed by bilateral SPS barriers

	Importers					
Exporter	United States	Brazil	EU	China	Japan	Russia
United States	—	No	No	Yes	Yes	Yes
Brazil	No	—	Yes	Yes	Yes	Yes
EU	Yes	Yes	—	Yes	Yes	Yes
China	No	No	No	—	Yes	Yes

There are several other sanitary restrictions on poultry trade among the six countries, in addition to the barriers faced by China mentioned above. The other three principal poultry exporters (the United States, Brazil, and the EU) impose restrictions *among themselves*. New food safety measures adopted in 1997 prompted the EU to shut off poultry imports from the United States (totaling about $50 million annually). The United States and Brazil have animal and human health restrictions in place that preclude any potential trade between the two countries. Intermittent outbreaks of poultry diseases in Brazil suggest that at best only certain regions could export to the United States, pending a thorough review by U.S. authorities, but so far no trade has been allowed. Regulators in the United States and Brazil also have each determined that the other's inspection system for poultry processing plants is not equivalent to its own, thwarting the possibility for trade in poultry parts between the two countries.

The pattern of sanitary trade barriers maintained on poultry by the six countries suggests that there are several differences in regulatory assessments about whether trade should be prohibited based on avian diseases. The EU, for example, does not block imports from Brazil because of END, while the United States does. Foodborne illness considerations further complicate the patterns of allowed trade, as in the case of the EU barrier against imports from the United States but, again, not Brazil. Both the sanitary barriers that are imposed and those that might be expected but are not enforced have implications for the flow of poultry products in world markets, and for how well world markets are able to arbitrage price differentials among subsets of countries that do not trade among themselves. It is interesting to note that Japan, which is widely viewed as highly protective of its domestic agriculture and very sensitive to sanitary and phytosanitary considerations, imports poultry products at low tariffs from a diverse set of countries including the United States, the EU, Brazil, and China, and thus may play an important arbitrage role in world poultry trade.

MODELS OF POULTRY TRADE

The United Nations trade database provides information on values and quantities for bilateral trade flows on a global basis. For poultry, the United Nations data distinguish among six SITC codes at the five-digit level. These SITC categories separate poultry (meat and edible offal of poultry fresh, chilled or frozen) among whole birds, cuts, and livers, and between fresh or chilled versus frozen, but do not provide a full characterization of traded products.[5] The dominant category of poultry trade is poultry cuts and offal (other than livers) frozen, SITC code 01235, accounting for 68.1 percent of world poultry trade (excluding intra-EU trade).

The values and quantities of bilateral trade flows for SITC code 01235 products in 1998 among the United States, Brazil, the EU, China, Japan, Russia, and aggregated groups of "all others" exporters and importers are shown in Tables 5 and 6, along with subtotals for the six specified countries and world totals. In value terms, the five exporters shown individually in Table 5 account for 80.1 percent ($2,913.5 million of $3,635.5 million) of the world's total exports of frozen poultry parts; and these five countries plus Russia account for 68.4 percent of world imports ($2,485.6 million of $3,635.5 million). The United States alone accounts for 42.2 percent ($1,536.2 million) of exports; while Brazil, the EU, and China have world market shares between 10 and 15 percent. Japan is the single largest importer on a value basis (23.2 percent of the world total), but China and Russia each import nearly twice as large a quantity of poultry products.

Among the exporting countries, the percentage of export value going to the six importers identified in Table 5 ranges from 48.8 percent ($241.2 million of $493.7 million) for the EU, to 100 percent for the very small value of exports by Japan ($8.5 million). The

Table 5. Value of 1998 world poultry trade, SITC code 01235: million dollars

	Importers									
								All others		
Exporter	U.S.	Brazil	EU	China	Japan	Russia	Subtotal	High value	Low value	Total
U.S.	—	0	0	317.6	84.6	490.6	892.8	5.6	637.8	1,536.2
Brazil	0	—	108.3	97.2	129.3	1.4	336.2	85.7	3.0	424.9
EU	0.1	0.1	—	130.9	7.2	102.9	241.2	0.3	252.2	493.7
China	0	0	0.2	—	365.9	0.5	366.6	83.6	0	450.2
Japan	0	0	0	8.5	—	0	8.5	0	0	8.5
Subtotal	0.1	0.1	108.5	554.2	587.0	595.4	1,845.3	175.2	893.0	2,913.5
All others										
High value	2.8	2.1	209.9	0	257.1	0	471.9	81.7[a]		722.0
Low value	0	0	59.3	100.6	0	8.5	168.4			
Total	2.9	2.2	377.7	654.8	844.1	603.9	2,485.6	1,149.9		3,635.5

[a]Data not tabulated to differentiate between high-value and low-value trade among unspecified countries in the categories of "all others" exporters and importers.
Source: International Bilateral Agricultural Trade Database, Economic Research Service, USDA, developed from United Nations Conference on Trade and Development bilateral SITC trade data.

Table 6. Quantities of 1998 world poultry trade, SITC code 01235: thousand metric tons

	Importers									
								All others		
Exporter	U.S.	Brazil	EU	China	Japan	Russia	Subtotal	High value	Low value	Total
U.S.	—	0	0.2	490.6	76.1	682.6	1,249.5	3.6	788.6	2,041.7
Brazil	0	—	43.2	135.5	66.6	2.6	247.9	48.3	6.3	302.5
EU	0.0	0.2	—	138.9	2.1	144.5	285.7	0.2	355.2	641.1
China	0	0	0.1	—	193.7	0.5	194.3	53.5	0	247.8
Japan	0	0	0	9.2	—	0	9.2	0	0	9.2
Subtotal	0.0	0.2	43.5	774.2	338.5	830.2	1,986.6	105.6	1,150.1	3,242.3
All others										
High value	1.3	1.1	64.3	0	124.8	0	191.5	38.3[a]		428.4
Low value	0	0	63.0	126.0	0	9.6	198.6			
Total	1.3	1.3	170.8	900.2	463.3	839.8	2,376.7	1,294.0		3,670.7

[a]Data not tabulated to differentiate between high-value and low-value trade among unspecified countries in the categories of "all others" exporters and importers.
Source: International Bilateral Agricultural Trade Database, Economic Research Service, USDA, developed from United Nations Conference on Trade and Development bilateral SITC trade data.

percentage of imports coming from the identified exporters ranges from 3.4 percent for the United States (a very minor importer) to 98.5 percent ($595.4 million of $603.9 million) for Russia. Nearly one-third of U.S. exports ($490.6 million) went to Russia, where the United States has over 80 percent of the import market and competes with the EU, which has most of the remaining market share. Both the United States and the EU also export substantial values of poultry to China (including Hong Kong). Brazil competes with the United States and the EU in the Chinese market and with the United States and China in the Japanese market. Brazil exports to the EU, but not to the United States or Russia. China exports almost exclusively to Japan (among the countries identified individually), where it has a higher market share than the United States and Brazil combined.

The distinction between high-value and low-value world markets for poultry products is apparent from the unit values of the bilateral trades, shown in Table 7. Russia and China import relatively low-value products from all of their sources. The average unit values of poultry imports by Russia and China (computed from import totals in Tables 5 and 6) are $719 per metric ton and $727 per metric ton, respectively. Unit values from its two main sources are very similar for Russia ($719 from the United States and $712 from the EU), with more variation for the small quantities it imports from Brazil, China, and all other countries. Similarly, the United States, Brazil, and the EU compete in the China market, although for China including Hong Kong the unit values of imports show more variability across countries of origin.[6]

In contrast to Russia and China, the EU and Japan import mostly high-value products. EU imports from Brazil and aggregated other exporters (under TRQs) have average unit prices of $2,505 per metric ton and $3,264 per metric ton, respectively. The products imported by Japan from its largest suppliers, Brazil and China and other exporters, have very similar unit values ($1,940 per metric ton, $1,890 per metric ton, and $2,060 per metric ton), which are lower than the unit values of imports by the EU.[7] Imports by Japan from the United States appear to have lower value on average ($1,112 per metric ton) than imports by Japan from Brazil, China, and other countries, while only a small quantity of high-value products are imported by Japan from the EU.

Table 7. Unit values in 1998 world poultry trade, SITC code 01235: dollars per metric ton

	Importers								
							All others		
Exporter	U.S.	Brazil	EU	China	Japan	Russia	High value	Low value	Wtd avg all exports
U.S.	—	—	—	647	1,112	719	1,555	808	752
Brazil	—	—	2,505	717	1,940	558	1,774	476	1,404
EU	—	894	—	936	3,358	712	1,500	710	770
China	—	—	2,400	—	1,890	894	1,563	—	1,816
Japan	—	—	—	924	—	—	—	—	923
All others									
High value	2,154	1,909	3,264	—	2,060	—	2,133		
Low value	—	—	936	798	—	885			
Wtd avg all imports	2,230	1,692	2,211	727	1,822	719			

— implies no trade or negligible quantities traded
Source: Authors' calculations from SITC value and quantity data.

For exporters, the pattern of trade that emerges is of the United States exporting mostly low-value products (averaging $752 per metric ton), and Brazil exporting mostly high-value products with some low-value products to China. EU export revenue from low-value products to Russia is about the same as its cost of imports of high-value products from Brazil. The EU is a net exporter in value terms, and, with mostly low-value exported products and high-value imports, it is a larger net exporter in quantity. China exports high-value products to Japan and various other countries. The world average unit value for high-value trade (computed from Tables 5 and 6 but not reported in Table 7) is $1,986 per metric ton, compared to an average unit value for low-value trade of $749 per metric ton. Thus, maintaining a distinction between the high- and low-value poultry markets conveys an important characteristic of world trade. Even though there is also substantial heterogeneity within each of the distinct high-value and low-value markets, price competition within each market seems evident in the aggregate data.[8]

To model poultry trade, we adopt the traditional spatial equilibrium framework with a specific empirical focus on product differentiation, sanitary barriers, and price arbitrage among countries that may not trade directly. Most previous models of the economic effects of technical barriers to trade have examined bans that preclude product movement across a single border (e.g., Orden and Romano 1996, Calvin and Krissoff 1998). Since no other trade opportunities are taken into account in these models, a bilateral ban forces prices in the importing country to an autarky level, with no limit on the extent to which the importer and exporter prices differ once the ban is in place. In contrast, in a model with multiple countries, trade "deflection" may occur when a ban precludes entry of a product from one exporter but leads to entry of that product from another country. A severe measure such as a ban may *look* to be not least trade distorting, in violation of WTO obligations. But well-arbitraged markets may imply that no trade would take place in equilibrium even without the ban or that alternative trade patterns might emerge with the ban, so the restrictive policy may not actually impede trade.[9]

The empirical model of poultry trade incorporates several basic simplifications. First, domestic supplies and demands are represented only by excess supply or excess demand functions for high-value or low-value products, centered on the observed traded quantities. Second, we utilize a linear specification in which each function (excess supply or demand) for a high- or low-value product is dependent only on the price of that product (own price), even though poultry products are jointly produced and there also may be cross-price effects in demand. In considering the effects of trade policies and alternative sanitary regulations, we utilize two sets of values for the elasticities of excess supply and demand: inelastic values (0.75, –0.75, respectively) that may be interpreted as short-run responses, and more elastic values (7.5 and –7.5, respectively) that are more representative of the long run.[10]

A third simplification is that, having distinguished between high-value and low-value poultry markets based on observed unit values of bilateral trades, the products traded within each market are treated as perfect substitutes. We center the model on representative prices for each of the quality types, and therefore assume—with one exception—that the price differences shown in Table 7 represent different product mixes at a more refined level than we model, not the effects of trade policies. More specifically, for low-value products, we take $720 per metric ton as a representative price and do not consider the effects of non-technical trade barriers among the countries in our model. For high-value products, we take $1,940 per metric ton as a representative price. The one exception to our assumption of perfect price arbitrage for substitutable goods is for the EU. We focus one counterfactual simulation on TRQs of the EU, which provide substantially higher prices (represented as $2,500 per metric ton) for those countries that have preferential access for high-value poultry products.

Results for the base model and various counterfactual policy simulations are reported in Tables 8 and 9. The basic table structure is to report the quantities exported and imported by each country in the relevant market (high-value or low-value), together with the world market price and any price differences among countries. For example, in the base model for the high-value market, exports by the United States, Brazil, China, and other exporters (all in thousand metric tons) are 79.7, 158.1, 247.2, and 189.1, respectively, as shown in Table 8. Prices are $2,500 per metric ton in the EU and $1,940 elsewhere. Because of our perfect substitutability assumptions, the individual bilateral flows are not uniquely determined within the world market—that is, there are arbitrage possibilities among those countries trading with each other.

The first policy simulation is relaxation of a nontechnical trade barrier (see Table 8). The EU is assumed to eliminate its TRQs, and to open up to trade with the rest of the world while retaining its sanitary restrictions on poultry from the United States and China. As a consequence of such a reduction of its trade constraints, the domestic EU price falls to a common level with the rest of the world, and imports by the EU expand, putting upward pressure on the initial world price and inducing more exports, and fewer imports, by other countries around the globe. Given our symmetric elasticity assumptions, the new equilibrium price is established at $1,975 in either the short-run or long-run simulation (up 1.8 percent from the base world price, and 21 percent below the EU base price). Quantity effects depend on the elasticities. In the short run (inelastic excess supplies and demands), EU imports expand from 107,500 tons to 124,500 tons (up 15.8 percent), while imports by Japan and others fall by 1.4 percent, and exports by the United States, Brazil, and China rise similarly. In the long run (elastic excess supplies and demands), EU imports rise to 277,900 tons—a more dramatic increase, but still accounting for only about 5 percent of EU consumption. Exports and imports by other countries also show larger quantity adjustments in the long-run model.

Next consider the simulated imposition of a sanitary barrier (not shown in Table 8). Assume that Russia imposes an embargo on imports from the United States, as threatened in 1996. This sanitary regulation applies in the market for low-value products, but the surprising result in the model is that it has no effect on the equilibrium total quantities of exports and imports of each country or on the world equilibrium price. Even with Russian imports comprising 13.4 percent of the total value of world poultry trade and 22.2 percent of the value of trade in low-value products, there are sufficient arbitrage possibilities among the various markets for trade deflection to offset the effects of the simulated Russian sanitary barrier. Such a disruption of established marketing channels might result in many real-world costs being incurred (especially in the short run) that our model does not take into account. But the model results also illustrate the important concept that multimarket arbitrage can mitigate the effects of seemingly onerous technical trade barriers as long as those barriers do not become too widespread.[11]

Table 8. Base model and EU liberalization simulation

		EU eliminates TRQ and opens up trade	
	Base model	Short run	Long run
Country	Quantities traded (thousand metric tons)		
High-value exporters			
United States	79.7	80.8	90.6
Brazil	158.1	160.3	179.8
China	247.2	250.6	281.1
Other exporters	189.1	191.7	215.1
High-value importers			
EU	107.5	124.5	277.9
Japan	461.2	454.9	397.8
Other importers	105.4	103.9	90.9
	Prices (per metric ton): EU: $2,500 Rest: $1,940	All: $1,975	

Table 9. Base model and simulated isolation of Brazil

		High-value imports from Brazil prohibited by:		
	Base model	U.S., EU	U.S., EU, Japan, China, and other exporters	All countries
Country	Quantities traded (thousand metric tons)			
High-value exporters				
United States	79.7	76.9	80.5	88.1
Brazil	158.1	152.6	126.5	0.0
China	247.2	238.6	249.6	273.4
Other exporters	189.1	182.5	190.9	209.2
High-value importers				
EU	107.5	64.3	64.3	64.3
Japan	461.2	477.2	456.7	412.2
Other importers	105.4	105.4	126.5	94.2
	Prices (per metric ton): EU: $2,500 Rest: $1,940	EU: $2,639 Rest: $1,930	EU: $2,639 Others not trading with Brazil: $1,942 Brazil and others trading with it: $1,888	EU: $2,639 Others not trading with Brazil: $1,967 Brazil: $1,681

A third set of simulations are related to the nontransitivity of sanitary barriers to poultry imports from Brazil and China by the United States, the EU, Japan, and other importers. The United States does not allow imports from Brazil or China, but does from the EU (Great Britain). If those regulations are appropriate, then it is surprising that the EU would allow imports from either Brazil or China—but it does from the former, yet not the latter. Meanwhile, Japan allows imports from both Brazil and China, as well as from both the United States and the EU. There is little evidence to suggest that Japan is an avian disease-ridden and food-safety-unconscious nation willing to trade with any rogue country, and much evidence to the contrary. So if Japan imports from Brazil and China, why does the United States (and the EU in the case of China) prohibit such imports? Why does Brazil prohibit imports from the United States?

The simulations in Table 9 explore alternative regimes related to these anomalies in the high-value poultry market. In the base model, imports from Brazil are prohibited only by the United States. Brazil may seek access to the U.S. market—and perhaps such access might eventually be granted—but one expects that such an outcome will be slow to be achieved and costly to pursue. The trade data suggest that if bilateral Brazil-U.S. access were mutually provided, there would be a small amount of trade induced but not a surge, because of the other market opportunities Brazil has and because of price arbitrage across markets. This may be the reason why neither Brazil nor the United States has pressed its case against the poultry barriers of the other country—multicountry arbitrage opportunities may be making two specific sanitary barriers less trade distorting than suspected based simply on the plausibility of the regulations per se.

More enlightening are the effects of sanitary regulations that increasingly adopt the current U.S. stance of prohibiting imports of poultry from Brazil or China. Results for three scenarios with respect to Brazil are shown in Table 9. In the first, it is assumed that the EU follows the U.S. lead and bans imports from Brazil, simultaneously cutting its total TRQ by an equivalent amount (as opposed to reallocating the Brazilian low-tariff access to other countries). In the second scenario, Japan also prohibits imports from Brazil, as do China and other exporters, if only because of concern about maintaining access to the Japanese market. Finally, in the third scenario, the aggregated other importers also prohibit imports from Brazil, forcing autarky on the Brazilian high-value poultry market.

In the first case, the world divides into three trading blocs that partly overlap. One bloc is the EU, which is isolated by its TRQ and over-quota tariff protection, as well as by some sanitary barriers. Another bloc is composed of Brazil and those countries (particularly Japan and the aggregated group of other importers, but also China and other exporters) still willing to import from Brazil and having limited access (in the case of other exporters) to the EU market. The third bloc is the United States, which prohibits imports from Brazil but has access, along with Brazil, to the markets of Japan and the aggregated other importers.

The results of the first scenario are shown in Table 9 for our long-run model. Prohibiting imports from Brazil and limiting its total import quantity pushes the EU price up from $2,500 per metric ton to $2,639 per metric ton (5.6 percent). The price in the rest of the world, to which Brazil still has access through Japan and other importers, is driven down slightly (from $1,940 per metric ton to $1,930 per metric ton). Total exports from Brazil, but also from the United States, China, and other exporters, decline; imports by Japan and other importers concurrently increase by less than the drop in EU imports.

When Japan, China, and other exporters join in prohibiting high-value poultry imports from Brazil, the world breaks more distinctly into separate trading blocs. The EU remains isolated as in the first scenario, with imports constrained and an equilibrium price of $2,639 per metric ton. The second bloc of countries is composed only of Brazil and the aggregated other importers willing to trade with Brazil; in the third bloc, only the United States, China, and other exporters have access to the market in Japan. Arbitrage opportunities for deflected trade from Brazil are limited to the markets of the aggregated other importers. This market is not sufficiently large to arbitrage away price differences in the (non-EU) world. Instead, imports by the other importers rise from 105,400 tons in the base model to 126,500 tons (20 percent), as these importers satisfy their excess demand with a low-priced supply from Brazil. Total exports by Brazil, which has no other opportunities, drop to 126,500 tons (80 percent of base model exports). The market price in Brazil and those aggregated other countries willing to import from Brazil is driven down to \$1,888 per metric ton (2.7 percent below the base model world price). In contrast, a slightly higher price than in the base model is paid by Japan, which has limited its sources to the United States, China, and the aggregated other exporters. Exports from the United States, China, and other exporters increase with the slightly higher price they receive, instead of decreasing due to a lower market price in the scenario in which only the EU imposed a new prohibition on Brazilian imports.

Finally, in the third scenario, Brazil is forced to autarky in the high-value poultry market and its domestic price falls to \$1,681 per metric ton. The EU remains isolated with the price of \$2,639 per metric ton. Because they now preclude imports from Brazil, the price in the aggregated other importers increases 4.2 percent, from \$1,888 per metric ton in the second scenario to \$1,967 per metric ton, the new (higher) world equilibrium price for those countries with limited access to the EU market and prohibiting imports from Brazil. Non-Brazilian exporters all gain from Brazil's increased isolation, receiving a higher price and exporting more than in the base model or the other two scenarios.

SUMMARY AND CONCLUSIONS

World poultry markets are one of the most rapidly growing sectors among food industries and are likely to remain so in coming years. International trade has been growing rapidly and now accounts for about 10 percent of world consumption, reflecting increased specialization among countries. The objective of this chapter has been to evaluate the effects of sanitary barriers related to avian and human health in the context of the broader set of economic factors and policy decisions that influence poultry trade flows.

To evaluate some of the effects on world trade, an equilibrium model was constructed to simulate the flow of poultry products among six key countries and aggregate rest-of-world exporting and importing regions. Among the wide range of traded products, the analysis focused on one SITC grouping, which accounts for nearly 70 percent of the value of world poultry trade. Within this category, we showed that a sharp distinction can be drawn between high-value poultry trade—going into Japan, the EU, and elsewhere—and low-value poultry products, which are imported primarily into China, Russia, and other countries. We modeled the trade outcomes maintaining this distinction between the high- and low-value poultry markets—the first global model, to our knowledge, to do so. Competition within each of these markets is apparent from comparisons of unit-value prices across bilateral trade flows in existing markets for high-value and low-value poultry products, although there remains substantial price variation that cannot be accounted for specifically. On the basis of the observed prices, we made competitiveness assumptions in our empirical model.

Results for a base model and several counterfactual policy simulations are presented above. For nontechnical barriers, we find that TRQs imposed on high-value poultry products by the EU somewhat reduce world prices and trade. For sanitary regulations, we derive a somewhat more unexpected result: that there are sufficient arbitrage possibilities in world markets for low-value poultry products to mitigate an imposition of sanitary restrictions on U.S. imports by Russia—as long as the restriction is not imposed on other exporters as well. We then examined the effects of an increase in the technical barriers imposed against exports of high-value poultry products by Brazil. We find that the direction of impact on various importers and other exporters depends again on how widespread such restrictions are assumed to become.

Our empirical results for world poultry markets suggest the importance of considering multicountry trade arbitrage in assessing the effects of sanitary regulations imposed by specific importers on products from specific exporters. Some of these sanitary barriers will not distort world trade as much as might be perceived based on assessment of a single barrier per se. This is not to argue that unnecessary sanitary regulations are harmless. Marketing channels are costly to establish in ways not captured in our empirical model, and there is also the serious risk of proliferation of unnecessary regulation to the point that it does become trade intrusive. Our analysis of poultry markets demonstrates that the world trading system has much to gain in avoiding such a result, and much work to do to achieve this desirable outcome.

NOTES

1. The EU is treated as a single "country" in our analysis of poultry trade, and intra-EU trade is not modeled. Hong Kong is considered part of China, though with somewhat different trade rules. Internal trade between Hong Kong and other parts of China has been netted out in the statistics shown here whenever a reasonable estimate of such trade is available.
2. See Henry and Rothwell (1995) and USITC (1998) for good descriptions of the world poultry industry.
3. See Swayne and Slemons (1997) for a discussion of HPAI outbreaks and eradication efforts. Lasley, Short, and Henson (1985) examine quarantine procedures and economic consequences of a major U.S. outbreak of HPAI in several eastern states in 1983; Wakenell and Jetter (1999) discuss a localized outbreak of END in California in 1998. As these and other case studies show, importing countries often respond to an outbreak of a List A poultry disease by imposing a regionalized and temporary quarantine but not by permanently blocking trade.
4. USDA does not rely on OIE information when making regulatory decisions, because the disease status of each country is self-declared and U.S. authorities have asserted that they are skeptical about some of these claims. The 13 countries recognized by USDA as END-free are Australia, Canada, Chile, Costa Rica, Denmark, Fiji, Finland, Great Britain, Iceland, Ireland, New Zealand, Sweden, and Switzerland. The five countries recognized by USDA as having equivalent poultry inspection systems are Canada, France, Great Britain, Hong Kong, and Israel. The two states in northwestern Mexico have recently been authorized to export poultry to the United States under WTO

regionalization provisions, upon confirmation that they meet U.S. animal health and food safety standards.

5. The six SITC codes for poultry, abbreviated descriptions, and value of world trade (excluding intra-EU trade) in 1998 are: 01231 poultry not cut in pieces, fresh or chilled, $181.1 million; 01232 poultry not cut in pieces, frozen, $1,054.6 million; 01233 fatty livers of geese or ducks, fresh or chilled, $61.7 million; 01234 poultry cuts and other offal, fresh or chilled, $403.5 million; 01235 poultry cuts and offal (other than liver) frozen, $3,635.5 million; and 01236, poultry livers frozen, $1.12 million.

6. Some of this apparent variability arises from aggregation of the two Chinese markets. When the markets are examined separately, Brazil and the EU receive similar average prices in China ($425 per metric ton and $474 per metric ton, respectively). Brazil and the EU (and also Thailand, supplying imports of $13.8 million) receive higher but, again, similar prices in Hong Kong ($987 per metric ton, $1,018 per metric ton and $972 per metric ton, respectively). Thus, the difference between the average price for Brazil and the EU in the combined China-Hong Kong market largely reflects different proportions of sales in the two locations. The United States, in contrast, sells in the China and Hong Kong markets at similar prices ($638 per metric ton and $648 per metric ton, respectively) which differ from Brazil and the EU in each market.

7. The comparison for aggregated exporters is on average across high-value products from nine other countries. Among these other countries, Thailand is the only one that supplies significant quantities to Japan ($246.9 million). Thailand also receives a higher unit price from the EU ($2,753 per metric ton for its sales of $91.2 million, versus $2,042 per metric ton in Japan). Other countries exporting high-value products to the EU include Hungary, Poland, and Canada; low-value exports to the EU came from a number of unidentified countries.

8. Less unit price variation might be expected among export destinations within more narrowly defined 10-digit harmonized tariff schedule codes for U.S. poultry exports, but this does not always turn out to be the case.

9. These concepts are developed in Roberts, Josling, and Orden (1999).

10. See Alston and Scobie (1987); Beck, Hoskins, and Mumey (1994); Koo and Golz (1994); Goodwin, Madrigal, and Martin (1998); Henry and Rothwell (1995); Kapombe (1997, 1998); Kapombe and Colyer (1998); Michel, Gempesaw, and Biery (1998); and Wang et al. (1998) for earlier models and discussion of elasticities of poultry supply and demand.

11. Pressing the claim of mitigation of a specific new sanitary barrier through trade re-routing might well confront challenge in trade policy debate. There was similar debate over a conclusion of this type in the congressionally mandated assessment regarding the effects of an earlier disruption of trade with Russia resulting from the U.S. embargo related to the Afghanistan war in 1980 (see ERS 1986).

REFERENCES

Alston, J. M., and Scobie, G. M., 1987, Differentiated goods model of the effects of European policies in international poultry markets, *Southern J Agric Econ* **19**(1):59–68.

Ames, G., 1998, Non-tariff barriers and political solutions to trade disputes: A case study of U.S. poultry exports to Russia, *Rev Agric Econ* **20**(1):238–247.

Beck, R., Hoskins, C., and Mumey, G., 1994, The social welfare loss from egg and poultry marketing boards, revisited, *Can J Agric Econ* **42**(1):149–158.

Calvin, L., and Krissoff, B., 1998, Technical barriers to trade: A case study of phytosanitary barriers and US-Japanese apple trade, *J Agric Resour Econ* **23**(Dec.):351–366.

Economic Research Service (ERS), U.S. Department of Agriculture, 1986, *Embargos, Surplus Disposal, and U.S. Agriculture*, Staff Report AGES860910, Washington, DC.

Food Safety and Inspection Service (FSIS), U.S. Department of Agriculture, 1995, *Focus on Chicken*, Consumer Education and Information Publication, http://www.fsis.usda.gov (accessed Apr. 29, 2001).

Goodwin, J. W., Madrigal, S., and Martin, J., 1998, *Supply and Demand Responses in the U.S. Broiler Industry*, Report 332, Arkansas Agricultural Experiment Station, Fayetteville.

Henry, R., and Rothwell, G., 1995, *The World Poultry Industry*, International Finance Corporation, Washington, DC.

Kahrs, R. F., 1996, The Threatened 1996 Russian Embargo on U.S. Poultry Meat Exports: Executive Summary and Recommendations, memo, Animal Plant Health and Inspection Service, U.S. Department of Agriculture, Washington, DC.

Kapombe, C. R., 1997, Broiler Exports: A Structural Time Series Approach, Ph.D. diss., West Virginia University, Morgantown.

———, 1998, Broiler exports: A structural time series approach, in: *Trade Policy and Competition: Forces Shaping American Agriculture*, Southern Cooperative Series Bulletin No. 390 (Nov.):31–58.

Kapombe, C. R., and Colyer, D., 1998, Modeling U.S. broiler supply response: A structural time series approach, *Agric Resour Econ Rev* **27**(Oct.):241–251.

Koo, W. W., and Golz, J. T., 1994, Competitiveness of broiler producers in North America under alternative free trade scenarios, *Agribusiness* **10**(6):503–511.

Lasley, F. A., Short, S. D., and Henson, W. L., 1985, *Economic Assessment of the 1983-84 Avian Influenza Eradication Program*, AGES841212, Economic Research Service, U.S. Department of Agriculture, Washington, DC.

Michel, K., Gempesaw, C. M., II, and Biery, C. S., 1998, *An Analysis of International Poultry Trade and Competitiveness*, FREC RR 98-01, Food and Resource Economics, University of Delaware, Newark.

Orden, D., and Romano, E., 1996, The Avocado Dispute and Other Technical Barriers to Agricultural Trade under NAFTA, paper presented at NAFTA and Agriculture Conference, Nov. 1, 1996, San Antonio.

Roberts, D., Josling, T., and Orden, D., 1999, *A Framework for Analyzing Technical Trade Barriers in Agricultural Markets*, Technical Bulletin No. 1876, Economic Research Service, U.S. Department of Agriculture, Washington, DC.

Swayne, D. E., and Slemons, R. D., eds., 1997, *Proceedings of the Fourth International Symposium on Avian Influenza*, United States Animal Health Association, Athens, GA.

U.S. International Trade Commission (USITC), 1998, *Industry and Trade Summary: Poultry*, Pub. 3148, Office of Industries, Washington, DC.

Wakenell, P., and Jetter, K., 1999, *Exotic Newcastle Disease Virus*, Agricultural Issues Center, University of California, Davis.

Wang, Q., Fuller, F., Hayes, D., and Halbrendt, C., 1998, Chinese consumer demand for animal products and implications for U.S. pork and poultry exports, *J Agric Appl Econ* **30**(1):127–140.

World Health Organization (WHO), 2000, Food Safety and Foodborne Illness, Fact Sheet No. 237, http://www.who.org (accessed Mar. 14, 2001).

World Trade Organization (WTO), 1997, United States—Measures Affecting Imports of Poultry Production: Request for Consultations by the European Communities, doc. symbol G/SPS/GEN/28, http://docsonline.wto.org (accessed Jul. 27, 2001).

———, 1995–2000, Committee on Sanitary and Phytosanitary Measures meeting summaries, doc. symbol G/SPS/R, http://docsonline.wto.org (accessed Jul. 27, 2001).

PRICE POLICIES AND THE DOMESTIC AND INTERNATIONAL DISTRIBUTION OF COMMODITY QUALITY

Theory and application to EU wheat

Julian M. Alston and Jennifer S. James*

Most studies of agricultural commodity price policies ignore quality responses.[1] Typically, it is assumed that the commodity of interest is homogeneous, and no allowance is made for any policy-induced changes in quality or in the distribution of quality (i.e., average quality).[2] This might be a good approximation in some cases. Recently, however, James (2000a) reported a closed-economy model of stereotypical domestic agricultural commodity policies, in which she found that quality responses might be significant and could substantially alter the welfare implications of policy alternatives.[3] In this chapter, we adopt the same general approach, and adapt and extend it to evaluate the quality impacts of both domestic and border policies applied to agricultural commodities in an open-economy setting.

We use a theoretical multimarket model to analyze price and quantity effects of various policies for specific qualities so that we can examine the effects on the quality distribution of production and consumption in aggregate and the quality specialization (in production and consumption) among nations. We decompose elasticity terms to illustrate the nature and importance of the errors caused by ignoring quality responses. In addition, we use numerical simulations to demonstrate some of the quality effects of wheat policy in the European Union (EU).

---

* Julian M. Alston is a professor in the Department of Agricultural and Resource Economics, University of California, Davis, and a member of the Giannini Foundation. Jennifer S. James is an assistant professor in the Department of Agricultural Economics and Rural Sociology, Pennsylvania State University. Senior authorship is not assigned. The authors gratefully acknowledge helpful comments from Tassos Haniotis, Daniel Sumner, and Stefan Tangermann.

Global Food Trade and Consumer Demand for Quality, edited by Krissoff *et al.*
Kluwer Academic/Plenum Publishers, New York, 2002.

A SMALL-COUNTRY MODEL

We begin with a simple model of quality responses to policies in a small trading country. We model the markets for two products (high and low quality of the commodity of interest) that are related in consumption and production.[4] Trade policies are represented as tax or subsidy equivalents, and Armington-type assumptions are used to define the elasticities of supply and demand in terms of more fundamental parameters.

Supply and Demand Models

A domestic supply (and demand) function is specified for each quality in which the quantity supplied (demanded) of each quality depends on its own price and the price of the other quality, as follows:

$$C_L = C_L(P_L^D, P_H^D) \tag{1}$$

$$C_H = C_H(P_L^D, P_H^D) \tag{2}$$

$$Q_L = Q_L(P_L^S, P_H^S) \tag{3}$$

$$Q_L = Q_H(P_L^S, P_H^S) \tag{4}$$

where C denotes quantity consumed, Q denotes quantity produced, and P denotes prices. Subscripts L and H refer to the low- and high-quality markets, respectively, and superscripts D and S refer to prices paid by consumers and producers, respectively.[5] In the market-clearing conditions, below, net imports are denoted by M and the exogenous world prices are denoted by P (without superscripts) for each of the two qualities. That is:

$$M_L = C_L - Q_L \tag{5}$$

$$M_H = C_H - Q_H \tag{6}$$

$$P_L^D = P_L(1 + t_L^D) \tag{7}$$

$$P_H^D = P_H(1 + t_H^D) \tag{8}$$

$$P_L^S = P_L(1 + t_L^S) \tag{9}$$

$$P_H^S = P_H(1 + t_H^S) \tag{10}$$

where t_L^D and t_H^D are proportional taxes on domestic consumption, and t_L^S and t_H^S are proportional taxes (or negative subsidies) on domestic production in the low- and high-quality markets; they are initially all equal to zero in the equilibrium displacement model. The different policies of interest are represented as different combinations of the consumption and production taxes, as shown in Table 1.[6]

Table 1. Combinations of domestic taxes and subsidies used to define policies

		Equivalent policy			
		Consumption tax		Production tax	
		Low quality	High quality	Low quality	High quality
Actual policy	Per unit rate	t_L^D	t_H^D	t_L^S	t_H^S
Output subsidy	T	0	0	$-T/P_L$	$-T/P_H$
Export subsidy (import tariff) for exporter (importer) of					
Both qualities	T	T/P_L	T/P_H	$-T/P_L$	$-T/P_H$
Low quality	T	T/P_L	0	$-T/P_L$	0
High quality	T	0	T/P_H	0	$-T/P_H$

Model Solutions

Totally differentiating Eqs. (1)–(10) yields:

$$\text{dln } C_L = \eta_{LL} \text{dln } P_L^D + \eta_{LH} \text{dln } P_H^D \tag{11}$$

$$\text{dln } C_H = \eta_{HL} \text{dln } P_L^D + \eta_{HH} \text{dln } P_H^D \tag{12}$$

$$\text{dln } Q_L = \epsilon_{LL} \text{dln } P_L^S + \epsilon_{LH} \text{dln } P_H^S \tag{13}$$

$$\text{dln } Q_H = \epsilon_{HL} \text{dln } P_L^S + \epsilon_{HH} \text{dln } P_H^S \tag{14}$$

$$\text{dln } M_L = (C_L/M_L) \text{ dln } C_L + (Q_L/M_L) \text{ dln } Q_L \tag{15}$$

$$\text{dln } M_H = (C_H/M_H) \text{ dln } C_H + (Q_H/M_H) \text{ dln } Q_H \tag{16}$$

$$\text{dln } P_L^D = \text{dln } P_L + t_L^D = t_L^D \tag{17}$$

$$\text{dln } P_H^D = \text{dln } P_H + t_H^D = t_H^D \tag{18}$$

$$\text{dln } P_L^S = \text{dln } P_L + t_L^S = t_L^S \tag{19}$$

$$\text{dln } P_H^S = \text{dln } P_H + t_H^S = t_H^S \tag{20}$$

where dln $X = dX/X$ denotes a proportional change in the variable X. Coefficients on the dln P terms in Eqs. (11)–(14) are elasticities: η_{ij} is the elasticity of demand for quality i with respect to the price of quality j, and ϵ_{ij} is the elasticity of supply of quality i with respect to the price of quality j.

In Eqs. (17)–(20), dln P_L and dln P_H are zero, since they refer to changes in world prices, which are constant and exogenous in this small-country case. Hence, the proportional changes in the domestic producer and consumer prices are as shown in Eqs. (17)–(20). Solving Eqs. (11)–(20) for the proportional changes in quantities supplied and demanded yields:

$$\text{dln } C_L = \eta_{LL}\, t_L^D + \eta_{LH}\, t_H^D \tag{21}$$

$$\text{dln } C_H = \eta_{HL}\, t_L^D + \eta_{HH}\, t_H^D \tag{22}$$

$$\text{dln } Q_L = -\epsilon_{LL}\, t_L^S - \epsilon_{LH}\, t_H^S \tag{23}$$

$$\text{dln } Q_H = -\epsilon_{HL}\, t_L^S - \epsilon_{HH}\, t_H^S \tag{24}$$

Solutions for the net imports or exports of each quality are linear combinations of the terms in Eqs. (21)–(24).

An Armington Approach to Defining Elasticities

The direction of change for each endogenous variable depends on the signs and, in some cases, the magnitudes, of the supply and demand elasticities (as well as the set of relevant tax rates). Imposing the assumptions of weak separability and homotheticity as described by Armington (1969), the elasticities of demand for the individual qualities with respect to individual prices can be expressed as:

$$\eta_{LL} = s_L^D \eta - s_H^D \sigma \tag{25}$$

$$\eta_{LH} = s_H^D(\eta + \sigma) \tag{26}$$

$$\eta_{HL} = s_L^D(\eta + \sigma) \tag{27}$$

$$\eta_{HH} = s_H^D \eta - s_L^D \sigma \tag{28}$$

where $s_i^D = P_i C_i / P^D C$ is the domestic consumption value-share of quality i, $s_L^D + s_H^D = 1$, $\eta \leqslant 0$ is the overall elasticity of demand (the elasticity of the aggregate quantity demanded, C, with respect to the aggregate consumer price, P^D), and $\sigma \geqslant 0$ is the elasticity of substitution between the two qualities.

A similar representation of the individual firm's profit maximization problem can be specified to derive expressions for the supply elasticities:

$$\epsilon_{LL} = s_L^S \epsilon - s_H^S \tau \tag{29}$$

$$\epsilon_{LH} = s_H^S(\epsilon + \tau) \tag{30}$$

$$\epsilon_{HL} = s_L^S(\epsilon + \tau) \tag{31}$$

$$\epsilon_{HH} = s_H^S \epsilon - s_L^S \tau \tag{32}$$

where $s_i^S = P_i Q_i / P^S Q$ is the domestic production value-share of quality i, and $s_L^S + s_H^S = 1$. These elasticities can be interpreted similarly to the elasticities of demand: $\epsilon \geqslant 0$ is the overall supply elasticity (the elasticity of aggregate quantity supplied, Q, with respect to the aggregate producer price, P^S), and $\tau \leqslant 0$ is the elasticity of transformation in production.

Because a model of a single commodity of constant quality implicitly ignores any substitution between the qualities, evaluating the expressions presented below as σ and τ approach zero is equivalent to imposing constant quality in the analysis. To complete the comparison between the two-quality and single-quality models, we must also define aggregate quantities and prices. We define these as:

$$C = C_L + C_H \tag{33}$$

$$Q = Q_L + Q_H \tag{34}$$

$$P^D = (P_L C_L + P_H C_H)/C \tag{35}$$

$$P^S = (P_L Q_L + P_H Q_H)/Q \tag{36}$$

Here, P^D is the average unit value of the two qualities consumed, and P^S is the average unit value of the two qualities produced, both defined at the initial equilibrium. These aggregate prices are implicitly assumed to be equal in a homogeneous goods model, as they would be in fact if quantity shares in production and consumption were equal, or if prices were equal across qualities.

EFFECTS OF POLICIES ON QUALITY

The general solutions in Eqs. (21)–(24) can be modified to represent the effects of a per unit import tariff or export subsidy under the assumption of homothetic separability by making the substitutions in Table 1 and Eqs. (25)–(32). After making the substitutions and simplifying, we find that an import tariff (or export subsidy) at a rate of T per unit has the following effects, expressed as proportional changes in the quantities consumed and produced in each market:

$$\text{dln } C_L = \eta(T/P^D) - s_H^D \sigma (T/P_L P_H)(P_H - P_L) \tag{37}$$

$$\text{dln } C_H = \eta(T/P^D) + s_L^D \sigma (T/P_L P_H)(P_H - P_L) \tag{38}$$

$$\text{dln } Q_L = \epsilon(T/P^S) - s_H^S \tau (T/P_L P_H)(P_H - P_L) \tag{39}$$

$$\text{dln } Q_H = \epsilon(T/P^S) + s_L^S \tau (T/P_L P_H)(P_H - P_L) \tag{40}$$

Note that the taxes and subsidies in Table 1 are defined as proportions of pre-intervention world prices, which are the same for consumers and producers. This is why the prices in the solutions in Eqs. (37)–(40) do not include superscripts. The same solutions hold for an export subsidy at a rate T per unit for a country that exports both qualities. For an output subsidy at a rate T per unit, there is no effect on domestic consumption of either quality ($t_L^D = t_H^D = 0$, and therefore dln C_L = dln $C_H = 0$); the results for domestic production are as given by Eqs. (39) and (40).

In each of Eqs. (37)–(40), the first term is equivalent to the effects found in a homogeneous goods model for a per unit import tariff (or export subsidy) of T, and initial producer and consumer prices of P^S and P^D. Hence, the second term in each equation is a measure of the error that would result from inappropriately assuming product homogeneity. Since, by definition, the price of the high-quality good is larger than that of the low-quality good—i.e., $(P_H - P_L) > 0$—we can determine the sign of the error.

Equations (37) and (38) show that the reduction in consumption of the low-quality good is greater and the reduction in consumption of the high-quality good is smaller than those predicted in a single-market model of a homogeneous good. Equations (39) and (40) show that the increase in production of the low-quality good is greater and the increase in production of the high-quality good is smaller than those predicted in a single-market model of a homogeneous good.[7] Interestingly, the quality-specific errors do not exactly offset each other, so estimates of the total demand or supply response to a policy from a model of a homogeneous good will also be incorrect.[8]

We can define average quality as C_H/C_L and Q_H/Q_L for consumption and production, respectively, and we can define the price premium for high quality as P_H/P_L. Then, the proportional change in average quality is given by the difference between the proportional changes in the quantities of high and low quality (similarly, the quality premium is given by the difference in the proportional price changes):

$$\text{dln } C_H - \text{dln } C_L = \sigma (T/P_L P_H)(P_H - P_L) > 0 \tag{41}$$

$$\text{dln } Q_H - \text{dln } Q_L = \tau (T/P_L P_H)(P_H - P_L) < 0 \tag{42}$$

$$\text{dln } P_H^D - \text{dln } P_L^D = -(T/P_L P_H)(P_H - P_L) < 0 \tag{43}$$

$$\text{dln } P_H^S - \text{dln } P_L^S = -(T/P_L P_H)(P_H - P_L) < 0 \tag{44}$$

The proportional reduction in consumption is smaller for high quality than low quality (in absolute terms), indicating that average quality consumed increases as a result of the import tariff or export subsidy—a variant of the standard Alchian-Allen result. Similarly, the proportional increase in production is smaller for high quality than low quality, indicating that average quality produced decreases as a result of the import tariff or export subsidy (or for an output subsidy). For both producers and consumers, the addition of a constant per unit subsidy (or cost) decreases the relative price of the higher quality good, causing a shift of consumption away from the lower quality good and a shift of production toward the lower quality good.

The effects of the various policies on the domestic quality premiums for consumers and producers, and in the average quality of domestic production and consumption, are summarized in Table 2. The results in this table provide unambiguous support for hypotheses about the quality effects of per unit border taxes or subsidies at the market level. They

Table 2. Effects of policies on quality premiums and average quality

	Consumption		Production	
Policy	Quality premium	Average quality	Quality premium	Average quality
Output subsidy	0	0	–	–
Export subsidy (import tariff) for exporter (importer) of				
Both qualities	–	+	–	–
Low quality	– –	+ +	– –	– –
High quality	+	–	+	+

Note: "– –" ("+ +") indicates a larger decrease (increase) relative to "–" ("+").

do, however, hinge on the Armington assumptions used to derive the elasticity decompositions. Under more general assumptions, quality effects are ambiguous.[9]

POLICIES AND QUALITY IN A LARGE COUNTRY

The model described above can be used, with minor modifications, to analyze the effects of similar domestic and trade policies for a large-country trader. In this case, world prices are endogenous, and so demand and supply conditions for each quality in the rest of the world (ROW) must be incorporated in the model, with corresponding changes to the market-clearing conditions. The analytics become much more cumbersome for the case of a large-country trader, since the number of endogenous variables increases to 16, and there are eight additional supply and demand parameters.[10]

The main implications for the large-country case with endogenous quality relative to the small-country case can be seen intuitively by combining some partial analyses. Consider the effects of a per unit tariff (or export subsidy) on the markets for each of the two qualities, assuming no interaction between the two. In the large-country case, an import tariff (or export subsidy) will increase the domestic consumer and producer prices, and reduce the consumer and producer prices in the ROW. This shifting of the incidence of the home-country policy would mean that, relative to the small-country case, the increases in domestic producer and consumer prices associated with the per unit import tariff (export subsidy) would be reduced. Nevertheless, since a larger proportional tax (or subsidy) is applied to the lower quality good, we would still expect the relative price of low quality to have risen on the domestic market, decreasing the domestic quality premium. As a result, the average quality of domestic consumption would increase, and the average quality of domestic production would decline.

Similarly, in the ROW, a proportionally larger price distortion (and a larger trade distortion) in the market for the lower quality good would give rise to a reduction in the ROW's relative price of the lower quality good, increasing the quality premium in the ROW. Accordingly, we would expect to see a shift in ROW consumption toward lower quality and a shift of ROW production toward higher quality—effects acting in the opposite direction to those in the home country. In both the home country and the ROW, the interactions between the markets for the different qualities modify the magnitudes of the effects, but would be unlikely to change the direction of any of them. In summary, the qualitative effects of the policies on average quality and the quality premium in the home country will be in the same direction as in the small-country case, only smaller in size, while the corresponding effects in the ROW will be in the opposite direction.

SIMULATION: EU WHEAT

To further illustrate our theoretical findings concerning the nature of the quality response to policies and to establish the potential quantitative importance of the effects, we use a simulation model of the EU wheat market and policy.

General Structure of Model

Our model is designed as an illustrative example and is somewhat stylized in its treatment of markets and policies. It has features in common with the model of de Gorter and Meilke (1987, 1989) and Meilke and de Gorter (1988), who disaggregated wheat consumed in the EU into high-quality imports and low-quality domestic production. They demonstrated the importance of distinguishing between the two primary policy instruments, because one applies to imports while the other applies to domestic production. Our model differs from that of de Gorter and Meilke in two important respects. First, we allow for EU production of both low- and high-quality wheat, rather than only low quality. This allows us to determine how the relative prices of the two types of wheat influence the average quality of wheat production as well as consumption. Second, we disaggregate wheat produced and consumed in the ROW into low and high qualities. This allows us to contrast the effects of the policy in the ROW between consumers and producers of low and high qualities.

In our model, the EU policy is represented simply as two price floors: (1) the "threshold price" for imports (supported by import tariffs, or variable levies, equal to the difference between the threshold price and the world price) defines the EU price of "high-quality" wheat; and (2) the "intervention" price (supported by export subsidies equal to the difference between the intervention price and the world price) defines the EU price of "low-quality" wheat. This representation makes sense if the EU imports only high quality and exports only low quality, such that the intervention price is binding only for low quality and the (higher) threshold price is relevant only for high quality.[11]

We use linear supply and demand equations, specified as follows:[12]

$$C_i^k = a_i^k + a_{iL}^k P_L^k + a_{iH}^k P_H^k \tag{45}$$

$$Q_i^k = b_i^k + b_{iL}^k P_L^k + b_{iH}^k P_H^k \tag{46}$$

for $i = L,H$ and $k = E,R$, where the notation used in previous sections is augmented with superscripts E and R to denote prices or quantities in the EU and the ROW, respectively. The market-clearing conditions ensure that total world consumption equals total world production for each quality. In this model, the exogenous EU prices determine the endogenous EU quantities produced and consumed of low- and high-quality wheat. These quantities, combined with the ROW supply and demand equations, determine the endogenous prices and quantities of both high- and low-quality wheat in the ROW.

Definition of Model Parameters

To define the parameters in this model, we used observed prices and quantities for the 1984–85 season, combined with estimates of the own- and cross-price elasticities of supply and demand. In turn, these elasticities were defined using estimates of the underlying overall elasticities of supply and demand for wheat in the EU and ROW, combined with estimates of the corresponding elasticities of substitution and expenditure elasticities in consumption and production. Then, we used the model to simulate a counterfactual scenario in which the two EU floor prices are eliminated (by solving for the free-market equilibrium of supply and demand).

Price and quantity data for 1984–85 were used to define the model parameters.[13] Total quantities refer to consumption and production of wheat used for human consumption (excluding durum wheat, used for pasta), measured in millions of metric tons.[14] Because these data were not available in a disaggregated form, we specified quantity shares of consumption and production of high and low qualities. For the EU, the production share was specified to reflect specialization in production of low-quality wheat, with some production of high quality. The quantity shares of high-quality consumption in the EU and the ROW were set equal to one-half. Finally, the quantity share of high-quality production in the ROW was implicitly defined by the other shares and the fact that the markets for the two qualities cleared. These quantity shares, and the implied value shares of consumption and production of each quality in the EU and the ROW, are provided in Table 3. Prices used to calculate the value shares are specified in U.S. dollars per metric ton, and are defined at the EU border.[15]

Table 3. Quantity shares used to parameterize the model, and implied value shares

	EU		ROW	
Share	Low quality	High quality	Low quality	High quality
Quantity shares of consumption	0.50	0.50	0.50	0.50
Quantity shares of production	0.80	0.20	0.41	0.59
Value shares of consumption	0.46	0.54	0.44	0.56
Value shares of production	0.77	0.23	0.36	0.64

Note: ROW includes all non-EU countries except the Soviet Union and China.
Sources: International Wheat Council (1987), Smith (1997), and authors' calculations.

The fundamental parameters used to define the model include various elasticities of supply and demand, which are assumed to be equal in the EU and ROW. The values used for these parameters are shown in Table 4 and imply the matrices of own- and cross-price elasticities of supply and demand at the initial (observed) market equilibrium shown in Table 5.

Simulation Results

The model described above was used to evaluate the effects of eliminating the two policy variables on the prices and quantities of each type of wheat in the EU and the ROW. Variables of particular interest include the quality premiums, average quality of production, and average quality of consumption, defined as P_H^k/P_L^k, Q_H^k/Q_L^k, and C_H^k/C_L^k, respectively, for $k = E,R$. The values of these variables at the observed equilibrium are listed in the first column of Table 6. Using the observed data, the quality premium is smaller in the EU than in the ROW. The difference between the intervention price and the world price of low-quality wheat is \$17 per metric ton, and this is one measure of support to EU producers of low-quality wheat. The difference between the threshold price and the world price of high-quality wheat is \$10 per metric ton, and can be similarly interpreted as the support to EU producers of high-quality wheat. These figures indicate that the distortion in the low-quality market is larger than the distortion in the high-quality market, both in absolute and relative terms.

Table 4. Values used for fundamental parameters

Parameter	Symbol	Value
Demand		
Overall price elasticity	η^k	−0.10
Elasticity of substitution	σ^k	3.00
Low-quality expenditure elasticity	μ_L^k	0.75
High-quality expenditure elasticity[a]		
European Union	μ_H^E	1.21
Rest of world	μ_H^R	1.20
Supply		
Overall price elasticity	ϵ^k	0.50
Elasticity of transformation	τ^k	−1.00
Low-quality expenditure elasticity	ψ_L^k	1.00
High-quality expenditure elasticity	ψ_H^k	1.00

[a] μ_H^k was computed using μ_L^k and the observed expenditure shares, combined with an Engel aggregation rule.

Table 5. Elasticities of supply and demand

	In EU w.r.t.		In ROW w.r.t.	
Elasticity of	P_L	P_H	P_L	P_H
Demand for				
Low quality	−1.67	1.59	−1.71	1.63
High quality	1.31	−1.43	1.27	−1.39
Supply of				
Low quality	0.61	−0.11	0.82	−0.32
High quality	−0.39	0.89	−0.18	0.68

w.r.t. = with respect to.

Using the model laid out above, we solved for the counterfactual market equilibrium that would have existed if the EU policy had been eliminated in 1984–85. The free-market prices and quantities, along with relevant quality variables, are presented in the second column of Table 6. The third column of that table shows the change in each variable that would have resulted from eliminating the policy (i.e., the difference between the second and first columns), expressed as a percentage of the observed value.

Not surprisingly, elimination of the EU policy would have caused the EU prices of both qualities to decrease and the ROW prices to increase. The simulated changes in total production and consumption are in the expected directions: a decrease in consumption and an increase in production in the EU; the converse in the ROW. The changes in quality and the quality premiums are also qualitatively consistent with our conjectures based on a model with equal per unit distortions in the prices of the two qualities. The quality premium in the EU would have increased while that in the ROW would have decreased if the EU policy had been eliminated. Corresponding to the noted changes in the quality premiums, there would have been a reduction in the average quality of consumption in the EU and an increase in the average quality of production. Conversely, for the ROW, the average quality of consumption would have increased, and the average quality of production would have decreased, if the EU policy had been eliminated.

Table 6. Wheat quantities and prices with and without EU wheat policy, for base parameter values

		After policy is removed			
	Observed	Two qualities		One quality	
Region and variable	market outcome	Value	% change	Value	% change
EU					
Price of low quality	156	143	-8.7	150	-9.1
Price of high quality	186	178	-4.1	150	-9.1
Consumption of low quality	13.0	14.0	7.9		
Consumption of high quality	13.0	12.3	-5.5		
Total consumption	26.0	26.3	1.2	26.2	0.9
Production of low quality	35.4	33.3	-4.9		
Production of high quality	8.8	8.8	-0.3		
Total production	44.2	42.5	-3.9	42.2	-4.5
Exports (low quality)	22.4	19.6	-12.3		
Imports (high quality)	4.2	3.5	-16.6		
ROW					
Price of low quality	139	143	2.5	150	2.4
Price of high quality	176	178	1.3	150	2.4
Consumption of low quality	84.2	82.5	-2.1		
Consumption of high quality	84.2	85.3	1.3		
Total consumption	168.4	167.8	-0.4	168.0	-0.2
Production of low quality	61.8	62.8	1.6		
Production of high quality	88.4	88.8	0.5		
Total production	150.2	151.6	0.9	152.0	1.2
EU					
Quality premium: P_H^E/P_L^E	1.19	1.25	5.0		
Average quality of consumption: C_H^E/C_L^E	1.00	0.88	-12.4		
Average quality of production: Q_H^E/Q_L^E	0.25	0.26	4.8		
Average quality of trade: M_H^E/M_L^E	0.19	0.18	-4.9		
ROW					
Quality premium: P_H^R/P_L^R	1.27	1.25	-1.1		
Average quality of consumption: C_H^R/C_L^R	1.00	1.03	3.5		
Average quality of production: Q_H^R/Q_L^R	1.43	1.41	-1.1		

Note: Wheat quantities are in millions of metric tons per year; prices are in dollars per million metric tons.

A more conventional analysis of such counterfactual policy scenarios would have used a model of a homogeneous good as an approximation. To evaluate the accuracy of the approximation, we also estimated the effects of eliminating the policy using a model of a single homogeneous commodity. In this model, supply and demand are linear, all substitution effects between low- and high-quality wheat are ignored, the aggregate quantity is defined as a simple sum of the quality-specific quantities, and the aggregate prices are weighted sums of the observed prices.[16] The estimated effects of eliminating the policy using this modeling approach are presented in the last two columns of Table 6. Because quality is ignored in this representation, the single-market model has nothing to say about the quality premiums or the average quality of production and consumption. Further, while the estimated effects on quantity aggregates from the single-market approximation are reasonably close to those predicted from the more detailed model, the approximation entails a considerable loss of information relative to the two-market model. One indicator of the importance of this lost information is the difference in the estimated welfare effects of the policy change between the two models. These effects are summarized in Table 7.

Table 7. Estimated welfare effects of eliminating EU wheat policy

Changes in	Two-quality model (million $ per year)	Single-quality model (million $ per year)	Percentage error
EU			
Consumer surplus	279.52	392.27	40.3
Producer surplus	–534.24	–648.76	–21.4
Taxpayer surplus	338.52	338.52	0.0
Net national surplus	83.80	82.02	–2.1
ROW			
Consumer surplus	–489.15	–602.30	–23.1
Producer surplus	425.40	541.15	27.2
Taxpayer surplus	0.00	0.00	0.0
Net national surplus	-63.75	-61.16	4.1
World			
Consumer surplus	–209.63	–210.03	–0.2
Producer surplus	–108.84	–107.62	1.1
Taxpayer surplus	338.52	338.52	0.0
Net national surplus	20.05	20.87	4.1

The last column of Table 7 includes the percentage error in each estimated welfare effect that was caused by ignoring quality variation. The single-good model understated the total welfare effect in the EU and overstated those in the ROW and the world. However, these errors are relatively small. The largest errors are in the distributional consequences among consumers and producers: the region-specific estimates of consumer and producer surplus from the single-good model under- or overstate the effects by at least 20 percent.

CONCLUSION

In the conventional analysis of agricultural commodity policies, heterogeneous goods are modeled as though quality is uniform and unaffected by policy. Effects of policies on the quality mix of production, consumption, and trade, and price premiums are implicitly assumed to be unimportant when we use a single-market model for a homogeneous good of constant quality as an approximation. The assumption of product homogeneity is convenient, but it is important to recognize that it may not always be appropriate. In particular, the implementation of some policies will induce changes in the relative prices of different qualities, and thus in the quality mix of units produced and consumed. If these quality effects are indeed relatively small, then the policy effects from a single-market model for an aggregate good may reasonably approximate the actual policy effects in markets for heterogeneous products. However, the larger are these quality effects, the less accurate will be the results from a model of a homogeneous good.

In this chapter, a model of agricultural commodity policy with two qualities developed by James (2000a) was extended to show the nature of the effects on the quality mix and the quality premium when various tax or subsidy policies are introduced by a small- or large-country trader. A per unit subsidy on production encourages a reduction in average quality produced, and a per unit tax on consumption encourages an increase in average quality consumed. Other producer price-support policies can be modeled as combinations of consumer taxes and producer subsidies. Based on this relatively simple framework, we were able to derive conjectures about the likely effects of stereotypical policies on price premiums and average quality, both in the country introducing the policy and in the rest of the world. This analysis could be extended readily to other policies (such as price discrimination and pooling schemes), and other market situations (such as more than two qualities, or more than two countries, or more than one country with policy distortions).

Our illustrative application to EU wheat in the mid-1980s indicates that the quality issue might be worthy of attention. The quality differences in wheat are significant but small compared with those of many other commodities. Nevertheless, significant errors arise in an analysis that treats wheat as a homogeneous commodity when policies distort the relative prices of low and high quality as well as the average price. Our model suggests that EU wheat policy may have encouraged an expansion of EU production and a shift in the direction of wheat varieties and production methods that would imply lower quality and higher yields. Ignoring the changes in quality causes substantial errors in the estimated welfare effects of the policy.

NOTES

1. Quality responses to conventional trade policies (such as tariffs, import quotas, and export subsidies) have been well documented in the economics literature for manufactured goods (e.g., work by Feenstra 1988 on U.S. import quotas on Japanese automobiles), but not for agricultural products. Work by Anderson (1985) on U.S. cheese import quotas is a notable exception.

2. For instance, various writers (including Johnson and Norton 1983 and Seagraves 1983) have claimed that the U.S. tobacco quota program encouraged an increase in U.S. tobacco quality and thus provided incentives for other countries to produce lower quality tobacco, but none have modeled this aspect of the policy.

3. The theoretical analysis was inspired by Alchian and Allen (1964) and Barzel (1976).

4. It would be straightforward to extend the model to include more qualities. An alternative would be to model a commodity as having continuous variation in quality, as suggested by the models of Houthakker (1952) and Theil (1952). James (2000b) discusses these alternatives.

5. Other demand and supply shifters, such as income, demographic variables, production technology, and input prices, are assumed to be fixed and are therefore not included as explicit arguments.

6. As shown by Alston, Carter, and Smith (1993), for example, many trade policies can be analyzed as equivalent combinations of subsidies and taxes on domestic production and consumption. Quantitative restrictions, too, could be analyzed as equivalent

per unit subsidies or taxes, so long as the rights were transferable, as discussed in James (2000c).

7. An output subsidy would give rise to the same production responses but would leave consumption unaffected.

8. For the simple-sum aggregates used here, the total demand response and the total supply response will be underestimated using a model of a homogeneous commodity. This can be seen by totally differentiating the aggregation rules in Eqs. (33) and (34), and substituting in the solutions for the proportional changes in quality-specific consumption and production from Eqs. (37)–(40), which yields:

$$\text{dln } C = \eta(T/P_D) - \sigma(T/P_D)[(P_H - P_L)^2/P_LP_H][(C_LC_H)/(C)^2]$$

$$\text{dln } Q = \epsilon(T/P_S) - \tau(T/P_S)[(P_H - P_L)^2/P_LP_H][(Q_LQ_H)/(Q)^2]$$

9. Beyond weak separability, the Armington decompositions impose homotheticity, which restricts the elasticities of demand for each quality with respect to changes in expenditure on the group to be equal to one. Similarly, homothetic separability implies that the elasticities of supply with respect to changes in total revenue (an expansion elasticity) are equal to one for both qualities. A more general assumption of weak separability (rather than homothetic separability) would allow the expenditure and expansion elasticities to differ between the two qualities; under this more general assumption, however, quality effects are ambiguous (see James 2000c for details).

10. Details of the model and analytical solutions for this case are available from the authors.

11. We do not make any explicit allowance for set-asides, which were introduced in the 1992 reform of the Common Agricultural Policy as a condition for receiving support. These would presumably be relevant only for producers of "low-quality" wheat, since all "high-quality" producers receive import protection regardless of their participation.

12. A specific (linear) functional form makes it convenient to use the simulation results to evaluate the economic welfare implications of the policies and is more convenient than a proportional change model for dealing with minimum price policies that are not always well approximated by ad valorem taxes and subsidies.

13. These data are provided in Table 6 along with the simulation results.

14. In the model as specified, in the absence of EU policy, price transmission elasticities between the EU and the ROW are equal to one. As an approximation, to reflect the fact that price transmission elasticities are generally less than one, the ROW was defined as including all non-EU countries apart from China and the Soviet Union. This is equivalent to assigning elasticities of price transmission of zero to China and the Soviet Union, and one to all other countries.

15. These prices are included in the first column of Table 6. The ROW price for low-quality wheat is the f.o.b. price of U.S. soft red wheat at the Gulf of Mexico port in Baton Rouge, Louisiana. The ROW price for high-quality wheat is the c.i.f. price of U.S. dark northern spring wheat, 14 percent protein, in Rotterdam.

16. Because these commodities are traded, within each region the total quantity consumed is not equal to the total quantity produced of either quality. Hence, a different price index is implied for producers than for consumers in a region if the quantity shares differ between production and consumption, and it is not entirely clear which weights should be used to calculate the aggregate price for the EU and the ROW. This in turn gives rise to questions about how to define the price wedges in ways that are consistent in some sense between the two-good and single-good models. We used the quantity shares of the sum of production and consumption to calculate the aggregate price in the EU, which was $165.33 per metric ton at the observed market outcome (i.e., $P_L^E(Q_L^E + C_L^E)/(Q^E + C^E) + P_H^E(Q_H^E + C_H^E)/(Q^E + C^E) = 165.33$). We opted to make the net EU taxpayer cost of the policy the same between the two models: $338.52 million, which seemed to be an important dimension in which to make the models consistent. The export subsidy per metric ton was defined as being equal to this taxpayer expenditure divided by the *net* export quantity for the EU, $18.60 per metric ton. This amount was then subtracted from the EU aggregate price, for a ROW aggregate price of $146.73 per metric ton.

REFERENCES

Alchian, A. A., and Allen, W. R., 1964, *University Economics*, Wadsworth Publishing Co, Inc., Belmont, CA.

Alston, J. M., Carter, C. A., and Smith, V. H., 1993, Rationalizing agricultural export subsidies, *Am J Agric Econ* **75**:1000–1009.

Anderson, J. E., 1985, The relative inefficiency of quotas: The cheese case, *Am Econ Rev* **75**:178–190.

Armington, P. S., 1969, A theory of demand for products distinguished by place of production, *Int Monet Fund Staff Papers* **16**:159–178.

Barzel, Y., 1976, An alternative approach to the analysis of taxation, *J Polit Econ* **84**:1177–1197.

de Gorter, H., and Meilke, K. D., 1987, The EEC's wheat price policies and international trade in differentiated products, *Am J Agric Econ* **69**:223–229.

———, 1989, Efficiency of alternative policies for the EC's common agricultural policy, *Am J Agric Econ* **71**:592–603.

Feenstra, R. C., 1988, Quality change under trade restrictions in Japanese autos, *Q J Econ* **103**:131–146.

Houthakker, H. S., 1952, Compensated changes in quantities and qualities consumed, *Rev Econ Stud* **19**:155–164.

International Wheat Council, 1987, *International Wheat Statistics*, London.

James, J. S., 2000a, Quality Responses to Agricultural Policies, paper presented at 44th Annual Conference of the Australian Agricultural and Resource Economics Society, Jan. 23–25, 2000, Sydney.

———, 2000b, Quality Responses to Commodity Policies, Ph.D. diss. (unpub.), Department of Agricultural and Resource Economics, University of California, Davis.

———, 2000c, Taxes and Quality: Theoretical Results from a Market-Level Analysis, paper presented at 44th Annual Conference of the Australian Agricultural and Resource Economics Society, Jan. 23–25, 2000, Sydney.

Johnson, P. R., and Norton, D. T., 1983, The social cost of the tobacco program redux, *Am J Agric Econ* **65**:117–119.

Meilke, K. D., and de Gorter, H., 1988, Impacts of the common agricultural policy on international wheat prices, *J Agric Econ* **39**:217–229.

Seagraves, J. A., 1983, The Life Cycle of the Flue-Cured Tobacco Program, Faculty Working Paper No. 34, Department of Economics and Business, North Carolina State University, Raleigh.

Smith, T. J., 1997, *European Agricultural Statistics*, Statistical Bulletin No. 937, Economic Research Service, U.S. Department of Agriculture, Washington, DC.

Theil, H., 1952, Qualities, prices and budget enquiries, *Rev Econ Stud* **19**:129–147.

THE IMPACTS OF LABELING ON TRADE IN GOODS THAT MAY BE VERTICALLY DIFFERENTIATED ACCORDING TO QUALITY

Brian Roe and Ian Sheldon*

Following Nelson (1970) and Darby and Karni (1973), analysis of asymmetric information and product quality has focused on the distinction between *search*, *experience*, and *credence* goods. In the case of search goods, information to aid consumers in their purchasing decisions is often plentiful; thus, market failure is not a significant problem, and government regulatory activity is relatively minor (Caswell and Mojduszka 1996). Most analysis has focused on experience goods (Stiglitz 1989), with significant contributions being made by Klein and Leffler (1981), Shapiro (1983), Allen (1984), and Riordan (1986). Results in this literature rely on quality being signaled to consumers via reputation effects. For example, Klein and Leffler show that if firms incur sunk costs by investing in firm-specific assets that are observable by consumers, high-quality goods will be supplied in equilibrium.

Typically, experience goods models rely on a repeat-purchase mechanism as a credible threat to discipline potentially cheating firms. It is assumed that, *ex post*, consumers will learn if they purchased a low-quality good at a high-quality price. This is then communicated to remaining consumers so that the cheating firm will be subject to a consumer boycott in future periods. There are two problems with this argument. First, it does not allow for uncertain product performance, which may result in a firm being permanently marked as a cheat even though there was no deliberate malfeasance on its part (Liebeskind and Rumelt 1989). Second, it assumes that consumers are actually able to assess quality even after consumption. Many goods are credence rather than experience goods; their quality is difficult to signal via private, reputation-type mechanisms (Caswell and Mojduszka 1996). In the case of credence goods, labeling, in its private or public form, has the ability to transform a market for credence goods from one plagued with a lemons-type informa-

* Brian Roe and Ian Sheldon are, respectively, an assistant professor and a professor in the Department of Agricultural, Environmental, and Development Economics, The Ohio State University. The authors acknowledge support from the Ohio Agricultural Research and Development Center.

Global Food Trade and Consumer Demand for Quality, edited by Krissoff *et al.*
Kluwer Academic/Plenum Publishers, New York, 2002.

tional problem into a fully functioning market. Specifically, labeling works where a reputable private or public certification agent is hired by firms to aid in the signaling of quality.

Interestingly, much of the literature on product differentiation has ignored the issue of imperfect information and product quality. Recently though, Bester (1998) introduced the notion of unobservable quality into a horizontal differentiation model of the type developed by d'Aspremont, Gabszewicz, and Thisse (1979), and showed that unobservable quality reduces firms' incentives for differentiation by relaxing price competition among firms in the sense that prices are a signal and include a quality premium. Bester suggested that such a result might also be generated in a vertical differentiation setting as developed by Shaked and Sutton (1982, 1983), but he did not develop the result. Boom (1995) introduced minimum quality standards into a vertical differentiation model, but did not address the issue of imperfect information and product quality.

In this chapter, we introduce continuous labeling into a vertical differentiation model under both autarky and free trade, where the quality of the good has credence attributes and is an endogenous decision of the competing firms. Under autarky, we show that, in the absence of a certified labeling scheme, there is market failure in that only the lowest possible quality will be supplied in equilibrium by a single firm that extracts monopoly profits given sunk costs of entry. If a continuous labeling system is implemented, and given specific assumptions about the distribution of income, consumer welfare is increased as a second firm enters the market and produces a higher quality good. We also establish that consumer welfare increases with trade and continuous labeling, although we are unable to predict the direction of trade.

The basic model used in the chapter is outlined in the following section. Next, we analyze the welfare effects of continuous labeling under, first, autarky, and then free trade. Finally, the chapter is summarized and conclusions are drawn.

THE BASE MODEL

Consumers, Firms, and Quality

Suppose in a specific country that consumers have a unit demand for a quality-differentiated product and utility is:

$$U = u(y - p) \tag{1}$$

where $u \in [\underline{u}, \infty)$ is the quality level of the differentiated good, $\underline{u} > 0$ is the minimum possible quality of the good, y is income, and p is the price of the differentiated good. If the consumer decides not to buy the differentiated good, $u = 0$; hence, the good is always purchased unless price exceeds income. Income is uniformly distributed on the interval $[a, b]$ with the simplifying assumption that $sN = b - a$ equals the population of the country under consideration; we shall normalize $s = 1$ when considering a single country's population.[1]

Firms produce only the differentiated product, and all firms share the same production technology characterized by zero production costs and a fixed quality-dependent cost, $F(u)$, which is sunk by the firm after entry. We assume:

$$F(u) = \epsilon + \alpha(u - \underline{u})^2 \qquad (2)$$

where ϵ and α are strictly positive constants. Sunk costs are convex and strictly increasing in the quality level.[2] Note also that a sunk cost of $\epsilon > 0$ must be expended to achieve even the lowest quality product.

The type of quality analyzed here occurs in a market characterized by vertical differentiation. Vertically differentiated goods have the following feature: if all products were priced at marginal cost, all consumers would choose the same quality. This clearly holds for the present utility and marginal cost of quality functions and will hold as long as consumer willingness to pay for quality increases more rapidly with quality than does the marginal cost of quality.

Game Structure

Firms maximize profit in the following one-shot, three-stage game described in Figure 1:

1. At the first stage, each firm decides to enter or not enter the market, incurring sunk costs ϵ if it chooses to enter.
2. At the second stage, firms that have entered simultaneously choose the quality level of their differentiated product, incurring the additional sunk cost for producing the chosen quality and also the costs of communicating that quality.
3. At the third stage, firms simultaneously set product prices.

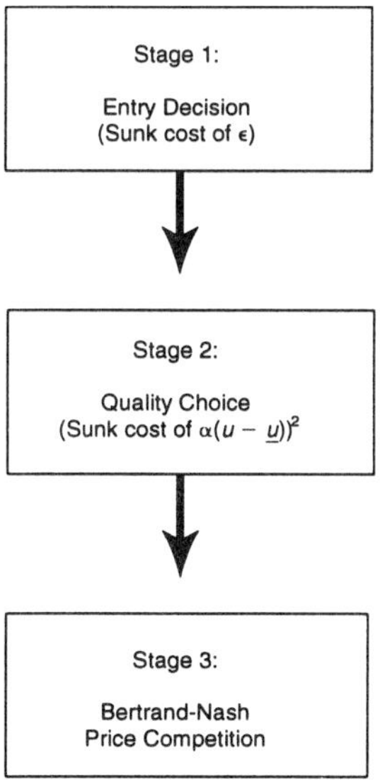

Figure 1. The three-stage game.

It is assumed that firms are perfectly informed about consumer preferences, income distribution, and all firms' technologies. We invoke the concepts of subgame perfect equilibrium and Bertrand-Nash competition for both the price- and quality-setting stages of the game.

Labeling Policy

This model differs from other vertical differentiation models in that the quality inherent in the product is a pure credence attribute. Hence, we assume no firm-based communication strategy can circumvent this problem and that all communication of quality occurs through a label that is administered by a separate, private firm or a government agency. Independent certification of product quality and labeling can either be voluntary or mandated by the government. We assume that the firm or agency monitors the quality of individual firms for a fee paid by the firms. Once the fee is paid, the quality monitoring firm assesses the production process and assigns a rating that perfectly corresponds with the quality; the labeling firm then precisely communicates each paying firm's rating to the consuming public.

Specifically, the fees paid by the firms producing the goods are:

$$\begin{aligned} I(u) &= I \text{ for } u > u \\ &= 0 \text{ for } u = \underline{u} \end{aligned} \tag{3}$$

where I is a positive constant representing the labeling firm's cost of administering the continuous labeling program. The second line of the definition reflects the fact that if a firm has no label, consumers assume that the product is of the lowest quality. Hence, a firm producing $\underline{u}$ will never pay for labeling. If more than one firm produced at a level above $\underline{u}$, we assume each firm is charged I—i.e., the cost of labeling involves no fixed costs, and there exist no economies of scale in providing this service.

Understanding the effect of a continuous labeling program is of particular, practical importance due to the popularity of such schemes in consumer goods markets. Continuous labeling of credence and experience attributes is common for many consumer durable goods (e.g., *Consumer Reports* ratings of durability); for complex service goods (e.g., report cards on health maintenance organizations); in nutrition contexts (e.g., the U.S. Food and Drug Administration's Nutrition Facts panel reports sodium content as a percentage of a recommended daily value); for energy conservation (e.g., the U.S. Environmental Protection Agency's energy efficiency ratings); and in environmental settings (e.g., ISO—International Organization for Standardization—14000 cradle-to-grave environmental labels and the New England Power Pool's environmental ratings of residential electricity services). In each setting, a vertical quality attribute that is difficult or impossible for a consumer to assess even after extensive experience with the good is revealed via a graduated scale as enforced by a governmental agency (e.g., the Food and Drug Administration or Environmental Protection Agency) or a private firm (e.g., *Consumer Reports*).

Entry and Number of Firms

Although solutions to multistage games typically begin with analysis of the third stage and proceed by backward induction, we draw upon previous results in the literature of vertical differentiation to make some initial remarks about the number of firms that will enter this market in the first stage of this game (see, e.g., Shaked and Sutton 1982, 1983; Motta 1993; Boom 1995; and Aoki and Prusa 1997). First, we assume the following:

$$4a > b > 2a \tag{4}$$

This assumption limits the dispersion of income across the population. With continuous labeling, this assumption ensures that exactly two firms will enter this market (as long as fixed costs plus labeling costs are not prohibitively high) and that each entrant experiences a positive market share in equilibrium—i.e., a natural duopoly. This restriction on income dispersion further ensures that all consumers will be at least indifferent between not purchasing the differentiated product and purchasing the lowest quality product (i.e., the market is covered). The proof follows from lemmas 1 and 2 in Shaked and Sutton (1982) and is sketched in the Appendix. Note that widening the income distribution will increase the number of firms that will enter the market so long as additional quality levels can be communicated by the labeling firm.

Price Equilibrium

We begin by solving the third stage of the game under the assumption that two firms have entered and chosen distinct, communicable quality levels ($0 < \underline{u} \leq u_1 < u_2$). Higher income consumers will choose the higher quality good. Define y_1 as the income at which the consumer is indifferent to buying either the high- or low-quality good:

$$y_1 = (1 - r)p_1 + rp_2 \text{ with } r = u_2/(u_2 - u_1) \tag{5}$$

where p_j is the price of the product with quality level j, and Eq. (5) is derived from Eq. (1). Also note that, given these prices, a consumer is indifferent between a product of quality u_1 and no product when $p_1 = y$. Given Eq. (5), profits of the two firms are:

$$\pi_1 = p_1(y_1 - \max[p_1, a]) - F(u_1) - I(u_1) \tag{6}$$

and

$$\pi_2 = p_2(b - y_1) - F(u_2) - I(u_2) \tag{7}$$

where $I(u_j)$ is the cost of communicating quality level u_j to consumers.

By taking first-order conditions of these profit functions, we can derive the Bertrand-Nash equilibrium. Three different equilibria could occur. The first is a *covered market* with equilibrium prices:

$$p_1^{cm} = (b - 2a)/3(r - 1) \tag{8}$$

$$p_2^{cm} = (2b - a)/3r \tag{9}$$

These hold if $p_1^{cm} < a$. This is equivalent to:

$$u_1 > [u_2(b - 2a)]/(b + a) \tag{10}$$

The second is a *corner solution* in which equilibrium prices are represented by:

$$p_1^{cs} = a \tag{11}$$

$$p_2^{cs} = [a(r - 1) + b]/2r \tag{12}$$

which holds if $p_1^{cm} \geqslant a \geqslant p_1^{uc}$; this condition is equivalent to:

$$[u_2(b - 2a)]/(b + a) \geqslant u_1 \geqslant u_2[(b - 4a)]/(b - a) \tag{13}$$

The third is an *uncovered market* with equilibrium prices of:

$$p_1^{uc} = b/(3r + 1) \tag{14}$$

$$p_2^{uc} = 2b/(3r + 1) \tag{15}$$

if $p_1^{uc} > a$; which holds if:

$$u_1 < u_2(b - 4a)/(b - a) \tag{16}$$

Equation (16) can never hold because of Eq. (4) and because $\underline{u} > 0$ by assumption. Hence, all consumers will have a choice between two distinct qualities offered by the two firms and will either always choose a differentiated product or be indifferent between the lowest quality and not purchasing a differentiated product.

The results concerning equilibrium prices will hold as long as $\underline{u} < u_1 < u_2$. These quality levels are assumed to be fixed during this third stage; hence, the quality levels need not have emerged from a second stage optimal choice by firms over all possible qualities but could also have emerged from firms' discrete choice over several communicable qualities.

Quality Equilibrium

If two firms enter and can communicate a continuum of quality, they will choose quality levels to maximize their profits. We now express the two profit functions as a function of qualities by utilizing Eq. (4) and equilibrium price expressions from Eqs. (8) and (9) or (11) and (12):

$$\pi_1(u_1;u_2) = \begin{cases} \pi_1^{cm} \equiv \dfrac{(b-2a)^2(u_2-u_1)}{9u_1} - F(u_1) - I(u_1) \text{ for } u_1 > \hat{u}_1(u_2) \\ \pi_1^{cs} \equiv \dfrac{1}{2}a(b-a-\dfrac{au_2}{u_2-u_1}) - F(u_1) - I(u_1) \text{ for } u_1 < \hat{u}_1(u_2) \end{cases} \tag{17}$$

$$\pi_2(u_1;u_2) = \begin{cases} \pi_2^{cm} \equiv \dfrac{(2b-a)^2(u_2-u_1)}{9u_2} - F(u_2) - I(u_2) \text{ for } u_2 < \hat{u}_2(u_1) \\ \pi_2^{cs} \equiv \dfrac{1}{4}\dfrac{((a-b)u_1+bu_2)^2}{u_2(u_2-u_1)} - F(u_2) - I(u_2) \text{ for } u_2 > \hat{u}_2(u_1) \end{cases} \tag{18}$$

The profit function changes at the same critical quality level as where the equilibrium price regime changes from a covered market to a market with a corner solution ($p_1 = a$). These quality thresholds are based upon the inequalities in Eq. (13) and are defined as follows:

$$\hat{u}_1(u_2) = [u_2(b - 2a)]/(b + a),\ \hat{u}_2(u_1) = [u_1(b + a)]/(b - 2a) \tag{19}$$

By Eq. (19), we can see that the qualities chosen in Stage 2 will determine if the price equilibrium established in Stage 3 is that of a covered or corner market.

First consider the quality choice of the low-quality firm (Firm 1). First-order conditions yield the following:

$$\frac{\partial \pi_1}{\partial u_1}(u_1;u_2) = \begin{cases} \dfrac{\partial \pi_1^{cm}}{\partial u_1} = -\dfrac{2(b-2a)^2}{9}\dfrac{u_2}{u_1^2} - F'(u_1) < 0 \text{ for } u_1 > \hat{u}_1(u_2) \\ \dfrac{\partial \pi_1^{cs}}{\partial u_1} = -\dfrac{a^2 u_2}{(u_2-u_1)^2} - F'(u_1) < 0 \text{ for } u_1 < \hat{u}_1(u_2) \end{cases} \tag{20}$$

Whether the market is a covered or corner equilibrium, the profits of the low-quality firm decrease as it raises its quality level. Increasing quality increases sunk costs, stimulates price competition with the higher quality firm (Firm 2) and requires a fixed expenditure to communicate quality via labeling. Furthermore, we have already shown that all consumers will buy the differentiated good; raising quality never pulls more customers into the market. Hence, Firm 1 always chooses:

$$u_1^{cm} = u_1^{cs} = \underline{u} \tag{21}$$

If the income distribution were broader such that the market were uncovered, increasing quality could draw more consumers into the market and may cause Firm 1's optimal quality to be interior.

Firm 2's optimal quality decision follows from differentiation of its profit function:

$$\frac{\partial \pi_2}{\partial u_2}(u_1;u_2) = \begin{cases} \dfrac{\partial \pi_2^{cm}}{\partial u_2} = \dfrac{(2b-a)^2}{9}\dfrac{u_1}{u_2^2} - F'(u_2) \text{ for } u_2 < \hat{u}_2(u_1) \\ \dfrac{\partial \pi_2^{cs}}{\partial u_2} = \dfrac{u_1}{2(u_2-u_1)^2}\left[\dfrac{(b-a)^2(u_2-u_1)^2}{2u_2^2} - \dfrac{a^2}{2}\right] - F'(u_2) \text{ for } u_2 > \hat{u}_2(u_1) \end{cases} \tag{22}$$

where the second derivative of π_2^{cm} is:

$$\partial^2 \pi_2^{cm}/\partial u_2^2 = -2/9[(2b - a)/u_2]^2(u_1/u_2) < 0 \tag{23}$$

and the second derivative of π_2^{cs} is:

$$\partial^2 \pi_2^{cs}/\partial u_2^2 = u_1/[2u_2^3(u_2 - u_1)^3]\,[a^2u_2^3 - (b - a)^2(u_2 - u_1)^3] - F''(u_2) \tag{24}$$

The negativity of Eq. (24) can be established in the following manner. First define $k = (b - a)/a$; by Eq. (4), we easily establish that $1 < k < 3$. Also note that π_2^{cs} is only of interest for $u_2 > \hat{u}(u_1) = u_1(k + 2)/(k - 1)$. A sufficient condition for Eq. (24) to be negative is: $k^{2/3}/(k^{2/3} - 1) < u_2/u_1$. If this holds for the smallest allowable u_2, and for $1 < k < 3$, then it will hold for all larger u_2. This reduces to verifying that $g(k) = 3k^{2/3} - k - 2 > 0$ for $1 < k < 3$ which, by visual inspection of Figure 2, holds. Hence, Firm 2's profit is a concave function of its own quality choice in the second stage. It can also be verified that Firm 2's profit function is continuous, as π_2^{cs} and π_2^{cm} are equal at $u_2 = \hat{u}_2(u_1)$.

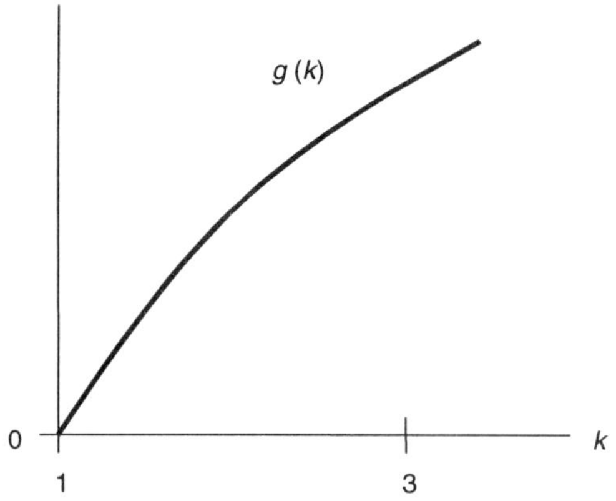

Figure 2. $g(k)$ is greater than zero in the relevant range.

Given that the low-quality firm always chooses $u_1 = \underline{u}$, Firm 2's optimal choice of quality is such that u_2 induces either a covered market price equilibrium:

$(\partial\pi_2/\partial u_{2)}\,(u_2;\underline{u}) = 0$ for $u_2 < \hat{u}_2(\underline{u})$

and a corner solution in prices:

$(\partial\pi_2/\partial u_2)\,(u_2;\underline{u}) > 0$ for $u_2 < \hat{u}_2(\underline{u})$, and $(\partial\pi_2/\partial u_2)\,(u_2;\underline{u}) < 0$ for $u_2 > \hat{u}_2(\underline{u})$

or an uncovered market:

$(\partial\pi_2/\partial u_{2)}\,(u_2;\underline{u}) = 0$ for $u_2 > \hat{u}_2(\underline{u})$

The equilibrium quality in a covered market is implicitly defined by:

$$u_2^{cm} = \left\{ u_2 \left| \frac{(2b-a)^2}{9}\frac{u_1}{u_2^2} - F'(u_2) = 0 \right. \right\} \tag{25}$$

In a corner solution, equilibrium is defined by:

$$u_2^{cs} = \hat{u}_2(\underline{u}), = [\underline{u}(b+a)]/2(b-a) \tag{26}$$

and, for an uncovered market, equilibrium is implicitly defined by:

$$u_2^{uc} = \left\{ u_2 \left| \frac{u_1}{2(u_2-u_1)^2}\left[\frac{(b-a)^2(u_2-u_1)^2}{2u_2^2} - \frac{a^2}{2}\right] - F'(u_2) = 0 \right. \right\} \tag{27}$$

The quality pairs of Eqs. (21) and (25), (21) and (26), or (21) and (27) represent a Nash equilibrium only if the low-quality firm has no incentive to leapfrog the high-quality firm—and, hence become the high-quality provider given that the high-quality firm has already chosen Eq. (25), (26), or (27). Boom (1995) has shown that such an incentive never exists if Eq. (25) holds; a unique Nash equilibrium exists in such a case. Otherwise, a unique equilibrium may consist of Eqs. (21) and (26) or (21) and (27), or a unique Nash equilibrium may not exist. The exact outcome depends on the severity of sunk costs, the lower threshold of quality, and the income distribution.

An Example: Continuous Labeling under Autarky

At this point, an explicit example will help solidify the model. Recall that $F(u_j) = \epsilon + \alpha(u_j - \underline{u})^2$ represents the structure of sunk quality costs and assume that $\underline{u} = 1$, $a = 4$, $b = 10$, $\alpha = 0.5$, and $\epsilon = 0.001$. Note that these assumptions satisfy Eq. (4). The results from this example are given in the second column of Table 1. The equilibrium in qualities is $u_1^{cm} = 1$, $u_2^{cm} = 3.42 < \hat{u}_2(1) = 7$. We verify that $u_1 = 1 > [u_2(b - 2a)]/(b + a) = 0.60$, which implies a covered equilibrium in prices. The price equilibrium is: $p_1^{cm} = 0.62$, $p_2^{cm} = 3.77$. Finally, we note that profits for the two firms are: $\pi_1^{cm} = 1.08$ and $\pi_2^{cm} = 17.20 - I$.

Firm 1's and Firm 2's profits are plotted in Figure 3 as a function of their own quality choices in the second stage of the game for this example.

Table 1. Welfare effects of labeling under autarky

	No labeling	Continuous labeling	Continuous labeling w/ trade
Low quality (u_1)	$\underline{u} = 1$	$\underline{u} = 1$	$\underline{u} = 1$
High quality (u_2)	None	3.42	4.21
Price of low quality (p_1)	5	0.62	0.68
Price of high quality (p_2)	NA	3.77	4.07
Income at which quality pref. switches (y_1)	$y < 5$ do not purchase	5.08	5.12
Low-quality firm's profits (π_1)	25	1.08	2.85
High-quality firm's profits (π_2)	NA	$17.20 - I$	$38.22 - I$
Total consumer welfare per country (CW)	12.5	67.61	76.12
Compensating variation to implement labeling policy per country (CV)	NA	19.10	18.42
Firms' increase in profits per country	NA	$-6.73 - I$	$-4.46 - I$
Firms' increase in profits + total consumer CV per country	NA	$12.38 - I$	$13.96 - I$

LABELING COST, ENTRY, AND WELFARE MEASUREMENT

In the example that ends the previous section, profits are positive for each firm; hence, the cost of the labeling program could approach π_2 and the entrance of both firms would still be guaranteed. The fact that labeling costs do not affect the entry decision of Firm 1 stems from the assumption made about the labeling program—i.e., a firm that produces the lowest possible level of quality does not need a labeling program to communicate its quality level effectively, and any firm producing a quality level above this must pay the full cost of the labeling program. Hence, a firm producing $\underline{u}$ will not pay for a voluntary program. A general result from the literature on vertically differentiated goods is that, when both firms enter the market, the high-quality firm will enjoy higher profits. Our example

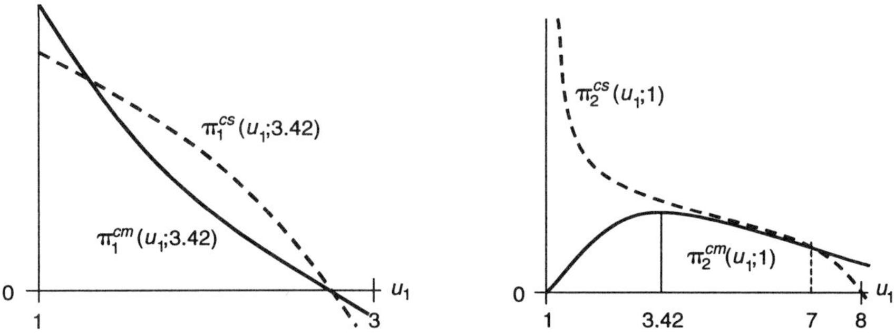

Figure 3. Firm 1's profits as a function of own quality are shown to the left; Firm 2's profits as a function of own quality are shown on the right.

can differ from this result; if the cost of the labeling program approaches π_2, the lower quality firm enjoys higher profits.

To gauge the effect of labeling on consumers, we compare consumer welfare both with and without labeling. First we establish the level of welfare obtained without labeling. Using standard arguments about market structure and price competition in the presence of exogenous sunk costs (Sutton 1991), we deduce that, in the absence of labeling, one firm enters the market, incurs a sunk cost ϵ, sells a product of quality $\underline{u}$, and charges a monopoly price—i.e., the second stage of the game in Figure 1 disappears. This follows from the fact that if a second firm were to enter at quality $\underline{u}$, Bertrand-Nash competition would drive the price to zero and firms would not cover their sunk costs.

The effects of the no labeling case using the specific assumptions from the previous example are reported in the first column of Table 1. Given the uniform income distribution, there exists a simple linear inverse demand function. Therefore, with zero marginal production costs, the monopoly price is $p^*_{nl} = \frac{1}{2}b = 5$, where the subscript *nl* refers to no labeling.[3] Also, because we have assumed that $\frac{1}{2}b > a$, the monopoly price with no labeling drives some portion of the income distribution out of the market as price exceeds this segment's incomes. The firm's profits are: $\pi^*_{nl} = s(b^2/4) - \epsilon \cong 25$.

Not surprisingly, the firm making monopoly profits in the case of no labeling is better off than if it were producing either low or high quality in the presence of continuous labeling. Total consumer welfare without labeling is considerably lower, however, than in the case with continuous labeling: $CW_{nl} = \int^b_{\frac{1}{2}b} \underline{u}(y - \frac{1}{2}b)dy = \frac{1}{8}\underline{u}b^2 = 12.5$.

Consumer welfare under continuous labeling is defined as:

$$CW_l = \int_a^{y_1} u_1^*(y - p_1^*)dy + \int_{y_1}^b u_2^*(y - p_2^*)dy \tag{28}$$

which equals 67.61 for the parametric assumptions used in the example. All consumers, regardless of income, benefit from higher quality.

INTERNATIONAL TRADE AND LABELING

We now consider a north-north trade scenario, such as in the European Union, in which two identical countries open up their markets for the credence good. By identical, we mean that the countries have the same income distributions and that firms face the same technology and cost of labeling, resulting in the same market structure in each country. Specifically, there are no orthodox reasons for trade to occur between the two countries.

Continuous Labeling

Under continuous labeling, the firms or agencies communicating quality in each country choose a common ratings scale or other means of continuous quality communication that is credible and comprehensible to consumers in both countries. To analyze such a case, we replicate the steps from the single-country, autarky case from above but modify the profit functions to accommodate that $b - a = sN$ where s will take on the value of 2 in the numerical example. This thickening of the population of possible buyers has no effect on the possible price equilibria and conditions listed in Eqs. (8)–(16).

The first thing to note is that exactly two firms will enter the unified market as the income dispersion is unchanged; hence, two firms that would have serviced the two markets under autarky will have to exit the integrated market. Which firms exit, and the location of the remaining firms, is completely arbitrary in the case considered here. Essentially, there is no underlying reason in terms of either technology, cost of labeling, or income distribution that would generate an incentive for firms to locate in one country as opposed to the other. Therefore, the direction of trade in the model is indeterminate, although the structure of trade may be intra-industry in nature if a firm in one country produces the low-quality good and exports it in exchange for the high-quality good produced by the other country (see Shaked and Sutton 1984, Beath and Katsoulacos 1991).

The profit functions change slightly in the case of trade to reflect the larger market populace:

$$\pi_1(u_1;u_2) = \begin{cases} \pi_1^{cm} \equiv \dfrac{s(b-2a)^2(u_2-u_1)}{9u_1} - F(u_1) - I(u_1) \text{ for } u_1 > \hat{u}_1(u_2) \\ \pi_1^{cs} \equiv \dfrac{sa}{2}(b-a-\dfrac{au_2}{u_2-u_1}) - F(u_1) - I(u_1) \text{ for } u_1 < \hat{u}_1(u_2) \end{cases} \tag{29}$$

$$\pi_2(u_1;u_2) = \begin{cases} \pi_2^{cm} \equiv \dfrac{s(2b-a)^2(u_2-u_1)}{9u_2} - F(u_2) - I(u_2) \text{ for } u_2 < \hat{u}_2(u_1) \\ \pi_2^{cs} \equiv \dfrac{s}{4}\dfrac{((a-b)u_1+bu_2)^2}{u_2(u_2-u_1)} - F(u_2) - I(u_2) \text{ for } u_2 > \hat{u}_2(u_1) \end{cases} \tag{30}$$

As in the case under autarky, the profit of Firm 1 is monotonically decreasing in its own quality for all $u_1 > 0$; hence $u_1^* = \underline{u}$. An example is given in Figure 4 for various sizes of the population.

Firm 2's profit is concave in the firm's own quality over the interval $[\underline{u},\infty)$. This can be verified in a manner similar to that used in the case of autarky. Again, we concentrate on the covered market equilibrium, which is defined by:

$$u_2^{cm} = \left\{ u_2 \left| \frac{s(2b-a)^2}{9}\frac{u_1}{u_2^2} - F'(u_2) = 0 \right. \right\}$$

Figure 4 offers a plot of profits and the different resulting quality levels under autarky and trade for the example used in this chapter.

The effects of free trade in the presence of continuous labeling are shown in the third column of Table 1. Clearly, if labeling is available, firms are better off under trade, as the variable s has a purely multiplicative effect on the profit functions listed in Eqs. (29) and (30): the profits of Firm 1 increase to 2.85, and those of Firm 2 to $(38.22 - I)$. Note, however, that total profits across firms are still smaller than monopoly profits with no labeling.

Trade induces competing effects with respect to consumer welfare. Higher quality is experienced for the segment of the population that purchases the labeled good but the price of this good also increases. Due to the higher price, fewer individuals purchase the higher quality good. For example, consider the consumer with income of 5.1. Under autarky, she purchases the high-quality good ($u_2 = 3.42$), pays price $p_2 = 3.77$, and experiences utility of $3.42*(5.10 - 3.77) \cong 4.55$. Under trade, she finds the lower quality good ($u_l = \underline{u} = 1$) preferable because the price of the high-quality good has increased to $p_2 = 4.07$. Purchasing the low-quality good at price $p_l = 0.68$ yields utility of $1*(5.10 - 0.68) \cong 4.42$, which is lower than under autarky. The net effect, however, as summed across individuals of all incomes, is that trade increases consumer welfare because the improvement in quality dominates the increase in prices. As reported in Table 1, *CW* increases from 67.61 under autarky to 76.12 under free trade.

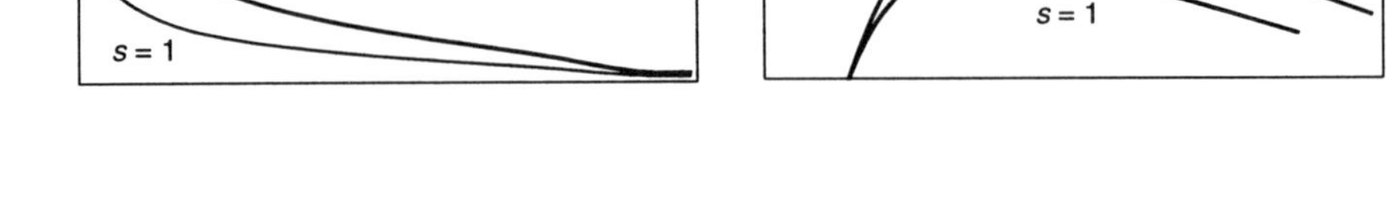

Figure 4. Firm 1's profits as a function of own quality with and without trade are shown on the left; Firm 2's profits as a function of own quality with and without trade are shown on the right.

SUMMARY AND CONCLUSIONS

This chapter focused on analyzing a model of vertical differentiation in the presence of credence goods. In the absence of a certified labeling scheme, there is market failure in that only the lowest possible quality will be supplied in equilibrium by a single firm that extracts monopoly profits given sunk costs of entry. If a continuous labeling system is implemented—and given specific assumptions about the distribution of income—consumer welfare is increased as a second firm enters the market and produces a higher quality good. This essentially replicates the results derived in the vertical differentiation literature when there is no credence good problem.

Unlike previous results from the vertical differentiation literature in which the higher quality firm earns greater profits than the low-quality firm in a vertical duopoly, we find that the firm that produces the high-quality good may earn profits that are greater than, equal to, or less than the profits of the low-quality firm. This emerges because the high-quality firm will choose to pay the cost of continuous labeling so long as profits over the three-stage game remain positive. One might imagine that, for costly quality and costly labeling, the low-quality firm may enjoy greater profits.

We also extended our analysis of continuous labeling from autarky to the case of free trade and established that aggregate consumer welfare increases with trade. However, a small segment of middle-income consumers may no longer afford the high-quality good and may experience a decrease in utility under trade. Total profits across firms increase under trade, although two firms service the integrated market whereas two firms serviced each market under autarky—i.e., two firms exit under trade. We are unable to predict the direction of trade, although its structure could be intra-industry in nature.

Given the specific assumptions made in this chapter, there are clearly two key directions in which this research could be taken. First, the assumptions concerning income distribution and technology need to be relaxed, allowing predictions to be made about the direction and structure of trade. For example, following Gabszewicz et al. (1981), overlapping income distributions could be assumed where one country has a higher mean income than the other, the former producing the high-quality good, the latter the low. Alternatively, either technology or the cost of labeling could be allowed to differ between countries. Introducing such differences would be particularly relevant in examining north-south trade and labeling in the presence of credence goods. Second, firms often use labeling in tandem with private communications to signal the quality of credence or experience attributes. Integrating nonlabeling communications (advertising or public relations campaigns) into the current model might improve our understanding of the interaction between firm-level and agency-level communications in establishing market structure and altering consumer welfare.

APPENDIX

We establish that, when $2a < b < 4a$, only two firms at most will enter the market. We follow closely the proofs from lemmas 1 and 2 in Shaked and Sutton (1982). Suppose three firms were to enter at the following distinct quality levels: u_1, u_2, and u_3. The following profit functions would emerge:

$$\pi_1 = p_1(y_1 - \max[p_1, a]) - \epsilon \tag{A1}$$

$$\pi_2 = p_2(y_2 - y_1) - F(u_2) - \epsilon \tag{A2}$$

$$\pi_3 = p_3(b - y_3) - F(u_3) - \epsilon \tag{A3}$$

where $y_1 = (1 - r')p_1 + r'p_2$ and $y_2 = (1 - r'')p_2 + r''p_3$, $r' = u_2/(u_2 - u_1)$, and $r'' = u_3/(u_3 - u_2)$. First-order conditions are:

$$\frac{\partial \pi_1}{\partial p_1} = \begin{cases} y_1 - a - p_1(r'-1) = 0 \text{ for } p_1 \leq a \\ y_1 - 2p_1 - p_1(r' - 1) = 0 \text{ for } p_1 \geq a \end{cases} \tag{A4}$$

$$\partial \pi_2 / \partial p_2 = y_2 - y_1 - p_2(r'' - 1) - p_2 r' = 0 \tag{A5}$$

$$\partial \pi_3 / \partial p_3 = b - y_2 - p_3 r'' = 0 \tag{A6}$$

From the definition of y_2, note that $p_3 r'' = y_2 - (1 - r'')p_2$; substituting this into Eq. (A6) yields:

$$b - 2y_2 - p_2(r'' - 1) = 0 \tag{A7}$$

which, by the fact that $r'' > 1$, implies that $b > 2y_2$. A similar substitution can be made into Eq. (A5), which yields:

$$y_2 - 2y_1 - p_2(r'' - 1) - p_0(r' - 1) = 0 \tag{A8}$$

which implies $y_2 > 2y_1$. Taken together, this implies that $b > 4y_1$. Our assumption that $4a > b$ implies that $4a > 4y_1$ or that $a > y_1$. This means that even the poorest consumer will not buy the lowest quality if all three firms were to enter and were allowed to choose prices simultaneously. Given the above, if three firms entered, at most two would obtain positive market share. Firms must at least cover their fixed costs if they are to enter at any given quality. Hence, at most, two firms will enter the market.

NOTES

1. Linearity of the utility function and a uniform distribution of income do not play a critical role in this type of vertical differentiation model (Shaked and Sutton 1983).
2. This form of cost function is very typical in the literature on vertical differentiation. The cost function's key characteristic is that the burden of quality improvement falls on fixed rather than variable costs and that fixed costs do not rise too rapidly.
3. Following Baumol, Panzar, and Willig (1982), if sunk costs were zero, the problem would reduce to that of a contestable market where the incumbent firm would price at zero given zero marginal production costs.

REFERENCES

Allen, F., 1984, Reputation and product quality, *Rand J Econ* **15**:311–327.
Aoki, R., and Prusa, T. J., 1997, Sequential versus simultaneous choice with endogenous quality, *Int J Ind Organ* **15**:103–121.
Baumol, W. J., Panzar, J. C., and Willig, R. D., 1982, *Contestable Markets and the Theory of Market Structure*, Harcourt Brace Jovanovich, San Diego.
Beath, J., and Katsoulacos, Y., 1991, *The Economic Theory of Product Differentiation*, Cambridge University Press, Cambridge, UK.
Bester, H., 1998, Quality uncertainty mitigates product differentiation, *Rand J Econ* **29**:828–844.
Boom, A., 1995, Asymmetric international minimum quality standards and vertical differentiation, *J Ind Econ* **43**:101–119.
Caswell, J. A., and Mojduszka, E. M., 1996, Using informational labeling to influence the market for quality in food products, *Am J Agric Econ* **78**(5):1248–1253.
Darby, M. R., and Karni, E., 1973, Free competition and the optimal amount of fraud, *J Law Econ* **16**(1):67–88.
d'Aspremont, C., Gabszewicz, J. J., and Thisse, J. F., 1979, On Hotelling's "stability in competition," *Econometrica* **47**:1145–1150.
Gabszewicz, J., Shaked, A., Sutton, J., and Thisse, J. F., 1981, International trade in differentiated products, *Int Econ Rev* **22**:527–535.
Klein, B., and Leffler, K. B., 1981, The role of market forces in assuring contractual performance, *J Polit Econ* **89**:615–641.
Liebeskind, J., and Rumelt, R. P., 1989, Markets for experience goods with performance uncertainty, *Rand J Econ* **20**:601–621.
Motta, M., 1993, Endogenous quality choice: Price vs. quantity competition, *J Ind Econ* **41**(2):113–131.
Nelson, P., 1970, Information and consumer behavior, *J Polit Econ* **78**(2):311–329.
Riordan, M. H., 1986, Monopolistic competition with experience goods, *Q J Econ* **101**:265–279.
Shaked, A., and Sutton, J., 1982, Relaxing price competition through product differentiation, *Rev Econ Stud* **49**:3–13.
———, 1983, Natural oligopolies, *Econometrica* **51**:1469–1483.
———, 1984, Natural oligopolies and international trade, in: *Monopolistic Competition and International Trade*, H. Kierzkowski, ed., Oxford University Press, Oxford, pp. 39–49.
Shapiro, C., 1983, Premiums for high quality products as returns to reputations, *Q J Econ* **98**:659–679.
Stiglitz, J. E., 1989, Imperfect information in the product market, in: *The Handbook of Industrial Organization*, R. Schmalensee and R. Willig, eds., North Holland, Amsterdam, pp. 769–847.
Sutton, J., 1991, *Sunk Costs and Market Structure*, MIT Press, Cambridge, MA.

LABELING BIOTECH FOODS

Implications for consumer welfare and trade

Elise Golan and Fred Kuchler*

Whether biotech agricultural products should be labeled has become an issue of contention both within the United States and between the United States and its trading partners.[1] Economists tend to argue that labeling and product differentiation of biotech and nonbiotech commodities and food products would expand consumer welfare. Such labeling would increase consumer choice and allow consumers to participate in determining the mix of biotech and nonbiotech products that are produced.

In this chapter, we note that although labeling and product differentiation may redress problems of asymmetric or missing information, they will usually not be successful in redressing problems of production externalities. As a result, biotech labeling is probably not a sufficient policy response to correct production externalities arising with biotech cultivation and production. Because of these externalities, we show that the introduction of biotech varieties could potentially result in a reduction in net consumer welfare under certain conditions. This result is unchanged even with mandatory labeling of biotech foods. We illustrate these theoretical results by examining potential changes to consumer surplus arising after the introduction of biotech soybeans.

Economic theory identifies a number of policy tools that may be more suited to redressing externalities than information. Bans, quotas, production regulations, or Pigouvian taxes may all be more successful than mandatory labels in adjusting consumption and production to better match socially optimal levels. The observation that labeling is not a "cure-all" solution has not been adequately acknowledged in the labeling debate, despite the observation that different countries have used different mixes of policies to address potential externality problems associated with biotech cultivation and food production. As a result, labeling has become a focal point in a debate that should be expanded to examine alternative policy tools.

---

* Elise Golan and Fred Kuchler are economists with the Economic Research Service, U.S. Department of Agriculture (USDA). The views expressed here are those of the authors and do not necessarily reflect official USDA positions.

Global Food Trade and Consumer Demand for Quality, edited by Krissoff *et al.*
Kluwer Academic/Plenum Publishers, New York, 2002.

In the first section of this chapter, we set up a comparative statics exercise to examine the impact of labeling and product differentiation in correcting for asymmetric or missing information. In the second section, we expand the analysis to examine the comparative statics results when externalities are introduced. We accompany the theoretical discussion with calculations of changes in consumer welfare triggered by the introduction of biotech soybean varieties. In the third section, we examine the reasons that labeling may not be successful in correcting externality problems. We conclude by discussing some of the reasons that labeling may continue to be a focal point of the biotech debate—and reasons to expect that a resolution to the labeling question will not end this debate.

LABELING AND PRODUCT DIFFERENTIATION INCREASE CONSUMER WELFARE: THE CASE OF ASYMMETRIC OR MISSING INFORMATION

When economists think of labels, they tend to think of trade. In fact, the raison d'être of labeling *is* trade. As noted by Susan Hadden in her 1986 book, *Read the Label: Reducing Risk by Providing Information*, "Trade beyond neighbors gave rise to the need for labels."[2] Quite simply, labels let us know what we're buying. As a result, labels play an important role in making the market work. Labels and the information they contain allow consumers to make purchases that best match their preferences. In this way, labels increase market efficiency: resources are allocated to the production of goods and services according to consumer preferences.

In this context, the question of whether consumers should have access to information about the biotech characteristics of food has a rather straightforward answer. If consumers value the information enough to cover the costs of supplying the information, they should have it.

In most cases, information of value to consumers will be supplied by the market. Private firms have an incentive to supply voluntarily *all* of the positive information that is relevant to consumers' purchasing decisions. Because skeptical consumers expect that labels are as optimistic as truth permits, they will infer that every attribute that the firm does not discuss is negative; either the product does not possess the desirable attributes or the attributes are of low quality (Grossman 1981). Competition among firms also works to inform consumers about both desirable and undesirable product characteristics. For example, the producer of a food product low in fat might voluntarily advertise that fact. A competitor with a similar product low in both fat and sodium would have an incentive to advertise its product's two desirable attributes. Consumers would then be suspicious of products that failed to make both claims. This competitive disclosure, which Ippolito and Mathios (1990a) named the "unfolding" theory, results in explicit claims for all positive aspects of products and allows consumers to make appropriate inferences about foods without claims.

The unfolding theory also leads to the conclusion that firms' advertising may inadvertently alert consumers to negative aspects of products. For example, absent any labeling requirements, the food product that advertises itself as "nonbiotech" alerts consumers to the probability that other food products contain biotech ingredients. The unfolding theory implies that the presence of advertising (including labels) is a signal of quality and that competitive products without such advertising are alerting consumers to its absence.

In some cases, the fact that information is not supplied by the market indicates that the information is not valuable to consumers in making their purchasing decisions. In other cases, information may not be supplied by the market because such information involves a negative credence attribute that is shared by a whole product category. That is, if no firm has the technical capability to eliminate the negative credence attribute, no firm will have an incentive to reveal this attribute. In these cases, one could argue that mandatory labeling is necessary to enhance market efficiency.

Whether due to voluntary market disclosure or mandatory labeling, information and product differentiation expand consumer choice, allowing consumers to make purchases that best match their preferences. Labeling thus increases market efficiency. It also reduces search costs for consumers, thus facilitating trade.

The typical narrative illustrating the process of differentiation describes a market in which the introduction of a new good expands choice and increases consumer welfare. For the biotech story, this narrative begins by assuming a market in which all products are some indistinguishable mix of biotech and nonbiotech commodities and products. Here, and in all of our examples, we restrict our analysis to first-generation biotech varieties. These varieties have cost-reducing producer attributes, but no consumer attributes. The majority of biotech varieties currently on the market are first generation.[3] If commodities are undifferentiated in the initial period, consumers are limited to one consumption choice: biotech foods. Assume perfectly competitive markets so that initially this market equilibrium is described by:

$$P_{o(biotech)} = MC_{o(biotech)} \tag{1}$$

Some consumers prefer to consume nonbiotech foods. To meet the nonbiotech demand, some producers market nonbiotech commodities and food products, and label them as such. By definition, first-generation biotech varieties are cost reducing, so producers specializing in nonbiotech commodities have higher production costs. As a result,

$$MC_{o(biotech)} < MC_{nonbiotech} \tag{2}$$

and eventually the market settles at two prices for two goods:

$$P_{o(biotech)} < P_{nonbiotech} \tag{3}$$

The introduction of the nonbiotech products creates gains for those consumers who value these quality attributes. Those who value the information about nonbiotech status pay for the information. Information and product differentiation lead to better matching of preferences with purchases and increase the efficiency of the market.

LABELING AND PRODUCT DIFFERENTIATION MAY NOT INCREASE CONSUMER WELFARE: THE CASE OF PRODUCTION EXTERNALITIES

Although labeling and product differentiation may lead to an efficient market outcome in the case of asymmetric or missing information, this may not necessarily be the case when production externalities are involved. Biotech cultivation and production may impose externality costs on nonbiotech producers. Some of these externality costs arise lock-step with product differentiation. Identity preservation of nonbiotech commodities will demand segregation from biotech commodities. At the farm level, farmers will have to take precautions to ensure that their crops are not cross pollinated by biotech crops. In fact, all along the production and distribution system, nonbiotech producers may need to absorb additional costs to ensure that their products remain nonbiotech. These costs may include those for separate storage and transportation facilities, additional cleaning expenses, and testing and certification services.[4]

These costs are not simply related to the scale of biotech cultivation. So long as there is one biotech farmer, there is a potential for mixing biotech and nonbiotech products. That is, to have nonbiotech products, nonbiotech industries and consumers must incur the same costs regardless of whether there is one biotech farm or whether biotech production methods predominate.

Because biotech production may impose externalities on nonbiotech producers, labeling and product differentiation may not lead to an efficient market outcome. To see this, suppose that the initial market equilibrium for a competitive market for a commodity is described by:

$$P_{o(nonbiotech)} = MC_{o(nonbiotech)} \tag{4}$$

Unlike the previous scenario, in this case, the initial period describes a situation in which all commodities and foods are nonbiotech. Then a first-generation, cost-reducing biotech variety of the commodity is introduced, where:

$$MC_{biotech} < MC_{o(nonbiotech)} \tag{5}$$

Through competitive market forces, at least some of the lower biotech production costs are eventually passed on to consumers in the form of lower prices, so that:

$$P_{biotech} < P_{o(nonbiotech)} \tag{6}$$

Some consumers do not view the biotech and nonbiotech products as equivalent and demand nonbiotech products. To meet the nonbiotech demand, some producers market nonbiotech commodities and food products. However, to ensure the nonbiotech quality of their products, these producers must now contend with a set of externalities generated by the cultivation and production of biotech commodities and foods. The externality costs imposed by biotech production lead to a higher marginal cost for nonbiotech production than in the initial period:

$$MC_{o(nonbiotech)} < MC_{nonbiotech} \tag{7}$$

Eventually these additional production costs will be passed to consumers and the nonbiotech market will settle at higher price than the initial nonbiotech price:

$$P_{o(nonbiotech)} < P_{nonbiotech} \tag{8}$$

In the final equilibrium, two different prices emerge:

$$P_{biotech} < P_{o(nonbiotech)} < P_{nonbiotech} \tag{9}$$

In the final equilibrium, those consumers who are indifferent between biotech and nonbiotech foods now pay $P_{biotech}$ for foods that they previously purchased at $P_{o(nonbiotech)}$. As compared with the initial equilibrium, these consumers benefit from the reduction in food prices, with the exact size of their welfare gain depending on the number of consumers and the intensity of their preferences. Those consumers who prefer nonbiotech foods now pay the higher price, $P_{nonbiotech}$, for the exact same foods that they previously purchased at price $P_{o(nonbiotech)}$. These consumers are worse off than before the introduction of the first-generation biotech technologies. If the decrease in consumer surplus arising from the increase in the nonbiotech price is larger than the increase in consumer surplus arising from the drop in the price of biotech foods, then the inequality in Eq. (9) describes a net decrease in consumer welfare with respect to the initial market equilibrium.

The final equilibrium condition described in Eq. (9) is very different from that described in Eq. (3). The equilibrium in Eq. (3) describes a situation in which consumer welfare necessarily rises. The equilibrium described in Eq. (9) explicitly accounts for the production externality and introduces the possibility that net consumer benefits may not be positive after the introduction of first-generation biotech foods—even if these foods are differentiated. Consumer welfare falls for those consumers preferring nonbiotech because biotech cultivation and production impose externalities on nonbiotech cultivation and production. The problem is not simply one of scale economies: it persists even if the nonbiotech market is the larger of the two. The gap between $P_{o(nonbiotech)}$ and $P_{nonbiotech}$ includes the precautions that biotech producers must take to ensure that cross pollination does not occur and that even a few grains of biotech commodity are not incorporated into their product.

The rise in the price of nonbiotech foods occurs whether the differentiation process is triggered by voluntary labeling of nonbiotech foods (and unfolding) or by mandatory labeling of biotech foods. This is because, currently, consumers who care most about the biotech status of a food are those who prefer to consume nonbiotech food. As a result, even if biotech producers are required to label their products with "May contain biotech material" or "Does contain biotech material," it will still be left to nonbiotech producers to certify that their products are indeed nonbiotech. Biotech producers do not have the incentive to strictly segregate, test, or certify that their products do not contain nonbiotech ingredients because their consumers are indifferent between biotech and nonbiotech products. In most cases, even with mandatory biotech labeling, nonbiotech producers and consumers will bear the costs of segregation, and labeling will not be a successful strategy for internalizing externality costs.

To get some idea of the magnitude of the types of changes in consumer surplus generated by the market equilibrium described in Eq. (9), we did some very rough, back-of-the-envelope calculations of the sort of trade-offs emerging or being predicted in the market for soybeans. To calculate consumer surplus gains due to lower prices arising from biotech adoption, we used biotech price change amounts based on results from Falck-Zepeda, Traxler, and Nelson (2000). This study develops a soybean world supply-demand model to examine the surplus created by the introduction of biotech soybeans.[5] Even including rather strong positive yield effects, the largest price decrease calculated in the Falck-Zepeda, Traxler, and Nelson study is $0.0009 per pound. We use this number for our "large biotech market effect" price change, as shown in row 1 of Table 1. If all consumers are indifferent between biotech and nonbiotech foods, then the consumer surplus generated by this price change would be $74 million. Although our calculations are less sophisticated, they are similar to the amounts calculated by Falck-Zepeda, Traxler, and Nelson ($76 million).

In the second row of Table 1, we consider the situation in which 5 percent of consumers prefer nonbiotech foods. The price premium for nonbiotech soybeans is taken from the upper end of the 1 to 5 percent premiums reported during the summer of 1999 (see ERS 2000). We set the "small nonbiotech market effect" price increase at $0.005 per pound, a roughly 4 percent increase over the $0.13 per pound base price.[6] This price increase triggers a decrease in consumer surplus of $21 million. The accompanying increase in consumer surplus due to the lower cost of biotech beans is $71 million. The net change is +$50 million.

If the dynamics of the market were such that more and more consumers preferred nonbiotech foods, then the relative size of the consumer welfare loss due to higher nonbiotech prices would begin to outweigh the gains due to the lower biotech price, as depicted in rows 3 and 4. This result is somewhat damped by the observation that as the nonbiotech market share grows, the price premium for nonbiotech would probably shrink (with processing economies of scale). This result is reinforced by the observation that, as the size of the biotech market shrinks, the yield and acreage effects that helped spur the large $0.0009 decrease would be diminished (as would processing economies of scale). Consequently, the biotech price decrease would probably not be as large as market share declined. The fact that the price decrease due to biotech is much smaller than even the small nonbiotech premiums that have been observed in the U.S. market implies that when as little as 25 percent of the market prefers nonbiotech, then losses to consumers may outweigh gains.

Although the trade-offs in consumer welfare are interesting in that they reveal the rather low level of nonbiotech demand and the small differences in relative prices that are capable of triggering a fall in net consumer welfare, these shifts in consumer surplus are actually relatively small. To give a notion of what these shifts really mean to the consumer in terms of the plate of food that he or she puts on the table every night, we translated these numbers into changes in the price of a pound of beef.

Table 1. Changes in price and U.S. consumer welfare due to market differentiation

Scenario	Biotech soybean price change ($/lb)	Nonbiotech soybean price change ($/lb)	Biotech consumer surplus ($ million)	Nonbiotech consumer surplus ($ million)
All consumers are indifferent between biotech and nonbiotech foods—large biotech market effect	–0.0009		+74	
5% of consumers prefer nonbiotech foods:				
Large biotech mkt effect	–0.0009		+71	
Small nonbiotech mkt effect		+0.005		–21
25% of consumers prefer nonbiotech foods:				
Large biotech mkt effect	–0.0009		+56	
Medium biotech mkt effect	–0.00045		+28	
Small nonbiotech mkt effect		+0.005		–104
50% of consumers prefer nonbiotech foods:				
Medium biotech mkt effect	–0.00045		+19	
Small biotech mkt effect	–0.0002		+8	
Medium nonbiotech mkt effect		+0.0025		–103
Large nonbiotech mkt effect		+0.001		–41

The first step was to calculate how much soy is in a pound of beef. About 3,000 pounds of grain are required to finish a feedlot steer under current feedlot technology. Most of this grain is corn, but not all. Some milo, or grain sorghum, barley, rye, oats, wheat, and other forms of grains or grain byproducts, such as corn gluten meal, are fed as substitutes for corn. Protein content is likely to be 15 to 20 percent of the feedlot diet. Protein may be in the form of legume hay and oilseed meals—cottonseed meal, soybean meal, linseed oil meal, and others. As the majority of feedlots are in the Midwest where soybean meal use is typical, we assumed that feedlots would feed 750 pounds of soybean meal, derived from 952.5 pounds of soybeans.

A feedlot steer weighs about 1,100 to 1,200 pounds coming out of the feedlot and produces about 470 pounds of mainly boneless retail beef at the grocery store. A cull cow weighs about 1,000 pounds and produces slightly less beef. The 3,750 pounds of corn and soybean meal fed to a steer translates into over 6 pounds of corn and 2 pounds of soybeans for each pound of retail beef.[7]

To translate these amounts into beef price changes, we make the simplifying assumption that the beef production, distribution, and marketing system is competitive and operates at constant marginal costs. On this basis, the entire calculated cost increase or decrease would be passed on to consumers. A price fall of $0.0009 per pound of biotech soybeans therefore results in a decrease in the price of beef of roughly $0.0018 per pound. A $0.005 per pound rise in the price of nonbiotech soybeans translates into an increase in the price of beef of $0.01 per pound.[8] These price changes are quite small. According to these calculations, the benefits of biotech soybeans do not translate into big changes for the consumer (these results would be larger, although still small, if biotech corn was also considered). The cost of nonbiotech soy-fed beef is also not very large.

To calculate consumer surplus changes from the beef price change numbers, we assumed a constant price elasticity of demand. The estimated price elasticity of beef demand was set at –0.6212 (Huang 1993). We calculated U.S. beef consumption by multiplying per capita consumption—67.9 pounds retail cut equivalent—by population—270,290,000 (both in 1998, Putnam and Allshouse 1999). We used an estimate of the 1998 retail price of choice beef of 277.1 cents per pound.[9] When 5 percent of the market prefers nonbiotech beef, the drop in consumer surplus due to the higher price of nonbiotech soy is $9 million (first row, Table 2). The accompanying rise in consumer welfare due to the drop in the

Table 2. Changes in price and U.S. consumer welfare due to product differentiation for beef, where changes are triggered by a price decrease in biotech soybeans ($0.0009/lb) and a price increase in nonbiotech soybeans ($0.005/lb)

Scenario	Biotech beef price change ($/lb)	Nonbiotech beef price change ($/lb)	Biotech beef consumer surplus ($ million)	Nonbiotech beef consumer surplus ($ million)
5% of consumers prefer nonbiotech foods	–0.0018	+0.01	+32	-9
25% of consumers prefer nonbiotech foods	–0.0018	+0.01	+25	–46
50% of consumers prefer nonbiotech foods	–0.0018	+0.01	+17	–93

price of biotech soy is $32 million. By the time 25 percent of the market prefers nonbiotech beef, the net consumer welfare change is negative, with a drop of $46 million and an increase of $25 million (second row, Table 2).

LABELING AND EXTERNALITIES: WHY DOESN'T IT WORK? WHAT ARE THE OTHER OPTIONS?

The fact that biotech production imposes externality costs on nonbiotech producers implies that labeling will not be a successful policy to maximize consumer welfare. Unfortunately, externality problems may actually be the main reason that many consumers and consumer groups are calling for labeling. Consumer surveys reveal that one of the primary reasons that consumers object to biotech foods is the potential for environmental damage, and one of the main reasons they support biotech agriculture is its potential to reduce chemical use in agriculture (Hoban 1999).

In externality cases, labeling advocates argue that social welfare may be maximized by a labeling choice that differs from the one generated by private costs and benefits. For example, the potential social benefits of providing dietary information on labels may include a healthier, more productive population and reductions in medical costs. These potential benefits may be larger than the increase in profits that compose a private firm's labeling benefits. As a result, the social benefits of labeling may outweigh the social costs even though the private benefits do not outweigh private costs. The opposite could also be true; the net social benefits of labeling could be negative, while the net private benefits could be positive. For example, the social costs of labeling alcoholic beverages with the information that a drink a day lowers the risk of heart disease may outweigh the private costs. The social costs of such a label could include increased rates of birth defects, car accidents, and alcohol-related health costs, while private costs simply include the costs of redesigning labels. The social costs associated with this label may outweigh the social benefits of a lower incidence of heart disease, though clearly, the private benefits of such a label (increased sales) may definitely outweigh the costs.

In externality cases where private firms do not supply relevant information, the government may decide to intervene in labeling decisions to try to maximize net social benefits. Government-mandated labeling can be a useful tool for achieving social objectives because of the potential power of information to influence consumption decisions. In this role, labeling falls into that category of government policy dubbed by Magat and Viscusi (1992) as "information provision programs to alter people's economic behavior."

Some consumer and producer groups argue that because of the potential externality costs of biotech cultivation and consumption, the government should require labeling of all biotech food products. They argue that consumers have a right to know if their food has been genetically engineered, and that if the potential social costs of biotech food production were considered in determining food consumption choices—including potential public health costs and environmental externalities—consumers would reduce their consumption of biotech foods.

One of the primary difficulties in trying to maximize net social benefits through labeling is that although individuals may alter their consumption behavior in response to information on social costs and benefits, this change will rarely reflect all social welfare effects.

Even if certain individuals alter their behavior to reflect social costs and benefits completely, the fact that different individuals place different values on different social objectives means that, again, these objectives will probably not be met. For example, although some consumers may only purchase free-range chickens, the fact that most consumers continue to purchase coop chickens means that the goal of more humane treatment of chickens is not achieved. Even if all individuals equally value the social objective, differing preferences for the targeted consumption good may lead to less than optimal results. For example, even if consumers agree that a slimmer, fitter population is a good social (and personal) objective, some consumers' preferences for fatty foods and inactivity may outweigh their valuation of the social objective.

Labels may also be unsuccessful in sufficiently changing behavior to meet a social objective if consumers opt to "free ride" on others' socially responsible behavior. For example, although a consumer may feel that sea turtles should be protected and that strict laws protecting their lives should be enforced, he or she may decide that partaking of one small bowl of turtle soup will not really make a difference. Labels may also be unsuccessful in reaching social goals because collective benefits are rarely evenly distributed. Even if individuals have similar preferences over the social outcome, the fact that some benefit more than others probably means that not everyone will change their consumption behavior to match the social optimum (Hadden 1986)

Proponents of mandatory labels often have ignored findings that it is difficult to convey information through labels. Magat and Viscusi (1992) argue that informational regulations such as labeling generally are not very effective and that there are some circumstances, such as when people do not read or do not care about the information on the label, in which they may not be effective at all. Empirical studies have found labels to be both successful (Ippolito and Mathios 1990b, 1995) and unsuccessful (Variyam, Blaylock, and Smallwood 1995, 1997; Moorman 1996) in educating consumers and changing consumption behavior.

Empirical studies highlight the observation that not just the information itself but also the format and context in which it is presented are important elements in maximizing the possibility that labeled information will reach its audience. Clear, concise labels are most successful at informing consumers. Labels that attempt to convey information about hazards or relationships that are ill defined will be less successful. Not only is it difficult to convey such information on a label, it is difficult for consumers to decipher it. Consumers have a particularly difficult time making sense of small probabilities or of information about an issue that does not have scientific or political consensus (for an analysis of how consumers react to risk information, see Slovic, Fischhoff, and Lichtenstein 1982; and Magat and Viscusi 1992).

Economic theory identifies a number of policy tools that may be more suited to redressing externalities than information (Just, Hueth, and Schmitz 1982). Bans, quotas, production regulations or standards, and Pigouvian taxes may all be more successful than mandatory labels in adjusting consumption and production to better match socially optimal levels. For biotech crops, such policy could include production regulations involving buffer strips and refuges. Different governments may use different mixes of policy tools to help regulate externalities. The extent to which any of these other tools are employed to control externalities leaves less of the task to labeling policy.

CONCLUSIONS AND IMPLICATIONS FOR TRADE

The existence of biotech production externalities weakens the strength of labeling and product differentiation to maximize market efficiency and increase consumer welfare. For the case of biotech soybeans, we show that after the introduction of biotech varieties, a net loss in consumer surplus can occur even when only 25 percent of the market prefers non-biotech foods. This result does not change with mandatory labeling of biotech crops and foods. However, these results could be changed by other policy tools.

Stakeholders in biotech trade disagree over many issues, including the extent of potential biotech externalities and the role of the government, scientists, and consumers in determining the proper level of regulation. These basic disagreements have contributed to complicating negotiations over trade in biotech foods and commodities. Labeling has become a flash point in these negotiations because of the lack of consensus on how to address externality concerns.

In many regulatory policy debates, there is little consensus on the appropriate regulatory response. Some groups may advocate complete product bans, while others advocate no government intervention at all. These debates could be national or international and could lead to difficult problems in harmonizing standards for a wide range of goods. In these cases, labeling may represent not just the best compromise solution but also the path of least resistance, both domestically and internationally. In this capacity, the labeling option has a political appeal that is independent of its merits (a point made by Magat and Viscusi [1992], with respect to hazard-warning programs).

The danger with using labeling to avoid political stalemate in the biotech debate is that not only will such labeling usually fail to correct externalities, it will also fail to provide consumers with any real information. This may particularly be the case when the lack of political consensus arises from a lack of scientific consensus. As pointed out by Hadden (1986), "Policymakers like labeling precisely because it leaves these difficult choices to the individuals who will benefit from or suffer the risk." She goes on to note that "It is unreasonable to expect individuals to process information that has confounded the experts."

NOTES

1. Agricultural biotechnology is a collection of scientific techniques, including conventional hybridization, that are used to modify or improve plants, animals, and microorganisms. Recently, the term biotechnology has been used to refer more specifically to products that have been genetically engineered (biochemical manipulation of genes or DNA). This is the meaning adopted here.

2. Hadden goes on to note that the very origin of writing has been traced back to tokens used in the ancient Near East to keep track of commodities and that the seals at sites of the ninth century B.C. Harappan civilization of South Asia indicate the owner and/or contents of the containers they closed (Hadden 1986).

3. An analysis of second-generation biotech varieties, those with attributes of value to consumers, would be quite different. Producers would have an incentive to label and

segregate these commodities and food products in order to gain any price premiums arising from their valuable attributes.

4. Other possible externalities that have been mentioned in the debate include resistance development in target and nontarget insects and weeds, the effect of pest-resistance crops on nontargeted species, and genetic flow from one species to another so that wild plant populations develop biotech traits such as herbicide and pest resistance. (For a comprehensive examination of potential health and environmental externalities, see Nelson et al. 1999.)
5. Moschini, Lapan, and Sobolevsky (2000) investigate similar questions.
6. This level of price increase is not without precedent: the price premium for food quality soybeans is about 20 percent (Bender et al. 1999).
7. Unpublished calculations by Ken Mathews, Economic Research Service, U.S. Department of Agriculture.
8. We calculated the beef price decrease brought about by the introduction of biotech soybeans as follows: 750 pounds soybean meal per 470 pounds of beef) × (1.27 pounds soybeans per pound of soybean meal) × (–$0.0009 per pound of soybeans) = –$0.00184 per pound of beef. The beef price increase faced by the nonbiotech consumers was calculated similarly: 750 pounds soybean meal per 470 pounds of beef) × (1.27 pounds soybeans per pound of soybean meal) × ($0.005 per pound of soybeans) = $0.01 per pound of beef.
9. Estimate provided by Larry Duewer, Economic Research Service, U.S. Department of Agriculture.

REFERENCES

Bender, K., Hill, L., Wenzel, B., and Hornbaker, R., 1999, *Alternative Market Channels for Specialty Corn and Soybeans*, AE-4126, Department of Agricultural and Consumer Economics, University of Illinois at Urbana-Champaign.

Economic Research Service (ERS), U.S. Department of Agriculture, 2000, *Changing Markets and the Government's Role*, http://www.ers.usda.gov/whatsnew/issues/biotechmarkets/governmentrole.htm (accessed June 25, 1999).

Falck-Zepeda, J., Traxler, G., and Nelson, R., 2000, Rent creation and distribution from biotechnology innovations: The case of Bt cotton and herbicide-tolerant soybeans in 1997, *Agribusiness* **16**(1):21–32.

Grossman, S. J., 1981, The informational role of warranties and private disclosure about product quality, *J Law Econ* **24**(3):461–483.

Hadden, S. G., 1986, *Read the Label: Reducing Risk by Providing Information*, Westview Press, Boulder.

Hoban, T., 1999, What Do Consumers Really Want and Need from Food Labels? Paper presented at AgBiotech Symposium on GM Foods, Nov. 10–12, Georgetown University, Washington, DC.

Huang, K., 1993, *A Complete System of U.S. Demand for Food*, Technical Bulletin No. 1821, Economic Research Service, U.S. Department of Agriculture, Washington, DC.

Ippolito, P. M., and Mathios, A. D., 1990a, The regulation of science-based claims in advertising, *J Consum Policy* **13**:413–445.

———, 1990b, Information, advertising, and health choices, *Rand J Econ* **21**:459–480.

———, 1995, Information and advertising: The case of fat consumption in the United States, *Am Econ Rev* **85**:132–156.

Just, R., Hueth, D., and Schmitz, A., 1982, *Applied Welfare Economics and Public Policy*, Prentice-Hall, Englewood Cliffs, NJ.

Magat, W. A., and Viscusi, W. K., 1992, *Informational Approaches to Regulation*, MIT Press, Cambridge, MA.

Moorman, C., 1996, A quasi experiment to assess the consumer and informational determinants of nutrition information processing activities: The case of the Nutrition Labeling and Education Act, *J Public Policy Mark* **15**(1):28–44.

Moschini, G., Lapan, H., and Sobolevsky, A., 2000, Roundup Ready® soybeans and welfare effects in the soybean complex, *Agribusiness* **16**(1):33–55.

Nelson, G., Josling, T., Bullock, D., Unnevehr, L., Rosegrant, M., Hill, L., with Babinard, J., Cunningham, C., De Pinto, A., and Nitsi, E., 1999, *The Economics and Politics of Genetically Modified Organisms in Agriculture: Implications for WTO 2000*, Bulletin 809, University of Illinois at Urbana-Champaign.

Putnam, J., and Allshouse, J., 1999, *Food Consumption, Prices, and Expenditures, 1970-97*, Statistical Bulletin No. 965, Food and Rural Economics Division, Economic Research Service, U.S. Department of Agriculture, Washington, DC.

Slovic, P., Fischhoff, B., and Lichtenstein, S., 1982, Facts versus fears: Understanding perceived risk, in: *Judgement Under Uncertainty: Heuristics and Biases*, E. Kahneman, P. Slovic, and A. Tversky, eds., Cambridge University Press, Cambridge, UK.

Variyam, J., Blaylock, J., and Smallwood, D., 1995, *Modeling Nutrient Intake: The Role of Dietary Information*, Technical Bulletin No. 1842, Economic Research Service, U.S. Department of Agriculture, Washington, DC.

———, 1997, *Diet-Health Information and Nutrition: The Intake of Dietary Fats and Cholesterol*, Technical Bulletin No. 1855, Economic Research Service, U.S. Department of Agriculture, Washington, DC.

CONSUMER EFFECTS OF HARMONIZING INTERNATIONAL STANDARDS FOR TRADE IN ORGANIC FOODS

Luanne Lohr and Barry Krissoff*

Worldwide markets for organic foods are expanding, with annual growth rates of 5 to 30 percent in the European Union (EU), the United States, and Japan for more than five years. Using 1997 sales data and annual growth rates from the International Trade Centre (ITC 1999), and assuming a linear trend, projected market size in 2010 will be at least $46 billion in the EU, $45 billion in the United States, and $11 billion in Japan. As many as 20 to 30 percent of consumers surveyed in Europe, North America, and Japan claim to purchase organic foods on a regular basis (Lohr 1998a). Yet "organic" does not mean the same thing to all these consumers, because organic food production and processing standards are not harmonized across countries. Certifiers of organic food production, processing, and handling use different rules according to regulatory, philosophical, and technical goals. This research compares the trade and welfare implications of harmonizing international standards for organic food certification with the status quo market response to differential standards.

We develop a partial equilibrium trade model to illustrate the gains and losses associated with international harmonization of organic standards. Market behavior is simulated under realistic assumptions about the evolution of a harmonized standard to obtain welfare results for comparison with the status quo market response to varying standards. We identify the conditions under which harmonization is beneficial to consumers and those under which it is harmful, and use this information to suggest how proposed U.S. standards will affect trade.

---

* Luanne Lohr is an associate professor, Department of Agricultural and Applied Economics, University of Georgia. Barry Krissoff is a senior economist, Economic Research Service, U.S. Department of Agriculture. This research was supported by USDA-ERS Cooperative Agreement 43-3AEK-7-80060. Helpful comments were provided by Katherine DiMatteo, Lewrene Glaser, Daniel Pick, and Mary Bohman. The views expressed here are those of the authors and do not necessarily reflect the positions of their respective institutions.

Global Food Trade and Consumer Demand for Quality, edited by Krissoff *et al.*
Kluwer Academic/Plenum Publishers, New York, 2002.

CURRENT STATUS OF INTERNATIONAL HARMONIZATION

No single international regulation establishes uniform standards for organic certification and no single agency or body is designated to accredit certifiers (ITC 1999). Exported goods must meet the production standards of the importing country as determined by the competent organic authority in that country, typically the national government body responsible for regulating domestic certification. Legal (federal, regional, state) standards supercede private (farmer-based or for-profit) standards. At least 100 regional or national standards have been enacted worldwide, and numerous private sector standards exist as well (ITC 1999). Inspection is carried out by public or private entities to verify that organic production processes meet standards. Certification confirms that standards are met so that buyers can be certain of product integrity. Accreditation recognizes the competence of certifiers to conduct inspections and offer certification. There are 30 organic accreditation bodies worldwide (ITC 1999).

An exporting country may apply to have its standards approved across the board for designated products, regions, or certifiers by the importing country or region. If not granted blanket equivalency, exporters must submit documents for contract-by-contract verification that certification standards applied to the product are compatible with prevailing standards in the importing country. The contract-by-contract approach is cumbersome and is associated with high transaction costs, including occasional rejection of shipments due to perceived incompatibility of standards. Exporters have evolved several certification alternatives to try to reduce transaction costs. These include using an independent local certifier accredited under international certification process standards International Organization for Standardization/International Electrotechnical Commission (ISO/IEC) Guide 65 or EU process standards EN 45011, using a local branch of an accredited international certifier, using local certifiers that have partnered with accredited international entities, using an international certifier or an entity in the importing country approved for third-country certifications, and subcontracting to processors or distributors certified in the importing country (ITC 1999).

Without national standards in place in the United States, there has been substantial effort on the part of private companies to develop certifier label recognition among importers and government authorities in the importing countries. This can reduce individual firm transaction costs by increasing knowledge about the certification and establishing its comparability to the importing country standards. An unpublished telephone interview of U.S. organic exporters and foreign importers conducted by the University of Georgia in July and August 1999 assessed certifier recognition in Europe and Japan. Of the dozens of active certifiers in the United States, only four for-profit certifiers, two farmer-based non-profit certifiers, and two state government certifiers were identified as having name recognition in foreign countries. Individual producers contribute to this awareness by providing information about the certification standards they adhere to whenever they conduct a transaction. Under uniform U.S. standards, exporting firms will still assume at least part of the cost of educating foreign buyers about U.S. standards during their transactions.

This situation has incited a call for harmonization of standards through international accreditation of certifiers to reduce marketing costs. Accreditation ensures that certifiers hold organic producers and processors to minimum industry standards. This provides the means for governmental and extra-governmental organizations to regulate organic processes without monitoring every single producer or processor within their geopolitical boundaries. By serving as accreditors, the entities that have the power to control international trade can review other countries' standards and negotiate acceptable standards for equivalency. Although a national government may also serve as a certifier, the system of accreditation introduces flexibility in the type of organization permitted to certify and the organic rules they apply to their clients or members.

Some progress has been made toward unified accreditation in both the private and public sectors. All allow for variation in specific standards as long as standard-setting and inspection guidelines are met. The International Federation of Organic Agriculture Movements (IFOAM) is a private sector umbrella association established in 1972 to encourage organic agriculture and trade (ITC 1999). With more than 100 members representing national associations, certifiers, traders, and processors, IFOAM is the largest and most influential organization of its type (Lohr 1998a). IFOAM's Basic Standards of Organic Agriculture and Food Processing have served as the framework for numerous certification programs, and its accreditation program assesses compliance with these standards. In 1999, 13 certification bodies were accredited by IFOAM with six more under review (ITC 1999). In 2000, 14 IFOAM-accredited certification bodies, including four private U.S. certifiers, took the additional step of signing a multilateral agreement to extend blanket equivalency to all other signatories, boosting the international credibility of IFOAM accreditation (IFOAM Accredited Bodies Sign Multilateral Agreement 2000). The effectiveness of this agreement in promoting harmonization is as yet unknown.

The IFOAM standards have been influential on work completed in 1999 by the Codex Alimentarius Commission's Committee on Food Labeling and Committee on Food Import and Export Inspection and Certification Systems to develop international guidelines for national standards (ITC 1999). Guidelines for crop production, marketing, and labeling have been approved by the commission, which will consider the committee's recommended livestock guidelines in July.[1] Codex is particularly concerned with preventing the use of national standards as trade barriers. While not envisioned as a basis for equivalency, these guidelines may be used by the World Trade Organization in settling disputes. An exporting country that adheres to these guidelines would be in a stronger position to demand access to an importing country's markets, even if its own national standards are less strict. These guidelines may result in harmonized standards by influencing trade dispute arbitration.

The most widely recognized organization associated with accreditation is the ISO, which promotes rationalization of standards to facilitate trade, product development, and research cooperation. ISO/IEC Guide 65 establishes generic principles for certification bodies and has been adapted for organic accreditation by IFOAM and Demeter, an international network of certifiers for biodynamic farming (ITC 1999). The EU's standardizing bodies have adapted ISO/IEC Guide 65 in EN 45011, their requirements for certifying bodies. Beginning in June 1999, all domestic and foreign certifiers approved by the EU had to meet these rules. In response to the needs of U.S. exporters to Europe, the Meat Grading and Certification Branch under the U.S. Department of Agriculture's (USDA's) Agricultural Marketing Service began accrediting U.S. certifiers according to ISO/IEC Guide 65. The ISO standards are seen as a stopgap measure for equivalency in organic production as they do not govern production methods, only production certification processes.

The United States moved closer to national accreditation with the posting of a final rule for national organic standards in December 2000. Once the final rule is implemented in 2001, the federal government will begin accrediting domestic and foreign certifiers selling product in the United States and will have standing to apply for blanket import approval in the EU. Although details of standards differ across countries, international harmonization appears to be inevitable.

IMPACTS OF HARMONIZATION ON CONSUMERS

A single minimum standard can reduce consumers' costs of obtaining information about the production process, an otherwise unobservable characteristic. Consumers, who pay premiums from 20 to 200 percent for organics in most countries, are protected from fraudulent assertions and mislabeled products (Michelson et al. 1999). Reducing the information asymmetry between seller and buyer should result in a gain in consumer welfare. Yet even fully informed consumers may differ in their perceptions of quality.

This welfare improvement depends on credibility of certification, internalized by the consumer as confidence in the organic label. Michelson et al. argued that the certification label is a generic requirement for sale of a good as organic rather than a brand cue, so consumers are not influenced by additional promotional expenditures to look for and purchase a particular organic label. There is almost no generic advertising to educate consumers about basic production principles and advantages of consuming organic foods (Michelson et al. 1999). As a result, underlying confusion about the nature of organic products makes consumers more dependent on labels as cues. This alters the branding aspect of particular certifier labels. Currently, in many countries, there is little competition by labels within a geographic market. As interregional and international trade expand the flow of organic foods, consumers are more likely to see multiple certifications competing in the same product category in the same outlet. Consumers faced with multiple certifications may revert to other signals for selecting goods, such as looking for domestic labels in which they have more confidence.

If both the importing and exporting countries view each other's certification as equivalent, organic product flow is optimized and the good is treated as homogeneous with respect to standards. Legal equivalency agreed upon by governmental accreditors does not mean that standards are identical, nor does it guarantee consumer acceptance of the legal designation. Even if standards are identical, consumers and buyers in the importing country are likely to view imports as subject to less stringent requirements, to be "less organic." To allow for flexibility in local conditions, production standards per se will not be harmonized. To the extent that philosophical, technical, or cost factors differ, standards will vary across countries. It is in the interest of beneficiaries of domestic production (farm organizations, trade groups, environmental groups) to encourage perceptions of differential quality. Given a preference for locally grown foods that already exists in many countries (ITC 1999), consumers are likely to believe that domestically produced organic foods are superior to imported foods in at least some attribute dimensions. At the extreme, consumers would reject imports altogether.

The relative difficulty of importing organics into a country is affected in large part by these concerns over perceived or real differences in standards. U.S. respondents in the

University of Georgia survey previously mentioned stated that they experience a high degree of difficulty importing to Austria, France, and Switzerland and a moderate degree of difficulty to Germany and Japan. Since Germany, France, and Switzerland are three of the four largest markets in the EU, and Japan is the second largest single-country market in the world behind the United States (ITC 1999, Wittenberg 2000), consumer perceptions in these countries are paramount to U.S. exporters.

There are several studies suggesting that credibility of foreign certification is questioned by consumers. Japanese consumers are highly skeptical of imported organic products, with consumer studies indicating that one reason for not purchasing these foods is that foreign certifications are untrustworthy (Wittenberg 2000). This perception is expected to be exacerbated when Japanese national organic standards are implemented in 2001. EU consumers voice similar concerns. Even though there is a single certification requirement for crop production and processing in the EU (European Council Regulation 2092/91), administration and marketing are left to each country's competent authority, no unified logo for labeling products was designated until 2000, and stricter regulations may be required by individual countries for domestic labels, which are most trusted by consumers. Michelson et al. (1999) reported cases of traders' refusal to handle foreign product or certifying bodies' refusal to permit entry of products from other countries, even when both the exporting and importing countries were in the European Union and subject to the same minimum organic standards. In those cases, there was concern about the erosion of domestic standards by importation of foods produced under (perceived) less strict requirements, which might result in a loss of consumer confidence. Michelson et al. (1999) stated that, while unified certification is necessary, it is not sufficient for market growth. Many consumers will still view their country's standards as stricter and "more organic," unless marketing campaigns are successfully conducted to contradict this perception.

In the importing country, harmonization to a minimum standard perceived to be less strict than the domestic standard could reduce demand for imported organic food, since it would be viewed as inferior. Alternatively, demand for imports could increase if a two-tiered demand develops, with lower priced, (perceived) lower quality imports being purchased by consumers who cannot afford foods that meet the stricter domestic standard but who want to participate in the organic market. Demand would then be segmented into import and domestic shares, with the possibility of price variability across quality groups and nonequal market shares for imports and domestically produced foods. The imports would be perceived as of different, and poorer, quality than domestically produced organic foods by some segment of the consumer population. This share of organic buyers would refuse to purchase the imports at any price. The remaining share would be indifferent between imported and domestically produced organics. They would purchase the lower priced of the two products, which would be the imports, if the second premise presented above holds.

With demand segmentation in the importing country, the slopes of the demand curves for the two groups are different from each other unless the share of consumers in each group is the same. Which slope is relatively steeper depends on whether a smaller percentage rejects or accepts imports, since the original market demand curve is partitioned by dividing these percentages into its slope. In previous applications of this model by Tauer (1994) to bST and non-bST milk and by Lohr (1998b) to three classes of eco-labeled foods, the percentages of consumers requiring particular quality characteristics were determined empirically.

If legal equivalence is accepted by consumers, imports are treated as homogeneous in the market. Similarly, in countries that do not have national standards, there is no widespread basis for judging the relative strictness of foreign and domestic rules, so discrimination against imports is less likely. Organic claims for imports into Canada and the United States are verified by importers rather than the government—if they are checked at all—because, as of the end of 2000, neither country had implemented national organic standards. In Japan, importation was assessed by the University of Georgia's survey as moderately difficult in 1999, but is expected to be much more difficult with the implementation of national standards in 2001 (Wittenberg 2000). Whether consumer acceptance of imports is less likely than consumer rejection in most industrialized countries depends on perceptions of equivalency between domestic and exporting country standards. These perceptions may be influenced by exporter behavior as well as by government action.

Consumers are aware that firms in the exporting country conform at least to the minimum international standard but not necessarily to stricter domestic standards in the importing country. Firms attempting to capture foreign market share could incur additional costs of certifying with a foreign entity to assure consumers in that country of the quality of their product. To avoid excess cost, these firms might opt out of their domestic certification programs altogether, leaving fewer domestic firms to share the fixed costs of certification and accreditation. The result would be a two-tiered supply in the exporting country segmented into domestic and export shares.

With supply segmentation of the type described, both the intercepts and the slopes of the supply curves for the two groups are different from each other. The market supply curve is partitioned according to the foreign market share captured by exporters, with the resulting export slope being steeper than the domestic supply slope if the foreign market share is less than 50 percent. The market intercept is adjusted upward separately for each supply segment according to the fixed cost of domestic certification (for domestic suppliers) and the cost of foreign certification (for exporters).

A combination of segmented demand and segmented supply could occur if exporters engaged in foreign certification but consumers in that country still rejected the import as inferior. This could conceivably happen if consumers are aware of the country of origin and distrust the foreign production system, even if domestic certification is granted. Alternatively, exporters could certify domestically and invest in educational programs to promote their certification or product quality to foreign consumers. Unless they already accept the imported product as homogeneous with the domestically produced version, it is unlikely that all foreign consumers would be convinced by such a campaign. Some percentage of those foreign consumers who would have rejected the certification outright will be convinced to buy the product, according to some function of educational spending by the exporters. This generates segmented demand in the importing country. Supply in the exporting country is partitioned according to the foreign market share captured by exporters, as explained previously, and the supply intercept for export supply is adjusted upward by the cost of educational spending. Again, both segmented demand and segmented supply would result.

SIMULATING CONSUMER WELFARE EFFECTS

To examine the possible outcomes of harmonization as described in the last section and the impacts on consumer welfare, we develop a concrete example of trade under varying assumptions about perceived product homogeneity. The autarky situation (no trade) is simulated as a baseline of comparison for all trade scenarios. In the current market environment, perceptions of consumers in the importing country dictate acceptance of imports. We consider six scenarios. The scenarios compared with the autarky baseline are summarized in Table 1 and explained below.

Table 1. Summary of scenarios compared with autarky baseline

	Exporter behavior in exporting country			Consumer behavior in importing country	
Scenario	Domestic certification w/ equivalency granted	Importing country certification	Domestic certification w/ education campaign	All accept imports	Some do not accept imports
1 (status quo)	[a]				X
2	X			X	
3	X				X
4		X		X	
5		X			X
6			X		X

[a] Under the status quo, prior to promulgation of the Final Rule for National Organic Standards, suppliers certify domestically, but equivalency cannot be granted due to lack of U.S. government regulations.

In Scenario 1, the exporting country standards are not granted equivalency by the importing country. Exporters incur additional transaction costs to access the import market. This is the status quo situation between the United States and the EU. In Scenario 2, the importing country and exporting country standards are perceived as equivalent, and the product traded is homogeneous.

In Scenario 3, the exporting country's standards are perceived as less stringent, and the product is no longer homogeneous. Demand in the importing country is segmented so that domestic demand is for a perceived higher quality good and import demand is for a lower quality product. The price differential between the two reflects in part the quality differentiation. In Scenario 4, supply in the exporting country is segmented into domestic and export supply shares. Exporters certify with an entity in the importing country and opt out of domestic certification in the exporting country. The domestic share in the exporting country incurs higher fixed costs because accreditation program costs are spread over fewer producers. It is assumed that consumers in the importing country are unable to distinguish imports from domestically produced organics when both display the same certification label, and so treat them as homogeneous.

Scenario 5 is the same as Scenario 4, except consumers are assumed to have information that enables them to identify imports, which they treat as lower quality. An example of such information is country-of-origin labeling. This results in two-tiered demand in the importing country and two-tiered supply in the exporting country. In Scenario 6, exporters certify with domestic entities, but invest in educational programs to promote their country's certification process. It is assumed that educational spending is less than 100 percent effective, but will increase the percentage of consumers in the importing country who will accept the imports. Demand is segmented in the importing country, and supply is segmented in the exporting country.

The simulation method used was adapted from Tauer (1994) and Lohr (1998b). Partial equilibrium models of linear supply and demand were constructed for each case for the importing and exporting countries. Systems of equations representing the trade scenarios were solved simultaneously using the nonlinear module of GAUSS™.[2] All demand and supply equations were set up in price-dependent form. The welfare calculations are similar to those used by Tauer (1994) and Lohr (1998b).

Social welfare improvements are measured by producer and consumer surpluses. Suppliers gain when the price they are paid is greater than their marginal cost of production. Consumers gain when the price they are charged is less than the amount they would be willing to pay for the good. In a typical equilibrium trade situation, a single price prevails for domestic markets in the exporting and importing countries. Trade enables the consumers in the importing country to buy at a price lower than domestic equilibrium, and suppliers in the exporting country to sell at a price higher than domestic equilibrium. Both groups gain surplus. However, sellers in the importing country and consumers in the exporting country lose surplus for the same reason. If the surplus gained is greater than the surplus lost, trade occurs.

Market segmentation introduces two equilibrium prices, one of which prevails within the country where segmentation occurs, that is, supply segmentation in the exporting country or demand segmentation in the importing country. The other price prevails in trade between the two countries and within the country with an unsegmented market. If there is segmented demand, then consumer surplus in the importing country must be calculated for each equilibrium and summed. With supply segmentation, producer surplus in the exporting country is similarly determined by both equilibria. Both surpluses in the country with an unsegmented market are calculated only from the prevailing trade price. Trade becomes less attractive the larger the differential between the equilibrium prices under segmentation because net surpluses decrease.

Each scenario is graphically presented, followed by a discussion of parameter values used for the scenarios. For all graphs in this section, the lowercase m refers to the importing country, and the lowercase x refers to the exporting country. ES and ED refer to excess supply and excess demand. All vertical axes are prices, and all horizontal axes are quantities. The left graph is for the exporting country, and the right graph is for the importing country. All cases are based on a "large-country" trade model, which is appropriate for the United States, Japan, and the EU as a whole and for most countries individually in the EU, since the largest organic markets are in these countries.

Scenario 1: Equivalency Not Granted (Status Quo)

If blanket equivalency is not granted to an exporting country, firms must negotiate certification equivalency for each contract. Figure 1 shows the extra cost incurred by the exporting country modeled as a tax equivalent imposed by the importer. Prices differ in the

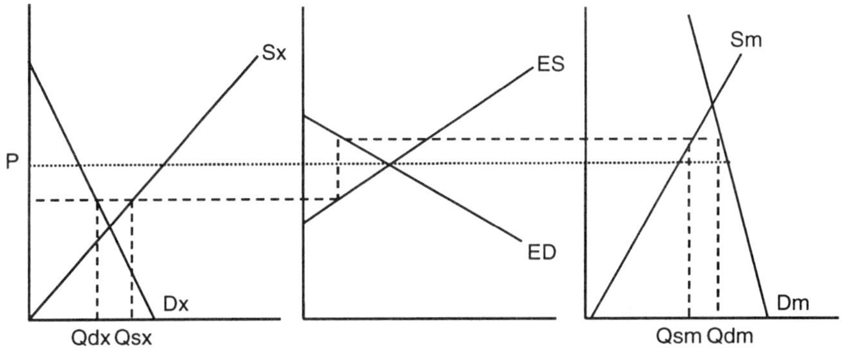

Figure 1. Equivalence versus no equivalence between exporting and importing countries.

importing and exporting countries because the cost differential of certification creates a wedge. Consumers in the importing country pay a higher price while the exporter receives a lower price because of the decrease in quantity demanded. The dashed line shows the implication of the excess costs.

Scenario 2: Equivalency Granted, Homogeneous Goods

The horizontal line at P in Figure 1 shows the equilibrium at ED = ES. This case should generate the greatest welfare improvement over autarky because there are no extra transaction costs. A single price, P, prevails in both countries, and consumers in the importing country treat the imported good as identical to the domestically produced version.

Scenario 3: Equivalency Granted, Imports Rejected

In Figure 2, demand in the importing country is segmented into domestic and import demand, Dmd and Dmm. There are two equilibria, one for the domestically produced quantity and its price and one for the imported quantity and its price. The market is segmented by assuming that more than 50 percent of consumers in the importing country refuse to buy imports because of perceived inferiority of the import good. This makes the price associated with imported quantity, Pmm, lower than the price for domestically produced quantity, Pmd. The sum of the imported quantity, Qmm, and the domestically produced quantity, Qmd, is the total amount consumed in the importing country. Domestic quantity is greater than import quantity despite the lower price of imports due to quality perceptions.

Figure 2 is a hybrid of the typical three-graph trade model shown in Figure 1. Here, the segmented demand of the importing country must be represented on both the right and middle graphs, while the left graph represents the exporting country. With segmented demand, a portion of consumers refuse to purchase imported organics. The demand for these consumers is met by domestic production. The right graph shows this equilibrium, which is determined entirely within the importing country.

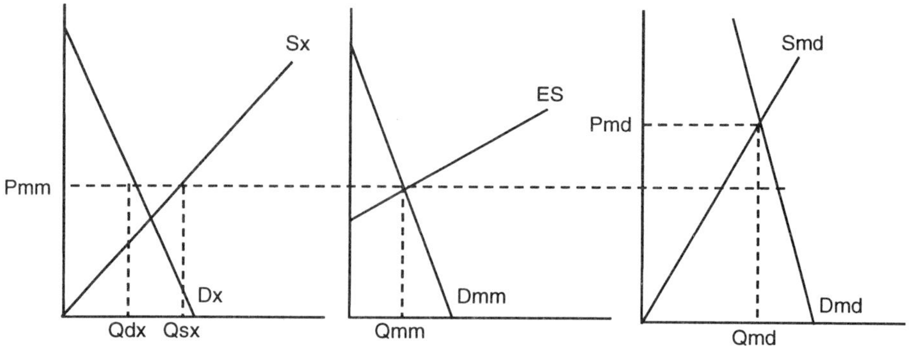

Figure 2. Imports rejected, segmented import demand.

The rest of the consumers in the importing country are indifferent between domestically produced and imported organics, and buy the lower priced imports. The availability of imports is the excess supply, the amount by which production exceeds consumption within the exporting country. From the left graph, excess supply can be mapped to the middle graph, so that the export supply can be compared with the demand for imports, and the equilibrium price for trade can be determined. The equilibrium in the middle graph is for the consumer segment in the importing country that is willing to buy imports. Excess demand exists for neither domestically produced nor imported organics because each segment generates its own equilibrium.

Consumer surplus in the importing country is the sum of the surpluses calculated for the domestic equilibrium price, Pmd, and the trade equilibrium price, Pmm, and their associated quantities, Qmd and Qmm. Producer surplus in the importing country is based only on the domestic price and quantity, Pmd and Qmd. Consumer and producer surpluses in the exporting country are calculated from the trade price and domestic quantities demanded and supplied, Pmm, Qdx, and Qsx. It is assumed that all excess supply at the trade price is sold to the importing country, so that Qsx − Qdx = Qmm.

Scenario 4: Exporters Certify in Importing Country, Homogeneous Goods

In this situation, shown in Figure 3, the exporting country is assumed to have segmented supply, with export supply, Sxx, differentiated from domestic supply, Sxd. No set share of supply is assumed to be exported. Instead, the model exploits the cost-increasing effects of the segregated domestic and international certification to solve for the share of production that is exported. Exporters certify with an entity in the importing country and do not share the domestic organic program costs. The foreign certification costs may be higher than domestic certification, which raises the fixed costs to exporters. Suppliers that remain in the domestic market incur higher fixed costs of accreditation and certification because exporters have opted out of the domestic program. If the domestic cost increase is

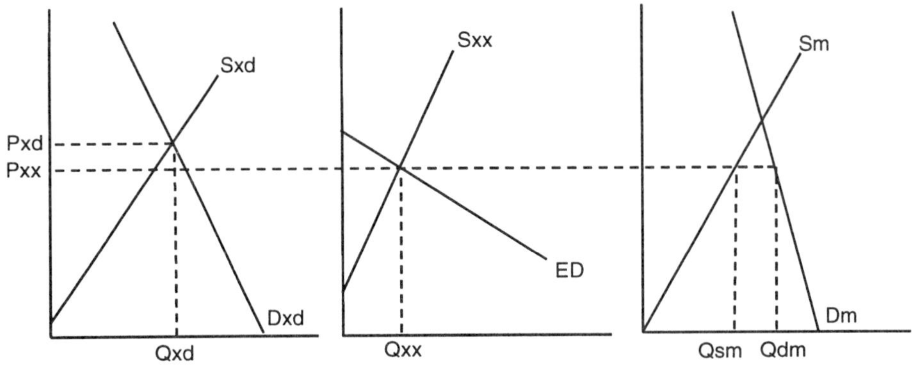

Figure 3. Exporters certify in importing country, homogeneous good.

less than the export cost increase, then the domestic price, Pxd, is higher than the export price, Pxx.

If foreign certification is a successful strategy, imports will be indistinguishable by certification label from domestically produced organic foods in the importing country. Consumers in the importing country will treat both as homogeneous, and thus, only one demand curve, Dm, exists in the importing country. Since the importing country partially satisfies its demand with domestic production, the imported quantity need not be large. Domestic quantity exchanged in the exporting country, Qxd, is greater than exported quantity, Qxx, which is determined by the excess demand in the importing country.

In a trade situation with segmented supply in the exporting country, the quantity of exports supplied is not set by excess domestic supply because exports and domestic production are segmented by costs. In this chapter, these costs were assumed to be related to certification and education as shown in Table 1. There are two equilibria, with the domestic market represented in the left graph and the export market represented in the middle graph. The domestic equilibrium is determined entirely by the domestic producers and consumers in the exporting country.

The exporter supply segment faces the excess demand from the importing country, mapped from the right graph to the middle graph. Consumers in the importing country purchase all they can domestically and make up the difference between their quantity demanded, Qdm, and domestic quantity supplied, Qsm, by importing the quantity provided by the exporters, Qxx. The trade price, Pxx, is less than what the equilibrium price would be in the importing country without trade, so this becomes the prevailing domestic price in that country as well. There is no excess supply in the exporting country because the domestic and export segments both reach equilibrium and the market segments clear. The total quantity supplied by producers in the exporting country is the sum of exports, Qxx, and domestic sales, Qxd.

Producer surplus in the exporting country is the sum of surpluses calculated for domestic equilibrium price, Pxd, and the trade equilibrium price, Pxx, and their associated quantities, Qxd and Qxx. Consumer surplus in the exporting country is based only on the domestic price and quantity, Pxd and Qxd. Consumer and producer surpluses in the importing country are calculated from the trade price and domestic quantities demanded and supplied, Pxx, Qdm, and Qsm. It is assumed that all excess demand at the trade price is satisfied by the exporting country, so that Qdm − Qsm = Qxx.

Scenario 5: Exporters Certify in Importing Country, Imports Rejected

This case has the same assumptions as Scenario 4—exporters certify in the importing country, leaving fewer domestic suppliers to share organic accreditation program costs and thus increasing domestic costs. However, in Scenario 5, it is assumed that additional information is available to consumers in the importing country so that they can identify which organic products are imported and which are domestically produced. As in Scenario 3, the imports are rejected by some share of consumers. Figure 4 shows this situation.

Both supply in the exporting country and demand in the importing country are segmented. There are now three equilibrium prices and quantities, one each in the domestic markets of the exporting and importing countries and one for the export supply and import demand curves. The domestic equilibrium prices and quantities in the exporting country and in the importing country are determined within those countries by the domestic producers and consumers, given the certification cost and consumer preference parameters specified. These equilibria represent only the domestic supply segment in the exporting country and the segment of consumers who reject imports in the importing country. The left graph in Figure 4 shows the exporting country, and the right graph shows the importing country. The domestic price in the exporting country, Pxd, is less than the domestic price in the importing country, Pmd, as in a typical trade model.

The middle graph represents the export supply segment from the exporting country, Sxx, and the consumer segment from the importing country, Dmm, that is willing to purchase imports. These curves are not excess supply in the exporting country and excess demand in the importing country, as in Figure 1, but are independent market segments for which the equilibrium determined is distinct from the domestic equilibria in each country.

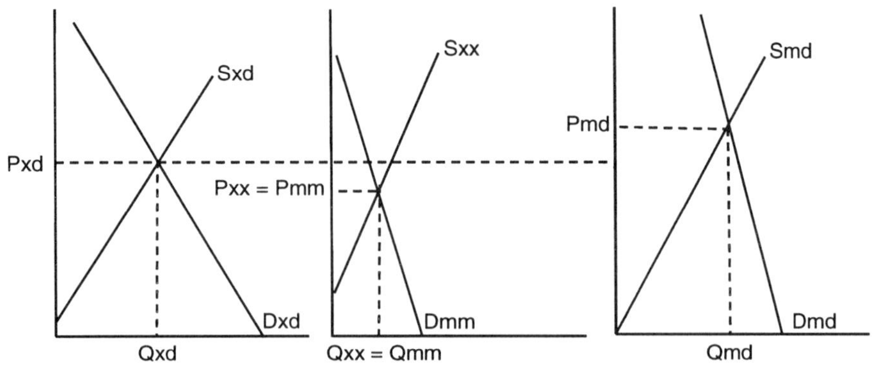

Figure 4. Exporters certify in importing country, imports rejected.

There is not a single prevailing price that clears all markets. The graph representing these segments equilibrates the export price, Pxx, with the import price, Pmm, and the export quantity, Qxx, with the import quantity, Qmm, so that the market clears. Both importing country and exporting country domestic prices, Pmd and Pxd, are greater than the trade price, and both domestic quantities, Qxd and Qmd, are greater than the quantity traded. This is an artifact of the condition that trade represents less than 50 percent of the share of total supply in the exporting country and of total demand in the importing country.

Consumer surplus in the importing country is the sum of surpluses calculated for the import and domestic segments of demand, Dmm and Dmd. Producer surplus in the exporting country is the sum of surpluses calculated for the export and domestic segments of supply, Sxx and Sxd. The three equilibria are used for these calculations. Producer surplus in the importing country and consumer surplus in the exporting country are based only on the domestic equilibrium prices and quantities, as was calculated in Scenarios 3 and 4.

Scenario 6: Exporters Pay Education Costs, Incomplete Import Acceptance

In Scenario 6, demand in the importing country and supply in the exporting country are both segmented. Exporters certify domestically, so cost differentials from Scenarios 4 and 5 between domestic and export suppliers in the export country are eliminated. However, exporters invest in education of consumers in the importing country about the quality of their products and certification with the aim of convincing consumers to accept imports. The efficiency of educational spending is assumed to be less than 100 percent, so that the share that reject imports is less than in Scenarios 3 and 5, but is not zero. The share that refuses to buy imports is variable, depending on exporters' educational spending and the efficiency of that spending.

This scenario is similar to that in Figure 4, except that the intercept for the domestic supply curve in the exporting country begins at the origin, there being no additional accreditation costs incurred. The intercept for the export supply curve shifts upward by the amount of educational spending, which is specified as a percentage of price. As described for Scenario 5, there are three equilibria used to calculate welfare effects.

The results that actually occur in the market depend on elasticities of demand, prices for imported and domestic organics, and costs of certification and accreditation. All the situations described are possible for the United States under current conditions. Since the United States will fully implement its national standards in 2002, the status quo scenario (Scenario 1) will not be maintained. Scenario 2 is the least likely to result across all countries to which the United States exports organic foods, since consumer acceptance of imports varies. Scenario 3 represents the initial situation that is likely following implementation of U.S. standards. Scenarios 4 and 6 are responses to rejection of U.S. exports certified domestically, with Scenario 4 being the more optimistic in terms of foreign consumer response. Scenario 5 would occur if foreign consumers distrust their own certification programs. This is a possible result with fragmented certification, where there are multiple certifiers in the country and none are sufficiently dominant to be credible throughout. Examples include Germany, with more than 50 certifiers, Austria with 22 certifiers, and Italy with eight control bodies. Also, Scenario 5 might result if consumers are aware of the origin of the import and, despite certification in their own country, distrust the production method and reject the import.

APPLICATION OF THE TRADE MODEL

The model was simulated for a two-country partial equilibrium with the United States exporting wheat to Germany. The United States is a major producer of organic wheat, calculated at 101,806 metric tons, based on 1997 acreage from Greene (2000) and yield from the Organic Farming Research Foundation (OFRF) (1999). Germany is the largest single market for organic food products outside the United States and a substantial producer of organic wheat in Europe. Domestic production was calculated at 59,880 metric tons, based on 1995 arable acreage from Foster and Lampkin (1999), percentage allocated to wheat, and yield per hectare from Offerman and Nieberg (2000). Prices differed markedly between the countries, with the 1997 farm price for U.S. organic wheat calculated at \$231.48 per metric ton, based on the per bushel price from OFRF (1999). The German farm price in 1995 was calculated at \$485.40 per metric ton, based on a per ton price in ECUs from Offerman and Nieberg (2000).

These prices and quantities, along with elasticities of supply and demand, were used to obtain the intercepts and slopes for the demand and supply curves. The demand elasticity for wheat in the United States was assumed to be –0.0255, consistent with the own-price elasticity for conventionally grown wheat (Barnes and Shields 1998). This is reasonable, since organic processors and consumers are unlikely to have more flexibility in substituting other grains for wheat than do conventional processors and consumers. While availability of substitutes in terms of quantity is probably more limited for organic processors, there is no solid information from which to choose a different elasticity. The German demand elasticity for wheat also was assumed to be –0.0255.

Both U.S. and German supply elasticities were set at 1.00. This forces the supply curve through the origin. It is reasonable to examine this case since both U.S. and German farmers sell some portion of certified organic wheat through conventional market channels. For German farmers, about 15 percent of wheat does not enter the organic market and so fails to return the expected price premium (Michelson et al. 1999). In the United States, about 20 percent of organic wheat acreage is sold as conventional (OFRF 1999). This flexibility in marketing permits organic growers to take advantage of price cost differentials, timing of market demand, and other factors that should increase responsiveness to price changes. The slopes and intercepts are presented in Table 2.

Table 2. Demand and supply equations

	Intercept	Slope
United States		
Supply	0.00	0.0023
Demand	9309.18	–0.0892
Germany		
Supply	0.00	0.0081
Demand	19520.64	–0.3179

The market curves represented in Table 2 assume that there is no substitution of conventional for organic wheat in either demand or supply. Although end consumers (households) may choose conventional wheat products when organic prices increase, processors and other intermediaries modeled here cannot, because EU regulations require that 95 percent of the ingredients of a product labeled "organic" be of certified origin (European Council Regulation 2092/91). The U.S. standards also stipulate this level of organic content. On the supply side, at least one year for the transition period is required in the EU countries and a three-year transition period is required in the U.S. rules, so farmers lose certification and must start over if they farm the land using conventional practices.

Other parameters were specified for the individual cases. Available information on market conditions was used to generate parameters; in all cases, the assumed values are conservative. In Scenario 1, transaction cost was assumed to be 5 percent of the equilibrium price. In Scenarios 3 and 5, the share of the German domestic market assumed to refuse to buy U.S. imports was 80 percent, which is also a conservative estimate. Cereals rank as the most important organic food group in Germany with organic holding 3.4 percent of total market share for cereals (Michelson et al. 1999). Organic bakeries, the main consumers of wheat, account for 8 percent of the total organic market, worth DM250 million; an estimated DM3 million is imported (ITC 1999). Another DM17 million worth of raw materials is imported for production of pasta and cereals. German consumers are considered among the most critical in the EU, and local sourcing is an important factor in their purchase decisions (ITC 1999). Importers must work extremely hard to meet these discerning standards and satisfy the German consumer.

In Scenarios 4 and 5, the accreditation cost increase to domestic suppliers was assumed to be 0.5 percent of the equilibrium price, based on program costs and the number of domestic producers estimated by USDA. The foreign certification cost increase to export suppliers was assumed to be 1.5 percent of domestic U.S. certification costs, based on costs in Germany and the United States (Offerman and Nieberg 2000). In Scenario 6, educational spending was assumed to be 5 percent of the equilibrium price, and educational efficiency was assumed to be 75 percent. Previous research by Lohr (1998b) suggested that these are realistic values for domestic education programs about eco-labels in the United States, but they probably overstate the cost effectiveness of a foreign education program given the strength of German attitudes.

Price and quantity equilibria for the six scenarios are shown in Table 3. The six cases were compared to autarky in terms of consumer, producer, and net surpluses; this is shown in Table 4. The results were consistent with the graphical analyses presented. In all cases, U.S. consumers were made worse off, while German consumers gained. Net surpluses were all positive, with Germany gaining 3 to 12 times as much as the United States from trade. Quantity traded and U.S. and German net surpluses were highest when the import good was treated as homogeneous with domestically produced organic wheat in Germany (Scenarios 2 and 4). U.S. consumers lost the most in these cases because of domestic price increases over autarky of 24.1 percent for Scenario 2 and 25.1 percent for Scenario 4.

The best situation for the United States (Scenario 2) yielded a net surplus of $697,670. In this case, 25,086 metric tons were exported, and domestic quantity demanded was 101,183 metric tons—0.6 percent lower than under autarky. Price was 24 percent higher for U.S. consumers with trade. The best result for Germany (Scenario 4) gave a net surplus of $2,501,082. With 25,156 metric tons imported and domestic quantity supplied at 48,144

Table 3. Price and quantity equilibria under trade scenarios

	Price ($/metric tons)	Domestic quantity[a] (metric tons)	Quantity traded[b] (metric tons)
Scenario 1. Equivalency not granted (status quo)			
United States	272.75	101,345	18,612
Germany	301.46	37,189	–18,612[c]
Scenario 2. Equivalency granted, homogeneous goods			
United States	287.10	101,183	25,086
Germany	287.10	35,418	–25,086
Scenario 3. Equivalency granted, imports rejected			
United States	258.35	101,505	12,119
Germany: Imports	258.35		–12,119
Germany: Domestic	390.26	48,144	
Scenario 4. Exporters certify in importing country, homogeneous goods			
United States: Exports	286.55		25,156
United States: Domestic	289.40	101,157	
Germany	286.55	35,350	–25,156
Scenario 5. Exporters certify in importing country, imports rejected			
United States: Exports	255.15		12,121
United States: Domestic	260.28	101,483	
Germany: Imports	255.15		–12,121
Germany: Domestic	390.26	48,144	
Scenario 6. Exporters pay education costs, incomplete import acceptance			
United States: Exports	276.93		14,377
United States: Domestic	263.09	101,452	
Germany: Imports	276.93		–14,377
Germany: Domestic	372.31	45,930	

Note: Under autarky, the U.S. equilibrium price for organic wheat was $231.38 per metric ton and quantity was 101,806 metric tons. In Germany, equilibrium price was $485.40 per metric ton and quantity was 59,881 metric tons.

[a] Domestic quantity demanded for the United States, domestic quantity supplied for Germany.

[b] Quantity traded is positive for the exporting country and negative for the importing country. When there is a single price for domestic and imported or exported quantity, quantity traded represents excess demand or excess supply for that country.

[c] Excess demand in Germany was 4,658 metric tons.

metric tons, total German consumption was 73,300 metric tons—22 percent higher than without trade. Price decreased by 41 percent from the autarky case.

The status quo situation described in Scenario 1 resulted in a net surplus for the United States that was only 55 percent of the surplus in Scenario 2. The net surplus for Germany was 86 percent of the best result described in Scenario 4. As a two-country model, the simulation results overstated the true trade conditions. The actual quantity of all cereals imported into Germany in 1997–98 was estimated at 25,000 metric tons, while the simulated quantity for organic wheat imported from the United States was 18,612 metric tons (Michelson et al. 1999). France, Canada, Italy, Australia, Czech Republic, and Hungary also export cereals to Germany; the total quantity imported is estimated at 10 percent of the domestic organic market share (Michelson et al. 1999). The simulated share of imports was 33 percent of domestic quantity demanded. Of key importance in the simulation results was the price effect in Germany, which, even with the extra transaction cost due to lack of equivalency, reduced the German domestic price by 38 percent. Maintaining a significant price differential with an importing country's domestic price improves the attractiveness of U.S. exports, even if they are not granted full equivalency by the importing country.

Table 4. Welfare changes compared to autarky

	Producer	Consumer	Net surplus
Scenario 1. Equivalency not granted (status quo)			
United States	4,575,655	–4,191,632	384,022
Germany	–8,927,537	11,067,710	2,140,173
Scenario 2. Equivalency granted, homogeneous goods			
United States	6,342,950	–5,645,280	697,670
Germany	–9,448,681	11,935,937	2,487,256
Scenario 3. Equivalency granted, imports rejected[a]			
United States	2,894,338	–2,731,518	162,820
Germany	–5,138,678	7,304,343	2,165,665
Scenario 4. Exporters certify in importing country, homogeneous goods[b]			
United States	6,560,908	–5,878,061	682,847
Germany	–9,468,156	11,969,238	2,501,082
Scenario 5. Exporters certify in importing country, imports rejected[c]			
United States	3,050,006	–2,927,191	122,815
Germany	–5,138,679	7,343,136	2,204,458
Scenario 6. Exporters pay education costs, incomplete import acceptance[d]			
United States	3,636,148	–3,211,957	424,190
Germany	–5,982,738	8,159,588	2,176,850

[a] Share of German domestic market assumed to refuse to buy imports was 80 percent.
[b] Share of exporting country supply traded was 20.21 percent.
[c] Share of exporting country supply traded was 10.95 percent.
[d] Share of exporting country supply traded was 12.32 percent.

In both cases (Scenarios 3 and 5) where a large percentage refused to accept the imports, gains were lower for the United States. The extra costs to both domestic and export suppliers in Scenario 5 resulted in only $122,815 net surplus to the United States, and the lowest price for U.S. exports at $255.15 per metric ton, 10 percent higher than autarky. In Scenario 3, net surplus was $162,820, at price $258.35. These cases resulted in the smallest loss to U.S. consumers, as domestic equilibrium quantity was greater than for the other scenarios. U.S. consumers are better off if the differential between domestic U.S. and German prices is large, but the differential between U.S. domestic and export prices is small. Scenarios 3 and 5 generated intermediate surplus values for Germany but the smallest quantities traded, at 12,119 metric tons for Scenario 3 and 12,121 metric tons with Scenario 5.

The low export-import prices were a reflection of the German unwillingness to buy imports that is built into the scenarios. With a higher level of resistance, import prices would be lower and domestic prices higher as autarky is approached. Erosion of this resistance would move prices toward the cases in which imports are viewed as homogeneous with domestically produced goods, with attendant benefits to U.S. producers and negative impacts on U.S. consumers.

Scenario 6 gave net surplus for the United States intermediate to the other cases at \$424,190, and produced an intermediate surplus result for Germany at \$2,176,850, improving on the status quo by 10 percent for the United States and 2 percent for Germany. This was the only case in which U.S. domestic price was below both the trade price and the German domestic price. Educational spending exerted downward pressure on the U.S. domestic price, and educational spending efficiency raised the trade price. As either or both of these increase, the effect would be magnified. If costs of education are borne by the government, exports would be favored even more.

The last scenario is the most complicated in terms of behavioral effects on market equilibrium. The share of Germans who will not buy U.S. organic wheat declines if either spending increases or efficiency increases, but the effects are not the same. The equilibria are related via the slopes for German demand curves due to shares imported (which depends on spending and efficiency), the shift in the U.S. export supply curve intercept due to education cost, and the slopes of U.S. supply curves due to shares exported (which is free to vary in this scenario) as explained in the case description. Thus, the results are not straightforward where there is two-tiered demand in the import country and two-tiered supply in the export country.

Sensitivity analyses conducted on the efficiency of education and educational spending parameters revealed that increased educational spending by U.S. exporters without increased efficiency drives up the trade price, depresses the German domestic price, and increases the U.S. domestic price. An educational efficiency gain magnifies the effect of a spending increase. The trade price rises higher as does the U.S. domestic price, but the German domestic price declines. The relative effects on slopes and intercepts of the demand and supply curves is such that the gap between German domestic and import prices becomes smaller, and the gap between U.S. domestic and export prices becomes greater. As a result, the export share of U.S. supply increases as more Germans perceive the import as equal in quality with domestically produced wheat.

Most of the results presented are subject to the parameters used to simulate the models. While realistic, conservative values were selected for these parameters. Different values could alter the relative rankings of the scenarios on the basis of surpluses. Of particular importance is the treatment of consumer resistance to imports in Germany. The status quo is usually considered a worst case situation by the industry because of the cumbersome transactions, but, in the simulations here, Scenario 1 implicitly assumed that German consumers would buy all the product offered at the higher "taxed" price. Exactly because of the extra costs incurred under the status quo system, care is usually taken to ensure that the contracts are fulfilled and delivery of product accepted, so the resistance to imports may be masked. Harmonization may generate a false sense of security among exporters, which will encounter lower transaction costs but reveal resistance to their products from consumers in the importing country.

CONCLUSIONS

Several conclusions may be drawn from the example provided for organic wheat trade between the United States and Germany. The status quo situation is not the best for either country. The U.S. organic industry and USDA are responding by developing accreditation standards that will permit the country to apply for EU equivalency. The status quo situation imposes extra transaction costs on exporters whose certification is not recognized with full equivalency in the importing country. Although trade does occur, there is excess demand in the importing country—which, in the real world, will be met by U.S. competitors.

German consumers would have improved welfare if they were less discriminating in their preferences for domestically produced wheat. However, consumer uncertainty and concern about food safety and fragmentation in German and U.S. certification authorities are likely to remain a continuing concern. Certification label branding is likely to evolve along with harmonization of standards. Consumers confronted with a multiplicity of organic labels will look for the familiar, which typically will be a domestic label. Depending on how distrustful they are of foreign certification, some consumers may continue to refuse imported organic foods. There are intangible gains to offering consumers greater choice, especially if the market is segmented into heterogeneous domestic production and imports. Consumers in the importing country who could not otherwise afford organic foods can buy imports because the import price is forced down.

As long as organic production, processing, and handling requirements are not identical across countries, some consumers will still view their country's standards as stricter and "more organic." Certification in the importing country offers a second-best solution to U.S. producers provided that no other information, such as country-of-origin labeling, undermines the camouflage of the domestic label. To the extent that costs of foreign certification are higher than U.S. certification, U.S. producers will incur an extra expense if they have to use this method of market entry.

Harmonization of accreditation standards alone is not sufficient to guarantee welfare maximization in international organic trade. If consumers do not accept the equivalency of imported and domestically produced organic foods, welfare gains cannot be maximized. Reassuring foreign consumers of U.S. certification quality and maintaining cost competitiveness are important factors in international marketing. Consumer perceptions of product homogeneity are critical whether developed through educational programs or foreign certification. The U.S. government conducts trade fairs to educate foreign buyers about U.S. organic products. Results here suggest that domestic producers may not gain significantly from education efforts if domestic consumers in the importing country are resistant to imports. The greatest welfare gains occur if equivalency is accepted, regardless of whether exporters certify domestically or in the importing country (Scenarios 2 and 4). In the absence of consumer acceptance, welfare improvements over the status quo are not significant for consumers in the importing country. For U.S. producers, surplus gains compared with autarky may actually be less if imports are rejected than the situation under the status quo without equivalency.

Currently, organic trade shows are conducted by the U.S. government only for purposes of product introduction. This de facto leads to a discussion between U.S. vendors and foreign buyers of the organic standards under which the product was certified. Whether or not the U.S. government provides educational programs about U.S. organic standards, firms will continue to promote their products and, of necessity, educate consumers about the standards to which their products conform. The organic industry has begun to develop export market assessments using a grant from the Foreign Agricultural Service made in 2000 under the Export Market Assistance Program. This is a step toward identifying reasons for resistance to U.S. organic products and ways to overcome consumer resistance in importing countries.

International trade in organics could benefit both U.S. consumers and producers. The welfare effects of importing into the United States should be explored. By simulating results for other countries and other crops, a view of the U.S. organic consumer's overall position may be developed and more general conclusions drawn.

NOTES

1. Katherine DiMatteo, executive director of the Organic Trade Association. Personal communication, by e-mail, September 4, 2000.
2. Aptech Systems, 1997, Nonlinear Equations-GAUSS™ Applications, Maple Valley, WA.

REFERENCES

Barnes, J. N., and Shields, D. A., 1998, The growth in U.S. wheat food demand, in: *Wheat Yearbook*, Economic Research Service, ed., WHS-1998, pp. 21–29, U.S. Department of Agriculture, Washington, DC.

Foster, C., and Lampkin, N., 1999, *European Organic Production Statistics 1993-1996*, Organic Farming in Europe: Economics and Policy, vol. 3, University of Hohenheim, Stuttgart.

Greene, C., 2000, Table 6: Certified organic grain crop acreage, by state, 1997, U.S. Organic Agriculture, Economic Research Service, U.S. Department of Agriculture, http://www.ers.usda.gov/Emphases/Harmony/issues/organic/table6.htm (accessed June 13, 2001).

IFOAM accredited certification bodies sign multilateral agreement, 2000, *Ecology and Farming* Mar.:35.

International Trade Centre (ITC) UNCTAD/WTO, 1999, *Organic Food and Beverages: World Supply and Major European Markets*, Geneva.

Lohr, L., 1998a, Implications of organic certification for market structure and trade, *Am J Agric Econ* **80**(5):1125–1129.

———, 1998b, *Welfare Effects of Eco-label Proliferation: Too Much of a Good Thing?*, FS 98-22, Agricultural and Applied Economics, University of Georgia, Athens.

Michelson, J., Hamm, U., Wynen, E., and Roth, E., 1999, *The European Market for Organic Products: Growth and Development*, Organic Farming in Europe: Economics and Policy, vol. 7, University of Hohenheim, Stuttgart.

Offerman, F., and Nieberg, H., 2000, *Economic Performance of Organic Farms in Europe*, Organic Farming in Europe: Economics and Policy, vol. 5, University of Hohenheim, Stuttgart.

Organic Farming Research Foundation (OFRF), 1999, *Final Results of the Third Biennial National Organic Farmers' Survey*, Santa Cruz, CA.

Tauer, L. W., 1994, The value of segmenting the milk market into bST-produced and non-bST-produced milk, *Agribusiness* **10**:3-12.

Wittenberg, A. E., 2000, *Organic Foods in Western Japan 2000*, Attaché Report AGR no. JA0712, Foreign Agricultural Service, U.S. Department of Agriculture, http://www.fas.usda.gov/scriptsw/attacherep/attache_lout.asp (accessed Jul. 27, 2001).

THE PUBLIC PROVISION OF INFORMATION

A welfare analysis of European products with geographical indications and products with designations of origin

Angelo Maria Zago and Daniel Pick*

Beginning with the 1992 MacSharry reform of the Common Agricultural Policy, the European Union (EU) initiated a series of policies aimed at increasing the diversification of agricultural production in order to achieve a better balance between agricultural commodity supply and demand. A concurrent objective has been to promote production with certain characteristics for the benefit of the rural economy, particularly less favored and remote areas.

One intervention in line with these broad objectives is the European Economic Community's Council Regulation No. 2081/92 on the protection of geographical indications and designations of origin for agricultural products and foodstuffs.[1] This regulation recognizes that consumers tend to attach great importance to the quality of foodstuffs and that "in order to be able to make the best choice they must be given clear and succinct information regarding the origin of the product..." The regulation aims to recognize, protect, and foster trade among member states of protected geographical indication (PGI) and protected designation of origin (PDO) products to secure higher incomes for farmers in return for a genuine effort to improve quality. The scope of the regulation is limited to those agricultural products or foodstuffs for which a link between product or foodstuff characteristics and geographical origin exists. The link and the specific quality, reputation, or other characteristics attributable to the area and to the product's production, processing, and preparation must be proven during the registration application and are evaluated by the EU.

* Angelo Maria Zago is a research associate in the Department of Economics, University of Verona; Daniel Pick is an economist with the Economic Research Service, U.S. Department of Agriculture. The authors wish to thank both the Department of Economics and the Economic Research Service for funding support provided to this project. We also thank Julie Caswell for thoughtful suggestions that helped improve the chapter. Any remaining errors are solely our responsibility.

Global Food Trade and Consumer Demand for Quality, edited by Krissoff *et al.*
Kluwer Academic/Plenum Publishers, New York, 2002.

In this chapter, we propose a welfare analysis of this approach to market regulation which aims, as explicitly stated by the regulator, to increase both consumer and producer welfare. Indeed, consumers with higher willingness to pay are sure to get what they are paying for, while producers find the incentives to provide the quality level sought by richer consumers and ensure themselves higher income levels. But if the motives are noble, we argue that the results of the regulation may not always increase welfare.

The impact on consumer welfare is in fact ambiguous and depends on the characteristics of the product and the extent of market power. For producers, the result is ambiguous too, since those in regions granted the right to use a label will gain, while other, less lucky, producers lose. Overall, the impact on total welfare may be mixed, depending on demand and production parameters and the costs of managing the granted label.

In the next section we review some of the literature and provide background information on the impact of the regulation for some of the commodities and regions that have benefited from it. We then introduce the model we use to represent the impact of the regulation. In selecting the model's underlying assumptions, we made the choices that are more optimistic about the impact of the regulation. In other words, we use a best case scenario approach for the regulation. We also consider the possibility that producers may exercise some market power after implementation of the regulation. After discussing the welfare impact of the regulation and offering possible extensions of the model, we provide some concluding comments.

THE REGULATION AND RELATED LITERATURE

Since 1992, many products have been proposed by producers and their organizations for PGI/PDO recognition. By the end of 1999, around 530 products had been granted the right to use either a PGI or PDO label. The major countries benefiting from the regulation are France (holding 22 percent of granted labels), Italy (20 percent), Greece and Portugal (14 percent each), and Germany (11 percent). In France and Germany, the majority of PGI/PDO products are local breads and beers; in Italy and other Southern European countries, these products include cheeses, meat products, fruits and vegetables, and olive oil.

Although quantified data are not available, many of the products that were first granted PGI/PDO labels were generally already well known by consumers at national and international levels—e.g., Parmesan cheese. For other products, the labeling was actively promoted and only granted on the basis of the opportunity given by the EU regulation. The value of these products compared to total agricultural turnover in, for example, Italy, is preliminarily estimated at about 10 to 15 percent. Many experts predict that the incidence of these protected differentiated products is likely to increase (Nomisma 2000). The economic importance of labeled products is an indirect testimony to the impact of the regulation on quality information provision by a public body.

The importance of information for the proper functioning of markets is well known and well documented. Since the pioneering work of Akerlof (1970) and Klein and Leffler (1981), economists have investigated the causes of and remedies to market failures due to the lack of information on product quality. It has been shown that the suboptimal equilibria resulting from these information problems may be improved through the emergence of different economic tools in the form, for example, of warranties, certification (De and Nabar 1991), and signaling and reputation (Kreps and Wilson 1982, Shapiro 1983).

It is common in the economic literature to distinguish goods according to the extent to which their quality can be identified by consumers. The quality of search goods is easily detected before consumption. For experience goods, consumers need to actually consume the good before being able to discern its intrinsic quality. For experience or trust goods, quality can never be known by consumers with certainty (Nelson 1970). And, although for search and experience goods, the emergence of market "remedies" for quality assurance can be relatively effective and can mitigate or eliminate market failures, in the case of credence goods the instances in which there are suboptimal equilibria are more common (Darby and Karni 1973).

Recent literature on food industries recognizes that many aspects of food quality and safety can be considered credence attributes (Caswell and Mojduszka 1996, Antle 1996). Although the theoretical contributions that deal with credence goods are relatively few, their applications to food industries are increasing. Bureau, Marette, and Schiavina (1998) consider the dispute over hormone-treated beef between the EU and the United States and the effects of trade liberalization with and without it being possible for consumers to recognize different beef qualities. They find that the positive effect on welfare following trade liberalization may be offset by the increase in imperfect information about product quality.

In a related paper, Marette, Crespi, and Schiavina (1999) investigate the impact of common labeling by a cartel of producers able to restrict output when there is asymmetric information about product quality. They find that with a high cost of labeling, a cartel that provides information about product quality may improve total welfare even where producers collude to reduce output. Anania and Nisticò (1999) consider different scenarios for a public regulation, according to which degree of "trust" or credibility the regulation can obtain from consumers. Using political economy arguments, they explain the relative weakness of regulations aimed at providing consumers with assurance regarding product quality. A fully credible regulation is preferred by producers with high-quality products, while a regulation that is only partially credible may also be profitable for low-quality producers since it allows them to mimic high-quality producers and thereby obtain higher prices.

Auriol and Schilizzi (1999) consider quality signaling through certification with fixed certification costs and find that the extent of fixed costs determines market structure. They also compare welfare levels that result from public and private certification programs and find that, the costlier the certification, the higher the need for public intervention. Kirchhoff (1999) considers the case of environmental labeling, i.e., the certification of technology "greenness." Using a two-period game with monitoring of firms' claims, she finds that firms may voluntarily overcomply—that is, produce high quality even when doing so implies giving up short-run profits. She explains why, in many cases, firms that pretend to be producing high-quality products may have an incentive to lobby for stricter monitoring.

THE MODEL

Our model builds on Bureau, Marette, and Schiavina (1998) and considers a vertically differentiated market. The starting point of the analysis is a situation in which a good may present different quality levels but appears undifferentiated to consumers. Indeed, we assume a credence good for which consumers are not able to distinguish among different variants of the same commodity. We also assume that the producers that are granted the label by the regulator are really producing a superior good—i.e., a good whose characteristics are not inferior to those of the other variants of the commodity. In other words, there are no regulatory capture or political economy arguments.

By introducing labeling, the superior version of the good becomes recognizable by consumers and can be distinguished from the lower quality variants. In practice, the labeling creates two distinct products: the one with the label, with higher quality, sold to consumers with the higher willingness to pay; and the other, with a lower quality level.

Consider then an agricultural commodity as a credence good. Its quality can vary and is not known by consumers either before or after consumption. Some consumers would be willing to pay more for a certain variant of the commodity, with characteristics that are linked to special features of the production technology and/or area of production, because they believe they would get higher utility from its consumption. The problem of asymmetric information can be alleviated by the regulator by granting a label to those producers that follow certain rules, thus helping them establish a reputation for higher quality. We assume that the regulator can perfectly understand which firm produces the high-quality product or the production areas from which the commodity comes. For this and other reasons, consumers trust public provision of certification.

We assume that the quality s of the good under consideration is exogenous: it can be either low (s_L) or high (s_H). Assume that there is an exogenous number of producers: n_L producers of the low-quality variety of the commodity and n_H of the high-quality. Producers from different areas share different production technologies and costs of production. We assume that producers specializing in the high-quality commodity use a more restrictive, i.e., costly, technology because they follow traditional techniques or simply because high quality requires more effort. We assume a quadratic functional form for the cost function: $0.5c_i q_{ij}^2 n_i$, where $q_{ij} \in \Re_+$ is the quantity level of the type $i = L, H$ commodity for the individual producer j, c_i is a cost parameter such that $c_L < c_H$, and n_i, the number of producers of quality type i, ensures constant return to scale technology.

To begin with, we assume that individual producers j are price takers. Their profit is given by the following:

$$\pi_{ij} = q_{ij} p_i - c_i(q_{ij}^2/2)n_i,\ i = L,H \tag{1}$$

The optimal level of individual production is $q_{ij} = p_i/(c_i n_i)$, while the aggregate supply is the summation of individual supplies:

$$Q_i(p_i) = n_i q_{ij} = p_i/c_i \tag{2}$$

Note that $Q(p) = Q_L(p_L) + Q_H(p_H) = (p_L/c_L) + (p_H/c_H)$.

To represent consumer preferences, and to keep things simple, we consider a demand structure similar to that used by Mussa and Rosen (1978). Consumers can choose one unit of the good with quality s_i. If they consume it, they receive the following utility:

$$V = \theta s - p \tag{3}$$

where θ is a taste parameter that represents different intensities of preference for quality, and p is the price of the good of quality s. Let us assume that the taste parameter θ is distributed uniformly over the interval $\theta \in [\underline{\theta}, \overline{\theta}]$ and normalize the distribution such that $\underline{\theta} = 0$ and $\overline{\theta} = 1$.[2] The consumers will consume as long as $\theta > p/s$.

The expressions for consumer and producer welfare are the following:

$$CS = \int_{\underline{\theta}}^{\overline{\theta}} (\theta s - p)\, d\theta,$$
$$PS_i = \int_{\underline{q}}^{\overline{q}} (p_i - c_i q)\, dq, \quad i = L, H \tag{4}$$

where $\overline{\theta}$, $\underline{\theta}$ and $\overline{q}$, $\underline{q}$ are generic integration intervals.

BEFORE THE REGULATION: THE UNDIFFERENTIATED MARKET

Consider the case before the regulation, when one indistinguishable variety of the good is offered. We assume that the equilibrium before the regulation is a market situation in which both types of the commodity are sold, but consumers are not able to distinguish between them. With a unique price in the market, consumers form expectations about the quality of the commodity they buy. Using rational expectations, we assume that consumers expect that the average quality of the undistinguished commodity is the weighted (by the relative quantity) average of the quality levels of the two varieties of the good. The expected quality is then the following:

$$\overline{s} = [Q_L(p_L)/Q(p)]s_L + [Q_H(p_H)/Q(p)]s_H = (s_L c_H + s_H c_L)/(c_H + c_L) \tag{5}$$

We may determine the demand for the good of quality $\overline{s}$ sold at price $\overline{p}$ by the following expression:

$$D(\overline{s}) = (\overline{\theta} - \theta_0)/\overline{\theta} \tag{6}$$

where θ_0 represents the consumer who is indifferent between buying and not buying the good, and it is such that $\theta_0 = \overline{p}/\overline{s}$. Recalling that $\overline{\theta} = 1$, we can determine that, when there is only one undistinguished good offered, the demand is $D(\overline{p}, \overline{s}) = 1 - (\overline{p}/\overline{s})$.

We can characterize the equilibrium quantity and price by setting the (aggregate) supply equal to the demand: $Q(p) = (p_L/c_L) + (p_H/c_H) = 1 - (\overline{p}/\overline{s}) = D(p)$. We then obtain the following:

$$q^{\overline{s}} = \overline{s}/(\overline{s} + \overline{c}), \quad p^{\overline{s}} = (\overline{s}\,\overline{c})/(\overline{s} + \overline{c}) \tag{7}$$

where $\overline{c} = (c_H c_L)/(c_H + c_L)$. Note that the superscript refers to an equilibrium, while the subscript refers to the different types, i.e., producers of the low-quality variety (s_L) of the commodity or of the high-quality variety (s_H).

The level of consumer and producer welfare can then be shown as:[3]

$$CSB = \int_{q_0}^{\bar{1}} (q\bar{s} - p^S)dq,$$
$$PSB_H = \int_0^{\bar{q}^S_H} (p^S - c_H q)dq, \tag{8}$$
$$PSB_L = \int_0^{\bar{q}^S_L} (p^S - c_L q)dq.$$

THE EFFECTS OF THE REGULATION

The Competitive Case

Now consider the case in which, after the regulation, consumers can distinguish between two goods offered at quality s_L and s_H, with $s_L < s_H$, and at prices of p_L and p_H, with $p_L < p_H$. In this case, we can consider two indifferent consumers. One, $\tilde{\theta}$, who is indifferent between the high-quality and the low-quality good: $\tilde{\theta}s_L - p_L = \tilde{\theta}s_H - p_H$ such that $\tilde{\theta} = (p_H - p_L)/(s_H - s_L)$. The other, θ_0, who is indifferent between buying the low-quality good and not buying at all: $\theta_0 s_L - p_L = 0$ such that $\theta_0 = p_L/s_L$. We can express the demand for the two goods in the following way:

$$D^H(s,p) = (\bar{\theta} - \tilde{\theta})/\bar{\theta} = 1 - (p_H - p_L)/(s_H - s_L),\ D^L(s,p) = (\tilde{\theta} - \theta_0)/\bar{\theta} = [(p_H - p_L)/(s_H - s_L)] - p_L/s_L \tag{9}$$

Following the regulation, two competitive markets emerge: one for the high-quality type of the commodity, and the other for the low-quality variant of it. The aggregate supplies in the two markets are $Q_L(p_L) = (p_L/c_L)$ and $Q_H(p_H) = (p_H/c_H)$. The equilibrium quantities and prices that emerge in both markets are denoted p^c_L, p^c_H, q^c_L, and q^c_H, where the superscript c refers to the competitive scenario equilibrium, while the subscript refers to the different quality levels, high and low. Given the equilibrium quantities and prices, the level of consumer welfare in the competitive scenario is the following:[4]

$$CSA^c_H = \int_{\theta}^{1} (\theta s_H - p_H)d\theta,$$
$$CSA^c_L = \int_{\theta_0}^{\theta} (\theta s_L - p_L)d\theta. \tag{10}$$

The regulation allows producers of a high-quality commodity to differentiate from other producers and production areas. The costs of program administration—i.e., the expenditures incurred in obtaining EU recognition, drawing up and administering the rules for production and trade, etc.—are to be borne by those high-quality producers that benefit from the program. We believe that it is reasonable to consider these costs to be fixed, as is common practice in the literature (see, e.g., Auriol and Schillizzi 1999, Ibanez 1998), and we set them equal to F. Welfare levels for producers, taking into account the equilibrium quantities and prices that emerge and the fixed expenditures for the program, are as follows:

$$PSA_H^c = \int_0^{q_H^c} (p_H^c - c_H q)dq,$$
$$PSA_L^c = \int_0^{q_L^c} (p_L^c - c_L q)dq. \tag{11}$$

Regulation and Market Power

One of the effects of the regulation is that it may allow the group of high-quality producers to initiate the process of recognizing the specific products to be labeled and to regulate and control the enforcement of the granted PDOs and PGIs. This group of producers may also be able to exercise some market power. These are differentiated products for which quantity and market volumes are often limited. It is plausible that, in some situations, the group of producers will be able to coordinate its activities and jointly decide some strategic variables, say the price of the higher quality commodity.[5]

When it is possible for producers to jointly determine the price of the high-quality commodity, they behave like a monopolist that fixes the optimal price at which to sell the commodity. The profit maximization problem for the choice of optimal price level becomes:

$$\max_{p_H} \pi = p_H D_H(p,s) - n_H[c_H(q_H^2/2)n_H] \tag{12}$$

By noting that the constant returns to scale technology imply that the aggregate supply of high-quality producers is just the summation of individual supplies, and that for market equilibrium we have $Q_H(p_H) = D^H(p,s)$, we solve for the optimal price and obtain the relevant p_H chosen by the group of producers.

Following the regulation, we have two different markets emerging: the high-quality one in which producers have some monopoly power, and a competitive market for the low-quality producers. The aggregate supply in the competitive market is, as in the previous section, $Q_L(p_L) = (p_L/c_L)$. The equilibrium quantities and prices in both markets, when there is market power in the high-quality segment, are denoted p_L^m, p_H^m, q_L^m, and q_H^m, where the superscript m refers to the scenario with monopoly power for the high-quality producers, while the subscript refers to the quality level.

The level of consumer welfare is the following:[6]

$$CSA_H^m = \int_{\tilde{\theta}}^{1} (\theta s_H - p_H^m)d\theta,$$
$$CSA_L^m = \int_{\theta_0}^{\tilde{\theta}} (\theta s_L - p_L^m)d\theta. \tag{13}$$

It is straightforward to show that since $p^c_H < p^m_H$, $CSA^m < CSA^c$. Consumer welfare is lower when producers have market power. Welfare for producers is the following:

$$PSA^m_H = \int_0^{q^m_H} (p^m_H - c_H q)dq,$$
$$PSA^m_L = \int_0^{q^m_L} (p^m_L - c_L q)dq. \tag{14}$$

Since $p^c_H < p^m_H$, $PSA^m > PSA^c$—that is, producer welfare is higher when they have market power.

ECONOMIC WELFARE AND THE DISTRIBUTION OF GAINS AND LOSSES

To evaluate the welfare impact of the regulation, we performed a simulation, mainly because analytical solutions—not reported here—are very complicated. In creating the scenarios of the model, we chose the ones that represented the best case scenario from the point of view of the regulator. In selecting the parameter values, however, we do not intend to represent exact EU market conditions. In fact, we calibrated the model to give some unintended (by the regulator) results, given that our aim is simply to show that there exist some cases in which the effects of the regulation are detrimental to welfare.

The regulation we are considering is intended to improve both consumer and producer welfare. Indeed, it is reasonable to expect that consumer welfare after the regulation in competitive markets should be greater than welfare prior to the regulation—i.e., $CSA^c > CSB$.[7] Before implementation of the regulation, due to imperfect information, consumers are constrained to consume a commodity for which the quality level is not certain. They expect the quality level to be equal to the weighted average of high and low quality. If a well-functioning regulation is introduced and markets remain competitive, consumers can make their choices according to the quality they prefer and for which they are willing to pay. For the high-quality consumers, given that the quality level is higher after the regulation, consumption and total welfare increase. For low-quality consumers, the quality level and quantity consumed are lower. In aggregate, the quantity and consumer welfare levels are higher after implementation of the regulation (see Tables 1 and 2). This result is very similar to that of Bureau, Marette, and Schiavina (1998).

The situation is different if we consider the case of market power. In this case, for a large range of parameter values, the welfare of consumers may decrease. Consumers are now able to make informed choices, but the exercise of market power by producers may make them worse off (Table 3). Here we obtain a different result than Marette, Crespi, and Schiavina (1999), who find that, in many instances, the welfare increase following the provision of information by the cartel of high-quality producers more than offsets the reduction in welfare due to output reduction by the cartel itself.

For producers, the impact of the regulation in the competitive scenario is less clear–cut, and the effect on their total welfare depends on parameter values. For low-quality producers, welfare decreases unambiguously because there is now a lower demand for their product. Given that after the regulation consumers are able to discern among commodities of different qualities, only low-quality consumers prefer low-quality products,

Table 1. Simulation of quantities, prices, and welfare levels for consumers and producers before regulation

Parameter values													
Quality level (type H)	s_H	1.1	1.1	1.15	1.15	1.2	1.2	1.1	1.1	1.15	1.15	1.2	1.2
Quality level (type L)	s_L	1	1	1	1	1	1	1	1	1	1	1	1
Cost parameter (type H)	c_H	1.25	1.5	1.25	1.5	1.25	1.5	1.25	1.5	1.25	1.5	1.25	1.5
Cost parameter (type L)	c_L	1	1	1	1	1	1	1	1	1	1	1	1
Fixed costs for labeling	F	50	50	50	50	50	50	100	100	100	100	100	100
Before the regulation, variable values:													
Quantity (type H)	q^s_H	2,901	2,537	2,922	2,554	2,943	2,571	2,901	2,537	2,922	2,554	2,943	2,571
Quantity (type L)	q^s_L	3,627	3,805	3,653	3,831	3,679	3,857	3,627	3,805	3,653	3,831	3,679	3,857
Quantity (total)	Q	6,528	6,342	6,575	6,385	6,622	6,428	6,528	6,342	6,575	6,385	6,622	6,428
Price	p^s	3,627	3,805	3,653	3,831	3,679	3,857	3,627	3,805	3,653	3,831	3,679	3,857
Consumer surplus	CSB	2,225	2,091	2,306	2,161	2,387	2,232	2,225	2,091	2,306	2,161	2,387	2,232
Producer surplus (type H)	PSB_H	526	483	534	489	541	496	526	483	534	489	541	496
Producer surplus (type L)	PSB_L	658	724	667	734	677	744	658	724	667	734	677	744
Producer surplus (total)	PSB	1,184	1,206	1,201	1,223	1,218	1,240	1,184	1,206	1,201	1,223	1,218	1,240
Total welfare	TWB	3,409	3,298	3,507	3,384	3,605	3,471	3,409	3,298	3,507	3,384	3,605	3,471

Table 2. Simulation of quantities, prices and welfare levels after regulation and with competitive markets

Parameter values													
Quality level (type H)	s_H	1.1	1.1	1.15	1.15	1.2	1.2	1.1	1.1	1.15	1.15	1.2	1.2
Quality level (type L)	s_L	1	1	1	1	1	1	1	1	1	1	1	1
Cost parameter (type H)	c_H	1.25	1.5	1.25	1.5	1.25	1.5	1.25	1.5	1.25	1.5	1.25	1.5
Cost parameter (type L)	c_L	1	1	1	1	1	1	1	1	1	1	1	1
Fixed costs for labeling	F	50	50	50	50	50	50	100	100	100	100	100	100
After the regulation with competition, variable values:													
Quantity (type H)	q^c_H	3,243	2,857	3,421	3,023	3,590	3,182	3,243	2,857	3,421	3,023	3,590	3,182
Quantity (type L)	q^c_L	3,378	3,571	3,289	3,488	3,205	3,409	3,378	3,571	3,289	3,488	3,205	3,409
Quantity (total)	Q^c	6,621	6,428	6,710	6,511	6,795	6,591	6,621	6,428	6,710	6,511	6,795	6,591
Price (H)	p^c_H	4,054	4,286	4,276	4,535	4,487	4,773	4,054	4,286	4,276	4,535	4,487	4,773
Price (L)	p^c_L	3,378	3,571	3,289	3,488	3,205	3,409	3,378	3,571	3,289	3,488	3,205	3,409
Consumer surplus (type H)	CSA^c_H	1,674	1,469	1,798	1,580	1,924	1,692	1,674	1,469	1,798	1,580	1,924	1,692
Consumer surplus (type L)	CSA^c_L	571	638	541	608	514	581	571	638	541	608	514	581
Consumer surplus (total)	CSA^c	2,245	2,107	2,339	2,189	2,437	2,273	2,245	2,107	2,339	2,189	2,437	2,273
Producer surplus (type H)	PSA^c_H	607	562	681	636	755	709	557	512	631	586	705	659
Producer surplus (type L)	PSA^c_L	571	638	541	608	514	581	571	638	541	608	514	581
Producer surplus (total)	PSA^c	1,178	1,200	1,223	1,244	1,269	1,290	1,128	1,150	1,173	1,194	1,219	1,240
Total welfare	TWA^c	3,423	3,307	3,562	3,433	3,706	3,564	3,373	3,257	3,512	3,383	3,656	3,514
Impact on welfare:													
Change in producer surplus	ΔPS^c	−6	−6	22	21	51	50	−56	−56	−28	−29	1	1
hange in consumer surplus	ΔCS^c	20	16	33	28	50	41	20	16	33	28	50	41
Change in total welfare	ΔTW^c	14	9	55	49	101	93	−36	−41	5	−1	51	43

and the quantity demanded and price received decline. For high-quality producers, the impact depends on the parameter values and the size of fixed costs. If the fixed costs are high enough,[8] the increase in profits of the high-quality producers is not enough to cover the decrease in the profits of the low-quality producers. The total effect on producers can then be negative, such as when there are small quality differences among producers (Tables 1 and 2).

When high-quality producers have market power after the introduction of the regulation, the welfare impact for producers is more likely to be positive, both for high-quality and low-quality producers. Indeed, high-quality producers exercise their market power by charging a higher price and sell a lower quantity. This translates to an upward shift of the demand for low-quality producers, which may sell a higher quantity at a higher price (Tables 1 and 3). These results confirm that "the interests involved in the introduction of a regulation...go well beyond those of the producers of the high quality good and involve other interests which may easily be stronger and more widespread" (Anania and Nisticò 1999, p. 10). This shows that, with fully credible certification, the distribution of benefits also depends on market structure and other parameter values.

To summarize, the introduction of the regulation followed by the emergence of two distinct competitive markets, for low and high quality, unambiguously leaves both consumers and high-quality producers better off. Producers of the low-quality commodity are unambiguously worse off. In some cases, in particular when fixed costs are relatively high and quality differences are low, the impact of the regulation on producer and total welfare can be negative. If the effect of the regulation is also that of giving some market power to high-quality producers, the effect on producers is more likely to be positive, but that on consumers is more negative.

Two things are worth noting given these results. First, the regulation is also intended to benefit rural communities in less developed areas of the EU. This can occur only if producers of high-quality commodities are located in these marginal areas. We believe that this is not always the case. If producers of high-quality commodities are located in less marginal areas—e.g., Parmiggiano-Reggiano (Parmesan cheese) and Prosciutto Crudo of Parma (Parma ham) in the Padana Valley, to name only some of the most prominent instances of this type of regulation—then low-quality producers in other areas could be worse off. In other words, in some instances the regulation could have opposite results from those intended in terms of fostering rural development in marginal areas.

A second point is that political economy considerations may induce policymakers and antitrust authorities at the EU and national levels to be more lenient toward monopolistic behavior by producers exercising some forms of market power. Indeed, with the exercise of market power by high-quality producers, the negative impact of the regulation on low-quality producers is attenuated. This could make the regulation more acceptable to producers in less favorable production areas. Consumers would be worse off, but they are often not sufficiently organized to make their voices heard, especially with regard to products that are often considered gourmet delicacies with a restricted and often local market.

Table 3. Simulation of quantities, prices, and welfare levels after regulation and with monopoly power

Parameter values													
Quality level (type H)	s_H	1.1	1.1	1.15	1.15	1.2	1.2	1.1	1.1	1.15	1.15	1.2	1.2
Quality level (type L)	s_L	1	1	1	1	1	1	1	1	1	1	1	1
Cost parameter (type H)	c_H	1.25	1.5	1.25	1.5	1.25	1.5	1.25	1.5	1.25	1.5	1.25	1.5
Cost parameter (type L)	c_L	1	1	1	1	1	1	1	1	1	1	1	1
Fixed costs for labeling	F	50	50	50	50	50	50	100	100	100	100	100	100
After the regulation with monopoly power, variable values:													
Quantity (type H)	q^m_H	3,077	2,727	3,170	2,826	3,256	2,917	3,077	2,727	3,170	2,826	3,256	2,917
Quantity (type L)	q^m_L	3,462	3,636	3,415	3,587	3,372	3,542	3,462	3,636	3,415	3,587	3,372	3,542
Quantity (total)	Q^m	6,539	6,363	6,585	6,413	6,628	6,459	6,539	6,363	6,585	6,413	6,628	6,459
Price (H)	p^m_H	4,154	4,364	4,439	4,663	4,721	4,958	4,154	4,364	4,439	4,663	4,721	4,958
Price (L)	p^m_L	3,462	3,636	3,415	3,587	3,372	3,542	3,462	3,636	3,415	3,587	3,372	3,542
Consumer surplus (type H)	CSA^m_H	1,642	1,447	1,743	1,541	1,840	1,633	1,642	1,447	1,743	1,541	1,840	1,633
Consumer surplus (type L)	CSA^m_L	543	615	500	574	460	536	543	615	500	574	460	536
Consumer surplus (total)	CSA^m	2,184	2,062	2,242	2,115	2,300	2,169	2,184	2,062	2,242	2,115	2,300	2,169
Producer surplus (type H)	PSA^m_H	636	582	729	669	825	758	586	532	679	619	775	708
Producer surplus (type L)	PSA^m_L	599	661	583	643	569	627	599	661	583	643	569	627
Producer surplus (total)	PSA^m	1,235	1,243	1,312	1,312	1,393	1,385	1,185	1,193	1,262	1,262	1,343	1,335
Total welfare	TWA^m	3,420	3,305	3,555	3,428	3,693	3,554	3,370	3,255	3,505	3,378	3,643	3,504
Impact on welfare:													
Change in producer surplus	ΔPS^m	51	37	111	89	175	145	1	–13	61	39	125	95
Change in consumer surplus	ΔCS^m	–41	–29	–64	–46	–87	–63	–41	–29	–64	–46	–87	-63
Change in total welfare	ΔTW^m	11	7	48	44	88	83	–39	–43	–2	–6	38	33

CONCLUDING REMARKS

In this chapter, we have considered the welfare impact of the introduction of the EU regulation that allows producers of agricultural commodities with specific characteristics to differentiate and label their products. With a simple model of vertical differentiation, we compared the situation before the regulation, in which consumers were unable to distinguish among the different quality levels of the commodities and could only form expectations about them, to what happens when distinction is made possible by regulation. With a fully credible certification system, we consider what happens when producers can differentiate themselves either on a competitive basis or with some market power.

We find that the introduction of the regulation and the emergence of two distinct competitive markets for the differentiated commodity leaves both consumers and high-quality producers unambiguously better off, while producers of low-quality are unambiguously worse off. In addition, when fixed costs are relatively high and quality differences low, the total impact of the regulation on producer and total welfare can be negative. If after the introduction of the regulation, high-quality producers find it easier to exercise some market power, the effect on producers is more likely to be positive, making the regulation more acceptable to producers in less favored production areas. However, the effect on consumers in this case is often negative.

Given its importance as stated by the regulator, we also discussed the links between the regulation and rural development. We argue that, in some instances, the regulation under examination could give the opposite result than that expected by those fostering rural development—clearly whenever low-quality producers are located in the marginal areas of the EU.

The model used for this analysis is relatively simple, and we believe it can be improved and enriched by taking into consideration some useful extensions. In particular, the choice of consumer expectations is a rather critical one. We use rational expectations for consumers but believe that, although this is a rather standard assumption in the literature, it is far from satisfactory. More efforts in this direction would likely give some fruitful extensions and new insights.

NOTES

1. A designation of origin is a region or specific place used to describe an agricultural product whose quality or characteristics are exclusively due to the natural and human factors existing within the particular geographic environment. Production, processing and preparation of the product take place in the defined area. A geographical indication is the name of a region or specific place used to describe an agricultural product that originated in that area. The product possesses a specific quality or reputation attributable to that area, and its production, processing, and/or preparation takes place in the defined area.

2. This corresponds to a situation in which the market is not covered, that is, some consumers prefer not to buy the commodity offered. We do not consider the other case, i.e., when the market is covered, here. When a market is covered, demand cannot be inverted and so quantity-competition à la Cournot cannot be used (Motta 1993, p. 116).
3. The letter B in the expressions *CSB*, PSB_H, and PSB_L stands for "before the regulation."
4. The letter A^c of CSA^c and PSA^c stands for "after the regulation under the competitive scenario." The equations for CSA^c are very complicated and are not reported here. They are available from the authors upon request.
5. Recently, the Italian Antitrust Authority investigated the Consorzio del Gorgonzola (the producer group in charge of regulating the production and trade of Gorgonzola cheese) because it imposed quantity restrictions on its members. Here we consider the case of price determination, not quantity determination, because price setting would likely be easier to enforce for the group and more difficult to detect and sanction for the antitrust authorities. In any case, the qualitative nature of the results presented here should be robust to this assumption.
6. The equations for CSA^m are very complicated and are not reported here. They are available from the authors upon request.
7. Analytical solutions are quite complicated and are not reported here. To derive the results presented in Tables 1 to 3, we performed numerical simulations using Mathematica 4 (Wolfram Research Inc.). Given normalization of the consumer taste parameter, such that $\underline{\theta} = 0$ and $\overline{\theta} = 1$, the quantity q_i and welfare levels are between 0 and 1. For ease of exposition, the values reported in the tables have been multiplied by a factor of 10,000.
8. Note that with typical products, we are often dealing with local markets—that is, markets of limited size—and the extent of the fixed costs can be high in relative terms in these situations.

REFERENCES

Akerlof, G. A., 1970, The market for "lemons": Quality uncertainty and the market mechanism, *Q J Econ* **84**(3):488–500.

Anania, G., and Nisticò, R., 1999, Public Regulation as an Imperfect Substitute for Trust in Quality Food Markets, mimeo, Department of Economics, University of Calabria, Italy.

Antle, J. M., 1996, Efficient food safety regulation in the food manufacturing sector, *Am J Agric Econ* **78**(5):1242–1247.

Auriol, E., and Schilizzi, S., 1999, Quality Signaling through Certification, working paper, Institut d'economie industrielle, Toulouse, France.

Bureau, J. C., Marette, S., and Schiavina, A., 1998, Non-tariff trade barriers and consumers' information: The case of the EU-US trade dispute over beef, *Eur Rev Agric Econ* **25**(4):437–462.

Caswell, J. A., and Mojduszka, E. M., 1996, Using informational labeling to influence the market for quality in food products, *Am J Agric Econ* **78**(5):1248–1253.

Darby, M. R., and Karni, E., 1973, Free competition and the optimal amount of fraud, *J Law Econ* **16**(1):67–88.

De, S., and Nabar, P., 1991, Economic implications of imperfect quality certification, *Econ Lett* **37**:333–337.

Ibanez, L., 1998, Competition in Environmental Labeling, working paper, Research Group in Mathematical and Quantitative Economics, University of Toulouse, France.

Kirchhoff, S., 1999, Overcompliance, Labeling, and Lobbying: The Case of Credence Goods, Ph.D. diss. (unpub.), Department of Agricultural and Resource Economics, University of Maryland, College Park, MD.

Klein, B., and Leffler, K. B., 1981, The role of market forces in assuring contractual performance, *J Polit Econ* **81**:615–641.

Kreps, D., and Wilson, R., 1982, Reputation and imperfect information, *J Econ Theory* **27**:253–279.

Marette, S., Crespi, J. M., and Schiavina, A., 1999, The role of common labelling in a context of asymmetric information, *Eur Rev Agric Econ* **26**:167–178.

Motta, M., 1993, Endogenous quality choice: Price vs. quantity competition, *J Ind Econ* **41**(2):113–131.

Mussa, M., and Rosen, S., 1978, Monopoly and product quality, *J Econ Theory* **18**:301–317.

Nelson, P., 1970, Information and consumer behavior, *J Polit Econ* **78**(2):311–329.

Nomisma, 2000, Prodotti tipici e sviluppo locale—VIII Rapporto Nomisma sulla agricoltura italiana, paper presented at 102nd Fieragricola, Verona.

Shapiro, C., 1983, Premiums for high quality products as returns to reputations, *Q J Econ* **98**:659–679.

INDEX

Accreditation
current status of, 210–212
organic food, 214, 215, 218, 221, 227
United States and, 212
Agricultural Marketing Service (USDA), 211
Animal welfare
domestic and international policy responses to, 92–94
economic impacts of higher standards for, 90–92
explanation of, 78–79
legislation related to, 85–87
multilateral issues regarding, 94–97
public concerns about, 79–85
Scottish Pig Industry Initiative and, 88–89
trade policies and, 10–11, 23
Animal Welfare Act (New Zealand), 93
Armington approach, 168–169
Association of Exporters of Non-Traditional Products (AGEXPRONT), 111
Australia, salmon import restrictions and, 5
Austria, animal welfare and, 87
Authenticity protection, 11–12

Bangladesh, shrimp and prawn exports from, 71
Basic Standards of Organic Agriculture and Food Processing (IFOAM), 211
Beef. *See also* Animal welfare
fluctuations in price of, 202–204
treated with growth-promoting hormones, 5, 6, 16–17, 35, 37, 40, 129, 140–141, 231
Uruguayan, 129–143
Belgium, animal welfare and, 87
Ben and Jerry's ice cream, 56
Bertrand-Nash equilibrium, 185
Biotech food labeling, 197–206
Bovine somatotropin, 87
Bovine spongiform encephalopathy (BSE), 3, 81, 88
Brazil, poultry trade and, 148, 152, 154, 156–162

Campylobacter jejuni, 151
Campylobacteria, 3
Canada
cyclosporiasis outbreaks in, 109, 110
organic imports in, 214
poultry trade and, 150, 152
Canadian Food Inspection Agency (CFIA), 114
Carne con Amore (Italy), 88
Cattle, 87. *See also* Animal welfare; Beef
Centers for Disease Control (CDC), 102, 109–113, 120, 125
Certification
issues related to cost of, 231
of organic foods, 210–228
Chile
impact of cyclosporiasis outbreak on, 121–124
raspberry exports from, 106–110, 113
China, poultry trade and, 148–150, 152, 154–161
Codex Alimentarius Commission, 5, 8, 9, 96, 140, 151, 211
Codex Committee on General Principles, 8
Committee on Food Import and Export Inspection and Certification Systems (Codex Alimentarius Commission), 211

Committee on Food Labeling (Codex Alimentarius Commission), 211
Commodity quality, 165
effect of policies on, 169–171, 176–177
EU wheat market and, 171–176
in large countries, 171
small-country model and, 166–169
Common Agricultural Policy, 229
Competition policy, 23–26
Consumer interface framework
dimensions of, 45
function of, 43–44
quality and, 45–49
quality perception framework and, 55–59
Consumers
governmental attention to preferences of, 40
impacts of harmonization on, 212–214
product origin information and, 229, 231
Consumption, 16–17
Continuous labeling
under autarky, 189
consumer welfare under, 190
effects of, 184, 185
implementation of, 182
international trade and, 191–192
Convention on Biological Diversity, 9
Cost-benefit analysis, 21, 23, 27
Council of Europe, 85
Council of European Communities, 86
Council Regulation No. 2181/92 (European Economic Community), 229
Credence goods, 181–182, 184, 193, 232
Cues
extrinsic, 50–51, 56
intrinsic, 50–51
quality, 49–50, 56, 57
Cyclospora
explanation of, 108–110
Guatemalan raspberries and, 102, 103, 107–108, 110, 115
tests for, 110
Cyclosporiasis
explanation of, 102, 108–110
impact on Chile of, 121–124, 126
impact on Mexico of, 124
impact on U.S. of, 119–121
Model Plan of Excellence and, 115–117
1996 outbreak of, 110–111
policy responses to outbreak of, 111–115, 125
raspberry industry and, 117–119
Czech Republic, animal welfare and, 93

Denmark, animal welfare and, 87, 88
Department of Agriculture (USDA)
Agricultural Marketing Service, 211
Food Safety and Inspection Service, 66, 102
foreign technical assistance and, 125
organic food accreditation standards and, 227
poultry market and, 152
Differentiation. *See* Horizontal differentiation; Product differentiation; Vertical differentiation
Dicose system (Uruguay), 129, 139, 140, 142, 143
Directive 81/602, 140
Disease. *See* Foodborne diseases
Domestic international sales corporations (DISCs), 34–35

East Asia, fresh food products from, 64
Egg production, 84, 86, 87, 90, 94
Elasticities, Armington approach to defining, 168–169
Environmental issues, genetically modified foods and, 7
Environmental labeling, 231. *See also* Labeling
Environmental Protection Agency (EPA), 120
Escherichia coli, 3
Ethics, genetically modified foods and, 8
Eurogroup for Animal Welfare, 85
European Court of Justice, 86
European Economic Community (EEC), 85, 229
European Union (EU)
agricultural production diversification and, 229
animal welfare and, 77–97 (*See also* Animal welfare)
ban on beef treated with growth-promoting hormones, 5, 6, 16, 35, 129, 140–141, 231
designations of origin information and, 229–241
export of fresh food products to, 64, 71
organic food market in, 209
organic standards and, 213
poultry trade and, 148, 149, 152, 154–161
process standards EN 45011, 210, 211
Uruguayan beef and, 129, 130, 134, 135, 138, 140

wheat policy in, 165, 171–177
Exotic Newcastle disease (END), 150, 152, 154
Experience goods, 181–182, 184
Experimental economics method, 25
Exporters of Snow Peas, 111
Extrinsic cues, 50–51, 56
Extrinsic quality indicators and cues, 56, 57

Farm-to-table management, 65–66
Finland, animal welfare and, 87
Five Forces model (Porter), 137
Food and Agriculture Organization (FAO) (United Nations), 64
Food and Drug Administration (FDA)
cyclosporiasis outbreak and, 111–114, 117, 123
food safety guidelines and, 64, 102
import detentions and, 64–65, 71
Food poisoning
costs of, 18
risk and, 19–20
Food production
public unease over, 4
views of agricultural biotechnology in, 7–8
Food safety
concerns regarding, 3
evaluation of public investments in, 67
fresh food products from LDCs and, 64–65
international standards for, 36
precautionary approach applied to, 6–7
produce, 101–126 (*See also* Fresh food products; Produce)
quality vs., 68
solutions to problems regarding, 104–105
trade issues and, 3, 18–20
trade with countries lacking controls for, 22
vertical differentiation and, 13
Food Safety and Inspection Service (USDA), 66, 102
Food Safety Initiative, 102, 125
Food safety standards
LDC exports and, 63–72
management issues and, 65–66
public and private actions to meet, 66–67
Foodborne diseases
from poultry, 150–151, 154
recent outbreaks of, 3
trade and, 18
Foot-and-mouth disease (FMD), 129, 133, 139
France
animal welfare and, 83, 84, 91
PGI/PDO labels and, 230
Freedom Food Ltd. (United Kingdom), 88, 89
Fresh food products, 64–66. *See also* Produce; *specific products*

General Agreement on Tariffs and Trade (GATT)
agriculture in framework of, 3
animal welfare and, 94–96
DISCs and, 35
function of, 34, 39
LDCs and, 64
production measures and, 10–11
Genetically modified (GM) foods, 7–8
Genetically modified organisms (GMOs), 37
consumer responses and, 40, 81
restrictions on, 39
Germany
animal welfare and, 83, 84
organic wheat market and, 222–227
PGI/PDO labels and, 230
Good agricultural practices (GAPs)
LDCs and, 64, 65
national guidelines on, 102, 112, 120, 122
Good manufacturing practices (GMPs)
LDCs and, 64, 65
national guidelines on, 102, 112, 122
Great Britain
animal welfare and, 83, 85, 87, 88, 90
poultry market and, 152
Greece, PGI/PDO labels and, 230
Growth hormones, beef treated with, 5, 6, 16–17, 35, 37, 40, 129, 140–141
Guatemala
raspberry exports from, 102–126
snow pea exports from, 70–71
Guatemalan Berry Commission (GBC), 111, 113, 116, 118

Hadden, Susan, 198
Harmonization. *See* International harmonization
Hazard Analysis Critical Control Points (HACCP)
as extrinsic indicator, 56, 58
poultry products and, 151, 152
raspberries and, 112, 122, 123
use of, 65, 66, 71, 112

Hazard prevention/control, 65–67
Health issues
food safety standards and, 69–70
genetically modified foods and, 7
poultry market and, 150–151
High-Level Commission for Food Safety (Guatemala), 113–114
Highly pathogenic avian influenza (HPAI), 150
Horizontal differentiation. *See also* Product differentiation
multidimensional models of, 49
product safety and, 13
quality and, 44, 47–48, 52, 54, 58
Hungary, poultry trade and, 150

Import detentions, 64–65, 71
Intellectual property rights, 11, 12
International Federation of Organic Agriculture Movements (IFOAM), 211
International harmonization
application of trade model and, 222–226
consumer welfare effects and, 215–222, 227–228
current status of, 210–212
impact on consumers of, 212–214
overview of, 209
International Office of Epizootics (OIE), 5, 150
International Organization for Standardization/International Electrotechnical Commission (ISO/IEC), Guide 65, 210, 211
International Organization for Standardization (ISO), 56, 65, 95, 211
International Plant Protection Convention, 5
International trade law
consequences of transformation in, 36–37, 41
mid- to late 20th century, 34–35
overview of, 33–34
pathology of problem cases in, 37–38
remedies for problem cases in, 38–40
Intrinsic cues, 50–51
Intrinsic quality attributes, 56, 57
Ireland, animal welfare and, 88
ISO 9000 certification, 56, 58
Italy
animal welfare and, 88, 90, 91
PGI/PDO labels and, 230, 239

Japan
fresh food products and, 64, 71
organic products and, 209, 213, 214
poultry trade and, 148–150, 152, 154, 156–161

Labeling
of biotech foods, 197–206
continuous, 182, 184–193
country-of-origin, 92
environmental, 231
for genetically modified foods, 8
objectives of, 198
PGI/PDO products and, 229–241
Lancasterian approach, 48–49
Latin America, fruit and vegetable exports from, 64, 65
Less developed countries (LDCs)
case examples addressing safety standards and, 70–71
food safety standards and exports from, 63–64, 72
fresh food export markets for, 64–66
market failure and exports from, 63, 66, 68–70
public and private actions to meet food safety standards and, 66–67
public investments in food safety and, 67
Listeria, 3
Listeria monocytogenes, 56, 151
Living modified organisms (LMOs), 10

McDonald's Corporation, 94, 97
MERCOSUR, 134–135, 137, 143
Mexico
food safety programs in, 124
integrated food safety investments in, 71
poultry trade and, 149, 152
raspberry exports from, 106–108, 121, 124
Microbiological contamination, 64, 65
Model Plan of Excellence (MPE), 115–117, 125
Multinational food corporations, 94, 97

New Zealand, animal welfare and, 93, 97
North America, export of fresh food products to, 64

Organic foods
certification standards for, 210–228
market for, 209

Organisation for Economic Co-operation and Development (OECD), 7, 28
Origin designations, 229–242

Perceived quality, 51–52
Pesticide residue, 64, 65
Pigs, 86, 88–89, 91
PIPAA (Integral Program of Agricultural and Environmental Protection), 116, 125
Poland, animal welfare and, 93
Portugal, PGI/PDO labels and, 230
Poultry markets
  animal welfare issues related to, 82, 86, 87, 90, 91
  growth in, 147, 149–150, 161
  health issues affecting, 150–151
  overview of, 147–149
  sanitary measures affecting, 151–153
  trade models and, 154–162
Prawns, 71
Precautionary principle, 6–7, 38, 40
Process control, farm-to-table, 65
Produce. *See also* Fresh food products; *specific produce*
  consumption of, 101
  quality attributes for, 103–104
  safety issues and, 104–105
Product differentiation. *See also* Horizontal differentiation; Vertical differentiation
  base model and, 182–189
  consumer welfare and, 198–204
  labeling and, 197–206
  multidimensional models of, 49
  quality and, 44–49, 52, 54, 182
  trade issues and, 13
Product quality. *See* Quality
Protected designation of origin (PDO) products, 229, 230, 235
Protected geographical indication (PGI) products, 229, 230, 235
Protocol on Biosafety, 9–10
PUL (Productores Unidos Cooperativa Agraria Ltda.), 141–143

Quality. *See also* Commodity quality
  biotechnology regulation and, 7-8
  competition policy and, 23–26
  consumer interface framework and, 44–49
  consumer uncertainty about, 103
  cost-benefit analysis and, 21, 23, 27
  economic aspects of, 12–13
  effects of policies on, 169–171
  explanation of, 27–28, 58
  food safety vs., 68
  framework for analyzing, 44
  imperfect quality information and, 14–18
  increased international trade and, 3–4, 18–20
  level of risk establishment and, 5–6
  market failure due to lack of information on, 230–231
  perceived, 51–52
  precautionary principle application and, 6–7
  socioeconomic concerns and, 8–12
  summary and conclusions regarding issues of, 26–27
  trade liberalization and, 13–14, 20–21
  World Trade Organization and, 4, 5, 23, 26
Quality assurance, 43, 44
Quality cues, 49–50, 56, 57
Quality equilibrium, 186–189
Quality perception framework
  consumer interface approach and, 55–59
  explanation of, 49–54

Raspberries
  Guatemalan exports of, 102–126
  U.S. market for, 105–108
Read the Label: Reducing Risk by Providing Information (Hadden), 198
Risk
  establishing level of, 5–6
  impact of, 12
  role of phantom, 37–38
  socioeconomic concerns and, 8–9
  trade producing increased, 18–20
Risk assessment
  basis for, 36, 37
  farm-to-table, 65
Royal Agricultural College, 138
Royal Society for the Prevention of Cruelty to Animals (RSPCA), 89
Russia, poultry trade and, 148, 149, 152–158, 161, 162

Safety. *See* Food safety
Salmon, Australian import restrictions on, 5
Salmonella
  poultry and, 151, 153
  recent outbreak of, 3
  shrimp and, 71
Salmonella enteritidis, 44, 151

Sanitary and Phytosanitary (SPS) Agreement
animal welfare and, 94
Article 5.7, 38
function of, 4, 5, 9, 114, 147–148, 151
international standards and, 36, 37
precautionary principle and, 6, 7, 38
Sanitary regulations
estimating benefits of, 24, 25
welfare effects of trading with countries lacking, 22
in world poultry markets, 147–162 (*See also* Poultry markets)
WTO and, 23, 27, 152
Saudi Arabia, poultry trade and, 149
Scottish Food Quality Certification Ltd., 89
Scottish Pig Industry Initiative, 88–89
Shrimp, 71
Snow peas, 70–71, 111
Socioeconomic concerns
animal welfare and, 10–11
limits of science and, 9
protecting quality and authenticity and, 11–12
Protocol on Biosafety and, 9–10
risk decisions and, 8–9
Standard Industrial Trade Classification (SITC), poultry and, 148, 154–156, 161
Staphylococcus aureus, 151
Statute of the International Court of Justice, 6
Strawberries, 120
Supreme Court, U.S., 36–37
Sweden, animal welfare and, 87
Switzerland, animal welfare and, 87

Tariff-rate quotas (TRQs), 148, 150, 158, 160, 161
Technical Barriers to Trade (TBT) Agreement, 4, 8
animal welfare and, 94, 96
requirements of, 39
standards and, 11
Technical Working Group on Food Safety (Mexico), 71
Thailand, poultry trade and, 149, 150
Total food quality model, 53–54
Total quality management, 65
Trade
continuous labeling and, 191–192
food quality issues and, 3–4
increased risk resulting from, 18–20
unified quality framework and, 58–59
Trade law. *See* International trade law
Trade liberalization
food safety and, 18–20
function of, 13
quality-cutting, 13–15
welfare and, 16–17, 20–21, 231
Trade regulations, 21, 23, 27
Treaty of Rome, 85

Unfolding theory, 198
Unified quality framework
advantages of, 58
explanation of, 55–58
trade and, 58–59
United Arab Emirates, poultry trade and, 149
United Kingdom. *See also* Great Britain
animal welfare and, 83, 85, 87, 88, 90
United States
cyclosporiasis outbreaks in, 109–111, 119–121 (*See also* Cyclosporiasis)
food safety standards in, 64, 102
national accreditation in, 212
organic food market in, 209
organic imports in, 214
organic wheat market in, 222–228
poultry trade in, 148, 149, 154, 156–161
raspberry market in, 105–108
shrimp and prawn exports to, 71
Uruguay
background of beef industry in, 129–131
beef consumption in, 129
beef export firms in, 138–141
case study of beef industry in, 141–143
industry analysis of beef industry in, 131–138
Uruguay Round
food quality and, 4
international trade law and, 34, 35
poultry market and, 147–148
requirements under, 36
U.S. Agency for International Development, 107
U.S. Meat Export Federation, 138

Veal calves, 86, 87
Vertical differentiation. *See also* Product differentiation
continuous labeling and, 182, 184–193
multidimensional models of, 49
product safety and, 13, 16
quality and, 44–46, 52, 54, 58, 183, 189

welfare impact of regulation and model using, 231–241

Welfare
harmonization and, 209, 212–222, 227
labeling and, 189, 198–204
market regulation and, 229–241
origin designations and, 229–241
trade liberalization and, 16–17, 20–21, 231
trade with countries lacking sanitary regulations and, 22
Westgren, R. E., 44
Wheat. *See also* Commodity quality
European Union policy regarding, 165, 171–177
organic, 222–226
World Trade Organization (WTO)
animal welfare and, 78, 95–97
compliance with rules of, 36, 38
dispute settlement and, 211
enforcement system of, 34
food quality issues and, 4, 5, 23, 26, 27
issues in survival of, 39–41
policy reform and, 34
risk assessment and, 37
SPS Committee, 152
trade agreements, 10, 39, 140